Industrial Organisation of High-Technology Markets

Industrial Organisation of High-Technology Markets

THE INTERNET AND INFORMATION TECHNOLOGIES

Stefano Comino
University of Udine, Italy

Fabio Maria Manenti
University of Padua, Italy

Edward Elgar
Cheltenham, UK • Northampton, MA, USA

© Stefano Comino and Fabio Maria Manenti 2014

First published in Italian as *Economia Di Internet E Delle Information & Communication Technology*
© Giappichelli Editore, Torino 2011
Translated by Stefano Comino, Fabio Maria Manenti and Miranda Lewis

Published by
Edward Elgar Publishing Limited
The Lypiatts
15 Lansdown Road
Cheltenham
Glos GL50 2JA
UK

Edward Elgar Publishing, Inc.
William Pratt House
9 Dewey Court
Northampton
Massachusetts 01060
USA

A catalogue record for this book
is available from the British Library

Library of Congress Control Number: 2013917976

MIX
Paper from
responsible sources
FSC FSC® C013056
www.fsc.org

ISBN 978 1 78195 198 9 (cased)
ISBN 978 1 78347 292 5 (paperback)
ISBN 978 1 78195 199 6 (eBook)

Printed and bound in Great Britain by T.J. International Ltd, Padstow

Contents

Contents in Full

About the Authors[*]

STEFANO COMINO

Stefano Comino is Associate Professor in Economics at the Department of Economics and Statistics, University of Udine – Italy. He obtained his Master of Science and his Ph.D. in Economics at the Universitat Autonoma de Barcelona, Spain. His research interests include various topics related to Industrial Organisation: strategic alliances, entry decisions, open source software and innovation in high-tech markets. His research has been published in *Games and Economic Behavior, European Economic Review, Research Policy, Journal of Economic Behavior and Organization* and other peer-reviewed journals.

FABIO MARIA MANENTI

Fabio Maria Manenti is Associate Professor in Economics at the Department of Economics and Management "Marco Fanno", University of Padua – Italy. He obtained his Master of Science and his Ph.D. in Economics at the University of York, U.K.; he also holds a Ph.D. in Economics from the University of Pavia, Italy. From 2001 he has been teaching the courses of Economics of Networks and of Regulation and Antitrust at the University of Padua. His research interests mostly concern Industrial Organisation applied to high-tech markets. His research has been published in various peer-reviewed journals such as *Games and Economic Behavior, Research Policy, Information Economics & Policy* and *Journal of Regulatory Economics*.

[*]The authors gratefully acknowledge the assistance of Miranda Lewis in drafting the manuscript.

Chapter 1

Industrial Organisation of High-Tech Markets

The aim of this book is to analyse the main economic aspects related to *Information & Communication Technologies* (ICT hereafter). In broad terms, ICT refer to the set of technologies used to manage information which is anything that can be digitised; in particular, ICT include technologies, either electronic or digital, which allow the processing, storage and transmission of information. Therefore, not only information technologies (computer technologies, both hardware and software) belong to ICT, but also telecommunications, electronics and digital media products. Just to give some examples, the components of a personal computer, the Internet and any device which allows us to surf the Web are classified as ICT. Likewise, even fixed and mobile telecommunications, electronic payment systems or video game consoles belong to the realm of Information & Communication Technologies.

ICT are all around us; it is undoubtedly true that such technologies have radically changed our everyday lives, from the way in which we interact with other people to the way in which we do business. Nowadays, more than two-thirds of Europeans surf the Internet and half of them are frequent users of Facebook, the well-known social network. In Italy, more than 50% of the population own a laptop and about one-third of them use an Internet key to access mobile Internet; three out of four Italians firmly believe that the Internet has improved the quality of their lives. Nearly 20% of European firms with more than ten employees purchase raw materials and services over the Internet and 13% sell their products on-line. The penetration of mobile telecommunications has soared in the last twenty years; nowadays, in Europe it has surpassed the 100% mark; in Italy, 87.4% of citizens state that they never part from their handset during day and night.

Moreover, Information & Communication Technologies contribute greatly to economic growth not only because they are extremely relevant industrial sectors, but also because high-tech products and technologies for data processing and transmission are crucial production inputs for manufacturing and service firms. In the last twenty years, the impressive increase in computing power, the associated decline in the price of information technologies combined with the boom of the Internet have stimulated firms to invest in ICT equipment and to rely on information technologies to organise and redesign their activities; these investments have led to an increase in labour productivity and, more generally, they have contributed to higher total factor productivity.

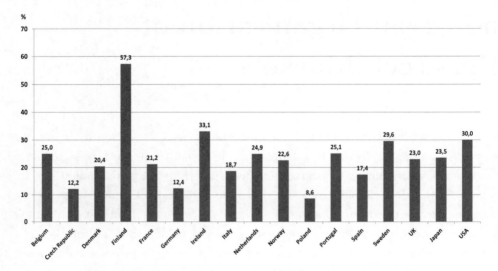

Figure 1.1: share of ICT investments in R&D for 2008[1]

However, ICT sectors have not escaped the economic crisis altogether; for instance, sales in the semiconductor industry, a good indicator for hardware technology business cycle, declined globally by about 40% between the end of 2008 and the beginning of 2009, but their recovery has been spectacular and by the end of 2009 global sales had already reached the pre-recession level (see EC, 2012). Despite the economic slowdown, high-tech industries have proved to be extremely dynamic; in recent years a great variety of innovative products and services, such as smartphones, app stores, e-readers, cloud computing, has been launched. Figure 1.1 shows the share of R&D investments in ICT industries compared to the total R&D expenditures for the year 2008 in some selected countries. Except for Poland, the figures are well above 10% and in most cases they lie between 20 and 30%, with the notable exception of Finland, where the figure is well above 50%. If one considers that, for instance, in Europe the

---

[1]Data shown in Figures 1.1, 1.2 and 1.4 are taken from the OECD Key ICT Indicators – www.oecd.org/sti/ICTindicators.

value added of ICT sectors is on average below 8% of the total value added, Figure 1.1 clearly proves that the sectors belonging to Information & Communication Technologies are extremely R&D intensive.

Box 1.1 – Small firms grow on-line

A report by the Boston Consulting Group studies the benefits which firms may obtain when using the Internet to promote their business or to re-organise their production activities; the study carried out in 2011 is based on a sample of 1,000 small and medium enterprises (SMEs) located in Italy.[a] The Boston Consulting Group classifies SMEs into three separate categories according to the intensity with which they use the Internet: *i)* active on-line firms, defined as those which carry out marketing activities and e-commerce, *ii)* on-line firms, defined as those which are endowed with a website only and *iii)* off-line firms, i.e. firms which do not have a company website. The results of this analysis are of great interest and emphasise the fact that the Internet is a powerful instrument not only to promote sales but also to increase productivity. In particular, the study shows that:

a) despite the economic slowdown, during the previous three years active on-line firms registered a 1.2% average increase in revenues. On-line and off-line firms, on the contrary, experienced a significant decrease in revenues (2.4% and 4.5%, respectively);

b) active on-line firms are the most export-oriented. They sell about 15% of their products abroad, a figure which is more than twice the percentage for on-line firms and more than three times the percentage for off-line firms;

c) during the previous five years, 34% of active on-line firms hired new personnel, while only 11% of off-line firms did so;

d) 65% of active on-line firms report that the Internet allowed them to increase productivity by simplifying transaction processes and by reducing time-to-market. This figure is more than twice the percentage reported by the other SMEs in the sample.

[a]See BCG (2011).

As already mentioned, ICT are not only important stand-alone sectors but they also represent so-called general-purpose technologies which are used to run virtually any business activity with the potential to reshape the economy and boost productivity across all sectors and industries. Consider the Internet; in 2008, almost 80% of European firms with at least 10 employees had broadband access to the Web and more than 60% of them had its own company website (see Figure 1.2). These figures show the pervasiveness of the use of the Internet in today's economy; nowadays, firms are employing the Web to promote their activities and to purchase and sell their products and services. On-line firms operate in a virtually unbounded market; geographical barriers are blurring and web-based firms may easily reach even distant customers. Figure 1.3 shows that e-commerce is one of the fastest growing markets in Europe; on average, the share of on-line revenues on total retail revenues has nearly doubled in the last two years. Changes in doing business have been so overwhelming that in the 90s the term *new economy* was coined to describe industries which rely on the Internet or on ICT to supply and distribute their products.

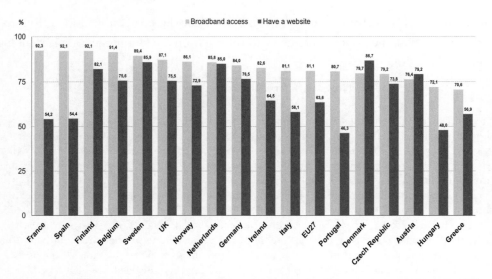

Figure 1.2: firms with broadband Internet access and company website (in %)

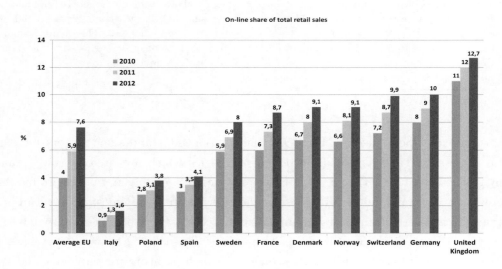

Figure 1.3: share of on-line revenues in European countries, years 2010–12[2]

Another relevant characteristic of the new economy is that a large share of the value generated derives from the production and distribution of so-called information goods. Music CDs, movies, video games and software are all examples of information goods whose value lies in the information they contain; a typical feature of an information good is that it can be digitised, copied and transferred on-line at virtually zero costs. This

---

[2]Data taken from the Centre for Retail Research (CRR).

is the reason why, unsurprisingly, the growth and diffusion of ICT and of the Internet have greatly stimulated the supply of information goods. Figure 1.4 shows the relative weight of on-line distribution channels for music, movies, newspapers, video games and advertising industries. In 2010 in OECD countries, the video games industry made 30% of its revenues from digital content (downloads, subscriptions, etc.) with a growth rate of 25%. The music industry, with overall falling revenues, generated one quarter of its earnings from downloads, streaming and bundled mobile services. In the same year, on-line revenues in the movie industry experienced a growth rate of more than one third.

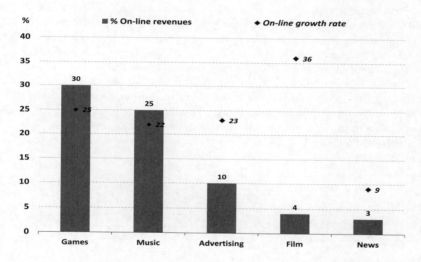

Figure 1.4: on-line distribution of digital goods in OECD countries

Contents of the book. ICT encompass a great variety of products and technologies affecting all dimensions of economic activities. The previous discussion reveals the possible roles which information technologies may play in modern economies. On the one hand, ICT are instruments used by firms to improve the efficiency of their production process, to promote their business, to remove geographical barriers and to reach new markets; e-commerce is a typical example of ICT used as an instrument. On the other hand, firms produce and sell high-tech products/services or information goods directly to consumers; for example, telecom operators offer communication services and access to the Internet to residential and business customers, while software houses develop new applications and distribute them to final users. Communication services, Internet access and software applications are all examples of ICT as a product.

Box 1.2 – Facebook: network effects in action

With more than 800 million active users in March 2012, Facebook is the most popular social network on the Internet. Founded in 2004 by Mark Zuckerberg and other fellow students at Harvard, Facebook is certainly one of the most striking examples to illustrate the power of network effects.

Facebook is a virtual social network connecting people and enhancing social interactions. In their Facebook walls, users communicate with friends and share content with them.

As in any community connecting people, each individual's willingness to join the network depends on the number of members: the more individuals are part of the network, the greater the opportunities for interactions. This is the mechanism which network effects are based on. Table 1.1 shows data on the diffusion of Facebook in ten countries where the social network is extremely popular; the last two columns show the two-year growth rate of Facebook users over the periods 2008–10 and 2010–12. All countries

are characterised by sustained adoption rates over the entire period taken into consideration; growth in the first two years was spectacular in all countries, with percentages of even four digits in Indonesia, Mexico and India. Clearly, growth slowed down in the period 2010–12 as the penetration of Facebook reached its saturation point. How can we explain such astonishing trends? Signing up for Facebook is completely free, but this is not enough to explain such figures. The most convincing explanation lies in the presence of strong network effects: as we shall study in Chapter 3, when network effects are strong, the so-called positive feedback kicks in. As the number of members increases the network becomes more and more attractive; other individuals sign up for membership, thus increasing network attractiveness even further.

This is exactly what happened to Facebook: new members induced other people to join the network, thus triggering exponential growth rates.

	Users		Two-year growth rate	
	31/12/2010	31/12/2012	2008–10	2010–12
U.S.	145,749,580	166,029,240	246.4%	13.9%
Indonesia	32,129,460	51,096,860	3481.7%	59.0%
U.K.	28,661,600	32,950,400	91.9%	15.0%
Turkey	24,163,600	32,131,260	204.5%	33.0%
France	20,469,420	25,624,760	210.7%	25.2%
Philippines	18,901,900	29,890,900	4738.0%	58.1%
Mexico	18,488,700	38,463,890	1183.4%	108.0%
Italy	17,812,800	23,202,640	218.9%	30.3%
India	17,288,900	62,713,680	1513.9%	262.7%
Canada	17,288,620	18,090,640	59.2%	4.6%

Table 1.1: the Facebook boom[a]

[a]Data available at http://www.nnickburcher.com.

Despite their ubiquity and the different roles which they may play (ICT as instruments or ICT as products), high-tech sectors share a common set of relevant economic features. In particular, Information & Communication Technologies are characterised by:

- **large economies of scale.** Typically, in ICT sectors, production is characterised by the presence of large fixed costs, on the one hand, and small, even negligible, variable/marginal costs, on the other; therefore, in most cases, ICT companies operate with a decreasing average cost function. Large fixed costs may arise for different reasons. Telecom companies, for instance, invest huge amounts of resources to deploy the physical infrastructure that they need to provide communication services. Similarly, the cost related to the realisation of the "first copy" of an information good is another example of a fixed cost generating economies of scale. Consider, for example, the movie or the music industry; producers incur significant costs for the realisation of the master copy of the movie/music CD, while the costs of reproduction and distribution are relatively small in magnitude. Furthermore, as mentioned above, ICT sectors are R&D intensive, another feature which implies the relevance of fixed costs over variable costs. Evans and Schmalensee (2002) provide clear evidence of the fact that production in new economy industries exhibits increasing returns to scale. According to the data presented by the two authors, in 1998 material expenses (variable costs) accounted for more than 50% of revenues in manufacturing industries overall; for ICT industries this figure goes down to less than 30%;

- **presence of network effects.** In many ICT sectors, the benefit an individual obtains when purchasing a product/adopting a technology increases with the number of users of the same product/technology; the term *network effects* (also known as *network externalities*) refers exactly to this feature: the utility enjoyed by a consumer when purchasing a product/technology increases with the size of the network of users. In the case of software, for example, the value of using an application is positively affected by the possibility of exchanging files with other individuals working with the same application or with a compatible one. Network effects are even more substantial in telecommunications or in social networks; here, the value of joining the network is essentially related to the possibility of getting in touch with other people;[3]

- **high innovation rates.** As argued in the previous discussion, ICT industries are R&D intensive and extremely innovative. In the case of several ICT sectors, companies are involved in winner-takes-all races, thus competing **for** the market rather than **within** the market. In these sectors, market dynamics are best described by the classical Schumpeterian model of *creative destruction* where market leaders

---

[3]In the literature, network effects are also referred to as demand-side economies of scale to distinguish them from the "traditional" supply-side economies of scale. While the latter refers to the fact that the average cost function decreases with the scale of production, with demand-side economies of scale, due to the fact that demand stimulates demand, it is the average revenue (i.e. the price) which increases with sales.

are bound to be soon replaced by the developer of the next superior technology. For example, cassette tapes replaced the 8-track, only to be replaced in turn by compact discs, which were undercut by MP3 players, which will in turn eventually be replaced by newer technologies. Large R&D investments are often associated with a sharp increase in firms' patenting activity;

- **substantial switching costs.** Many ICT products and technologies are char-acterised by the presence of significant costs when moving from one supplier to another or when changing products or technologies. Switching costs do not nec-essarily have only a monetary nature. For instance, consider the overall cost of switching from an Apple computer to a PC running the Windows operating system; the user not only has to pay the price of the new computer and of new software applications, but she/he also incurs substantial non-monetary expenses related to the time and the effort needed to learn how to use the new machine and the new software. When switching costs are large enough, customers are *locked-in* to their current provider.

The typical features of ICT sectors that we have briefly reviewed turn out to have im-portant consequences for market outcomes. For instance, the presence of large economies of scale implies that prices cannot converge to the marginal cost of production; if they do, companies cannot compensate the fixed costs they incur. For this reason, firms typi-cally engage in price discrimination strategies aimed at setting prices as close as possible to consumer willingness to pay.

We devote Chapter 2 to the analysis of price discrimination and the associated price dispersion in on-line markets. As suggested in Box 1.4, digital markets seem to be particularly suited for implementing discriminatory strategies; firms operating on-line can collect relevant information about consumer preferences and habits more ef-fectively, thus making it easier to set prices as close as possible to consumer willingness to pay.

In Chapter 3, we discuss some of the most interesting issues related to markets exhibiting network effects; in particular, we analyse how network effects influence the demand for high-tech products and market equilibrium. Part of the chapter is devoted to discussing the dynamics of technology adoption and to examining how a technology imposes itself as the market standard; we complete the analysis by studying oligopolistic interactions in network markets and by focusing in particular on compatibility strategies among rival firms.

Two-sided markets/networks are the main argument of Chapter 4. A market is said to be two-sided when two conditions are met: *i*) firms (platforms) intermediate between two separate groups of agents (the two sides of the market) and *ii*) the utility of an agent increases with the number of agents belonging to the other group (cross-side network effects). Video game consoles are a typical example of two-sided markets; the console producer is the intermediary (the platform) while the two sets of agents are consumers and video game developers. Consumers are not interested in buying the console if only a few games are available and, similarly, developers are not willing to write new games if only few consumers have purchased the console. Therefore, the console producer needs to induce both sides of the market to join the platform, for instance, by setting appropriate prices for the two groups of agents.

Box 1.3 – There's an app for that

Since the launch of Apple's iTunes app store in 2008, the segment for smartphone/tablet mobile applications (the so-called apps) has become one of the most dynamic high-tech markets. According to the website 148apps.biz, in May 2013, more than 880,000 applications, which had been developed by approximately 236,000 publishers, were available for download from the iTunes app store; the most popular app categories were games, education and entertainment (16.6%, 10.8% and 8.8% of the total number of apps respectively). Several companies, such as Google, RIM, Nokia, Samsung and Amazon just to mention some of the most important, tried to replicate the business model of iTunes. Today, the second biggest on-line app store is Google's Android market with nearly 700,000 applications (see www.appbrain.com/stats).

App stores are a typical example of two-sided platforms (see Kouris, 2011); they intermediate between software developers (the publishers), who create new applications and publish them in the app store, and smartphone/tablet users, who connect to the relevant store to download their favourite apps.

Stores provide publishers with software development kits and other tools that facilitate the creation of new apps; publishers, in turn, are entitled to set the price they wish for their apps.

App pricing is an extremely interesting issue. According to an article published in *The Wall Street Journal* on 3 March 2013, for apps "free is still king"; for instance, about 58% of iTunes apps are available to consumers free of charge. A recent study by Distimo reported that the average price for a paid app in iTunes is $3.18 (apps for iPhone) and $4.4 (apps for iPad); prices for paid apps in other stores are about 30% lower (e.g. $3.06 in the case of Android and $2.84 in the case of Amazon.com Inc's app store).

Developers generate revenues through advertising or by employing sophisticated pricing strategies; this is the case, for instance, of *freemium*, a strategy according to which publishers release a basic version of the app for free and set a price for more advanced versions of the software. This strategy appears to be suitable for certain categories of software, such as game apps, in particular.

Telecommunications, probably the most important sector in ICT, is the main subject of Chapter 5. This sector, which includes voice telephony, Internet access as well as radio and television broadcasting, is extremely dynamic with firms continuously launching new services and products; on top of that, the industry has been at the core of a radical liberalisation process during the last twenty years. Consequently, the industry structure is moving from the traditional *one-way access* model, whereby new telecom operators need access to the physical copper-network controlled by the incumbent firm, to *a two-way access* model characterised by the presence of competing infrastructured operators; these changes are currently posing new challenges for regulators whose intervention is no longer aimed at granting access to an essential infrastructure (the network controlled by the incumbent) but rather at favouring interconnection among rivals' networks.

Box 1.4 – Google: the new Big Brother?

Do you frequently visit sport websites when you surf the Internet? If your answer is yes, then probably you will have noticed that most of the ads that pop up on your screen are about sport products.

The reason why this occurs is related to the fact that modern technologies allow on-line firms to target their ads. Internet operators, in fact, are able to track users anonymously as they move around the web and to collect a series of relevant data (such as users' IP addresses, visited websites, date and time of access and other information on their habits and characteristics) revealing information on their preferences; this information is stored in so-called cookies, small text files saved on users' PCs, which can be used by firms for commercial purposes.

On-line vendors may use the behavioural data stored in cookies to price discriminate users, thus setting prices as close as possible to their willingness to pay; on top of that, these technologies have made targeted advertising more and more pervasive. For example, Facebook can gather information from members' profiles and select the ads that appear on their screens. Similarly, Internet search terms determine the next ad which a user can see on the pages of search results.

The ease with which on-line firms can collect and store personal information currently is posing serious concerns for individuals' privacy. For example, in the U.K., according to *The TRUSTe 2012 Consumer Data Privacy Study*, consumer concern about on-line privacy is growing: 94% of consumers are worried about their on-line privacy, a percentage which is almost twice that of 2011. The study suggests that the impact on businesses could be significant since consumers are likely to engage less with the companies that they don't trust.

For these reasons, more and more sites are adopting measures to protect users' personal information. Facebook, for example, has introduced privacy settings for all registered members. These settings include the possibility of blocking certain individuals from seeing one's profile, the opportunity of choosing one's friends and the possibility of restricting the content which one can access. Privacy settings are also available on other sites such as Google Plus and Twitter. Still, even a hint of data being collected surreptitiously can trigger a firestorm of bad publicity for a company; both heavyweights Microsoft and Intel have been forced to eliminate the features which allowed them to track customers over the Internet.

Nonetheless, all these efforts are considered insufficient to restore Internet trustworthiness; Google's experience is emblematic: despite all the measures taken to guarantee individual privacy, in April 2013, Google was fined 145,000 euros for what a regulator called "one of the biggest data protection rule violations known". The fine came after it had been proven that Google's Street View cars had been illegally collecting data from open Wi-Fi networks between 2008 and 2010.

In 2006 David Steele, a former service officer for the CIA, said that Google is "in bed with" the CIA, accusing the company of sharing information with the intelligence services. We do not know whether Steele was right or not; what is certain is that protection of personal information is one of the most critical issues concerning the Web.

High-tech firms often accumulate large patent portfolios; according to the European Patent Office (EPO), in 2011 more than 22% of the total number of patent applications at the EPO are related to ICT sectors. For some countries, these figures are even larger; in particular, more than 25% of French applications filed at the EPO belong to ICT sectors and this figure soars to more than 40% in the case of Sweden and Finland. In high-tech industries, the innovation process is highly cumulative with follow-on inventions building on earlier innovations; therefore, the whole process is characterised by a sequence of incremental steps where later innovations represent improvements of previous inventions. With cumulative innovation, patents may have conflicting effects on R&D incentives; we devote Chapter 6 to a detailed analysis of this topic. In particular, we focus on the design of the optimal patent policy in the case of cumulative innovation, an issue which is attracting more and more attention from policy makers and regulators. In Chapter 6, we also argue that in high-tech industries firms often employ patents strategically as "legal weapons" against competitors. According to some scholars this evidence urges for a thorough revision of the current patent and copyright system.

Chapter 7 is devoted to the analysis of possible departures from the traditional approach to protect intellectual property. Several high-tech sectors are experiencing striking innovation rates despite the low propensity of companies towards patenting, thus suggesting that there may be alternative forms to stimulate and protect innovation. A remarkable example of how innovation can flourish without exploiting patents and copyright is given by open source software, presented in detail in the second part of Chapter 7.

In the final chapter of the book we discuss some of the most interesting antitrust issues in ICT. The presence of substantial economies of scale combined with the effect of network externalities and the high innovation rates along with the common practice of filing several patent applications are all features which are likely to induce the emergence of dominant firms; for this reason, antitrust authorities must pay particular attention to the functioning of these markets.

Audience. This is a textbook of industrial organisation of ICT sectors; it blends theory with real-world applications. The theoretical models are presented in a clear and accessible way; through all the chapters of the book a series of boxes complements the presentation with additional anecdotal/empirical evidence.

The book is aimed at advanced undergraduate students with a background in microeconomics and game theory. It may represent a good reference also for more advanced courses in industrial organisation; in this case, the book should be complemented with additional material such as research articles. The volume can be useful also for practitioners in regulatory authorities or in consultancies interested in grasping the main economic issues of high-tech markets.

The materials of the book have been organised in order to create self-contained chapters which can be studied in isolation. Therefore, parts of the book are suitable to be used within courses which are not specifically dedicated to the economics of ICT (e.g. economics of networks, economics of innovation, applied microeconomics etc.).

Chapter 2

Digital Markets

2.1 Introduction

As mentioned briefly in the Introduction to this book, one of the most significant aspects of the so-called *new economy* lies in the fact that nowadays companies heavily rely on Information & Communication Technologies (ICT) to organise and manage their activities. This is true not only for already established businesses which often use these technologies to improve their efficiency, but also for entrepreneurs who, thanks to ICT, now have the opportunity to develop innovative business models.

The boom of e-commerce is one of the most evident examples of the relevance of ICT; an increasing number of firms uses the Internet not only to provide customers with better information on their products but also as an additional distribution channel. Progress in hardware and software technologies, more powerful telecommunication infrastructures along with the resulting growth of the Internet have led to the emergence of so-called "digital marketplaces", namely virtual (on-line) markets where consumers and suppliers meet to exchange products and services.

Nowadays, we can buy anything on-line: music CDs, books, software, electronic and ICT products, plane and train tickets, insurance policies and much more. According to a study by the European Commission, in 2011 more than 40% of European citizens used the Internet to buy products and services; the same study reveals that this figure is expected to increase to over 50% in 2015. In Europe, the United Kingdom and Germany are the two countries where individuals use the Internet most frequently to make their purchases; British and Germans make, respectively, 13.5 and 7.1% of their purchases on-line.[1] Amongst emerging economies, China's e-commerce continues to expand; with almost 600 million Internet users in 2012, in just a couple of years China's on-line

---

[1] These figures are taken from a research by the Boston Consulting Group.

shopping sales are expected to be worth more than 250 billion euros and possibly to exceed the size of the U.S. e-commerce market. Countries in the Middle East have experienced a similar exponential trend; the region is now home to more than 60 million Internet users and their preferred e-commerce segments are travelling and gambling.

One of the main reasons for the success of e-commerce is certainly the ease with which on the Web individuals can access relevant information on prices and products. However, this is not the only feature of digital marketplaces which we want to focus on; on the Internet:

1. companies can gain information on competitors' pricing strategies and products;

2. on-line sellers can react quickly to changes in market conditions; prices can be adjusted almost instantaneously without incurring substantial costs;

3. there are no physical boundaries; on-line, retailers and consumers can get in contact with each other even if they are far away.

These characteristics are the main reasons why many observers have thought of digital markets as a good approximation of perfect competition: these markets are transparent, frictionless and highly competitive. According to this view, prices on digital markets should be cost-oriented; the lack of frictions along with the abundant information which is available to all participants should lead to lower prices and greater efficiency.

Box 2.1 – E-commerce in Italy: looking for better deals?[a]

Every year Casaleggio Associati, an Italian consulting company, analyses the e-commerce market in Italy. The 2012 report was conducted through on-line questionnaires, telephone interviews and meetings involving more than 300 Italian e-commerce companies.

According to the study, e-commerce is particularly relevant for entertainment and leisure products and services (among these, on-line gambling is the most significant); in 2011 they accounted for more than a half of the total amount of on-line sales (56.9%), followed by tourism (24.8%) and electronics (5.3%).

Despite the economic downturn, in Italy, as in other countries, the total amount of on-line sales has greatly increased since 2008; in 2011, on-line revenues accounted for nearly 19 billion euros, with an average annual growth rate of around 40%.

Why do more and more consumers purchase on-line? The results of a series of interviews with some e-commerce companies shed light on this issue. According to Casaleggio Associati (2012), customers buy on-line because of the comfort of making purchases directly from home (31%), because of the ease with which they can compare several different offers (21%), or because some offers are available only on-line (9%).

It is interesting to note that for about a quarter of the respondents the main motivation behind on-line shopping is the expectation of finding lower prices.

[a]From Casaleggio Associati (2012).

The Economist and *Business Week*, two of the most influential economic magazines, totally agreed with this view; during the early days of the new economy they wrote:

> The explosive growth of the Internet promises a new age of perfectly competitive markets. With perfect information about prices and products at their fingertips, consumers can quickly and easily find the best deals. In this brave new world, retailers' profit margins will be competed away, as they are all forced to price at cost. (*The Economist*, November 1999)

> The Internet is a nearly perfect market because information is instantaneous and buyers can compare the offerings of sellers worldwide. The result is fierce price competition, dwindling product differentiation, and vanishing brand loyalty. (*Business Week*, May 1998)

Did these predictions turn out to be accurate? More than ten years have passed since they were made, so the time has come to assess whether or not they were correct. This is the aim of this chapter; before proceeding further, it is useful to briefly discuss the meaning of market efficiency and the possible ways of measuring it.

2.2 Market efficiency

Market efficiency can be assessed both in static and dynamic terms. From the static point of view, a market is efficient when firms minimise production costs (productive efficiency) and when market prices equal marginal costs (allocative efficiency); when a market is efficient, all individuals willing to pay a price which covers production costs actually buy the good and social welfare is maximised. Dynamic efficiency, instead, refers to innovation incentives for the development of new production processes or products. In this chapter we focus on static efficiency.[2]

Information plays a crucial role in determining market efficiency. From standard industrial organisation models, we know that, with homogeneous goods and price competition, the market is efficient provided that consumers are fully informed about prices and product characteristics. Fully informed consumers purchase the good from the firm charging the lowest price, thus inducing companies to adopt "undercutting strategies", i.e. to set prices below those charged by rivals in the attempt to increase their market share. Firms undercut each other until the market price equals the marginal cost of production; at this price social welfare is maximised and, therefore, market equilibrium corresponds to the perfectly competitive outcome.

---

[2]Chapters 6 and 7 focus on the issue of dynamic efficiency in high-tech markets.

Perfectly efficient markets do not exist in the real world; nonetheless, the quotes from *The Economist* and *Business Week* suggest that the advent of the Internet and of e-commerce have made markets become closer to the perfectly competitive paradigm. It is, therefore, interesting to study the effect of the Internet on market efficiency; as discussed by Smith et al. (2000), four indicators can be used to assess market efficiency: price levels, price elasticity of demand, relevance of menu costs and price dispersion. In particular, a market is said to be efficient when:

1. **prices are cost-oriented.** As discussed above, social welfare is maximised when prices equal marginal production costs. Therefore, the more prices are oriented to costs, the more efficient markets are;

2. **price elasticity of demand is high.** The price elasticity of demand measures how sensitive consumers are to changes in prices. A large price elasticity induces firms to price aggressively and to adopt undercutting strategies in order to increase their market shares. For this reason, high levels of elasticity of demand are associated with greater market efficiency;

3. **menu costs are low.** Menu costs are the expenses which a firm incurs when changing its prices. They may include the costs of informing distribution channels, of hiring consultants to design new pricing strategies, of updating computer systems or of retagging items, as well as the literal costs of printing new menus. Large menu costs make markets less competitive since they reduce the incentives for firms to adopt undercutting strategies;

4. **price dispersion is low.** According to standard models of competition, with homogeneous products and fully informed consumers, the same good cannot be sold at different prices: if a firm charges a price above its competitors it sells nothing. In a fully efficient market, retailers charge the same price for the same good. In general, price dispersion is used to measure market efficiency: the lower price dispersion, the more efficient the market.

If digital markets were more efficient than brick-and-mortar ones, then we expect lower prices, larger price elasticity of demand, firms which are more willing to change their menus, and less price dispersion on-line than off-line. The next section presents a review of the empirical literature on these issues.

2.2.1   Empirical evidence

In recent years, several authors have investigated the efficiency of digital markets; as documented below, empirical evidence does not always support the view according to which electronic markets are more efficient than brick-and-mortar ones. In this section, we present a brief review of some of the main contributions on this topic.

Price levels. The first empirical studies on this issue did not find clear evidence supporting the idea that prices on digital markets are substantially lower than on brick-and-mortar ones; the articles by Bailey (1998a) and Bailey (1998b) focus on markets for software, CDs and books, while Lee (1998) analyses auction data. Quite surprisingly, these studies find out that, for the same type of product, on-line prices tend to be generally higher than those charged on traditional markets.

More recent contributions reach the opposite conclusion: for consumers, on-line deals are better than off-line ones. Among these works, we recall the articles by Brown and Goolsbee (2002) (insurance products) and Brynjolfsson and Smith (2000) (books and CDs). A particularly interesting analysis is the one carried out by Scott-Morton et al. (2004) on the retail car industry; the authors provide evidence that consumers who use Internet referral services purchase products at lower prices (approximately by 2.2%). Finally, in a study on the publishing sector, Clay et al. (2002) find that there seems to be no significant price difference between on- and off-line markets.

Price elasticity of demand. The literature on price elasticity reaches mixed conclusions too. On the one hand, both Goolsbee (2000), in a detailed study on the behaviour of more than 25,000 on-line consumers, and Ellison and Ellison (2009), in an investigation on retail markets of hardware products, confirm the hypothesis of higher price elasticity for Internet purchases; likewise, using data from a major shopbot (price comparison website) for books, Brynjolfsson et al. (2010) find that on-line price elasticity is relatively high compared to off-line markets. On the other hand, Degeratu et al. (2000) (several mass-market products) and Pozzi (2009) (breakfast cereals) find that on-line consumers are less price sensitive than off-line ones.

Menu costs. Menu costs are difficult to measure; for this reason, the empirical literature often proxies them with the frequency with which firms change their prices. Various studies, including those by Bailey (1998a), Bailey (1998b) and Brynjolfsson and Smith (2000), agree on the fact that on-line retailers adjust price lists more frequently than off-line ones. Even though the frequency of price adjustments is only an indirect measure of menu costs, the evidence just presented provides a pretty clear indication according to which, at least in this respect, digital markets perform better than traditional ones.

Price dispersion. The last dimension used to assess the efficiency of on-line markets is price dispersion; most empirical studies do not support the hypothesis of lower on-line dispersion. The literature on this issue is quite well developed and it could not be otherwise; the topic is closely connected to the way firms form their prices strategies and it is extremely fascinating for economists. Furthermore, prices are more easily observable than, let's say, menu costs or price elasticity of demand and, therefore, dispersion is much simpler to study. The articles by Brynjolfsson and Smith (2000) (books and CDs), Clay et al. (2001) (books) and Clemons et al. (2002) (air tickets) are among the most interesting and they all agree on one point: on digital markets, the degree of price dispersion is not lower than on brick-and-mortar ones. In a more recent paper, Bounie et al. (2012) show that on-line price dispersion increases with the number of sellers; the authors explain this evidence by arguing that new sellers price their product significantly below the price charged by incumbents.

This brief review reveals that digital markets are not as efficient as one would expect; further support for this evidence comes from a very interesting research by Michael Baye, John Morgan and Patrick Scholten. These three scholars monitored the prices of more than 5,000 products sold on-line from August 2000 to February 2007. Thanks to the great amount of observations collected, it was possible for the three authors to build a series of indicators aimed at measuring digital market efficiency. Figures 2.1 and 2.2 show two such indicators.[3] The Internet Competitiveness index (Figure 2.1) is a comprehensive measure of the level of on-line competition. Increases of the index reveal more competitive pricing, while decreases signal a weakening of competition. The Relative Price Dispersion index (Figure 2.2) is the coefficient of variation in the prices charged by different sellers for the same products. It is zero when all sellers charge the same prices.

The Internet Competitiveness index does not follow a particular trend, neither upwards nor downwards. The Relative Price Dispersion index, instead, exhibits a slightly decreasing trend; nevertheless, it is still well above zero, suggesting that on digital markets price dispersion is high and persistent.

To summarise, the empirical evidence we have briefly reviewed does not seem to support the widespread opinion according to which digital markets are the best real-world approximation of perfect competition.

Therefore, a natural question arises: why are digital markets so far from efficiency despite satisfying many of the conditions required for perfect competition to emerge? This is an issue of great interest which has recently attracted the attention of many scholars both in economics and in management. The following sections review some of

---

[3]We thank Michael Baye for the permission to show these diagrams. Other data and figures are available at URL www.nash-equilibrium.com.

the most compelling contributions of this literature.

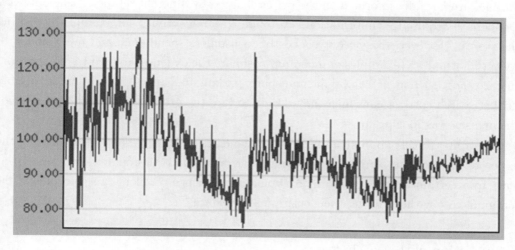

Figure 2.1: Internet Competitiveness index (from 28/08/2000 to 16/02/2007)

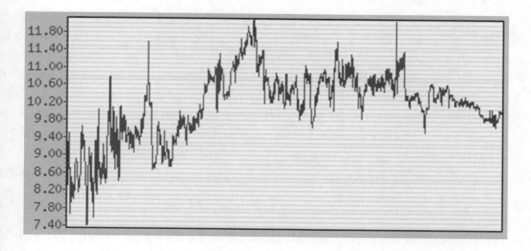

Figure 2.2: Relative Price Dispersion index (from 28/08/2000 to 16/02/2007)

2.3 Price dispersion on digital markets

2.3.1 Search costs

One of the explanations provided by the economics literature for the inefficiency of potentially competitive markets is based on the existence of so-called search costs.

The basic idea of search cost models is that in most cases potential consumers of a product are not fully informed on the prices charged by different retailers. The only way for them to acquire this information is through a search activity, for example by visiting the stores. However, this activity is costly: consumers spend time and even money to collect information (examples of monetary costs are the expenses related to moving from shop to shop, such as petrol, public transport, parking fees and so on). In order to avoid further search costs, a consumer may decide to buy the product even if the price is not the one she was looking for.

According to this approach, market inefficiencies can be explained as an effect of the expenses of searching activities: consumers do not search thoroughly and remain, at least to a certain extent, uninformed about prices, hence retailers can price above the marginal cost without losing their entire market share.

Competition with search costs

A simple model can be used to highlight the role of search costs.[4] Consider two stores, A and B, that sell a homogeneous product and compete in prices. Suppose that store A has just been opened. Store B, instead, has been selling the product for some time and, therefore, has a number of "loyal" customers. These consumers are willing to purchase the product from B regardless of the price charged. Besides loyal consumers, demand also consists of a number of "unloyal" customers, who may buy the product from any of the two shops, depending on the price they charge. Unloyal consumers are uninformed on prices; however, before purchasing they may undertake a search activity in order to collect information to find out which is the most convenient store.

In what follows, η_B denotes the mass of consumers loyal to store B, while the mass of unloyal consumers is assumed to be 1. Therefore, the entire market amounts to $1 + \eta_B$ consumers.

Let p_A and p_B be the prices charged by store A and store B, respectively. We assume that store B cannot discriminate between loyal and unloyal consumers and, therefore, it charges p_B to everybody. This assumption implies that in equilibrium $p_A \leq p_B$. Store B has lower incentives than A to cut prices in order to attract unloyal consumers; if it does so, it suffers from a reduction of revenues collected from loyal consumers. Therefore, we can focus only on the case where p_A is smaller than or equal to p_B.[5]

---

[4]We present a simplified version of the model by Shy (1996).

[5]Note that we are assuming that unloyal consumers are unaware of the existence of consumers who are loyal to store B. If, instead, they were aware, they would anticipate that $p_A \leq p_B$ and, therefore, they would purchase from store A without searching at all.

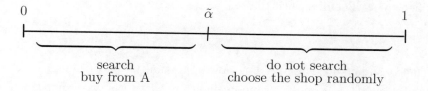

Figure 2.3: market segmentation of unloyal consumers

In order to acquire information on p_A and p_B, unloyal consumers need to devote a certain amount of time $s > 0$ to search activities. Searching, of course, implies an opportunity cost: the time spent collecting information on prices may be alternatively used for more enjoyable activities. We assume that consumers have heterogeneous preferences with regard to their opportunity cost of time. In particular, we assume that: $i)$ search costs are αs, with α measuring the opportunity cost of time, and $ii)$ α is uniformly distributed over the interval $[0, 1]$. Therefore, consumers who are not severely hurt by searching are characterised by a low level of α, while those who do not like to go shopping have a high level of α.

Let's now determine the demand functions of the two stores. Consider an unloyal consumer of type α. She has two options: either she does not search (thus saving αs) or she searches in order to find which is the store with the best deal. In the former case, the consumer does not know where she can find the product at the lowest price and so she is indifferent between the two stores. Assuming that she visits each store with probability $1/2$, her expected utility is:

$$U_{ns}(\alpha) = k - \frac{p_A + p_B}{2},$$

where k is the consumer's evaluation of the good (or gross utility) and $(p_A + p_B)/2$ is the price she expects to pay; subscript ns denotes the fact that we are referring to the case of no search activities.

If the consumer chooses to search, she incurs costs αs and obtains all the necessary information in order to purchase at the cheapest price. As mentioned earlier, store A offers the best deal in equilibrium, therefore the net utility for the consumer of type α who searches is:

$$U_s(\alpha) = k - p_A - \alpha s.$$

How many unloyal consumers decide to search? To answer this question we need to identify the indifferent consumer, i.e. the consumer who is indifferent between searching and not searching at all. From the condition $U_{ns}(\alpha) = U_s(\alpha)$, the indifferent consumer is identified by a value of α such that:

$$\tilde{\alpha} = \frac{p_B - p_A}{2s}.$$

All the consumers for whom $\alpha \leq \tilde{\alpha}$ (low opportunity cost of time), search, while the others, those with $\alpha > \tilde{\alpha}$, make a random choice between the two stores (see Figure 2.3). Following the assumption according to which α is uniformly distributed over $[0, 1]$, the mass of customers who searches equals $\tilde{\alpha}$; the remaining customers, $1 - \tilde{\alpha}$, choose the store randomly: $(1 - \tilde{\alpha})/2$ buy from store A and $(1 - \tilde{\alpha})/2$ from store B. Recalling that in equilibrium $p_A \leq p_B$, the demand functions of the two stores are:

$$D_A(p_A, p_B) = \tilde{\alpha} + \frac{1 - \tilde{\alpha}}{2} = \frac{1}{2} + \frac{p_B - p_A}{4s}, \qquad D_B(p_A, p_B) = \eta_B + \frac{1 - \tilde{\alpha}}{2} = \eta_B + \frac{1}{2} - \frac{p_B - p_A}{4s}.$$

Store A's demand is made up of unloyal consumers only: all the $\tilde{\alpha}$ consumers who search (and find out that $p_A \leq p_B$) and half of the consumers who choose the store randomly. Store B's demand, instead, consists of the loyal consumers and half of the unloyal ones who do not search.

For simplicity, we assume that production costs for both stores equal zero; therefore, the profits of the two stores are:

$$\pi_A(p_A) = \left(\frac{1}{2} + \frac{p_B - p_A}{4s} \right) p_A, \qquad \pi_B(p_B) = \left(\eta_B + \frac{1}{2} - \frac{p_B - p_A}{4s} \right) p_B.$$

By differentiating π_A with respect to p_A and π_B with respect to p_B and then by solving the system of first order conditions, we determine the equilibrium prices:

$$p_A^* = \frac{2}{3} s \left(3 + 2\eta_B \right) > 0, \qquad p_B^* = \frac{2}{3} s \left(3 + 4\eta_B \right) > 0. \tag{2.1}$$

Expressions (2.1) deserve some comments. Firstly, B's price is larger than A's, thus confirming the previous arguments. Secondly, both prices are positive; this fact implies that they exceed the marginal production costs (assumed equal to zero in this model). Moreover, prices increase with s. Therefore, prices are above marginal production costs and they get larger as search costs increase. Finally, note also that price dispersion enlarges with s; formally, $p_B^* - p_A^* = (4s\eta_B)/3 > 0$ is increasing in s. Summarising:

Result 1. *With search costs: i) prices exceed marginal production costs, ii) there is price dispersion.*

Despite its simplicity, this model is extremely interesting because it shows that if consumers are not fully informed and if searching is costly, a potentially competitive market turns out to be inefficient with firms enjoying market power: they can price above marginal production costs without losing all of their customers.

At this point, it is useful to interpret the results of the model in relation to digital markets. The question is the following: how informative is this model in explaining price dispersion in digital markets? Probably not very much. On-line search costs are likely to be negligible: thanks to Internet search engines, it is extremely simple for anyone to collect information on prices and products; moreover, comparing offers on-line is even easier thanks to specialised websites (known as "shopping bots") which directly collect information about prices and compare them on behalf of customers.

On the basis of the above results, negligible search costs lead to very low prices and to minor price dispersion. However, as discussed earlier in this chapter, empirical evidence has shown that, both the level and the dispersion of on-line prices are high. This evidence implies that search costs do not represent a convincing explanation for price dispersion in the case of digital markets.

2.3.2   A model of sales

As argued in the previous section, search costs cannot explain on-line price dispersion. Thanks to the Internet consumers can collect information on prices instantly and for free. Furthermore, price dispersion due to search costs cannot possibly be long-lasting. As time passes by, information on prices becomes common knowledge and, therefore, consumers are soon aware of where they can get the best deal.

An alternative explanation to price dispersion is provided by Hal Varian in a famous article published in 1980 in the *American Economic Review*. According to this work, retailers choose their prices "randomly" thus leading to equilibria with price dispersion. Varian's work originates from the observation of retail markets. Stores frequently change their prices over time (for instance because of "sales") or they inform customers of the limited duration of their special offers. Two are the main features of these kinds of practises which are important for our analysis: *i)* variations in prices are frequent; *ii)* offers do not seem to be related to specific market conditions or pricing strategies but they often appear as the result of random choices.

In the analysis, Varian shows that it may actually be optimal for retailers to randomly choose prices. This fact produces two main consequences. Firstly, since the probability of different stores randomly choosing exactly the same price is zero, then market equilibrium is characterised by price dispersion. Secondly, consumers cannot be informed on prices even if search costs are null: firms continuously change their prices and this means that a consumer cannot infer any information about current prices from past ones; each store makes its choice randomly so new prices are not related in any way whatsoever to past ones.

From this brief introduction, it is clear that Varian's approach is particularly suitable for digital markets. Even though the article was published before the Internet had been properly developed, the model actually includes two typical aspects of digital markets: little menu costs (therefore the possibility to change prices frequently) and negligible search costs.

The model

Consider a large number of consumers who wish to purchase a single unit of a product which is available at $n \geq 2$ stores. For simplicity, we assume that consumers have homogeneous preferences and that they receive a gross utility $k > 0$ from the product. Before making her purchase, each consumer can collect information on prices charged by all retailers without incurring any search cost. We assume that I consumers acquire information on prices and purchase the product at the cheapest store (we refer to these as "informed consumers"). The remaining consumers, denoted by D, do not look for any information; they choose the store at random and purchase the product if the price is lower than or equal to their willingness to pay, k (we refer to these as "uninformed consumers"). We also assume that uninformed consumers are spread evenly across the various stores; therefore, $D/n \equiv NI$ is the fraction of uninformed consumers which visits each store. Finally, we assume that if all stores charge the same price, also informed consumers are spread evenly across stores.

Let's now move to the retailers. We assume that their cost function exhibits economies of scale: retailers incur high fixed costs (such as rent, salaries and so on) while their marginal costs are relatively small. Formally, let $C(q)$ denote the retailers' cost function; we assume that the average cost, $AC(q) = C(q)/q$, is decreasing in q. Finally, in order to represent a competitive scenario, we assume that the market is characterised by free entry.

Assumption. *On the market there is free entry.*

The lack of barriers to entry implies that as long as expected profits are positive, new stores enter the market; the entry process makes the market more and more competitive and it stops only when there is no more room for additional stores. Consequently, expected profits in equilibrium are zero; formally, $E[\pi_i] = 0$ where π_i denotes store i's profits while E is the expected value operator.

The aim of our analysis is to characterise the retailers' pricing strategies; we start by determining the upper and lower bounds of price p. A retailer never charges a price exceeding consumer willingness to pay: with $p > k$ no single unit of the product is sold; therefore, the upper bound of the price equals k. At the same time, a store never charges

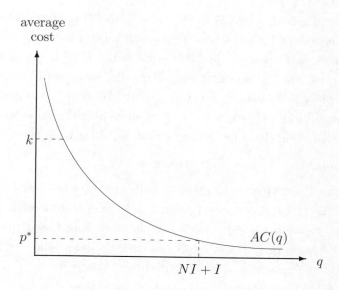

Figure 2.4: the costs of production

a price below its average production cost, $AC(q)$. On the basis of our assumptions on consumer behaviour, $NI+I$ is the maximum number of consumers that a store may hope to serve: at most a retailer can sell the product to its fraction of uninformed consumers (NI) and to all the informed ones (I), provided that it charges the lowest price. Since $AC(q)$ is decreasing in q, the minimum level of average production cost in equilibrium equals $AC(NI+I)$ (see Figure 2.4). This implies that the lower bound of the price is $AC(NI+I) \equiv p^*$. Summarising, each retailer chooses a price such that $p \in [p^*, k]$.

The n retailers are identical; therefore, we focus on symmetric equilibria in which all of them play the same pricing strategy. The first important result we prove is the following:

Result 2. *An equilibrium in pure strategies in which all stores charge the same price does not exist.*

The proof of this result is rather straightforward. Suppose that all retailers charge the same price p. Consumers, informed and uninformed, are evenly spread across the n stores; therefore, each retailer sells $I/n + NI$ units of product incurring an average cost $AC(I/n + NI)$. Note that p cannot be lower than $AC(I/n + NI)$ because, otherwise, each retailer would make losses. Consider, therefore, a price $p \geq AC(I/n + NI)$. This cannot be the equilibrium price neither: for a retailer it would be profitable to marginally decrease its price; in this way, it would increase sales up to $I + NI$ (i.e. it would serve its fraction of uninformed consumers and all the informed ones) and it would reduce its average cost from $AC\,(I/n + NI)$ to $AC\,(I + NI)$. These arguments are enough to prove that there is no equilibrium where all retailers charge the same price p.

Result 2 implies that the only possible equilibrium is in mixed strategies. Each retailer sets the price in a probabilistic way. Formally, each retailer chooses $p \in [p^*, k]$ on the basis of a probability density function denoted by $f(p)$.[6] It is interesting to note that even if the equilibrium is symmetric and retailers play the same strategy $f(p)$, the probability of two of them charging the same price equals zero. Therefore:

Result 3. *In equilibrium there is price dispersion.*

Now we proceed by characterising the equilibrium in mixed strategies. The first step is to determine retailers' expected profits. Consider store i setting price p. Two events may occur: $a)$ all the $n - 1$ rival stores charge a price larger than p, $b)$ at least one rival store charges a price below p. Given that all the n stores choose their price according to the same $f(p)$, event $a)$ occurs with probability equal to $(1 - F(p))^{n-1}$, where $F(p) = \int f(p)dp$ is the cumulative density function associated with $f(p)$. Therefore, with probability $(1 - F(p))^{n-1}$, store i charges the lowest price, it sells to all the informed consumers (in addition to its fraction of uninformed consumers) thus obtaining:

$$\pi^a(p) = p\,(I + NI) - C(I + NI).$$

Event $b)$, where at least one rival store charges a price lower than i's, occurs with probability $1 - (1 - F(p))^{n-1}$. In this case, store i serves its fraction of uninformed consumers only, thus obtaining:

$$\pi^b(p) = p\,NI - C(NI).$$

By putting all these arguments together, store i's expected profits when charging p are:

$$E\,[\pi_i] = \int_{p^*}^{k} \left\{ \pi^a(p)(1 - F(p))^{n-1} + \pi^b(p)\left(1 - (1 - F(p))^{n-1}\right) \right\} f(p)dp.$$

From the free entry assumption, the expected profits for each retailer in equilibrium equal zero, $E\,[\pi_i] = 0$. Moreover, following the definition of mixed strategies, each retailer is indifferent among any price within the support of $f(p)$; this fact, along with condition $E\,[\pi_i] = 0$, implies that for any $p \in [p^*, k]$ expected profits are zero. Formally:

$$\pi^a(p)(1 - F(p))^{n-1} + \pi^b(p)\left(1 - (1 - F(p))^{n-1}\right) = 0, \quad \forall p \in [p^*, k].$$

---

[6]Note that the support of the density function corresponds to the entire interval $[p^*, k]$. This fact can be proved by contradiction; suppose the support is $[p^*, \bar{p}]$ with $\bar{p} < k$. In this case, by definition, $F(\bar{p}) = 1$: by charging $p = \bar{p}$, the retailer sells only to its fraction of uninformed consumers, thus obtaining profits equal to $\bar{p}NI - C(NI)$. However $\bar{p}$ cannot be the equilibrium price: by increasing the price to $p = k$, the retailer still sells to NI uninformed consumers, thus obtaining $kNI - C(NI) > \bar{p}NI - C(NI)$. A similar argument can be used to prove that the lower bound of the interval is p^*.

Box 2.2 – Varian's model in action[a]

The theoretical predictions of Varian's model of sales have been empirically tested by Michael Baye, John Morgan and Patrick Scholten in an article published in 2006.

The authors observed the evolution of prices of the 36 most popular high-tech products classified into the following three categories of homogeneous items: software, computers and electronic devices. Data was collected from `Shopper.com`, one of the most visited price comparison sites, over a period of 18 months (from November 1999 to May 2001).

In particular, the authors wanted to test the two main predictions of Varian's model: i) the presence of persistent price dispersion in on-line markets (see Result 3) and ii) the tendency of price dispersion to be smaller the lower the consumer reservation value. Prediction ii) is a natural extension of the analysis we have discussed in the text: in equilibrium retailers randomly select prices according to the probability density function $f(p)$ defined over $[p^*, k]$; clearly, the support of $f(p)$ reduces for smaller values of k (the consumer reservation price) which implies lower price dispersion.

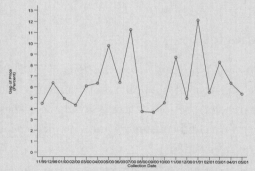

Figure 2.5: price dispersion on `Shopper.com`

As far as prediction i) is concerned, the authors computed several indexes of price dispersion; all the indicators show a significant and persistent dispersion. Just to take a relevant example, Figure 2.5 shows the evolution of the index of price dispersion calculated as the percentage difference between the highest and the lowest price for the same product; this index fluctuates be-

tween 7% and 10% and it features no particular trend.

Consider now prediction ii). Since consumer willingness to pay cannot be directly observed, Baye, Morgan and Scholten used an indirect approach. They moved from the consideration according to which high-tech products have a relatively short life cycle and, consequently, as products get older, consumer reservation values decline; hence, to test prediction ii) it is sufficient to observe how price ranges evolve over time. More specifically, the authors defined two dummy variables: D_1 is a dummy variable for whether the observation comes from six to ten months from the end of the data set; D_2 is a dummy variable for whether the observation comes from the last five months of the data set. Therefore, D_1 includes products that are newer than those of D_2; if prediction ii) is correct, the price range for products observed in D_2 should be smaller than the price range for products in D_1.

By using GLS (*Generalised Least Squares*) to correct for the presence of heteroscedasticity in the error term, the authors estimated the following equation:

$$RANGE_{it} = \beta_0 + \beta_1 D_1 + \beta_2 D_2 + \beta_r M_{it} + \gamma X_i + \epsilon_{it}$$

where $RANGE_{it}$ is the range in prices for product i on date t, M_{it} is the manufacturer's suggested retail price for product i on date t, and the vector X_i consists of dummies for the type of product (software, peripherals, or accessories) to control for systematic biases. The coefficients of interest are β_1 and β_2: a negative value implies greater price "compression" (smaller price range).

The estimated values of β_1 and β_2 are negative and statistically significant ($\beta_1 = -4.58$ and $\beta_2 = -12.59$). These results suggest that the prices of the products included in D_2, the less recent ones, fluctuate within a smaller range (prices more compressed) than those included in D_1 (newer products). All this seems to confirm the prediction of Varian's model, namely that a lower price dispersion is associated with a lower consumer willingness to pay.

---

[a]From Baye et al. (2006).

On the basis of this condition, it is easy to derive the strategy played by each retailer; formally, the equilibrium strategy is represented by the following cumulative density function:

$$F^*(p) = 1 - \left(\frac{\pi^b(p)}{\pi^b(p) - \pi^a(p)} \right)^{\frac{1}{n-1}}.$$

Varian's model shows that it is optimal for firms to choose prices randomly.[7] This result is important for two reasons. First, it proves that there can be price dispersion despite the absence of search costs. Second, it is consistent with the fact that price dispersion is a persistent phenomenon. To understand this latter point, we need to interpret Varian's model dynamically. Prices charged in the past are uninformative: future prices are chosen randomly according to the equilibrium strategy. Past and future prices are, therefore, uncorrelated. Hence, consumers can never be fully informed on the commercial strategies adopted by retailers and this makes price dispersion a long-lasting phenomenon.

As mentioned earlier, the absence of both menu and search costs makes Varian's model particularly appropriate to study digital markets. For this reason some authors have recently extended Varian's analysis in order to investigate several features of digital markets. In the following section, we present one of these extensions.

2.3.3   Competition and infomediaries

Baye and Morgan, in an article published in the *American Economic Review* in 2001, extend Varian's model in order to examine the role of shopping bots, namely price comparison websites which automatically search for the lowest prices available. These websites can be seen as intermediaries between firms and consumers and, for this reason, they are commonly known as infomediaries or gatekeepers.

Infomediaries are not a completely new phenomenon. For instance, in the housing market, real estate agencies act as intermediaries between buyers and sellers of real estates in a certain area. However, it is clear that the widespread use of the Internet has greatly increased both the number and the importance of information gatekeepers. The reasons for this are twofold: on the one hand, on-line retailers can reach a larger set of potential consumers, as compared to what happens when using more traditional means of communication and, on the other hand, consumers can compare prices more easily.

---

[7]Morgan and Sefton (2001) extend Varian's analysis to study the impact of an increase in the number of uniformed consumers on the equilibrium prices; they show that the average price increases with D and therefore market efficiency reduces with the number of uninformed consumers.

In what follows, we present a simplified version of the original model by Baye and Morgan. The analysis is interesting since it clarifies the role of gatekeepers in improving the diffusion of relevant information, thus enhancing market efficiency.

Consider two firms selling a homogeneous product; they produce the good with the same technology characterised by a constant marginal cost, c. Each firm operates in a local market; absent the gatekeeper, the geographical distance between the two markets is such that consumers can purchase from the local firm only which, therefore, operates as a monopolist. For simplicity, we assume that:

- in each market there is a mass equal to 1 of consumers with homogeneous preferences;

- each consumer's demand function is denoted by $d(p)$;

- each consumer who decides to visit the store of the local monopolist incurs search costs equal to s.[8]

Absent the gatekeeper, each monopolist chooses the price in order to maximise the profits generated in the local market: $\pi(p) = (p - c)d(p)$. In what follows, p^m and π^m denote the equilibrium price and profits of the monopolist, respectively. Finally, we assume that the surplus which a consumer obtains when purchasing the quantity $d(p^m)$ at price p^m exceeds search costs s; this means that for a consumer it is convenient to visit the local store and purchase.

Let's consider now what happens if there is a gatekeeper. Two are the main effects related to the presence of this operator. First, a gatekeeper removes the geographical barriers between the two markets; thanks to the gatekeeper: i) firms can provide information on their prices not only to local consumers but also to those "living" in the other market, and ii) consumers can purchase also from the firm located in the distant market. The second effect related to the presence of a gatekeeper is that consumers can obtain information on prices, and eventually buy products, without incurring search costs, since they do not need to physically visit the local store.

The gatekeeper is a profit-maximising business; it offers intermediation services which both consumers and firms pay a fee for. Let ϕ denote the advertising fee that firms pay the gatekeeper in order to post their prices on the website, while ψ is the subscription fee for consumers to access the website and observe prices.

---

[8]Note that similarly to the model presented in Section 2.3.1, looking for information in local markets implies a positive search cost.

Box 2.3 – AutoScout24

AutoScout24 is the largest on-line marketplace for buying and selling new and used cars in Europe. It was founded in Germany in 1988 and it expanded abroad very soon. Today the site is active in almost all European countries with more than 1 million visitors per month; in Italy, for example, almost all car dealers advertise their offers on AutoScout24 and consumers that visit the website access a virtually unlimited catalogue: if one considers both new and second hand cars there are more than two million different vehicles available!

The website's success is also due to the extreme flexibility of its search engine; for example, when searching for a second hand car, it is possible to specify: brand, model, fuel type (gasoline, diesel, hybrid), price range, registration year and much more (see Figure 2.6). It is possible to view only the offers which include photos of the vehicle, or only those made by dealers or by privates. One can also refine the search according to many other criteria (colour, comfort, safety and environment, optionals and so on).

Thanks to this powerful search interface, the visitor is guided in her choice so that she can easily compare prices and models and quickly find the car she is looking for.

Figure 2.6: AutoScout24

According to the model by Baye and Morgan, the timing of the game is the following:

$t = 0$: the gatekeeper chooses ϕ and ψ;

$t = 1$: consumers decide whether or not to subscribe to the gatekeeper's site;

$t = 2$: firms choose the price of their product and decide whether or not to post it on the gatekeeper's website. As in Baye and Morgan (2001), we assume that firms cannot discriminate between consumers who buy the product on-line (through the gatekeeper's website) and those who purchase off-line (by visiting the local store). In other words, the price posted on the website has to be the same as the price charged in the local store;

$t = 3$: consumers decide whether or not to purchase, from which of the two firms and whether to buy on-line or off-line.

Given the dynamic nature of the game, in order to define the equilibrium, we proceed by backward induction: first we characterise the optimal decision of consumers in the last stage of the game and then we determine what happens in the previous stages.

Consumer behaviour ($t = 3$)

The optimal decision of a consumer in $t = 3$ depends on whether she has subscribed to the website and on whether firms have posted their prices on-line. We prove that the optimal strategy for a consumer is the following:

  i) a consumer who has not subscribed to the gatekeeper's site purchases from the local firm;

  ii) a consumer who has subscribed to the gatekeeper's site: a) visits the website and b) chooses the best price which is available on-line;

  iii) if a consumer visits the gatekeeper's website and no firm has posted its price on-line, then she purchases off-line from the local store.

The proof of points i) and iii) is straightforward. Since it is not profitable for firms to charge a price above p^m (the monopoly price) then, by purchasing off-line, a consumer obtains a surplus which is large enough to cover search costs s, as argued previously. Also the proof of point iia) is straightforward; a consumer who has already paid the subscription fee ψ can observe on-line prices without incurring any further costs.

The proof of point iib) is more articulated. If some prices are posted on-line, three are the scenarios that a consumer may face: 1) only the local firm's price is posted (the other firm has not paid the advertising fee), 2) only the other firm's price is posted (the local firm has not paid the advertising fee), or 3) both prices are posted. In case 1) it is clear that the consumer purchases on-line in order to save search costs. Case 3) is straightforward too: if both firms advertise prices on-line then the consumer chooses the lowest.

Consider case 2) which occurs when only the other firm's price is posted on-line; once the consumer has observed the price posted by the other firm, she may decide to spend s and visit the local store. This latter option is desirable only if the consumer expects the local firm to charge a price substantially cheaper than that posted on-line. In particular, the local price should be low enough to compensate the consumer for search costs s.

The question, therefore, is the following: is it profitable for the local firm to charge such a low price? The answer is negative and the argument goes as follows. Consider a consumer who has visited the local store and, therefore, has already spent s. When deciding whether to buy from the local store or on-line, she simply compares the two prices, without considering s: search costs have already been incurred and are, therefore, sunk. This means that the optimal choice for the local firm is to charge a price which is only marginally lower than the rival's. In this way, the product is sold to all consumers who visit the store (and who have sunk s). Therefore, when operating only in the local market, it is not profitable for a firm to charge a price substantially below the rival's. Consequently, if only the other firm's price is posted, then the consumer is better off by purchasing on-line without visiting the local store (point *iib)*).

Firm behaviour $(t = 2)$

Let us move to the firms' decision to advertise their prices on-line or not. For the sake of simplicity, we restrict the analysis to the case of symmetric equilibria where the two firms: *a)* decide to post prices on the gatekeeper's website with the same probability $\alpha \in [0, 1]$ and *b)* adopt the same pricing strategy.

Let $\mu > 0$ denote the percentage of consumers who, in each market, subscribe to the website;[9] therefore, the overall amount of subscribing consumers is 2μ. Firms take their decisions by comparing expected profits when posting their price on-line and when acting off-line only.

Firm's expected profits when it posts the price on-line. Suppose that a firm has decided to advertise its price on-line. The first important result shown by Baye and Morgan is summarised by the following observation:

Observation 1. *A firm that advertises its price on-line plays mixed strategies and chooses p randomly according to the probability density function $f(p)$.*

To prove this result we use the same arguments as in Varian's model of sales. When a firm posts the price on-line, its cost function exhibits economies of scale (decreasing average cost): the firm produces at constant marginal cost c and, in addition, it incurs a fixed cost ϕ, the advertisement fee owed to the gatekeeper. As in Varian's model, this fact implies that there cannot be an equilibrium in which firms choose prices deterministically. This can be proved by contradiction: if the two firms choose the same price, then each of them serves half of the 2μ subscribers; thus for a firm it is profitable to undercut the rival in order to sell to all of the 2μ subscribers: by reducing the price, the firm increases sales and lowers the average production cost. As mentioned above, following

---

[9]The case of $\mu = 0$ is trivial: if no consumer subscribes to the website then it is not profitable for a firm to advertise prices on-line (see Result 5).

the same arguments as in the model of sales, when a firm operates on-line it plays mixed strategies, i.e. it chooses the price on the basis of a probability density function $f(p)$. Clearly, even though they play the same pricing strategy, since the probability of the two firms selecting the same price is zero, then Observation 1 also implies that there is price dispersion.

Let $F(p)$ denote the cumulative density function associated with $f(p)$; from Observation 1, it follows that the expected profits for a firm which advertises prices on-line and charges p are:

$$E\left[\pi^{on}(p)\right] = \underbrace{(1 - \mu)\,\pi(p)}_{\text{off-line}} + \underbrace{2\mu\left[(1 - \alpha)\,\pi(p) + \alpha(1 - F(p))\pi(p)\right]}_{\text{on-line}} - \phi.$$

The first term of this expression represents the expected profits from the local market (off-line): a mass $(1 - \mu)$ of consumers does not subscribe to the website and purchases the good from the local store. The second term represents the expected profits from on-line sales, a potential market made up of 2μ consumers. In particular, the firm knows that with probability $1 - \alpha$ the rival does not advertise its price on-line and, hence, in this case, the firm serves all the subscribers. Alternatively, with probability α also the rival posts its price on the gatekeeper's website and, in this case, the firm sells to all the subscribers only if it charges the lowest price; this event occurs with probability $(1 - F(p))$. Finally, ϕ is the advertising fee owed to the gatekeeper.

Note that, since firms play mixed strategies when choosing prices, any p belonging to the support of the cumulative density function $F(p)$ yields the same expected profits $E\left[\pi^{on}(p)\right]$.

Expected profits when operating in the local market only. On the basis of the optimal consumer behaviour in $t = 3$, when the firm does not post its price, it sells the product only to local consumers who cannot purchase from the other firm either because they have not subscribed to the gatekeeper's website or because the rival firm does not advertise its price on-line. Clearly, the optimal price charged by the firm in this case is p^m, the monopoly price.

Observation 2. *The optimal price for a firm which sells the product only locally (off-line) is p^m.*

Following this observation, we can determine the expected profits of a firm operating exclusively in the local market:

$$E\left[\pi^{off}(p^m)\right] = (1 - \mu)\pi^m + \mu\,(1 - \alpha)\,\pi^m.$$

As argued above, this expression shows that the firm serves local consumers only: all the $(1 - \mu)$ non-subscribing ones and the μ subscribers only if the rival has not posted its price on-line (an event which occurs with probability $1 - \alpha$).

Advertising prices on-line or not? When deciding whether or not to advertise prices, a firm compares $E\left[\pi^{on}(p)\right]$ with $E\left[\pi^{off}(p^m)\right]$; this comparison is not straightforward. As we illustrate later on, Baye and Morgan prove that when the advertising fee is not too large, the only possible equilibrium is such that firms decide to post prices on-line with a certain probability, i.e. they play mixed strategies also when taking their advertising decision.[10] Consequently, in equilibrium, the expected profits from the two alternatives must be the same; formally, $E\left[\pi^{on}(p)\right] = E\left[\pi^{off}(p^m)\right]$. From this equality we derive the cumulative density function $F(p)$ which characterises the optimal pricing strategy for a firm operating on-line:

$$F^*(p) = \frac{(1 + \mu)\,\pi(p) - \phi - \pi^m\,(1 - \mu\alpha)}{2\mu\alpha\pi(p)}.$$

Baye and Morgan prove that the support of $F^*(p)$ is the interval $[p_0, p^m]$, where the lower bound p_0 exceeds the marginal cost, $p_0 > c$.

Recalling that $E\left[\pi^{on}(p)\right]$ is constant for all the prices belonging to the support of $F^*(p)$, the equilibrium condition $E\left[\pi^{on}(p)\right] = E\left[\pi^{off}(p^m)\right]$ can be rewritten as $E\left[\pi^{on}(p^m)\right] = E\left[\pi^{off}(p^m)\right]$; from this latter condition, we determine the probability of each firm advertising prices on-line:[11]

$$\alpha^* = 1 - \frac{\phi}{\mu\pi^m}.$$

Note that $\alpha^* < 1$ if $\phi < \mu\pi^m$. The following result summarises the arguments we have discussed so far.[12]

Result 4. *If the advertising fee is not too large ($\phi \leq \mu\pi^m$):*

   - each firm advertises its price on-line with probability $\alpha^* = 1 - \phi/(\mu\pi^m)$;

---

[10]It can be proved that there is no symmetric equilibrium where both firms advertise with probability 1. By choosing not to advertise when the rival is certainly on-line, a firm obtains $(1 - \mu)\,\pi^m$. If, on the contrary, the firm decides to advertise its price, we know that *i*) p^m is one of the optimal prices, and *ii*) given that p^m exceeds the rival's price, the firm serves only the local non-subscribing consumers, thus gaining profits equal to $(1 - \mu)\,\pi^m - \phi$. These considerations imply that, if the rival advertises with probability 1, then for the firm it is profitable not to post its price on the website. Similar arguments can be used to prove that, if ϕ is not too large, it is not possible to have an equilibrium where both firms decide not to advertise with probability 1.

[11]The value of α^* follow from condition $F^*(p^m) = 1$.

[12]To determine the firm's profits we substitute α^* either in $E\left[\pi^{off}(p^m)\right]$ or in $E\left[\pi^{on}(p^m)\right]$.

- *a firm advertising its price on-line chooses it on the basis of the cumulative density function $F^*(p)$ with support $p \in [p_0, p^m]$;*

- *a firm operating only locally (off-line) charges the monopoly price p^m;*

- *each firm obtains profits equal to $\phi + (1 - \mu) \pi^m$.*

From this result, which represents the main contribution of Baye and Morgan's work, several interesting observations can be drawn:

(a) the on-line market exhibits price dispersion. As in Varian's model, this occurs because the on-line prices are randomly selected within the interval $[p_0, p^m]$ on the basis of the cumulative density function $F^*(p)$;

(b) on-line prices are lower than p^m, the price charged by firms operating on the local market only. This result is due to the fact that on-line the two firms compete against each other: each of them knows that, with probability α^*, also the rival sells on-line;

(c) the probability of each firm advertising prices on-line, α^*, is increasing in the number of subscribing consumers, μ, while it is decreasing in the advertising fee ϕ;

(d) the equilibrium profits for each firm, $\phi + (1-\mu)\pi^m$, are increasing in ϕ and decreasing in μ. This observation, apparently counterintuitive, can be easily explained by recalling how μ and α affect the probability of the competitor advertising on-line. As argued in point (c), the probability α^* is lower when the advertising fee is large and increases with the number of subscribers; therefore, a large ϕ and a small μ imply a lower probability of facing the competitor and, therefore, larger profits.

Subscription decision ($t = 1$)

Working backwards, we now determine whether or not it is optimal for consumers to subscribe to the gatekeeper's website. In exchange for the payment of ψ, a consumer enjoys two benefits from subscription: she can observe the prices which firms have posted on the gatekeeper's website and she can save search costs s. Clearly, the larger the probability of firms advertising on-line (the larger α), the greater the expected benefits that consumers derive from subscription.

Baye and Morgan prove that the subgame starting at $t = 1$ has three possible equilibria; formally:

Result 5. *When the fees ψ and ϕ are not too large, the subgame starting at $t = 1$ has three symmetric equilibria:*

1. *no on-line market:* $\mu^* = 0$ *and* $\alpha^* = 0$. *No consumer and no firm access the gatekeeper's website and firms act as local monopolists;*

2. *an on-line market emerges but only some consumers subscribe to the website (partial consumer participation):* $\mu^* < 1$. *The probability of each firm advertising prices on the gatekeeper's website is* $\alpha^* = 1 - \phi/\left(\mu^* \pi^m\right)$;

3. *an on-line market emerges and all consumers subscribe to the website:* $\mu^* = 1$ *(total consumer participation). The probability of each firm advertising prices on the gatekeeper's website is* $\alpha^* = 1 - \phi/\pi^m$.

Equilibrium 1 is the least interesting of the three: if there are no subscribers, then there is no reason for the firms to pay ϕ and post their prices on-line. In this case, the on-line market does not emerge and all transactions take place locally. Equilibria 2 and 3 are characterised by a partial or total consumer participation to the on-line market, which, in turn, implies an increasing participation of firms. In both cases, the equilibrium displays on-line price dispersion, as stated in Result 4.

Before moving to the initial stage of the game, it is interesting to observe that consumers and firms have opposite preferences towards which equilibrium is played in $t = 1$. Consumers prefer Equilibrium 3, the most competitive one characterised by the greatest probability of firms advertising on-line, hence by fiercer competition and lower prices. Firms, on the contrary, prefer equilibrium 1: with no on-line market, firms operate locally as monopolists and gain larger profits. More generally, as α increases so does competitive pressure; this fact reduces the equilibrium prices thus benefiting consumers and harming firms.

After having described the equilibrium strategies of firms and consumers, we can now determine the equilibrium of the game by defining the gatekeeper's optimal pricing strategy.

The gatekeeper's pricing strategy $(t = 0)$

To make the intermediation service attractive, the gatekeeper needs to define the fees ϕ and ψ in order to stimulate subscriptions from both consumers and firms. Indeed, consumers' benefits deriving from subscription increase with the probability of firms advertising on-line; similarly, firms' willingness to pay for posting prices on-line increases with the number of subscribers. Formally, the gatekeeper maximises expected profits:

$$E\left[\pi_{GK}\right] = 2\,\alpha^*\,\phi + 2\mu^*\,\psi - H,$$

with $H > 0$ representing the gatekeeper's costs,[13] while $2\,\alpha^*\,\phi$ and $2\,\mu^*\,\psi$ are the ex-

---

[13]To provide the intermediation service, a gatekeeper needs software and hardware to run the website

pected revenues from the sales of the intermediation services to firms and consumers, respectively. Clearly, gatekeeper's profits depend on which of the three equilibria in Result 5 is played. As in Baye and Morgan (2001), we assume that at $t = 1$ consumers and firms play Equilibrium 3; following this assumption, the authors prove that the gatekeeper's profits are maximised when:

i) the subscription fee for consumers is lower than their willingness to pay for the intermediation service. This implies that all consumers subscribe to the gatekeeper's website (full consumer participation): $\mu^* = 1$;

ii) firms post their prices on the website with a probability strictly lower than 1 (partial firm participation).

The gatekeeper maximises its profits by reducing ψ so that all consumers subscribe to the website (point *i*)). In fact, the authors prove that the smaller revenues from consumer subscriptions are more than compensated by the larger gains from the advertising fees: as argued previously, as μ increases so does α, the probability of firms advertising their prices. While it is optimal to stimulate full consumer participation, it is profitable for the gatekeeper to have partial firm participation (point *ii*)): an increase in α augments competitive pressure and makes it less convenient for firms to advertise their prices.

2.4   Versioning and bundling

The main argument of the previous section is that price dispersion represents a persistent phenomenon in on-line markets. In this section, we focus on another important aspect of digital markets which affects their efficiency; the Internet, in fact, represents an effective tool that firms may employ to segment the market and to price discriminate, thus allowing them to retain a substantial market power.

On the Internet not only can consumers easily compare the various offers available, but also retailers may take advantage of the opportunity of acquiring detailed information on customers; in this way, they can "tailor" products and prices to consumer preferences.

Dell Computer is a typical example of a firm employing these kinds of strategies. On the company website, consumers can assemble the PC that best suits their needs by selecting their preferred combination of a series of components (such as microprocessor, capacity of memory, hard-disk, monitor, etc.). This strategy, known as *mass*

---

and it also needs to access the network infrastructure. Typically, the use of these inputs does not vary with the level of intermediation services provided by the gatekeeper. Therefore, the gatekeeper is characterised by a large fixed cost, as shown in expression $E[\pi_{GK}]$.

customisation, is possible since Dell assembles the selected product only after the order has been placed. The key ingredient to the success of this strategy consists in moving product customisation downstream in the production process, leaving it completely to customers: by using new flexible computer-aided manufacturing systems, the on-line retailer waits for the consumer request and then it assembles the product with the required components. In Italy Vodafone, the well known mobile telecommunications operator, launched the campaign *Di che colore sei? Colora il tuo piano!* (literally, "What colour are you? Colour your tariff plan!") in which customers were given the opportunity to select on-line the price plan that best suited their needs.

Note also that these customisation strategies can be adopted much more easily by on-line retailers than by traditional ones; in fact, while a brick-and-mortar shop is limited by the physical constraints, such as shelf size, an on-line vendor does not face any physical limitation and it can display a virtually unlimited number of different products.

Versioning and *bundling* are certainly two of the most common on-line price discrimination strategies. They are not exclusive to digital markets; nevertheless, it is thanks to the Internet that they have become extremely popular.

2.4.1   Versioning

The first commercial practice which we focus our attention on is known as versioning. This is a second degree price discrimination strategy according to which a firm produces several versions of its product, each targeted at a specific market segment.

For example, an editor who is publishing the latest novel of a popular author can sell the book in a special hard-cover/gift edition intended for the author's loyal and regular readers and then offer a pocket/paperback (cheaper) version a few months later. Similarly, a software producer can make two versions of the same application available to consumers: a fully-fledged version, designed for a professional audience and a version lacking some functionalities designed for low-end users. More generally, in the case of software, it is possible to create different versions by varying several dimensions such as user interface, image resolution, processing power, completeness, customer care services, warranty and so on.

Before proceeding with the economic analysis of versioning, it is useful to briefly recall why price discrimination may be profitable. In Figure 2.7, p^m represents the price charged by a monopolist who does not discriminate consumers. The figure shows that a firm adopting price discrimination strategies may increase profits for two reasons: on the one hand, it may charge a price larger than p^m to customers with a high willingness to pay (segment I in the figure); on the other hand, the firm may enlarge its sales by selling at lower prices to consumers whose willingness to pay is lower than p^m but greater than

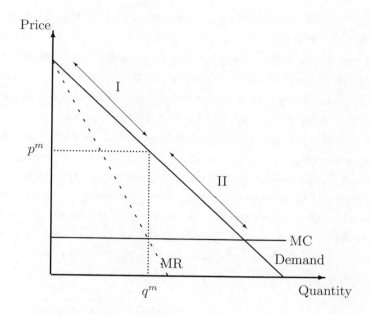

Figure 2.7: the aims of price discrimination

the marginal cost MC (segment II in the figure). This distinction between the two basic aims of price discrimination will help us to interpret better our results.

The most delicate aspect of a versioning strategy is to design the different versions of the product so that consumers self-select, that is, they are induced to choose the version which is specifically targeted at them. A simple numerical example helps us understand this issue better.[14] Consider an editor who is about to launch a new novel and needs to decide which strategy to adopt for the distribution of the book. Following thorough marketing investigations, the editor is aware of the fact that the market is made up of two distinct groups of readers; some "loyal" readers who are eager to buy the author's latest novel as soon as possible and other "normal" readers who, instead, don't mind waiting. Clearly, the editor's aim is to segment the market in order to sell the book to the loyal readers at a higher price than the one charged to normal readers.

If the editor knew the exact type of each reader (loyal or normal), the task would be rather easy: the editor would be able to price discriminate perfectly and to charge each customer a price equal to her willingness to pay. Nonetheless, firms do not possess such precise information about their clientele: they do not know which type of user each consumer belongs to. Going back to our example, we represent this information asymmetry by assuming that the editor knows how the population of customers is distributed

---

[14]This example is taken from Varian and Shapiro (1999).

between loyal and normal readers (namely, it is able to assess their percentages) but it does not know exactly who is who.

How should the editor proceed to segment the market? One possible strategy is versioning, i.e. to print two different editions: a gift/hardcover edition, more expensive and designed for loyal readers, and a pocket/paperback edition, published some months later and targeted at normal readers. The editor differentiates the two versions of the book along two dimensions: i) time, i.e. when to sell each version of the book, and ii) prices of the two editions.

More specifically, suppose that the market is made up of 100 readers, 40 loyal and 60 normal. It is natural to assume that all readers, regardless of their type, are willing to pay more for the gift edition than for the paperback; furthermore, we assume that loyal readers are willing to pay more for both versions of the book in comparison to normal readers. The following table presents the readers' willingnesses to pay for the two versions of the book:

	Loyal readers N=40	Normal readers N=60
Gift/hardcover edition	110	60
Pocket/paperback edition	50	40

Table 2.1: readers' willingnesses to pay

The editor decides whether or not to sells both versions of the book and at what prices; for simplicity, let us assume that production costs of both versions are equal and normalised to zero. Clearly, if the editor publishes only one version of the book, then it would be the hardcover edition: it costs the same and it is more valuable for consumers. In this case, the optimal price to charge is 60: all consumers buy the book and profits equal 6,000.

Can the editor do better? The answer would certainly be yes if the editor were able to price discriminate perfectly. In this case, it would sell the gift edition only, charge a loyal reader 110 and a normal reader 60, thus realising profits equal to 8,000. Nonetheless, as mentioned above, this strategy is not feasible because the editor cannot determine whether a customer is a loyal or a normal reader.

However, market segmentation can still be achieved if the editor, rather than selling the gift version only, adopts a versioning strategy. As described by Varian and Shapiro (1999), the editor may try to segment the market by offering two versions of the book at different prices; the crucial aspect of versioning is self-selection: prices for the two versions need to be such that loyal readers are induced to select the gift edition while normal readers select the paperback.

Hence, given the preferences shown in Table 2.1, the optimal versioning strategy requires:

1. the paperback version to be sold at 40, the willingness to pay of normal consumers;

2. the hardcover version to be sold at 100, namely the price that makes loyal readers indifferent between the two editions. One can easily check that loyal readers receive the same net utility from the purchase of the paperback edition at 40 (net utility $50 - 40$) and from the hardcover edition at 100 (net utility $110 - 100$).

By assuming that in the case of indifference, normal readers purchase the gift version, then at prices 40 and 100 self-selection occurs: loyal readers purchase the gift edition while normal readers buy the paperback version at a lower price. Overall the editor's profits are 6,400, larger than those obtained when selling the gift version only. Going back to Figure 2.7, this example illustrates a case where versioning is profitable since it allows the editor to charge a higher price to consumers with a larger willingness to pay. In other words, the editor benefits from selling the two versions of the book even though it does not increase sales.

At this point of our discussion, it is interesting to stress that versioning is less profitable than perfect price discrimination (6,400 instead of 8,000) since the paperback and the hardcover editions compete against each other. Competition entails two negative effects on firm's profits. On the one side, with versioning, normal readers purchase the paperback edition at 40 instead of the hardcover at 60; with respect to this group of consumers the paperback version cannibalises the market for the gift edition. On the other hand, in order to induce loyal readers to purchase the hardcover version, the editor must reduce the price from 110 to 100.

Despite being extremely simple, this example highlights the crucial role played by consumer self-selection. The basic rule that the editor needs to follow is relatively straightforward and consists in the following "two-step procedure": i) identify the characteristics and price of the low-end version, which, in our example, consists in charging for the paperback a price equal to the willingness to pay of normal readers, ii) determine the features and price for the high-end version so that loyal consumers are indifferent between the two versions; in our example this means charging for the gift edition the price that makes loyal readers indifferent between the two versions.

2.4.2   Versioning to increase the market

Let's move now to the second reason why versioning may be profitable, namely the possibility of increasing sales.[15] Consider a monopolist operating in a market where consumers have heterogeneous preferences. As in the example of the editor, we assume that the firm knows only the aggregate distribution of consumer preferences but it does not observe the exact type of each consumer. Perfect price discrimination is, therefore, not feasible but there is still room for strategies aimed at market segmentation to extract consumer surplus.

Suppose that the monopolist produces a good of quality m; for example, m may represent the speed of calculation in the case of a software for mathematics or the quality of the connection in the case of broadband Internet access. Consumer preferences towards m are represented by a taste parameter θ. We assume that θ is uniformly distributed over the interval $[0,1]$; consumers who do not value m very much are characterised by a low θ, while those who care a lot for product quality have a large θ. Formally, the utility that a consumer derives from the good is the sum of a basic willingness to pay $k > 0$, common to all consumers, plus θm, the personal valuation that the consumer of type θ attaches to quality m.

As mentioned earlier, the firm operates under asymmetric information: it knows that the taste parameter θ is uniformly distributed over $[0,1]$ but it does not observe the exact value of θ that characterises each consumer.

Finally, we assume that the firm may sell two versions of its product (version 1 and version 2). The two versions are characterised by a different quality, which we denote by m_1 and m_2, respectively. Therefore, the net utility for a consumer of type θ purchasing version $i = 1, 2$ at price p_i equals: $U(\theta, m_i, p_i) = k + \theta m_i - p_i$.

Clearly, consumer utility is increasing in product quality; therefore, if $p_1 = p_2$ consumers prefer the highest quality version. For example, all other conditions being equal, a PC with a more powerful processor is preferred to the others.

In what follows, we assume that version 2 is the "high-quality" one: $m_2 > m_1$. For simplicity, production costs are normalised to zero for both versions of the product.

One version of the product

Suppose that the monopolist sells only one version of the product, in other words no versioning strategy is adopted. Clearly, in this case, it is profitable for the firm to produce the high-quality version (version 2): it costs the same and it is more valuable for consumers. Let p_N denote the price charged by the monopolist (subscript N recalls the fact that we are dealing with the case of no versioning).

---

[15]In what follows we provide a simplified version of Belleflamme (2005).

Each consumer observes p_N and decides whether or not to buy. The indifferent consumer is characterised by a taste parameter such that the two options yield the same utility; formally, θ is such that $U(\theta, m_2, p_N) = 0$. Letting $\tilde{\theta}(p_N)$ denote the taste parameter of the indifferent consumer, it follows that:

$$\tilde{\theta}(p_N) = \frac{p_N - k}{m_2}.$$

Therefore, given p_N, all consumers with a taste parameter greater than or equal to $\tilde{\theta}(p_N)$ purchase the product, while the others do not; given that θ is uniformly distributed over the interval $[0, 1]$, a mass $1 - \tilde{\theta}(p_N)$ of consumers purchase the product. Therefore, the monopolist's profit function is:

$$\pi_N(p_N) = p_N \left(1 - \tilde{\theta}(p_N)\right) = p_N \left(1 - \frac{p_N - k}{m_2}\right).$$

By differentiating $\pi_N(p_N)$ with respect to p_N and by solving the first order condition, we determine the optimal price charged by the firm and the equilibrium profits:

$$p_N^* = \frac{k + m_2}{2}, \qquad \pi_N^* = \frac{(k + m_2)^2}{4m_2}.$$

Finally, by substituting p_N^* into $\tilde{\theta}(p_N)$ it follows that the mass of consumers who actually purchase the product equals:

$$\frac{1}{2} - \frac{k}{2m_2}.$$

Two versions of the product

Suppose now that the monopolist sells the two versions of the product: version 1 of quality m_1 and version 2 of quality m_2, with $m_2 > m_1$. The most important aspect of versioning is consumer self-selection: prices p_1 and p_2 need to be such that consumers with a high taste parameter are induced to select the high quality version, while those characterised by a low θ go for the low quality one.

In order to determine the prices charged by the monopolist, we start by defining the demand functions for the two versions of the good; in other words, given prices p_1 and p_2, we need to determine how many consumers buy the high quality version and how many the low quality one.

Similarly to the previous section, the first step is to define the two indifferent consumers: i) the consumer who is indifferent between purchasing the high-quality and the low quality version, whose taste parameter is denoted by $\tilde{\theta}_{1,2}$; ii) the consumer who is indifferent between buying the low quality version and not buying at all, taste parameter $\tilde{\theta}_{0,1}$. The following conditions identify these consumers:

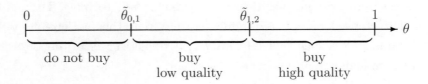

Figure 2.8: market segmentation with versioning

i) $U(\theta, m_1, p_1) = U(\theta, m_2, p_2), \quad \Rightarrow \quad \tilde{\theta}_{1,2}(p_1, p_2) = \frac{p_2 - p_1}{m_2 - m_1},$

ii) $U(\theta, m_1, p_1) = 0, \quad \Rightarrow \quad \tilde{\theta}_{0,1}(p_1) = \frac{p_1 - k}{m_1}.$

Consumers self-select provided that $0 \leq \tilde{\theta}_{0,1} < \tilde{\theta}_{1,2} < 1$: those characterised by a high taste parameter, $\theta \in [\tilde{\theta}_{1,2}, 1]$, buy the high quality version, while those with $\theta \in [\tilde{\theta}_{0,1}, \tilde{\theta}_{1,2})$ buy the low-quality version. Finally, consumers who have a very low taste parameter do not purchase at all (see Figure 2.8).

Since θ is uniformly distributed over $[0, 1]$, we can compute the demand function for each version of the product and define the monopolist's maximisation problem; formally, the firm chooses p_1 and p_2 in order to solve:[16]

$$\max_{p_1, p_2} \pi_V(p_1, p_2) = p_2 \left(1 - \tilde{\theta}_{1,2}(p_1, p_2)\right) + p_1 \left(\tilde{\theta}_{1,2}(p_1, p_2) - \tilde{\theta}_{0,1}(p_1)\right) =$$

$$= p_2 \left(1 - \frac{p_2 - p_1}{m_2 - m_1}\right) + p_1 \left(\frac{p_2 - p_1}{m_2 - m_1} - \frac{p_1 - k}{m_1}\right).$$

From the first order conditions, we determine the equilibrium prices for the two versions of the product and then we can compute the profits obtained by the monopolist:

$$p_1^* = \frac{k + m_1}{2}, \; p_2^* = \frac{k + m_2}{2} \quad \text{and} \quad \pi_V^* = \frac{2km_1 + m_2 m_1 + k^2}{4m_1}.$$

By substituting p_1^* into $\tilde{\theta}_{0,1}$, it follows that the mass of consumers who actually purchases one of the two versions of the product equals:

$$\frac{1}{2} - \frac{k}{2m_1}.$$

By comparing this expression with its equivalent in the case of no versioning, it immediately follows that the firm serves more consumers when selling both versions of the product. Thanks to this market enlargement effect, the firm is able to increase profits; formally, it is easy to prove that:

$$\pi_V^* = \pi_N^* + \frac{k^2(m_2 - m_1)}{4m_1 m_2} > \pi_N^*$$

The following result summarises these arguments:

---

[16]Subscript V recalls the fact that the monopolist is adopting a versioning strategy.

Result 6. *If the monopolist offers the two versions of the product, then sales increase and profits are larger.*

The above result, which is indeed the most relevant in Belleflamme (2005), illustrates the second reason why firms adopt versioning: when offering also the low-quality version, the firm is able to sell to consumers with a relatively low taste parameter who, absent versioning, would not have purchased the product at all.

It is interesting to note that the low quality version cannibalises, at least partially, the high quality one. Some consumers shift from the high quality version (in the case the firm does not adopt versioning) to the low quality one (in the case of versioning). Therefore, restricting the attention to these consumers only, the firm reduces its revenues when adopting the versioning strategy because it obtains $p_1^* < p_N^*$. Result 6, however, suggests that the positive effect of versioning, due to market enlargement, dominates the negative effect of cannibalisation.

Finally, it is also interesting to note that in the setting we are examining the only benefit of versioning is due to the market enlargement effect. In other words, when selling both versions of the product, the monopolist is not able to charge a larger price to consumers with a high taste parameter; by looking at the prices charged for the high quality version when the firm adopts versioning with the price in the case of no versioning, one can easily observe that $p_N^* = p_2^*$.

2.4.3 Limits of versioning

In the previous sections we have illustrated how an appropriate versioning strategy allows firms to segment the market, expand sales and increase profits. However, it is important to stress the fact that versioning is not always profitable: firms benefit from selling different versions of their products only when consumer preferences meet certain conditions. Therefore, it is important to determine which conditions need to be satisfied in order to make versioning profitable. Let's go back to the example of the editor; we now assume that readers' willingness to pay for the two versions of the book are as described in Table 2.2:

	Loyal readers N=40	Normal readers N=60
Gift/hardcover edition	110	60
Pocket/paperback edition	80	40

Table 2.2: readers' willingness to pay

As in the previous section, we assume that the market is made up of 40 loyal readers and 60 normal readers. Following the same arguments as above, the optimal versioning strategy requires: a price of 40 (i.e. equal to the willingness to pay of normal readers) for the paperback and of 70 (i.e. the price that makes loyal readers indifferent between the two versions) for the gift edition. With these prices readers self-select (loyal readers purchase the gift edition, while normal readers purchase the paperback) and the editor obtains profits equal to 5,200.

However, the editor does better by selling only the gift edition at a price of 60. In this case, all readers (loyal and normal) purchase the book and the editor enjoys profits equal to 6,000. Hence, versioning is not profitable!

At a first glance, this result may seem quite surprising; nonetheless, it can be easily explained by looking in greater detail at readers preferences in Table 2.2. Compared to the previous example (see Table 2.1), loyal readers attach a relatively larger value to the paperback edition (80 compared to 50 in Table 2.1). In this case, in order to induce loyal readers to self-select, the editor needs to substantially reduce the price of the gift edition. In other words, in the case we are now analysing the gift and the paperback edition are very close substitutes: the paperback edition is very attractive for loyal readers who are induced to purchase the gift edition only if the price is low enough. In this case, the cannibalisation effect associated with the sale of the paperback edition dominates.

In a recent article, Bhargava and Choudhary (2008) generalise the analysis of Tables 2.1 and 2.2. In a more general setting, they look for the conditions which make versioning a profitable strategy. Their framework is similar to that proposed by Belleflamme (2005): a firm can sell two versions of the product (a low quality version, m_1, and a high quality version, m_2, with $m_2 > m_1$) and consumers have heterogeneous preferences towards quality. The main result shown by Bhargava and Choudhary suggests that in order to verify whether versioning is profitable, one needs to compare the number of consumers served by the firm when it sells the low quality version only with the number of consumers purchasing the product in the case the firm sells the high quality version only. More specifically:

Result 7 (Bhargava and Choudhary, 2008). *Versioning is (is not) a profitable strategy when the number of consumers served when the firm sells only the high-quality version is lower (higher) than the number of consumers served when the firm sells only the low quality one.*

Bhargava and Choudhary explain this result in terms of market enlargement (i.e. with versioning the firm serves customers who would not purchase otherwise) *vs* cannibalisation (i.e. with versioning some individuals purchase the low quality version at a lower price rather than the high quality one). With versioning, besides the high quality version, the firm sells also the low quality one; according to Result 7 this strategy is profitable only when the potential market share of the low quality version is large enough, i.e. when there is a large mass of consumers purchasing the product in the case of the firm selling the low quality version only. Under these circumstances, the market enlargement effect is strong enough to compensate cannibalisation.

Result 7 can be applied to Belleflamme's analysis. When the firm sells only the high quality version, sales amount to $1 - (1/2 - k/(2m_2))$; similarly, it is straightforward to verify that when the firm offers only the low-quality version, $1 - (1/2 - k/(2m_1))$ individuals are served. Since $m_2 > m_1$, the number of consumers that purchase the low quality version (when only this one is available) is higher than the number of consumers that purchase the high quality one (when only this version is available); hence, Result 7 applies and confirms the fact that in this case versioning is profitable.

2.4.4 Bundling strategies

The second example of a price discrimination strategy commonly adopted by on-line retailers is bundling, namely, the sale of two or more products bundled in a single package. Both bundling and versioning are strategies used by many firms and not only by on-line retailers. Some common examples of bundling are: television networks offering a wide range of combinations of channels (pay-per-view channels, video on demand, free channels, international channels, pay-TV, DTTV (digital terrestrial television) etc.); publishers offering both on-line and printed versions of a magazine in the same subscription; software companies selling packages consisting of several applications. Even though bundling strategies are commonly used by many companies, they are very appealing to on-line retailers who can easily and cheaply bundle several products.

The question we want to address in this section is the following: when is bundling profitable for a firm? As argued by Schmalensee (2001), the main aim of bundling is to reduce heterogeneity in consumer preferences. The following example may help us understand better how bundling works. A software company produces two different applications: a text editor called *Wordy* and a spreadsheet called *Calc*. For simplicity, we assume that market demand consists of two different consumers, a writer and an accountant. Their preferences are heterogeneous and negatively correlated: the writer has a high valuation for the text editor and a low valuation for the spreadsheet, while the accountant values *Calc* more than *Wordy*. Finally, we assume that the valuation for the bundle *Wordy+Calc* equals the sum of the valuations for each single application.

The following table summarises the valuations of both consumers for the two applications and for the bundle:

	Wordy	*Calc*	*Wordy+Calc*
writer	11	2	13
accountant	3	7	10

Table 2.3: willingness to pay for the software

Suppose that perfect price discrimination is not possible and consider what happens when the software company sells the two applications separately (so-called separate selling). Given consumer preferences and under the simplifying assumption of zero production costs, it is clear that the optimal strategy for the company is to charge a price equal to the highest willingness to pay for each application: 11 for *Wordy* and 7 for *Calc*. In this case, the company sells one unit of each application: the writer purchases one copy of the text editor and the accountant buys one unit of the spreadsheet. Therefore, with separate selling the software company gains profits equal to 18.

Consider now bundling. One can check that the optimal price for the bundle *Wordy + Calc* is 10. At this price, both consumers purchase the bundle and the company obtains profits equal to 20, which are larger than those achieved with separate selling. This example is useful to understand in which cases bundling is profitable: when consumer valuations for each product are heterogeneous but they cluster around a common value for the entire package, then the company profits from adopting a bundling strategy. Table 2.3 represents exactly this case: consumer valuations for each application are very dispersed (e.g. *Wordy* is worth 11 for the writer and only 2 for the accountant) while they are much more clustered for the bundle (the bundle is worth 13 for the writer and 10 for the accountant). The writer and the accountant have negatively correlated preferences with respect to the two applications and, therefore, their valuations for the bundle are more concentrated around a common value.

In the previous example, we presented the case of pure bundling, namely when a firm only sells bundles of products. However, it is possible for a firm to do better by adopting more articulated strategies. Retailers may offer both bundles and products sold separately, thus mixing separate selling and pure bundling; the following example is useful to understand the advantages of such strategy, commonly known as mixed bundling.

Consider the case of a television network broadcasting three different channels: an entertainment channel, E, a sports channel, S and a news channel, N. The marketing department of the TV network has grouped consumers into four categories: **A**, **B**, **C**, **D**. Each category is made up of one consumer and the categories differ according to their willingness to pay, as in Table 2.4; the willingness to pay for a subscription to two or more TV channels equals the sum of the valuations for each single channel.

On the basis of the preferences in the table, one can check that in the case of separate selling, the TV network obtains profits equal to 46.[17] Alternatively, the TV network may adopt a pure bundling strategy and sell the subscription to the three channels in one package. From Table 2.4, we know that the bundle is valued 12 by consumers **A** and **C** and 15 by consumers **B** and **D**. The optimal choice for the TV network is to charge 12 for the bundle, thus obtaining profits equal to 48. As in the case of the software company, bundling is more profitable than separate selling.

	Channel S	Channel E	Channel N
A	10	1	1
B	9	1	5
C	1	10	1
D	1	9	5

Table 2.4: willingness to pay for the TV channels

However, the TV network can do even better by employing a mixed bundling strategy. In particular, the firm maximises its profits by offering the subscription to:

- the bundle $E + S$ at price 10;

- channel N at price 5.

With mixed bundling the TV network obtains profits equal to 50: consumers value the bundle $E + S$ 10 (consumers **B** and **D**) or 11 (consumers **A** and **C**) and therefore they all purchase it; moreover, **B** and **D** also subscribe to the news channel since its price equals their willingness to pay.

The case we are analysing is interesting because it suggests which products should be bundled together and which should be sold separately; by looking at Table 2.4, we can see that consumer valuations for the bundle $E + S$ are very similar (10 or 11) while the valuations for the bundle $E + S + N$ are more dispersed (12 and 15).[18] Therefore, for the TV network it is profitable to exclude channel N from the bundle.

An interesting article by Bakos and Brynjolfsson published in 1999 in *Management Science* illustrates the advantages of bundling strategies when a firm offers a very large number of products in the same package. The analysis presented by the authors is in

---

[17]With separate selling, the TV network charges 9 for E and for S and 5 for N. Consumer **A** subscribes to channel S, consumer **C** subscribes to channel E, while **B** subscribes both to S and N and **D** both to E and N. Therefore, the firm sells six subscriptions, two for each channel.

[18]One can easily check that consumer valuations for bundles $E+N$ and $S+N$ are even more dispersed and the TV network cannot benefit from selling them.

line with the two examples we have presented above: an increase in the number of products included in the package reduces heterogeneity in consumer preferences. Therefore, bundling together a large number of products makes it much easier for firms to predict consumer valuations and thus to extract a larger portion of consumer surplus. Bakos and Brynjolfsson refer to this fact as the "predictive value of bundling".

Formally, the two authors consider a large number of consumers who purchase at most one unit of the n products sold by a monopolist. The marginal cost for each product is zero and therefore social welfare is maximised when each consumer buys one unit of all the n products. For each consumer the authors assume that:

Assumption. *For each consumer the valuations of the n products are independent.*

As in the previous examples, we also assume that the valuation of the bundle equals the sum of the valuations of each single product. Under these conditions, the authors prove the following result:

Result 8 (Bakos and Brynjolfsson, 1999). *When the number of products included in the bundle tends to infinity ($n \rightarrow \infty$) then all consumers buy the bundle and the firm extracts the whole consumer surplus.*

This result is very interesting and highlights the profitability of bundling strategies when the number of products bundled together is very large. Note that, according to Result 8, as n goes to infinity, the firm is able to replicate the same outcome as under perfect price discrimination: there is no deadweight loss (all consumers buy the bundle) and the firm gains the whole social welfare (i.e. it extracts the entire consumer surplus).

Bakos and Brynjolfsson prove this result by employing the "law of large numbers": as the number of products included in the bundle increases, the mean valuation for each product clusters around a common value; consumers have similar valuations for the bundle[19] and, as n approaches infinity, the bundle is worth exactly the same for all consumers. In this case, the firm extracts the entire consumer surplus by charging a price equal to the common valuation for the bundle.

Figure 2.9, taken from the article by Bakos and Brynjolfsson, provides a graphic interpretation of this result. Suppose that for each consumer the valuations of the n products are independent and uniformly distributed over $[0, 1]$. In this case, the market demand for a single product sold separately is $q = 1 - p$, where p denotes the price charged by the firm and 1 is the highest willingness to pay of consumers (panel (i) of Figure 2.9).

---

[19]Formally, let $k_{j,i}$ denote the valuation of consumer j for product i which is included in the bundle. Therefore, the mean valuation of a single product which the firm offers in the bundle is: $(1/n)\Sigma_{i=1}^{n}k_{j,i}$.

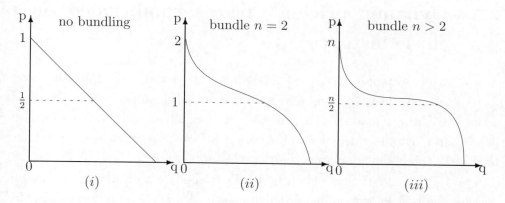

Figure 2.9: demand for the single product and for the bundle of n products

The second panel of Figure 2.9 represents the market demand for a bundle made up of 2 products, while in panel (*iii*) we can observe the demand for bundles including $n > 2$ products. To determine these demand functions we need to define the distribution of consumer valuations for the bundle. Consider the case where $n = 2$: the valuation of the bundle is a random variable equal to the sum of two random variables (representing the valuations of the separate products). One can check that consumer valuations for the bundle cluster around 1; very small (close to 0) and very large (close to 2) valuations are less frequent.[20]

For this reason the market demand flattens around the central value 1 (see panel (*ii*) of Figure 2.9). We can extend this argument to cases where $n > 2$; as the number of products included in the bundle increases, the demand function becomes flatter and more elastic around the mean consumer valuation ($n/2$); as n grows, the monopolist serves an increasingly larger number of consumers and it extracts most of their surplus by charging a price equal to $n/2$ (panel (*iii*), Figure 2.9).

---

[20]To convince the reader that this is true, let's imagine the following experiment. Suppose you are rolling a dice and that the number appearing on the face represents the valuation of the product. If there are two products the valuation of the bundle equals the sum of the numbers which come out when throwing the dice twice. Now, we can calculate the probability for each possible value of the bundle. It is clear that the intermediate valuation (i.e. the total score when rolling the dice twice is 7) is the most likely to happen, while the smallest (i.e. 2) and the largest (i.e. 12) possible valuations have the lowest probability of occurring. Going back to the example provided by Bakos and Brynjolfsson and recalling some basic notions of statistics, we can say that the valuation of the bundle can be obtained through the convolution of the two distribution functions for each product. Since both distributions are uniform, it follows that the distribution of the valuations of the bundle is triangular ranging from 0 to 2, centred in 1 and with maximum value 1. Therefore, intermediate valuations of the bundle are those with the highest probability of occurring, thus generating a demand function as in panel (*ii*) of Figure 2.9.

2.5 Dynamic pricing: prices conditioned on purchase history

As we have repeatedly pointed out in the previous sections, the Internet allows firms to employ sophisticated pricing strategies that would be difficult, if not impossible, to adopt in traditional markets. Therefore, we conclude this chapter by focusing on another price discrimination strategy which has became very popular among on-line retailers: the practice of conditioning prices on purchase history.

It is useful to start this section by briefly recalling a story involving Amazon.com, perhaps the best known on-line distributor of books, DVDs and music CDs. In 2001, Amazon was caught charging customers different prices for the same product; thanks to an on-line forum where customers compared their purchasing experiences, some of them realised that they had been charged a significantly higher price than others for the same article. But the most disturbing fact was that Amazon was charging regular customers much higher prices than occasional visitors. The accusation to Amazon was that, having recorded their on-line behaviour (namely their previous purchases), Amazon discriminated its regular customers accordingly; this practice is known in the literature as "dynamic pricing". Within two weeks, following a fierce reaction of its customers, Amazon.com was forced to apologise for its behaviour and to refund them.

Like Amazon, any on-line vendor can obtain valuable information on consumer preferences, on their individual characteristics and on their habits; this information is extremely useful for discriminating customers and to adopt dynamic pricing strategies. There are several ways through which a vendor can gather information on the visitors of its on-line shop. The most common device is represented by so-called *cookies*, namely text files saved on the user's computer where several information on her preferences (i.e. past purchases, pages visited and so on) and characteristics are stored. In this way, each time the user accesses the website, the server reads the cookies and personalises the webpage in order to meet visitors' tastes, interests and habits.[21]

The vendor keeps track of and stores specific information concerning the users who access the website thanks to the use of cookies. In this way it is possible to know whether a user is visiting the website for the first time or if she is a loyal customer; in this case the vendor knows which pages she has visited previously (clickstream) and which products have been added to the various shopping carts. Therefore, firms can condition

---

[21]Firms can also use other devices besides cookies in order to obtain information on consumers and on their preferences; for instance, a firm can keep track of the purchase history of a consumer and therefore identify her preferences by means of static IP addresses, credit card numbers and authentication mechanisms.

pricing strategies on the basis of the range of information gathered on customers, thus discriminating different users by distinguishing between first time or second time visitors, between consumers who have already made on-line purchases or not and even on the basis of which products they have already bought; to sum up firms can easily segment the market.

Box 2.4 – The power of trust

Consumer trust represents one of the biggest challenges for on-line retail. When a customer visits an on-line retailer she may have little information on the owner of the website, on his physical address, telephone number, or email address. Nevertheless, the customer still selects a product and electronically transfers payment to the e-commerce business without receiving anything in return right away.

But, what if the retailer were to never send the good? What if he simply overcharges the customer's credit card? What if he collects credit card information to sell it to fraudsters? What if he sends the customer the wrong or even a non-functional product?

Trust is important in any business transaction but in the case of e-commerce it is all the more so. One way for retailers to develop trust is through quality certifications.

The economics literature on quality certifications is well developed; it is highly acknowledged that such certifications can reduce information asymmetries between buyers and sellers. In this way, they may remedy to the "lemons" problem which causes transactions to break down. This explains why quality certifications are a common feature in several "traditional" markets (e.g. consumer retail, firm-to-firm trade, medical treatment, auto repair and many others).

Elfenbein et al. (2013) study empirically the effects of the seller-quality certification program on the U.K. eBay platform, eBay's second most active marketplace after the US-based one.

To improve reputation and trust, eBay introduced Detailed Seller Ratings (DSRs) in 2007 and the eBay Top-Rated Seller (eTRS) program in 2009. Under the DSR, program buyers are asked to rate sellers along four dimensions (i.e. Was the item received as described by the seller? Was the

seller's communication effective? Was the product shipped in a timely manner? Were shipping and handling charges reasonable?). To become a Top-Rated Seller, retailers have to meet a number of requirements concerning the time the account has been active, the volume of transactions, the percentage of positive feedbacks and DSR ratings. Sellers who receive a sufficiently high score are assessed as Top-Rated and receive a badge which appears on their listings. To stimulate sellers' good practices, eBay offers discounted fees to eTRS.

Elfenbein, Fisman and McManus are interested in assessing the way in which seller and market characteristics affect consumer response to quality certification; they use a large data set obtained from the U.K. eBay platform including data on individual listings (detailed information on sellers and products), collected from 29 September 2009 (the first day of the eTRS program) to 31 October 2010. Listing data are complemented with a panel of seller-level data including information on the annual and quarterly amount of transactions and revenues. Overall, the sample is made up of 16 million observations for over 8,000 eBay product categories.

The results obtained by Elfenbein, Fisman and McManus are of great interest: for a seller, gaining eTRS certification increases the probability of successfully concluding a transaction by 7%; consumers are willing to pay eTRS-badged items a higher price (up to 7% more) and, on aggregate, eTRS earned an additional £26.8 million in the year following the introduction of the eTRS program (roughly £1,110 per certified seller). The authors also find that the impact of certification is greater in categories with few other certified listings and that the eTRS badge has greater effects in less concentrated markets.

It is interesting to analyse which are the effects of dynamic pricing (i.e. conditioning prices on purchase history) on the market equilibrium, on firms' profits and on social welfare; these issues are addressed in the model by Acquisti and Varian (2005) which focuses on the interactions between consumers and firms when technologies such as cookies are used in order to identify, recognise and therefore discriminate consumers.[22]

The model by Acquisti and Varian

With dynamic pricing retailers charge different prices depending on whether a consumer has already purchased in the past or not. In what follows, we present a simple model of dynamic pricing based on Acquisti and Varian (2005).[23]

Consider an on-line monopolist operating in two periods. Each consumer visits the firm's website twice, once in each period and decides whether to purchase and when to do so. Four possible events may occur: the consumer purchases on her first visit, on her second visit, during both visits or she does not buy at all.

The benefit derived from the purchase depends on k, the valuation of the good, and on m_i, where the subscript $i = 1, 2$ denotes whether the consumer purchases at her first or second visit. Parameter m_i refers to the benefits derived from the additional services that a customer may exploit by purchasing on the Internet: on-line it is very easy to complete transactions and usually purchases can be made by credit card or by other electronic means of payment, thus enhancing their attractiveness. The two basic assumptions of the model concern parameter m_i:

Assumption. *Consumers have: i) heterogeneous preferences with respect to m_i and ii) the benefit increases when the product is purchased on the second visit: $m_2 > m_1$.*

The interpretation of assumption *ii*) is the following; the second visit to an on-line store is more efficient than the first for two reasons. The consumer learns how to find her way through the website and wastes less time; moreover, the on-line retailer often provides additional services to second time visitors (such as further information, targeted recommendations, loyalty rewards etc.).

---

[22]It is important to highlight that Acquisti and Varian also analyse another interesting aspect which we do not include in our presentation; on-line customers, or at least those who are more sophisticated, may protect themselves from being discriminated for instance by disabling cookies, an option which is available in almost all web browsers. In this way a strategic interaction between the user and the website emerges. On the one hand, the vendor needs to choose whether or not to condition prices on the basis of the information included in the cookies and on the other hand, the consumer can take action in order to avoid being identified and recognised.

[23]We present a simplified version of the model as in Belleflamme (2005).

Formally, the net utility from purchasing during visit i is:

$$U(\theta, m_i, p_i) = k + \theta m_i - p_i,$$

where p_i denotes the price charged by the on-line retailer while θ is the taste parameter which measures consumer preferences with respect to m_i. Following assumption i), consumers have heterogeneous preferences towards m_i; formally, we assume that θ is uniformly distributed over the interval $[0, 1]$. Therefore, a consumer who, for instance, is characterised by a very small taste parameter θ does not enjoy purchasing on-line very much (namely, she does not obtain a significant benefit from the on-line retail services).

Benchmark: no price discrimination. The aim of Acquisti and Varian's work is to determine the optimal dynamic pricing strategy, namely the prices that the firm charges in the two periods; we start by considering the case of no price discrimination: the monopolist charges the same price p in both periods. Consumers observe p and decide whether to purchase or not; for each period, we determine the consumer who is indifferent between purchasing and not purchasing. Formally, the indifferent consumer is identified by the condition $U(\theta, m_i, p) = 0$ and is characterised by a taste parameter:

$$\tilde{\theta}(m_i, p) = \frac{p - k}{m_i}, \quad \text{with} \quad i = 1, 2.$$

Given p, all consumers characterised by $\theta \geq \tilde{\theta}(m_1, p)$ purchase the product in period 1; consumers with $\theta \geq \tilde{\theta}(m_2, p)$ buy from the monopolist in period 2. Following the assumption of zero production costs, the monopolist's profits are:

$$\pi_N(p) = p\left(1 - \tilde{\theta}(m_1, p)\right) + p\left(1 - \tilde{\theta}(m_2, p)\right) = \frac{p}{m_1 m_2}\left(2m_1 m_2 - (p - k)(m_1 + m_2)\right),$$

where subscript N denotes the fact that we are considering the case of no price discrimination.

From the first order condition, we define the monopoly price, p_N^*; by substituting this expression into $\pi_N(p)$, we determine the equilibrium profits:

$$p_N^* = \frac{k}{2} + \frac{m_1 m_2}{m_1 + m_2}, \quad \text{and} \quad \pi_N^* = \frac{(2m_1 m_2 + k(m_1 + m_2))^2}{4m_1 m_2 (m_1 + m_2)}.$$

Cookies and dynamic pricing. By using the information provided by cookies, the monopolist can price discriminate: it may condition prices on the history of purchases.

Clearly, in period 1, all consumers visit the retailer's website for the first time, cookies have not been created yet and the firm cannot discriminate. Things change in the second period. When consumers visit the website for the second time, cookies already contain information which the firm can use to infer their preferences; a consumer purchasing in period 1 is characterised by a large θ. Vice versa, if the consumer did not buy the product then her preferences are characterised by a small θ. Therefore, thanks to the information stored in the cookies, the firm can discriminate between two categories of consumers, those that value m a lot and those that value m little.

In order to define the optimal pricing strategy for the monopolist, we need to determine three prices: one for period 1 and two for period 2. In period 1, consumers are all alike from the monopolist's point of view (no cookies are available) and for this reason the firm sets only one price, denoted by p_o. In period 2, the monopolist can condition prices on purchase history: let p_b denote the price charged to consumers who bought the product in period 1 and p_{nb} denote the price charged to those who did not purchase.

Consumers who purchased during their first visit are characterised by a large θ; therefore, in period 2, it is profitable for the monopolist to charge them a large price p_b. At this price, some of them purchase also in period 2, while others do not.

The choice of p_{nb} is more articulated and entails two effects. Consumers who did not purchase during their first visit are characterised by a small value of θ; therefore, in order to induce them to buy, the firm should charge a small price in period 2. However, the firm knows that p_b and p_{nb} also affect consumers' choices in period 1. In particular, by charging a large p_b and a small p_{nb} the firm discourages consumers from buying during their first visit: if they do so, then they are charged a large p_b in period 2 while if they do not purchase during their first visit, they can obtain the product at a low price p_{nb} in the following period. This second effect suggests that the vendor should charge a sufficiently large p_{nb} to induce some consumers to buy in period 1.[24]   It is possible to prove that this second effect is the dominant one and, therefore, it is optimal for the monopolist to set an extremely large p_{nb} (e.g. infinite). Therefore, to define the monopolist's optimal pricing strategy we only need to determine the values of p_o and p_b.

On the basis of the above arguments, as shown in Figure 2.10, consumers can be segmented into three categories: consumers with a large θ who purchase in both periods; consumers with intermediate values of θ who buy in period 1 only, and, finally, consumers characterised by a low θ who do not purchase at all.

To define the optimal pricing strategy, we first need to determine the demand function; namely, how many consumers buy during their first visit and how many buy during their second visit. As shown in Figure 2.10, we proceed by identifying two indifferent consumers. We let $\tilde{\theta}_L(p_o)$ denote the taste parameter of the consumer who is indiffer-

---

[24]Implicitly, we are assuming that the firm can credibly commit to this pricing strategy; Acquisti and Varian (2005) also analyse the case where commitment is not credible.

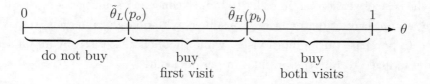

Figure 2.10: market segmentation with dynamic pricing

ent between purchasing in period 1 at p_o and not purchasing at all; from the condition $U(\theta, m_1, p_o) = 0$, it follows that:

$$\tilde{\theta}_L(p_o) = \frac{p_o - k}{m_1}.$$

The second indifferent consumer is identified by the taste parameter $\tilde{\theta}_H(p_b)$; this consumer is indifferent between buying the product during both visits and buying only in period 1. Formally, $\tilde{\theta}_H(p_b)$ is derived from the condition $U(\theta, m_1, p_o) + U(\theta, m_2, p_b) = U(\theta, m_1, p_o)$, that is $U(\theta, m_2, p_b) = 0$:

$$\tilde{\theta}_H(p_b) = \frac{p_b - k}{m_2}.$$

From the above discussion, when the monopolist discriminates consumers on the basis of the purchase history, the profit function is:

$$\pi_D(p_o, p_b) = p_o \left(\tilde{\theta}_H(p_b) - \tilde{\theta}_L(p_o)\right) + (p_o + p_b)\left(1 - \tilde{\theta}_H(p_b)\right) = p_o\left(1 - \frac{p_o - k}{m_1}\right) + p_b\left(1 - \frac{p_b - k}{m_2}\right)$$

By differentiating $\pi_D(p_o, p_b)$ with respect to p_o and p_b and by solving the system of first order conditions, we derive the equilibrium prices and profits:

$$p_o^* = \frac{k}{2} + \frac{m_1}{2}, \quad p_a^* = \frac{k}{2} + \frac{m_2}{2} \quad \text{and} \quad \pi_D^* = \frac{(k^2 + m_1 m_2)(m_1 + m_2) + 4k m_1 m_2}{m_1 m_2}.$$

Comparing the equilibrium profits with and without price discrimination, we obtain the following result:

Result 9. *The firm profitably discriminates consumers by conditioning prices on purchase history, $\pi_D^* > \pi_N^*$.*

The interpretation of Result 9 is straightforward and resembles the arguments we presented when discussing versioning. The monopolist segments consumers on the basis of their valuations. The optimal strategy consists in reducing the price for first time visitors (p_o) and in increasing it for consumers who have already purchased the product (p_b). One can easily verify that $p_o^* < p_N^* < p_b^*$.

As in the case of versioning, in order to induce consumer self-selection, the difference between p_o^* and p_b^* cannot be too large: consumers with a large willingness to pay should be induced to purchase during both visits, while those characterised by an intermediate θ should be induced to buy the product in period 1 only.

Chapter 3

Network Externalities

3.1 Introduction

Information & Communication Technologies (ICT) play a crucial role in modern society. Besides the numberless electronic and telecommunication devices such as computers and mobile phones that all of us use in our everyday lives, nowadays the provision of many essential services rely on ICT. Loosely speaking, ICT enable us to write documents with a personal computer, to watch a film on-line, to download music with iTunes and to connect with other users, for instance by talking on the phone, sending an email and chatting with an instant messenger.

A basic economic feature of ICT relates to the benefit each consumer enjoys when purchasing a product or when adopting a technology; in ICT markets, the more consumers adopt a certain technology (purchase a certain product), the larger the utility they enjoy. In other words, the benefit obtained increases as the network of users becomes larger and larger. For example, if we consider a text editor, it is clear that the utility which a consumer derives from purchasing the software also depends on the possibility of exchanging files with others who work either with the same application or with one which is compatible. A more striking example of the importance of the size of the network of users is provided by the case of telecommunication technologies, such as telephone, email or instant messenger: the network physically connects individuals and their utility exclusively depends on the possibility of communicating with each other; therefore, the value which individuals obtain increases with the size of the network.

Another important aspect of ICT is that when choosing whether to adopt a certain technology, a consumer does not take into account the fact that her decision affects network size and therefore the benefit that other users enjoy. In the economics jargon, this is referred to as an "externality", which in the case of ICT is better known as network externality, or network effect.

In this chapter, we provide a general description of the main features of markets with network externalities. In particular, we show that the fact that consumer willingness to pay for network products increases with the number of users has relevant consequences for the shape of the demand function and, therefore, for the strategies firms adopt when competing in high-tech markets. We also discuss in greater detail topics such as positive feedback, standardisation, compatibility and the role of consumer expectations in determining the dynamics of high-tech markets.

3.2　Network externalities and critical mass

As mentioned in the introduction, a market exhibits network externalities when the utility enjoyed by individuals increases with the number of users of the product/technology. The literature distinguishes between two different types of network externalities:

- *direct network externalities*: when the utility (the valuation of the product) increases directly with the number of users of the same product or of a compatible one;

- *indirect network externalities*: when the valuation of the product is determined by the availability of complementary products; in this case the utility from consumption is only indirectly influenced by the number of users.

Direct network effects are typical of communication networks, such as fax and telephone. In these cases the more people you can interact with, the larger the utility of having a fax/telephone.[1]

Network effects are said to be indirect when the utility derived from technology adoption depends on the availability of complementary products; hence, the number of users of the technology affects utility but only indirectly: the larger the network of users the higher the number of complementary products available on the market and therefore the greater the utility from technology adoption. For example, the more widespread a certain operating system is, the larger the range of available applications and therefore the greater the utility derived from purchasing a personal computer running that specific operating system.

---

[1]Suppose an additional individual subscribes to a phone network made up of n users. This generates a positive externality for all users: the network becomes bigger, each subscriber can now communicate with an additional person and, therefore, n new channels of communication are created. This idea, formally known as the Metcalfe Law (after the name of one of the co-inventors of the Ethernet), describes how networks work. Since the individual benefit is proportional to the number of users, the social value of the network is n times the individual benefit, formally n^2: the social value of a network increases more than proportionally with n.

Internet features both types of network externalities. Internet users can interact with each other through email or social networks, thus benefiting from direct network externalities. An important role is also played by indirect network externalities: the more people access the Internet, the greater the number of products and services available on-line, thus increasing the overall value for consumers.[2]

As mentioned earlier, consumer expectations play a central role in technology markets. Take software for example: when we decide which application to adopt, we tend to prefer the one which is expected to become the most widespread. This fact implies that network externalities depend on the future prospects of the technology. Consumer expectations are particularly relevant for new technologies/products; clearly, when launching a new technology there is no installed base of users yet and, therefore, adoption decisions are greatly influenced by expectations concerning the future size of the network of users.

Let us now formalise these arguments by presenting a simple model. Consider a consumer who is deciding whether or not to buy one unit of a network good; in jargon, we say that the consumer is deciding whether or not to access/connect to the network. Her willingness to pay for the good depends on two dimensions: i) the basic utility, that is a stand-alone benefit derived from the use of the technology, formally denoted by $k > 0$, and ii) the network effects related to the expected future dimension of the network of users, i.e. the so-called expected installed base of users, denoted by y^e. For instance, in the case of a text editor, the basic utility is related to the possibility of drafting letters and documents, while the network effects are associated with the opportunity of exchanging files with other users of the same software.

Let $U(k, y^e)$ be the gross utility, i.e. the benefit which a consumer derives from purchasing the good (accessing the network), gross of the price paid; this utility increases both with k, the stand-alone benefit, and y^e, the expected network size. Formally:

$$\frac{\partial U}{\partial k} > 0 \quad \text{and} \quad \frac{\partial U}{\partial y^e} > 0.$$

Before discussing the effects of network externalities, it is useful to make a methodological clarification. As discussed previously, consumer expectations play a crucial role in markets featuring network effects; nevertheless, formalising them within a model makes the analysis rather complex. For this reason, for the sake of simplicity, we assume in some cases that consumers act "myopically" and take their adoption decisions on the

---

[2]ICT markets are not the only ones where network externalities play an important role. For instance, consider a consumer who is deciding which car to buy. The benefit she enjoys from the purchase is also associated with the number of consumers who have chosen the same model: the more widespread the model is, the easier it is to find expert mechanics or spare parts. Therefore, indirect network effects characterise also traditional markets. Several observers have criticised the definition of indirect network externalities claiming it is too loose (see Liebowitz and Margolis, 1994).

basis of the current network size rather than on the expected one. We introduce this simplification only when it is without loss of generality, i.e. when the results obtained are valid also when consumer expectations are taken into consideration.[3]

3.2.1   The demand with network externalities

We now proceed step-by-step to define the demand function for the network good.[4] Suppose there is a mass equal to 1 of (potential) consumers of the good; each individual decides whether or not to purchase at most one unit of the good. For the sake of simplicity, we assume that the gross utility of a consumer, $U(k, y^e)$, is separable in its two arguments and takes the following functional form:

$$U(k, y^e) = k + v(y^e),$$

where k is the stand-alone utility and $v(y^e)$ is the benefit from the network externality, which depends on the expected installed base of users, y^e. Throughout this chapter, we assume that consumers are heterogeneous with respect to the stand-alone value; formally, k is uniformly distributed over the interval $[0, 1]$: consumers characterised by a small (large) k derive a little (great) basic utility from the network good. On the contrary, we assume that the benefit from the network externality is common to all consumers.[5]

We assume that the benefit from the network externality increases with y^e but at a decreasing rate; formally, $v' > 0$ and $v'' < 0$. The interpretation of the negative sign of the second derivative is the following; consider the effect produced by a new user connecting to the network: when y^e is small, the new user has a substantial impact on the size of the network and, therefore, on the utility of other users; when y^e is large, the additional user joining the network has little effect on network size and consequently also the utility of other users varies marginally. Finally, when the network is of size zero, there are no externalities; formally, $v(0) = 0$.

The first step to define the demand function for the network good is to determine the so-called indifferent consumer, that is, the individual who, given p and y^e, is indifferent between purchasing and not purchasing the product (between joining and not joining the network). This consumer is characterised by a stand-alone benefit $\tilde{k}$ such that her net utility from the purchase equals zero; formally, $k + v(y^e) - p = 0$, that is:

$$\tilde{k} = p - v(y^e).$$

Recalling that $U(k, y^e)$ increases with k, then consumers with a stand-alone utility $k \geq \tilde{k}$ purchase the good, while those with $k < \tilde{k}$ do not. Since k is assumed

---

[3]See Gandal (2002) for a thorough discussion on this issue.

[4]This section is based on Economides and Himmelberg (1995).

[5]We also assume that consumers hold the same expectations y^e about the future size of the network.

to be uniformly distributed over the interval $[0, 1]$, it follows that, given p and y^e, the overall number of individuals who buy the product, $y(p, y^e)$, equals $1 - \tilde{k}$, that is $y(p, y^e) = 1 + v(y^e) - p$. Therefore, the inverse demand function is:

$$p(y, y^e) = 1 + v(y^e) - y. \tag{3.1}$$

This expression represents the maximum price which the indifferent consumer is willing to pay when expected network size is y^e. By differentiating $p(y, y^e)$ with respect to its two arguments, we observe that the willingness to pay of the indifferent consumer decreases with quantity, y, and increases with expected network size, y^e; formally:

$$i) \quad \frac{\partial p}{\partial y} = -1 < 0 \quad \text{and} \quad ii) \quad \frac{\partial p}{\partial y^e} = v'(y^e) > 0.$$

Condition $i)$ highlights the standard negative relationship between price and quantity: as y increases, p decreases. Condition $ii)$ highlights the role played by network effects: the larger the expectations on future network size, the higher the price which consumers are willing to pay to join the network. As we point out later, conditions $i)$ and $ii)$ determine the shape of the demand function.

However, expression (3.1) does not identify the demand function yet: p depends not only on y but also on consumer expectations y^e. To determine the demand function, $p(y)$, we need to define how consumers form their expectations; following a typical approach used in the literature, we assume that consumer expectations are *ex post* correct (in jargon, fulfilled expectations):

Assumption. (fulfilled expectations) *Consumers are rational and form expectations which are correct in equilibrium:* $y^e = y$.

This assumption may seem rather strong but its explanation is actually very intuitive: if consumers expect the good to become popular and to spread quickly on the market, they will be more willing to purchase it, thus determining its actual success. Vice versa, if consumers are convinced that only a few users are interested in purchasing the good, then only a small fraction of them will join the network; in this case, the network does not build up and the good "does not take off". In both scenarios, consumer expectations are fulfilled (*ex post* correct).

By substituting $y^e = y$ into expression (3.1), we obtain the demand function for the network good (also known as demand with fulfilled expectations):

$$p(y) = 1 + v(y) - y.$$

Let's look at the shape of this demand function. Consider different levels of consumer expectations y_1^e, $2y_1^e$, $3y_1^e, \ldots$, where each level is K times y_1^e with

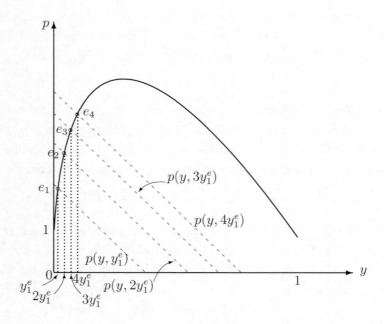

Figure 3.1: demand with network effects and fulfilled expectations

$K = 1, 2, 3, \ldots$. Different values of the function (3.1) are associated with these expectations: $p(y, y_1^e), p(y, 2y_1^e), p(y, 3y_1^e), \ldots$. By plotting these functions in a (y, p) plane and recalling conditions i) and ii), we observe that: these functions are parallel and negatively sloped and they shift outwards as K increases; moreover, since $v(\cdot)$ is a concave function, the vertical shift decreases as K increases.

Now look at Figure 3.1; the dashed lines represent the various $p(y, Ky_1^e)$ functions. For each function we identify the point e_K where expectations are fulfilled. For instance, point e_1 lies on $p(y, y_1^e)$ in correspondence to $y = y_1^e$, point e_2 lies on $p(y, 2y_1^e)$ in correspondence to $y = 2y_1^e$, and so on. By connecting all the e_K points we obtain the demand function with fulfilled expectations. As shown in Figure 3.1, this function has an inverted U-shape: when y is small, the demand function slopes upwards (positive relationship between price and output) while for larger values of y the demand slopes downwards (negative relationship between price and output).

This rather peculiar shape of the demand function can be explained on the basis of conditions i) and ii) seen above; by differentiating $p(y)$, it follows that:

$$\frac{dp}{dy} = v'(y) - 1.$$

The sign of this derivative depends on the relative strength of conditions i) and ii). Condition i), which, as in conventional markets, implies a negative relationship between price and quantity, prevails when $v' < 1$; since $v'' < 0$, this occurs when network size is large enough, namely when y is relatively high. On the contrary, condition ii), according to which price increases with quantity, dominates when network size is small: when y is low, an additional user joining the network substantially increases the externality effect, thus augmenting consumer willingness to pay; this fact explains the positive slope of the demand function for sufficiently small network size.[6] Summarising:

Result 1. *When the network is small-sized (small y), the price increases with y: the (positive) effect of the externality prevails on the standard (negative) price–quantity relationship. Consumer willingness to pay increases with y and the demand function is positively sloped. The opposite occurs when the network size is large (large y).*

Finally, it is important to note that the demand function with fulfilled expectations includes also part of the vertical axis. This fact can be easily explained; suppose that consumers expect no-one to join the network, $y^e = 0$. When $p \geq 1$, this expectation is actually fulfilled: with such a large price, no consumer, not even the one with the highest stand-alone utility $k = 1$, is willing to purchase the good ($y = 0$). Therefore, the vertical axis where $p \geq 1$ is also part of the demand function with fulfilled expectations.

3.2.2   Multiple equilibria, critical mass and positive feedback

The inverted U-shape of the fulfilled expectations demand function has important consequences on market equilibrium. Suppose that the good is supplied by a large number of perfectly competitive firms; with an inverted U-shaped demand function more than one equilibrium may emerge. In particular, as shown in Figure 3.2, demand and supply cross three times and therefore there are three possible market equilibria:

- E_0: equilibrium where no one adopts the network good, $y^* = 0$ (no adoption);

- E_l: equilibrium where few individuals adopt the network good, $y^* = y_l$ (low adoption);

- E_h: equilibrium where many individuals adopt the network good, $y^* = y_h$ (high adoption).

As highlighted in later sections of this chapter, multiple equilibria are typical of markets with network externalities. Note, however, that only two of these equilibria are long-run/stable. According to standard market dynamics, the quantity sold by

---

[6]Note that in order to have an inverted U-shaped demand function, the following conditions need to be satisfied: $v'(0) > 1$ and $v'(1) < 1$.

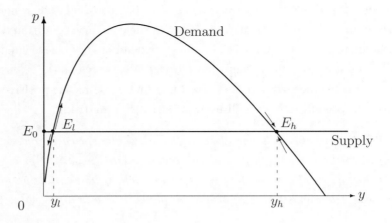

Figure 3.2: multiple equilibria with network externalities

firms increases when demand exceeds supply and decreases otherwise; therefore, it is straightforward to check that only the "no adoption" and the "high adoption" equilibria are stable. The "low adoption" equilibrium, instead, is actually unstable since a small perturbation drives the market away from E_l. To understand this fact, suppose that, for some reason, the demand increases slightly above y_l; as shown in Figure 3.2, when this occurs some additional consumers join the network since their willingness to pay now exceeds the market price. As the installed base of users gets larger, externalities make adoption even more attractive, thus creating a "snowball effect" according to which additional individuals are induced to join the network. This process, known as "positive feedback", continues until the market has achieved the stable equilibrium E_h. Likewise, E_l is unstable to perturbations that reduce the quantity demanded below y_l. In this case, some consumers drop out of the network since the market price is now above their willingness to pay; this time the feedback effect goes in the opposite direction inducing further individuals to exit the network. This drop out process leads the market to the stable equilibrium E_0.

The quantity y_l (the output level in the "low adoption equilibrium") represents an important threshold, known in the literature as the *critical mass*. If quantity demanded is above y_l the positive feedback "kicks in", further demand is generated and the market converges to the high adoption equilibrium. If instead, the critical mass is not achieved, the good does not take off and the market falls back to the stable zero-demand/zero-supply equilibrium.

Result 2. *The minimum network size is known as **critical mass**. If the network reaches this size then the positive feedback kicks in and the market converges to the stable* *equilibrium E_h; otherwise, the network does not build-up. In the long run, small-sized networks (with $0 < y < y_l$) are not observed.*

Box 3.1 – Network externalities in the computer spreadsheet market[a]

One of the first scholars who empirically estimated the existence and intensity of network effects in high-tech markets was Neil Gandal; in an article published in 1994, Gandal estimated the demand function for spreadsheets. Since the 80s, the market for spreadsheets was dominated by Lotus 1-2-3 with the homonymous product, the de facto standard at the time. Other relevant producers were Microsoft (with Multiplan and then Excel), Computer Associates (SuperCalc) and Borland (QuattroPro).

The aim of the study was to find the main determinants of the price of the various software available on the market and to this end the author used the information provided by Datapro Research Group for the period 1986–91. The various software were classified according to a set of features including: computing power, graphics and printing capabilities, easiness of data processing, compatibility with the dominant spreadsheet platform (Lotus), availability of access to external databases and, finally, capability of linking independent users through a local area network (LAN).

With network externalities the last three features were expected to have a positive and significant effect on the price of the software. For example, compatibility with the dominant standard Lotus enlarged the installed base of users, thus increasing the price that consumers were willing to pay for a software.

The following table presents the estimated coefficients and the t-test statistics obtained by Gandal for the three features potentially generating network effects:

Dependent variable: Log Price

Feature	Coefficient	t-stat
Compatibility with Lotus	0.76	5.30
Access to data bases	0.52	3.10
LAN	0.25	1.62

n. of observations 91, $R^2 = 0.86$

Table 3.1: intensities of network effects (Gandal, 1994)

The table shows that in all three cases the coefficient was positive and statistically significant, indicating that users were willing to pay a premium for a software incorporating these features. In particular Gandal found that consumers were willing to pay a significantly higher price for spreadsheets compatible with the dominant Lotus software and for spreadsheets offering links to external databases; the premium was smaller (but still positive and statistically significant) for spreadsheets offering local area network compatibility.

Gandal's findings strongly support the hypothesis that the computer spreadsheet market was significantly affected by network externalities.

---

[a]From Gandal (1994).

Consumer expectations play a crucial role in determining which equilibrium is going to emerge; the market converges either to E_0 or to E_h depending on expectations regarding network size. If consumers believe that the good is not going to be successful then no-one buys it and the equilibrium quantity converges to $y^* = 0$. If, on the contrary, consumers expect the others to "join the network", then they purchase it and the good will certainly take off. It is, therefore, vital for firms producing network goods to be able to influence consumer expectations in order to reach the critical mass of adopters and to ignite the positive feedback.[7]

The above discussion highlights another typical feature of high-tech markets, i.e. the problem of "coordination" among operators in the case of multiple equilibria. The two stable equilibria E_0 and E_h have very different characteristics; E_h is the most desirable from the social point of view: it is beneficial not only to firms whose technology takes off but also to consumers who enjoy the presence of a widespread network. The other stable equilibrium, E_0, represents the worst scenario for everybody: firms' technology does not take off and consumers do not enjoy any network benefit. In economic jargon E_0 is said to be Pareto-dominated by E_h.

In similar circumstances it is interesting to address the following questions: how can consumers coordinate their decisions in order to prevent the market from reaching the Pareto-dominated equilibrium where nobody adopts the technology? Which of the two stable equilibria is actually achieved by market forces? Consumer expectations concerning future network size play a crucial role and, therefore, it is very important for firms to influence them in order to avoid the risk of the market converging towards the non-adoption equilibrium. Alternatively, industrial policies aimed at subsidising or imposing the adoption of a specific technology may induce consumers to coordinate their decisions.

These issues allow us to introduce the second part of this chapter which analyses in greater detail the main features of technology diffusion and adoption.

3.3   The dynamics of technology adoption

The analysis presented in the previous paragraphs is based on several simplifying assumptions: first of all, since the model is essentially static, it does not take into consideration the dynamic features of a technology adoption process; for example, the model predicts the existence of multiple (stable) equilibria but it does not say anything about which one prevails in the long run. Secondly, it describes a market with only one technology. However, consumers often may choose among several competing technologies; for

---

[7]While the theoretical literature on the dynamics towards the equilibrium in network markets is quite rich, the empirical literature is still relatively scarce due to the difficulties to estimate the effects of externalities in dynamic models. Among the most relevant empirical works, it is worthwhile mentioning the seminal paper on the demand for telecommunication services by Rohlfs (1974), the works by Economides and Himmelberg (1995) (fax machines) and by Goolsbee and Klenow (2002) (personal computers); for a recent review on the empirical literature on networks see Birke (2009). For a comprehensive surveys on the economics of networks see Economides (1996b) and Matutes and Regibeau (1996).

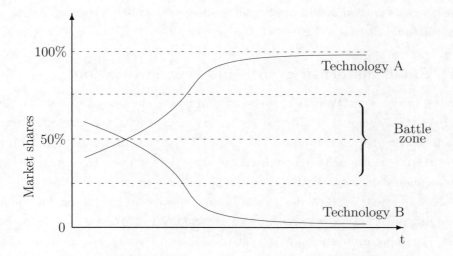

Figure 3.3: typical dynamics of technology adoption

example at the end of the 70s/beginning of the 80s, VHS (produced by JVC), Betamax (produced by Sony) and, to a minor extent, Video2000 (produced by Philips) were struggling for the leadership on the market of videotape recorders. More recently, Microsoft, Sony and Nintendo have been competing with their game consoles (Xbox, PlayStation and GameCube) in the market for video games. Hence, it is of great interest to study the dynamic process of technology adoption when consumers have the opportunity of choosing among different technologies.

Markets exhibiting network externalities are often referred to as *winner takes all* markets, that is markets where a single technology rises to dominance and competing technologies are forced to a marginal position. Operating systems for PCs are an example of this kind of market; there is one leading technology, Microsoft Windows, which has gained nearly the entire market share.

Figure 3.3 shows the typical pattern of an adoption process: at the beginning, the two technologies compete against one another in order to increase their own installed base of users (this is the so-called "battle zone"). After some time, one of the two technologies acquires a leading position, which, due to the effect of the externality, becomes so strong that the dominant technology is able to capture the entire market. Just to take a relevant example, this kind of dynamics has been observed in the market of videotape recorders in the 70s–80s; as shown in Figure 3.4, VHS, initially less popular, gained the leadership and after a few years forced Betamax to exit the market.

The aim of this section is to examine the adoption process when different technologies compete for market leadership. The literature on this topic is extremely rich; in this section we focus on two of the most significant works, namely those by Arthur (1989) and by Katz and Shapiro (1986).

3.3.1   Small historical events and standardisation

Most of us know about QWERTY, the most common modern-day keyboard layout. The name QWERTY comes from the first six letters (keys) of the top left letter row of the keyboard of personal computers.[8]   The QWERTY design, however, is not born with modern PCs. It first appeared in typewriters in the late nineteenth century; created for the Sholes and Glidden typewriter, it became popular with the success of the Remington No. 2 of 1878. The QWERTY design was chosen in order to slow typing down and avoid key-jamming problems. Nowadays, we still use the QWERTY even though there are no more key-jamming problems and alternative keyboard layouts have proven to be more efficient in terms of typing speed (we refer, for example, to DSK, the Dvorak Simplified Keyboard). The reason why the QWERTY design is still used today is due to the existence of network externalities; for example, the manager of an office who wants to buy a new computer, will prefer the QWERTY design for the keyboard because typists are accustomed to using this kind of layout.

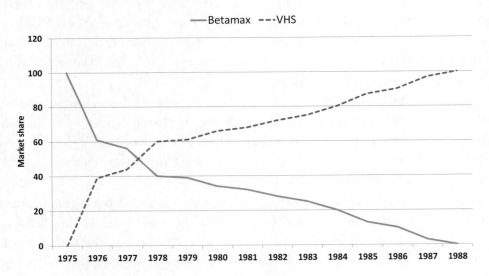

Figure 3.4: VHS *vs* Betamax – market shares[9]

The story of QWERTY is instructive for at least two reasons. The first thing we note is that the decision taken a long time ago by the producers of type-writers to adopt

---

[8]See David (1985) for greater details.

[9]Data obtained from Cusumano et al. (1992).

the QWERTY layout has forced society to standardise on an inferior technology: more efficient layouts are actually available, but nevertheless we still use QWERTY. Arthur (1989) refers to this case as an example of inefficient adoption process.

A simple numerical example helps us understand better Arthur's argument. Consider a market where there are two incompatible technologies (A and B) competing for adoption; consumers line up sequentially: at each instant of time t a new consumer arrives in the market and chooses which technology to adopt. For simplicity, we assume that consumers are "myopic": the adoption decision is based on the current size of the two networks rather than on their expected future sizes; in other words, consumer t decides which technology to adopt on the basis of how many consumers have already adopted technology A and how many technology B. In particular, we assume that the utilities enjoyed by consumers when adopting technologies A and B are:

$$U_A = 10 + n_A \quad \text{and} \quad U_B = 4 + 3n_B,$$

where n_i denotes the number of users who have already purchased technology i=A, B. Table 3.2 shows the utility enjoyed by a consumer adopting technology i at time $t = 1, 2, \ldots, 6$, under the assumption that all previous consumers have adopted the same technology.

One can observe that, as the adoption process goes on, technology B becomes superior due to stronger network effects ($3n_B$ compared to n_A). As shown in Table 3.2, the utility enjoyed by consumer t when adopting B, provided that also all previous individuals have adopted B, is initially smaller than the utility obtained by adopting A, provided that previous consumers have adopted A; however, this occurs only up to the fourth adopter. From the fifth consumer onwards, technology B yields larger benefits. Nevertheless, B is never chosen: the first consumer compares 4 with 10, therefore she opts for technology A. A fortiori, subsequent consumers also adopt technology A, which delivers an increasing benefit due to its growing installed base of users (the second user compares 4 with 11); the result is that the efficient technology B is kicked out of the market, while the inefficient technology A becomes the standard. This is what is meant by inefficient standardisation.

	consumer at time t					
	1	2	3	4	5	6
Technology A	10	11	12	13	14	15
Technology B	4	7	10	13	16	19

Table 3.2: individual utility from adoption

Going back to QWERTY, there is another important lesson we can learn from the story of the keyboard layout: "small events" may have major consequences in determining the winning technology. As mentioned previously, it was the need to slow down the speed of typing and to avoid key jams on the first typewriters that led producers of typewriters to choose the QWERTY standard. In other words, a small event or a "historical accident", namely something that took place about 150 years ago, is still producing effects on our everyday life. Using a common jargon, economic outcomes that depend on past events rather than simply on current conditions, are said to be *path-dependent*; when, as in the QWERTY example, past conditions/events determine an inefficient standardisation, the adoption process is said to be *path-inefficient*.

The case of the QWERTY keyboard is only one of the possible examples of inefficient standardisation. Several authors consider Microsoft Windows another example of social lock-in to an inferior technology; according to them, Windows is clearly inferior to other alternative operating systems, such as Linux, but despite its inferiority it is by large the dominant technology.

The model by Arthur

Consider a market where two incompatible technologies are competing for adoption;[10] consumers can be of two different types, α and β. Consumers of type α have a natural preference for technology A: they enjoy a larger stand-alone utility from adopting technology A rather than B. On the contrary, consumers of type β derive a larger stand-alone utility from technology B. Consumers line up sequentially: at each instant of time, a new consumer chooses to adopt one of the two technologies. We assume that with equal probability $1/2$ a consumer is of type α or of type β; once the adoption decision has been taken, the consumer is committed to the chosen technology, in other words she cannot switch to the other technology in later periods.

As in the previous model, we assume that consumers have myopic preferences, that is they base their decisions on the current network size (and not on the expected one). Table 3.3 shows the utility of the consumer who chooses at time t; the utility depends on her type and on the installed base of users of the two technologies at time t. In particular:

- $\alpha_i > 0$ identifies the stand-alone utility which consumers of type α derive from adopting technology $i = $ A,B. As argued previously, we assume that consumers of type α have a natural preference for technology A and, therefore, $\alpha_A > \alpha_B$;

---

[10]The model we present is based on Arthur (1989).

- $\beta_i > 0$ identifies the stand-alone utility which consumers of type β derive from adopting technology $i = $ A,B; following the assumption according to which these consumers have a natural preference for technology B, then $\beta_A < \beta_B$;

- $n_i(t) > 0$ identifies the installed base of users of technology i at time t;

- θ measures the intensity of the network externality; as θ increases so does the importance of the installed base of users.

		Technology A	Technology B
Consumer	α	$\alpha_A + \theta\, n_A(t)$	$\alpha_B + \theta\, n_B(t)$
type	β	$\beta_A + \theta\, n_A(t)$	$\beta_B + \theta\, n_B(t)$

Table 3.3: individual benefit from adoption

We now determine the dynamics of technology adoption represented by the stochastic process $x(t)$; in particular, $x(t) \in [0,1]$ identifies the market share of technology A at time t. The way in which the process $x(t)$ evolves over time depends on the preferences (i.e. the type) of consumers lining up for adoption.

Consumer adoption decisions depend on their natural preferences and on the difference between the installed base of users of the two technologies. For instance, consumers of type α, who have a natural preference for technology A, may, instead, choose B if, in the past, this technology had a much higher adoption rate than A; in this case, the effect of the network externality more than compensates the lower stand-alone benefit that the consumer enjoys by adopting technology B. Formally, a consumer of type α chooses technology B if $\alpha_A + \theta n_A(t) < \alpha_B + \theta n_B(t)$, that is, if

$$n_A(t) - n_B(t) < \frac{\alpha_B - \alpha_A}{\theta}.$$

Note that if at time t consumers of type α prefer technology B, then a fortiori consumers of type β prefer B too. Therefore, the above condition implies that from t onwards all consumers choose technology B.

Similarly, a consumer of type β chooses A, despite B being her naturally preferred technology, if

$$n_A(t) - n_B(t) > \frac{\beta_B - \beta_A}{\theta}.$$

Once again, this condition implies that from t onwards all consumers choose technology A.

For simplicity, we define these two thresholds as follows: $\Delta_\alpha \equiv (\alpha_B - \alpha_A)/\theta$ and $\Delta_\beta \equiv (\beta_B - \beta_A)/\theta$, with $\Delta_\alpha < 0$ and $\Delta_\beta > 0$; these two expressions are important

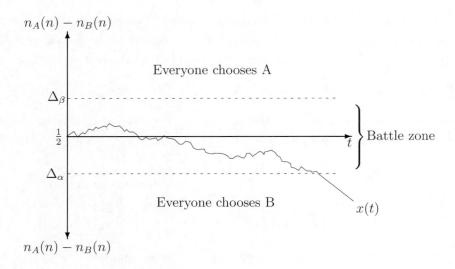

Figure 3.5: technology B becomes the standard

because they determine the dynamics of the technology adoption process: if at time t the difference between the installed base of users for the two technologies is not too large, that is, if $n_A(t) - n_B(t) \in [\Delta_\alpha, \Delta_\beta]$, then each consumer taking the adoption decision in time t will choose the technology she naturally prefers. Vice versa, if the difference between the installed bases of users is large enough, then each consumer adopts the leading technology regardless of her natural preference; therefore, if at a given time t $n_A(t) - n_B(t) < \Delta_\alpha$, then from that period onwards all consumers entering the market adopt technology B which becomes the standard. Alternatively, if at t $n_A(t) - n_B(t) > \Delta_\beta$ all individuals lining up for adoption choose A which becomes the standard technology.

For example, Figure 3.5 provides a graphical representation of standardisation on technology B. Following the previous arguments, as soon as $n_A(t) - n_B(t)$ crosses the threshold Δ_α, all consumers adopt technology B and $x(t)$ converges to 0.

Now, we focus our attention on what happens when $x(t)$ lies between the two thresholds Δ_β and Δ_α, that is when $n_A(t) - n_B(t) \in [\Delta_\alpha, \Delta_\beta]$. This is the so-called battle zone where there is no dominant technology. Arthur (1989) proves that in the battle zone, the $x(t)$ behaves according to the following stochastic process:

$$x(t) = \frac{1}{2} + \frac{n_A(t) - n_B(t)}{2t}. \tag{3.2}$$

The dynamics of $x(t)$ represent the heart of Arthur's model; it is clear that $x(t) > 1/2$ when the installed base of users of technology A is larger than that of B, that is when $n_A(t) - n_B(t) > 0$, while it is lower then $1/2$ when B is the more adopted technology. It is interesting to note that, as shown by expression (3.2), the difference between the installed base of users of the two technologies has a greater impact on the dynamics of adoption when t is small, that is at the early stages of the technologies' life. This is a relevant feature of the adoption process; suppose, in fact, that a small number of consumers of the same type (let's say type α who have a natural preference for technology A) lines up sequentially at the beginning of adoption process. In this case, this event may have a great impact on the dynamics of adoption, eventually inducing the market to standardise on technology A. On the contrary, if the same event occurs when t is large (that is when technologies are mature), the impact on the dynamics of adoption is much less relevant in the sense that it hardly induces standardisation. Therefore, the analysis by Arthur (1989) confirms that the effect of a small event (such as a sequence of consumers of the same type lining up for adoption) is less important if it occurs in later phases of the process, but it may play a crucial role if it takes place in the earlier stages. As mentioned previously, dynamic processes with this property are known as path-dependent because their long-run behaviour is determined by past events.

Figure 3.5 represents the typical behaviour of an adoption process $x(t)$: within the thresholds $[\Delta_\alpha, \Delta_\beta]$, $x(t)$ increases or decreases randomly according to the type of consumers entering the market; when $x(t)$ crosses one of the thresholds, standardisation occurs and all consumers, from that time onwards, choose the leading technology regardless of their natural preferences. Arthur proves that eventually the stochastic process $x(t)$ crosses one of the two thresholds and that standardisation on one of the two technologies is bound to take place.[11] Markets where only one technology survives in the long-run are commonly known as tipping or winner takes all markets.

Note the role of θ, the intensity of network externalites. The larger θ, the smaller the difference between Δ_α and Δ_β;[12] thus, when θ is large, the battle zone where technologies compete is narrower or, equivalently, standardisation (the moment when $x(t)$ crosses one of the thresholds) takes place earlier: when network effects are strong it does not take much time for a standard technology to emerge, while when externalities are weak both technologies tend to coexist for a longer period. To conclude, the main results of Arthur's analysis are the following:

Result 3. *With network effects:*

- *in the long-run the two technologies cannot coexist: one technology becomes the standard;*

- *historical small events may have a great impact on the dynamics of adoption;*

- *technology adoption may be path inefficient.*

---

[11]In technical jargon, $x(t)$ is referred to as a random walk with absorbing barriers Δ_α and Δ_β.
[12]One can easily check that both Δ_α and Δ_β are decreasing in θ.

3.3.2   Adoption decisions and technological progress

The story of the QWERTY keyboard design and Arthur's analysis highlight a typical feature of markets with network effects, that is the risk of standardisation on an inefficient technology. Before Arthur, several authors had already discussed this topic; in this section, we focus on the analysis provided by Katz and Shapiro (1986) which is particularly interesting because it focuses on technology adoption in a context characterised by technical progress, a natural feature of ICT industries. In fact, high-tech markets are characterised by ongoing technological progress with firms regularly introducing new products embodying the latest technologies. Consumers when choosing between an (old) established technology and a new but less popular one take their decision by balancing two opposing effects: on the one hand, the new product lacks an installed base of users but it is technologically more advanced; on the other hand, the (old) established technology is technically inferior but it is endowed with a larger installed base of users.

In this scenario, two different forms of inefficiency of the adoption process may arise:

1. **excess inertia** which occurs when consumers stick to an old and inferior standard even though a new and socially more desirable technology is available;

2. **excess momentum** which occurs when consumers switch to a new technology even though the old one is still socially more desirable.

In the first case, society is locked into an inferior technology, even if better products are available; this is typical of markets exhibiting network effects as described previously. The second type of market failure goes exactly in the opposite direction: society switches to the new technology too quickly, even if the old one is still socially more efficient.

Examples of excess inertia are rather frequent. QWERTY is an evident case of this kind of market failure; as mentioned previously, several authors argue that Microsoft Windows, the dominant operating system, is inferior to other alternative technologies and it can be considered a case of excess inertia. Examples of excess momentum can be found in software applications especially when companies launch updated versions of existing software: often when a number of key players switch to a new version of a software application, other users are also induced to switch for reasons of compatibility, even if they are satisfied with the old version. Updated versions, in fact, are often incompatible with the previous ones, thus forcing users to switch, even though the old version is still fully satisfying.

The model by Katz and Shapiro

The model by Katz and Shapiro (1986) analyses the main features of technology adoption with technical progress. In this section, we present a simplified version of the model in order to focus on the most important aspects and, in particular, on the possible forms of social inefficiencies that may emerge in a process of technology adoption.

Suppose that two incompatible technologies are competing for adoption; these two technologies are supplied by many firms in a perfectly competitive regime. We consider a two-period game and we assume that in each period there is a homogeneous generation of consumers choosing between the two technologies; for simplicity, we assume that each generation is made up of a single consumer. The total market amounts to two users: user 1 who makes her adoption decision in period 1 and user 2 who chooses a technology in period 2.

The utility enjoyed from adoption depends on $i)$ the quality of the technology at the moment of the adoption decision and $ii)$ the impact of network externalities; formally, the gross utilities enjoyed by consumers 1 and 2 from the adoption of either technology A or technology B are as follows:

$$U_{A,t} = \alpha_t + \theta y_A, \qquad U_{B,t} = \beta_t + \theta y_B, \quad \text{with} \quad t = 1, 2,$$

where α_t and β_t denote the quality of technology A and B at time $t = 1, 2$, i.e. the quality enjoyed by consumer t, while y_A, y_B denote A and B's network sizes at $t = 2$, with $y_A = \{0, 1, 2\}$ and $y_A + y_B = 2$; note the difference with Arthur's model: consumers are not myopic and their preferences depend on the overall size of the two networks.[13] As in the previous model, parameter θ denotes the intensity of network externalities.

Technological progress implies that the second generation of both technologies (available in $t = 2$) is more advanced and, hence, of higher quality. Formally, technological progress is represented by assuming $\alpha_2 > \alpha_1$ and $\beta_2 > \beta_1$.

In what follows we focus on the most interesting case where one technology, B for instance, is of lower quality at $t = 1$ and, thanks to technological progress, it becomes of higher quality in period 2. Formally, we assume that:

Assumption. *i) At the beginning technology A is the most advanced, $\alpha_1 > \beta_1$, and ii) over time, technology B becomes qualitatively superior, $\beta_2 > \alpha_2$.*

---

[13] We solve the game by backward induction and we look for the subgame perfect Nash equilibrium; alternatively, we could have modelled consumers' preferences based on expectations concerning future network size. In this case, we could have looked at the equilibrium with fulfilled expectations as in Section 3.2.1; one can check that in the simple setting we are considering, subgame perfection implies fulfilled expectations.

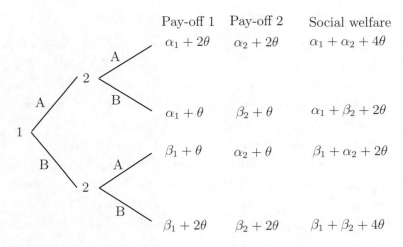

Figure 3.6: the game tree

Katz and Shapiro refer to technology B as the "emerging technology". Two scenarios need to be considered: a) despite being the declining technology, A is globally superior, that is, considering the two periods, technology A has a larger overall quality, $\alpha_1 + \alpha_2 > \beta_1 + \beta_2$; b) technology B is not only emerging but also globally superior, that is $\beta_1 + \beta_2 > \alpha_1 + \alpha_2$.

For the sake of simplicity, let Δ_1 and Δ_2 denote the difference between the quality of the two technologies in period $t = 1$ and $t = 2$ respectively; formally: $\Delta_1 \equiv \beta_1 - \alpha_1$ and $\Delta_2 \equiv \beta_2 - \alpha_2$, with $\Delta_1 < 0$ and $\Delta_2 > 0$, since B is assumed to be the emerging technology. Finally, if B is globally superior, then $\Delta_2 > -\Delta_1$.

Consider now the supply-side of the market. As mentioned at the beginning of this section, we assume that both technologies are produced in a perfectly competitive environment; by normalising the marginal cost of production to zero for both technologies, it follows that equilibrium prices also equal zero; therefore, $U_{A,t}$ and $U_{B,t}$ represent consumer net utilities.

Figure 3.6 represents the extensive form of the adoption game. In $t = 1$ consumer 1 chooses between A and B; in $t = 2$, consumer 2 observes the decision taken by consumer 1 and then decides which technology to adopt. When both consumers adopt the same technology, there is standardisation. The first two columns of Figure 3.6 show the net utilities enjoyed by consumers depending on their adoption decision;[14] for each adoption pattern, the last column shows social welfare, that is the sum of the utilities of the two consumers.

---

[14]Even though consumer 1 adopts in period 1 and obtains benefits in both periods, for the sake of simplicity, we assume that she enjoys a utility in period 2 only, after consumer 2 has taken her decision.

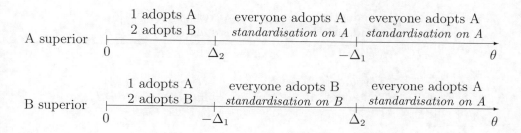

Figure 3.7: equilibrium of the adoption game

We are now ready to determine the equilibrium of the game; we proceed by backward induction and we start by analysing the choice of consumer 2 who, after having observed the decision taken by consumer 1, decides whether to adopt A or B in order to maximise her net utility. The optimal strategy for consumer 2 depends on: the decision taken by consumer 1 in the first period, the strength of network externalities and the quality of the two technologies. By observing the game tree and consumer 2's pay-offs, it is straightforward to show that the optimal strategy for this consumer is the following:

- if $\theta < \Delta_2$, consumer 2 adopts B, no matter which technology consumer 1 has chosen;

- if $\theta \geq \Delta_2$, consumer 2 mimics 1's decision: if consumer 1 has adopted A, then consumer 2 chooses A too, if consumer 1 has chosen B then consumer 2 does likewise.

Consumer 2's behaviour can be easily interpreted. When network externalities are weak, that is when $\theta < \Delta_2$, the effect of the installed base of users does not affect her decision; in this case, consumer 2 adopts B, the more advanced technology, regardless of consumer 1's choice. On the contrary, if $\theta \geq \Delta_2$, network externalities have a strong impact and it is optimal for consumer 2 to mimic the decision taken by the other consumer in order to enjoy the benefit of a larger installed base ("copycat" strategy).

Now let's consider consumer 1; she knows that her adoption may affect the decision taken by the other consumer. In particular, consumer 1 anticipates that if $\theta < \Delta_2$, consumer 2 chooses technology B, while if $\theta \geq \Delta_2$, consumer 2 plays a copycat strategy; therefore, by looking at her pay-offs, the optimal behaviour of consumer 1 is the following:

- when $\theta < \Delta_2$, consumer 1 chooses technology A if $\theta < -\Delta_1$, while she chooses B if $\theta \geq -\Delta_1$;

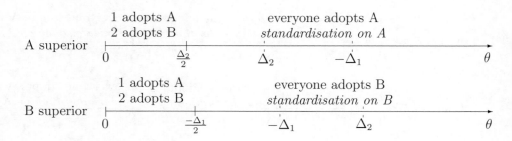

Figure 3.8: socially optimal adoption paths

- when $\theta \geq \Delta_2$, consumer 1 chooses technology A, the most advanced technology in $t = 1$.

We can now define the equilibrium of the game; Figure 3.7 shows that two cases need to be considered, depending on which technology is globally superior. Katz and Shapiro prove the following result:

Result 4. *If the intensity of network externalities, θ, is small, technology A and B coexist in equilibrium. On the contrary, if the intensity of network externalities is large, there is market standardisation on one technology.*

Once again network externalities play a crucial role; similarly to Arthur's model, when the intensity of network externalities is small, the two technologies coexist in equilibrium. Vice versa, when θ is large, only one technology survives and the adoption path yields standardisation either on A or on B.[15]

It is now interesting to consider whether the market equilibrium is efficient or not and, in the latter case, to determine the sources of inefficiency. The first step in order to perform this analysis is to compare the social welfare associated with each possible pattern of technology adoption (see the last column of Figure 3.6) and determine the socially optimal one. Figure 3.8 shows that when the intensity of network externalities is not too strong, then social welfare is maximised when consumer 1 adopts A while consumer 2 adopts B (no standardisation). Vice versa, when θ is large, the socially optimal adoption pattern requires standardisation on technology A (when technology

---

[15]Result 4 has been obtained under the assumption that the two technologies are supplied by perfectly competitive firms. Katz and Shapiro's article also includes the case where each technology is sold by one firm only, the so-called sponsor. The authors prove that in period 1, it may be profitable for the sponsor to adopt an aggressive pricing strategy, by charging a price below production costs. This makes the product appealing for consumers in $t = 1$ thus increasing the installed base of users; the reduction in profits obtained in period 1 is more than compensated by the higher profits the firm earns in period 2, when it can substantially increase its price to exploit the larger installed base of users.

A is globally superior) or on technology B (when B is globally superior). By comparing Figures 3.7 (market equilibrium) with 3.8 (socially optimal adoption pattern) two different types of market inefficiencies arise:

- *lack of standardisation*: two technologies coexist in equilibrium even if standardisation is optimal from the social point of view;

- *standardisation on the wrong technology*: the market selects the globally inferior technology as the standard.

Lack of standardisation occurs in two cases, both characterised by moderate intensity of network externalities (θ takes intermediate values). Consider the case where A is the globally superior technology; by comparing Figures 3.7 and 3.8, when $\theta \in (\Delta_2/2, \Delta_2)$, the two technologies coexist in equilibrium despite standardisation on A being socially preferable. Recalling the notions of excess inertia and excess momentum introduced at the beginning of this section, this form of inefficiency is an example of the latter: future users (consumer 2 in the model) adopt the emerging technology even if the old one is socially preferable. Therefore, the inefficiency is caused by future users who do not internalise the effect of their adoption decision on the benefit enjoyed by older users (consumer 1 in the model).

The second case of lack of standardisation occurs when technology B is globally superior and $\theta \in (-\Delta_1/2, -\Delta_1)$: in equilibrium, consumers 1 and 2 choose different technologies despite standardisation on B being socially preferable. In this case market failure is due to excess inertia: older users choose technology A which is superior in $t = 1$ but is globally inferior to technology B. Therefore, in this case, market failure accrues from older users not internalising the effect of their choices on the utility of future users.

Standardisation on the wrong technology occurs when the intensity of network externalities is large (θ takes large values) and technology B is globally superior: in equilibrium all consumers choose A despite standardisation on B being socially optimal. This market inefficiency represents an extreme case of excess inertia which is due to the behaviour of older users who adopt the old (globally inferior) technology and induce future users to do the same. This last case is very much in line with the spirit of Arthur's model: early adopters select the inferior technology and cause a social lock-in, thus imposing future users to standardise on the wrong technology.

Standardisation and public intervention

The risk of market failures is one of the main motivations for public intervention in a market economy: when governments or regulatory authorities are better informed than consumers on the characteristics of the various available technologies, industrial policies may be used in order to induce the market to adopt the best standard. For example in 1986, thirteen European governments agreed to develop and deploy the GSM technology for second generation digital cellular networks. The decision to adopt a continental standard had an immediate effect and created a unified, standard-based network. In the United States, instead, the federal government did not take similar actions and several incompatible standards coexisted for a long period of time, thus slowing down the adoption of wireless technologies.[16]

Quite surprisingly, despite the importance of the topic, the economic literature on the role of governments in the determination of technology standards is rather underdeveloped. Among the few authors who discuss the issue, the work by Cabral and Kretschmer (2007) is one of the most interesting. These two authors extend Arthur's model in order to analyse the effects of government's intervention on the dynamics of adoption.

As in Arthur (1989), the adoption process is represented as a sequence of consumers lining up for adoption. Cabral and Kretschmer extend this framework assuming that, at each instant of time, a welfare-maximising government may decide to support one of the available technologies. Public support may take different forms; for example, the government may subsidise adoption or it may shift demand by mandating the adoption of the technology in public offices, schools and so on.

The authors analyse two possible scenarios characterised by different time horizons and preferences: *i*) the government intervenes to favour consumers who are currently adopting or have already adopted a technology (myopic or impatient government with short-term preferences) and *ii*) the government focuses on the welfare of future users (patient government with long-term preferences). In the first scenario, the government is not interested in the welfare of future users; the authors prove that in this case it is optimal for the government to intervene immediately by supporting the leading standard. In the second scenario, when the policy maker focuses on the welfare of future users, it may prefer to delay its intervention or to support the lagging standard.

Clearly, these scenarios represent two extreme cases; the authors highlight that when the government cares both for current and for future users, then the best policy would be ... to have no policy at all! In other words, no intervention may be preferable to any intervention.

---

[16]In the U.S.A. there were three technologies competing in the market for mobile telecommunications: Global System for Mobile telecommunications (GSM), Time Division Multiple Access (TDMA) and Code Division Multiple Access (CDMA). See Varian and Shapiro (1999) for further details on the case.

Box 3.2 – Inefficient standardisations[a]

History is full of examples of inferior technologies which have become the market standard; Foray (1994) provides a series of such examples including the case of the technology for the production of nuclear energy and the one related to video-recording systems.

Nuclear power. The story of the technology for the production of nuclear energy dates back to the post-war period. At that time, the technology based on pressurised water-cooled reactors was selected instead of the one based on gas-cooled reactors, which today is unanimously considered as superior.

The "historical accident" which led to the adoption of pressurised water-cooled reactors can be traced back to the post-war purchase order by the US government from Westinghouse and General Electric for the construction of a submarine reactor. The need to build very compact reactors for submarines led engineers from both companies to select the technology based on cooled-water reactors, which was more suitable for military purposes, despite being less efficient. This choice steered subsequent decisions related to nuclear generators for civilian purposes, even though other technologies were undoubtedly more efficient.

Video cassette recorders (VCR). The story of video recorders goes back to the late 70s and the protagonists were Sony with its Betamax technology and JVC with its VHS system.

Betamax, launched in the Japanese market in June 1975, was the first VCR system in history; a short time later, in September 1976, JVC challenged Sony by launching its VHS technology. From the technical point of view, Sony Betamax format was undoubtedly superior, especially with respect to image quality; yet, it was VHS which penetrated the market. The story ended in 2002 with Sony abandoning the production of Betamax.

According to Foray, the VCR battle can be divided into two distinct phases: an initial one, until the early 80s, during which the two technologies coexisted, and a later phase in which JVC definitely took the lead of the market and VHS became the standard.

How can we explain these dynamics of adoption? Foray offers a very interesting interpretation by suggesting that the second phase began with the creation and diffusion of pre-recorded video tapes and with the emergence of the video rental market in the second half of the '80s. Pre-recorded video cassettes are, in fact, complementary to the video recording system and, as we know, the availability of complementary products generates indirect network externalities.

Therefore, the explanation given by Foray for the two-phase adoption path is the following: up to the 80s, pre-recorded video cassettes were not available and, for this reason, video recording systems exhibited poor network externalities; this explains why in the first period the two technologies coexisted. With the spreading of pre-recorded video cassettes, network externalities became much more intense, thus changing the very nature of the dynamics of adoption; as in Arthur (1989), in the presence of strong network externalities, the adoption process exhibits a winner takes all market dynamics, with a technology that inevitably becomes the standard. JVC successfully exploited its market leadership and transformed it into market dominance by igniting the feedback effect.

[a]From Foray (1994).

This consideration allows us to assess the U.S. experience in mobile telecommunications from a different perspective. As mentioned above, the decision not to intervene in support of one of the competing technologies may have delayed the emergence of a standard, and, at first sight, it may appear to be a wrong decision. Nonetheless, the analysis by Cabral and Kretschmer suggests that, on the contrary, this decision may have been right. Nowadays the penetration of mobile phones in the U.S. market is comparable to the one in Europe. On top of that, the new (third) generation of mobile telecommunications we are now using is an evolution of the CDMA standard which is the technology that, without any public intervention, succeeded in the race for adoption in the U.S.A.

In more general terms, the analysis by Cabral and Kretschmer suggests that the optimal policy also depends on the expected life span of technologies. A patient attitude by the government may be optimal in the case of technologies with a long expected life span; on the contrary, the optimal government action for shortly-lived technologies that soon become outdated because of rapid technological progress is to intervene immediately, as an impatient policy maker would do. To support this latter argument, the authors recall the story of the DAT (Digital Audio Tape), a tape-recording technology launched by Sony in 1987. Digital recording is a high-tech segment which, since the 80s, has been undergoing rapid technological progress; more specifically, in the late 80s, DDS and DataDAT competed against DAT for market leadership. In this scenario, Cabral and Kretschmer suggest that policy makers interested in welfare maximisation should intervene by supporting the leading technology.

3.4   Competition, compatibility and standardisation

In the previous sections we focused on consumers and on their demand for technology in order to discuss how network externalities affect standardisation processes. In this perspective, we did not however take the supply side of the market into account.

In this section, we shift our focus and we concentrate on firms and on how their behaviour affects market dynamics. This change of perspective will allow us to discuss which strategies firms competing in high-tech markets should follow in order to succeed; as we see later, among the most important decisions that a firm needs to take, there is certainly the one concerning compatibility between its product and those of rivals.

To discuss this topic, we begin by presenting the well-known model of oligopolistic competition in markets with network externalities proposed in 1985 by Michael Katz and Carl Shapiro.

3.4.1   Oligopolistic competition with network externalities

Consider a market for a network good supplied by n firms competing *à la Cournot*. Consumers choose whether or not to purchase the good and from which company. Firms offer a homogeneous product which may or may not be compatible with those supplied by rivals. In order to keep things as simple as possible, we analyse two "compatibility regimes": i) the regime of perfect compatibility, where technologies are based on a common standard (this regime is indexed by $T = c$) and ii) the regime of incompatibility where each firm employs a technology based on its own standard (indexed by $T = nc$). As we clarify later, the type of compatibility regime is relevant to determine the sizes of the networks of users.

The demand function faced by a firm depends on consumer expectations on network sizes; as in Section 3.2.1, we assume that consumer expectations are fulfilled in equilibrium, that is they are correct *ex post*.

More specifically, the timing of the game involving both firms and consumers is as follows:

$t =$1: consumers form expectations on the amount of sales for each firm, and, consequently, on the size of the networks of users; let $x^e_{T,i}$ denote consumer expectations concerning the sales of firm i under compatibility regime T, while $y^e_{T,i}$ represents consumer expectations on the size of the network of firm i, with $i = 1 \ldots n$. As clarified later, sales do not necessarily coincide with network size;

$t =$2: given consumer expectations, under compatibility regime T each firm chooses its output level denoted by $x_{T,i}$, $i = 1 \ldots n$;

$t =$3: equilibrium prices, quantities and profits of the n firms are determined.

Given consumer expectations on network sizes, the demand function faced by the representative firm i is:[17]

$$p_i(X_T, y^e_{T,i}) = 1 + v(y^e_{T,i}) - X_T, \qquad (3.3)$$

where $X_T = \sum_{i=1}^{n} x_{T,i}$ represents the total output produced by the n firms under compatibility regime T, given that each firm actually sells $x_{T,i}$. The function $v(y^e_{T,i})$ represents

---

[17]The setting we are considering is very similar to the one of Section 3.2.1 with consumers deriving a stand-alone utility k and a network benefit $v(y^e_{T,i})$ when purchasing the product from firm i. The main difference with respect to the previous section is that in Katz and Shapiro (1985), even though firms produce a homogeneous good, the size of the networks of users may be different. This fact implies that, in equilibrium, firms charge the same expected hedonic price, that is the same price adjusted for the network size; formally, in equilibrium, it must be $p_i - v(y^e_{T,i}) = p_j - v(y^e_{T,j}) \equiv \phi$, for each pair of firms i, j. Only those consumers with a stand-alone utility such that $k \geq \phi$ purchase the good. Under the assumption that k is uniformly distributed over $[0, 1]$, the total number of consumers, X_T, who join the network equals $1 - \phi$; expression (3.3) follows from these arguments.

the effect of the externality which, in turn, depends on the expected size of the network of firm i, $y_{T,i}^e$; as in Section 3.2.1, we assume that $v' > 0$ and $v'' < 0$.

By assuming that production costs equal zero, it follows that the profit function of firm i under compatibility regime T is:

$$\pi_{T,i}(x_{T,i}, y_{T,i}^e) = \left(1 + v(y_{T,i}^e) - X_T\right) x_{T,i}. \tag{3.4}$$

As mentioned previously, firms compete à la *Cournot*: given consumer expectations, each firm chooses the quantity to produce in order to maximise profits. By differentiating $\pi_{T,i}(\cdot)$ with respect to $x_{T,i}$ for each firm $i = 1 \dots n$, and by solving the system of the n first order conditions, the optimal quantity for firm i, given consumer expectations, is:[18]

$$x_{T,i}^*(y_{T,1}^e, \dots, y_{T,n}^e) = \frac{1 + nv(y_{T,i}^e) - \sum_{j \neq i}^n v(y_{T,j}^e)}{n+1}. \tag{3.5}$$

To proceed further in the analysis of the model and to determine the market equilibrium, we need now to clarify the implications of the two compatibility regimes. When technologies are perfectly compatible, each individual can interact with any other user, regardless of which firms they have purchased from. Therefore, the actual network size is given by the sum of the sales of all the n firms on the market. Good examples of compatible technologies are software applications which share the same format or fully interconnected communication networks; in the former case, users can exchange files and data regardless of which application they have. In the latter case, individuals are able to communicate independently of which firms provide access. Vice versa, if firms produce incompatible products, a consumer can interact only with those who have purchased the good from the same firm; for example, users of a software application that adopts a proprietary and incompatible format, can exchange files only with users of the same application. In this case, network effects depend only on the sales of each single firm.

These arguments highlight the crucial role played by compatibility: with compatible products, consumers are interested in the sum of the sales of all the n firms, while with incompatibility each firm has its own, independent, network of users. On the basis of these observations, it follows that:

- when technologies are perfectly compatible ($T = c$), it is as if on the market there were a single network, whose expected size equals the sum of expected sales of

---

[18]To convince the reader that expression (3.5) represents the equilibrium output for firm i, let's see what happens in the most simple scenario, that is when $n = 2$; the first order conditions of the two firms are respectively $d\pi_{T,1}/dx_{T,1} = 1 + v(y_{T,1}^e) - 2x_{T,1} - x_{T,2} = 0$ and $d\pi_{T,2}/dx_{T,2} = 1 + v(y_{T,2}^e) - 2x_{T,2} - x_{T,1} = 0$. By solving the system of equations in $x_{T,1}$ and $x_{T,2}$, we obtain expressions as in (3.5).

all the n firms; formally, $y_{c,i}^e = \sum_{i=1}^n x_{c,i}^e$. Note that in case of compatibility the expected network size is the same for each firm;

- when technologies are incompatible ($T = nc$), there are n networks; the expected size of each network coincides with the expected output of each firm: $y_{nc,i}^e = x_{nc,i}^e$. Note that with incompatible technologies firms may have different expected network sizes.

Market equilibrium with compatible technologies. Consider the case of compatible technologies. Since the n firms are symmetric (they supply a homogenous good and incur the same cost of production), in equilibrium they produce the same level of output, x_c^*; therefore, total industry output is nx_c^*. Under the assumption of fulfilled expectations, the condition $y_{c,i}^e = n\,x_c^*$ holds and expression (3.5) is reduced to:

$$x_c^* = \frac{1 + v(nx_c^*)}{n+1}. \tag{3.6}$$

By substituting x_c^* into expression (3.4) one can easily determine the equilibrium profits for each firm:

$$\pi_c^* = \left(\frac{1 + v(nx_c^*)}{n+1}\right)^2. \tag{3.7}$$

Market equilibrium with incompatible technologies. When technologies are incompatible, the size of firm i's network coincides with its sales; given that firms are symmetric, and under the assumption of fulfilled expectations, it follows that $y_{nc,i}^e = x_{nc}^*$, for $i = 1, \ldots, n$, where x_{nc}^* denotes the equilibrium output produced by each firm. From expressions (3.5) and (3.4) we obtain the equilibrium output and profits of each firm under the incompatibility regime:

$$x_{nc}^* = \frac{1 + v(x_{nc}^*)}{n+1}, \tag{3.8}$$

and

$$\pi_{nc}^* = \left(\frac{1 + v(x_{nc}^*)}{n+1}\right)^2. \tag{3.9}$$

By comparing the market equilibrium under the two regimes, it follows that:

Result 5. *With compatible technologies, each firm produces a larger output and gains larger profits than with incompatible technologies.*

This result can be proved by following a simple graphical analysis. Figure 3.9 plots expressions (3.6) and (3.8); the equilibrium outputs x_c^* and x_{nc}^* are represented in

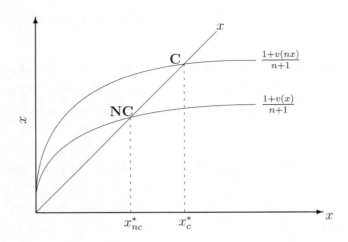

Figure 3.9: compatibility *vs* incompatibility

points **C** and **NC** which lie on the intersections of the $45°$ line with the functions $(1 + v(nx))/(n+1)$ and $(1 + v(x))/(n + 1)$, respectively. These latter expressions are increasing and concave since $v' > 0$ and $v'' < 0$; moreover, since $nx > x$, $(1 + v(nx))/(n + 1)$ lies above $(1 + v(x))/(n+1)$. Following these observations, we have that $x_c^* > x_{nc}^*$ i.e. under the compatibility regime firms produce more. Finally, given that firms' profits are equal to the square of the equilibrium quantity (see expressions (3.7) and (3.9)), it follows that they are larger under compatibility.

Result 5 is very important since it highlights the reason why technological compatibility may be profitable. When technologies are compatible, each consumer interacts with all the other users, regardless of which firm she has purchased the product from; consumers benefit from large network externalities and this fact increases their willingness to pay. Therefore, in equilibrium, firms' sales and profits are larger than with incompatible technologies.[19] In other words, Result 5 suggests that firms benefit from making their technologies compatible in order to exploit the positive effects accruing from larger network externalities.

Katz and Shapiro show that also consumers benefit from compatibility. This can be easily proved; in fact, given X_T, the total output under compatibility regime T, consumer

---

[19]In this analysis we restrict our attention to the case of symmetric equilibria (firms produce the same quantity in equilibrium). It is worthwhile noticing that, under incompatibility, if consumers expect the sizes of the networks to be different, then asymmetric market equilibria may arise; in this case, Result 5 needs to be reconsidered. In fact, when the equilibrium is asymmetric, firms able to attract a larger share of consumers may prefer the regime of incompatible technologies. For further details see Katz and Shapiro (1985) and the discussion in Section 3.5.

surplus equals $X_T^2/2$.[20] Since the equilibrium quantity is larger under compatibility then also consumer surplus is larger.

Competition and network effects: the paradox of Economides

The equilibrium of the model presented in the previous section has several interesting implications, one of which is known as the "paradox of Economides", named after the economist who formulated it.[21]

This paradox concerns the impact of competition on firms' profits when technologies are compatible. From expression (3.7), we know that π_c^* is a function of n, the number of firms or, equivalently, the degree of market competition. What we are interested in is how the equilibrium profits vary when n increases, that is, when the market becomes more competitive. Taking the derivative of π_c^* with respect to n, we obtain:

$$\frac{d\pi_c^*}{dn} = \underbrace{\frac{\partial \pi_c^*}{\partial n}}_{\text{direct effect}} + \underbrace{\frac{\partial \pi_c^*}{\partial v(\cdot)} \frac{dv(\cdot)}{dn}}_{\text{indirect effect}}.$$

With compatible technologies, an increase in n has two effects on equilibrium profits. The first is the typical negative effect of competition on firms' profits (direct effect): the more competitive the market, the lower the profits. The second effect is due to the presence of network externalities $v(\cdot)$ (indirect effect): as n increases, so does network size; therefore, a larger n translates into a higher consumer willingness to pay due to a larger externality $v(\cdot)$. Economides shows that, if the effect of the network externalities is strong enough, the indirect (positive) effect dominates the direct (negative) one, thus generating the paradoxical result according to which firms actually benefit from an increase in competition:

Result 6 (Paradox of Economides). *With compatible technologies, if the network effects are strong enough and if competition is not too fierce, then an increase in the number of competitors yields larger profits.*

To prove this result, we need to determine the sign of the derivative $d\pi_c^*/dn$. From expression (3.7), we know that equilibrium profits equal the square of the output. Therefore, Result 6 holds provided that $dx_c^*/dn > 0$; after some algebraic manipulation, we

---

[20]Consumer surplus is represented by the area below the demand function. Given price p, this area equals $(1 + v(\cdot) - p)X_T/2$; recalling that $p = 1 + v(\cdot) - X_T$, it follows that consumer surplus is $X_T^2/2$.
[21]See Economides (1996a), but note also that the existence of the paradox had already been suggested in the original paper by Katz and Shapiro.

obtain:[22]

$$\frac{dx_c^*}{dn} = x_c^* \frac{v' - 1}{1 + n(1 - v')},$$

which is positive if network externalities are sufficiently strong, that is if $v' > 1$, and if the market is not too competitive, $n < \frac{1}{v'-1}$.

To summarise, when network externalities are strong enough and competition is not too fierce, the positive effect of an increase in n dominates the negative one.[23] When these conditions are satisfied, it may be profitable for a firm which has a proprietary control on a technology to "invite" new competitors to enter the market.

The paradox of Economides helps us to interpret better the counterintuitive behaviour of potential monopolists inviting competitors to enter the market. This is what IBM did in 1987 with MCA (Micro Channel Architecture), its technology for the architecture of personal computers; a short time after launching this new technology, IBM, instead of exploiting its market power, announced its intention to license MCA for free to any rival wishing to enter the market with the same standard (see Economides, 1996a). More recently, in 2013 Google announced its "Patent Non-Assertion Pledge" through which it invited new firms to enter the market by making ten patents related to the MapReduce technology freely available for the development of open source software.

Standardisation and product differentiation

Katz and Shapiro (1985) highlight one of the most striking aspects of markets with network externalities: firms may find it profitable to pursue "cooperative" strategies (such as technological compatibility or invitations to enter the market) in order to benefit from an enlarged installed base of users. The analysis presented by the two authors is based on some simplifying assumptions which need to be discussed (see also Section 3.5); for instance, Katz and Shapiro assume that firms supply homogeneous goods, regardless of the compatibility regime.

However, high-tech markets are often characterised by a certain degree of product differentiation and it is natural to expect the existence of a trade-off between technological compatibility and product variety. Firms may find it more difficult to differentiate their products when they adhere to a common standard, i.e. when there is technological compatibility. In this case, firms cannot differentiate their products by acting on

---

[22]By differentiating (3.6) with respect to n, we obtain $\frac{dx_c^*}{dn} = \frac{\left((x_c^* + n\frac{dx_c^*}{dn})v'(nx_c^*)\right)(n+1) - 1 - v(nx_c^*)}{(n+1)^2}$; by solving for dx_c^*/dn, the expression in the text follows.

[23]The paradox does not apply when firms compete in prices instead of in quantities; competition in prices is, in fact, fiercer than competition in quantities, hence the negative effect due to an increase in n dominates the positive one.

the technical specifications but only on other product dimensions such as guarantees, customer services, complementary goods and so on.

In the light of these arguments, we should re-consider the firm's decision on technological compatibility. The relevant trade-off that firms face is the following: on the one hand, as explained by Katz and Shapiro, firms benefit from compatibility since it allows them to enjoy larger network effects but, on the other hand, they also benefit from incompatibility since it allows them to differentiate their products more effectively thus reducing the intensity of competitive pressure. When this second effect is particularly strong, firms may no longer benefit from technological compatibility.

3.5   How to compete? Strategies towards standardisation

In the previous section, following Katz and Shapiro, we have seen how compatibility may increase social welfare; not only do firms benefit from standardisation, but also consumers are better off. When products adhere to a common standard there is a unique large network, consumers are free to interact with all other adopters and the positive effects of network externalities are maximum. Nevertheless, despite compatibility being socially desirable, firms often prefer to produce incompatible goods and to fight "standard wars" rather than coordinating on a common technology. Examples of this kind of behaviour abound: recently, a format war took place between Blu-ray and HD DVD to define the technological standard for storing high definition video and audio data (see Box 3.3). Another example comes from the US mobile telecommunications industry where three incompatible technologies (GSM, TDMA and CDMA) competed to become the market standard.

Hence, the issue that we want to investigate in this section is the following: why do firms produce incompatible technologies and fight a standards war in certain markets, while preferring to coordinate on a common technology in others? In other words, why do firms in some cases compete "for the market" and try to impose their own standard while in other cases they coordinate on a common technology and compete "within" the market?

The analysis presented in Section 3.4 represents a useful starting point to begin thinking about technological compatibility. It is now time, however, to discuss and remove a couple of important simplifying assumptions of the model by Katz and Shapiro. The first important assumption concerns the relationship between the compatibility regime and the degree of competition; more specifically, Katz and Shapiro assume that firms compete *à la Cournot* with homogenous products regardless of the compatibility regime. As already mentioned, the choice between compatibility and incompatibility may affect the extent of product differentiation which in turn impacts the intensity of competition. The second important ingredient driving the results shown by Katz and Shapiro is the assumption according to which firms are symmetric, they operate with the same cost function and their installed bases of users are of equal size. Asymmetric firms, for example firms with different installed bases of users, may have diverging objectives and they may pursue different strategies with respect to compatibility.

This section focuses on firms' decisions on technological compatibility and considers a more general setting than the one studied in Section 3.4. Our aim is to describe the main strategies which firms should follow when competing in a market with network externalities. To begin with, it is useful to recall some of the main features of network markets that we have highlighted throughout this chapter and that crucially affect firms' strategies:

1. the coexistence of more than one technology is often temporary and unstable. In the long run, a single winning standard dominates the market (tipping or winner takes all market);

2. consumer expectations on the size of the networks are crucial to determine the winning technology;

3. history matters: the pattern of technology adoption in earlier periods affects current adoption decisions (path dependency).

These characteristics imply that competing in high-tech markets is a very complex and articulated matter. Typical sources of competitive advantage, such as producing a high quality good or being at the technological frontier, may not be enough for a firm to succeed. A firm must also be able to rapidly establish a sufficiently large installed base of users before its competitors. In this respect, for instance, the ability of a firm to affect consumer expectations about future network sizes can be a key factor to impose market leadership. Moreover, it is important to stress that the stakes on these kinds of markets are typically much higher because the firm winning the standards war takes the whole market while losers are forced to a niche position.

In order to discuss the strategic interactions among firms which choose whether to impose their own technology or to promote compatibility, it is useful to resort to a game-theoretic analysis as in Table 3.4. Consider two firms, A and B, which are choosing one of two incompatible technologies: technology 1 and 2. If they go for the same technology, then there is compatibility and firms compete within the market. Alternatively, if firms

Firm B

Technology 1   Technology 2

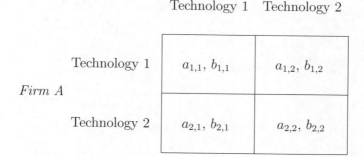

	Technology 1	Technology 2
Technology 1	$a_{1,1}, b_{1,1}$	$a_{1,2}, b_{1,2}$
Technology 2	$a_{2,1}, b_{2,1}$	$a_{2,2}, b_{2,2}$

Table 3.4: the compatibility game

choose different technologies (standards war), there is incompatibility; in this scenario firms fight to impose their own technology and compete for the market. Formally, $a_{i,j}$ is the pay-off of firm A when it chooses technology i given that firm B chooses technology j; on the diagonal, firms adopt the same technology (standardisation occurs), while off the diagonal they go for different technologies (standards war).

Which is the equilibrium of the game? Or, in other words, under which conditions do firms adopt the same technology and compete within the market? Or, alternatively, when does a "standards war" break out? The answers to these questions depends on the characteristics of the two technologies, on how compatibility impacts the intensity of competition and on the relative dimensions of firms' installed bases of users. Following the discussion presented Besen and Farrell (1994), three different strategic scenarios may emerge.

Scenario 1: standards war. As discussed above, when firms adhere to the same technical standard, they are hardly able to differentiate their products; therefore, compatibility may imply fierce competition and low profits. In this scenario, firms prefer to compete to impose their own standard. In terms of Table 3.5, this case occurs when the off-diagonal pay-offs exceed the on-diagonal ones; in other words, when technologies are compatible, competition drives firms' profits below those obtained when involved in a standards war. Formally: $a_{1,1} < a_{2,1}$ and $a_{2,2} < a_{1,2}$ for firm A, and $b_{1,1} < b_{2,1}$ and $b_{2,2} < b_{1,2}$ for B; Table 3.5 depicts an extreme case of standards war; when A and B choose the same technology (compatibility between A and B) products are very similar and competition is so severe that profits are driven down to zero.

One can easily observe that in Table 3.5 there are two Nash equilibria characterised

Firm B

	Technology 1	Technology 2
Technology 1	0, 0	100, 10
Technology 2	10, 100	0, 0

Firm A (label to the left of the rows)

Table 3.5: standards battle

by firm A and firm B going for different technologies; each firm attempts to impose its standard thus engaging in a standards war. As recalled earlier, this is what happened in the US mobile telecommunications industry where firms adopted incompatible technologies. Firms were aware of the fact that standardisation would have resulted in more homogeneous products, fiercer competition and, hence, lower profits; therefore, they preferred not to coordinate on a common transmission technology but rather to compete for the market. Other examples of standards wars are the well known battle between Betamax and VHS in the video-tape recorders industry or, more recently, the one between HD DVD and Blu-ray in the high definition DVDs.

Besen and Farrell identify four strategies which may be used by firms to impose their technology:[24]

1. build an early lead before competitors establish a large installed base of users; this lead must be strong enough to reach the critical mass and trigger the positive feedback;

2. sign agreements with the suppliers of complements in order to induce them to produce compatible goods and services. This increases the value of the network and attracts a larger number of consumers;

3. preannounce the launch of new products in order to induce consumers to expect a rapid take-off of the technology;

4. commit not to increase prices in the future (e.g. through contractual clauses) in

---

[24]See also Varian and Shapiro (1999) for greater details.

order to reassure prospective consumers that they will not be locked-in on a very expensive technology.

Firm B

Technology 1   Technology 2

		Technology 1	Technology 2
	Technology 1	100, 10	0, 0
Firm A			
	Technology 2	0, 0	10, 100

Table 3.6: cooperation *vs* incompatibility

Scenario 2: agreement on compatibility. The second scenario occurs when compatibility *i)* is overwhelmingly important for consumers and *ii)* firms are able to differentiate their products and gain profits despite adhering to a common standard. In this case, firms prefer to employ compatible technologies and compete within the market.

In this scenario, there are two possible cases. In the first one, one of the two technologies is clearly superior to the other and firms simply need to coordinate on the adoption of such standard; coordination may be obtained, for instance, through formal standard-setting organisations which support the development of common technical standards that apply industry-wide. In the second case, firms are still willing to coordinate on a common technology but they do not agree on which one is the best. This happens, typically, when each firm has proprietary control on a technology which, therefore, is preferred to the others. In this case, the strategic interaction among firms resembles the one described by the well-known game of the "battle of the sexes", as in Table 3.6; even though firms agree that compatibility is needed for the market to take-off, their preferences for the two technologies are not aligned: firm A prefers technology 1 while firm B prefers technology 2.

As in a typical battle of the sexes, there are two Nash equilibria in the game shown in Table 3.6: both firms choose either technology 1 or technology 2. Therefore, in both cases there is standardisation but on a different technology.

There are several examples of strategies which firms may employ to foster technological compatibility. For instance, they may form a patent pool, a consortium of companies agreeing to cross-license different patents related to the same technology which becomes the industry standard. Another interesting way of coordinating on a standard is by making the technology available to the public domain or, in the case of the software industry, by releasing the code of the software as open source. For example, this seems to be the strategy adopted by IBM. "Big Blue" decided to release a certain number of its patents to the public domain; moreover, it also started Eclipse, a project for a software development environment which was later released as open source.

Box 3.3 – Blu-ray *vs* HD DVD

On 19 February 2008, Toshiba announced that it was going to abandon the development of HD DVD and dismiss the related activities; this decision put one of the most exciting standards battles of recent history to an end.

The battle was for the leadership in the market for high definition DVDs; the two "fighters" were Sony with its Blu-ray system and Toshiba with the HD DVD technology. Even though the two technologies are not compatible with each other, they both are evolutions of the traditional DVD technology: they use the laser at lower wavelength, thus providing them with a larger storage capacity.

The two technologies are qualitatively extremely similar; while Blu-ray has a larger storage capacity, HD DVD is backward compatible with the DVD technology: DVD discs can be read in HD DVD players thus allowing HD DVD adopters to enjoy the large amount of content available for the earlier technology. However, this advantage proved to be transitory, since several manufacturers started quite soon to supply backward-compatible players also for the Blu-ray technology.

Since the very beginning of the battle it was clear that strategic alliances were going to play a crucial role. Both Sony and Toshiba sought agreements with content and hardware producers in order to gain the lead and to win the standards war; Sony, besides embedding the Blu-ray technology in its PlayStation 3 game console, signed agreements with several movie stu-

dios, including 20th Century Fox, Disney and MGM, aimed at distributing their content; similarly, Toshiba reached agreements with Universal, Paramount and Warner. Furthermore, Toshiba, at least initially, allied with Microsoft which agreed to install HD DVD players in its Xbox 360 game console.

Many aspects of this story recall what happened in the 80s during the battle between VHS and Betamax (see Box 3.2); however, unlike this earlier case, in the battle between Blu-ray and HD DVD the strategic alliances with producers of complementary products played a crucial role since the very beginning. Therefore, from the outset, the market has been influenced by the presence of relevant (indirect) network externalities related to the availability of complementary products; as a consequence, the dynamics of adoption has been that of the winner takes all market type since the beginning.

Sony, which was defeated in the earlier VHS *vs* Betamax battle, seems to have learned the lesson; there is no doubt that it has benefited from the success of PlayStation 3 that, as mentioned previously, embeds the Blu-ray technology. In combination with a very effective strategy of alliances and an aggressive pricing policy, this has allowed Sony to win the battle.

As far as Toshiba is concerned, many observers have judged the company as being too confident in its strengths; sure of the ultimate victory, it has often maintained an attitude of sufficiency seen by many as the main cause of its defeat.

Scenario 3: asymmetric firms. In Scenarios 1 and 2, firms are characterised by strategic symmetry, i.e. they find it optimal to choose the same kind of strategy. In Scenario 1, each firm struggles to impose its own technology as the industry standard; in Scenario 2, they select the same technology and compete within the market.

However, we often observe cases of firms pursuing different strategies. For instance, market leaders controlling a large installed base of users may benefit from fighting a standards war which they are likely to win; followers, instead, prefer to coordinate on the same technology of the leaders in order to exploit their larger installed bases of users.

In the 80s Atari, the US producer of video game consoles, was lagging behind its competitor Nintendo; in order to increase its market share, Atari introduced an adapter to make its technology compatible with Nintendo's. Similar attempts were made in other industries by followers. Borland, for instance, enabled its software to import files created with Lotus 1-2-3, the market leader in the spreadsheet segment. Still in the 80s, Apple was unable to keep pace with IBM-compatible PCs and their MS-DOS operating system; for this reason Apple installed on its computers the Hyper drive, a driver that allowed its users to read MS-DOS floppy disks.

Market leaders typically react in the attempt to maintain technological incompatibility thus exploiting their competitive advantage. For instance, Nintendo denied Atari access to its platform by asserting the proprietary rights protecting its technology. In other cases, leaders change their technologies frequently (i.e. by launching new versions of their products) in order to make it difficult for competitors to keep up-to-date.

Table 3.7 provides a representation of the strategic interaction characterising Scenario 3. Looking at the pay-off matrix, one can check that A, the follower firm, is willing to

Firm B

		Technology 1	Technology 2
	Technology 1	30, 10	10, 20
Firm A			
	Technology 2	10, 30	20, 10

Table 3.7: asymmetric firms

coordinate with the leading firm B; in turn, B prefers to "run away" from A and to choose a technology which is different from the competitor's.

3.6   Switching costs and network externalities

We cannot conclude our discussion without mentioning another crucial aspect of high-tech markets, namely the presence of so-called switching costs. The term "switching costs" refers to those costs which consumers incur when changing suppliers, brands or products.

In most cases, switching costs involve a monetary payment and are relatively easy to measure; this is the case of, for instance, contractual obligations that an individual must pay to her/his current supplier as a compensation for breaching the contract. Nevertheless, they often involve also psychological, effort- and time-based costs which do not necessarily imply a direct monetary payment. Psychological switching costs are, for example, those incurred when a consumer switches from a familiar provider to one whose quality is unknown (Klemperer, 1995).

Switching costs play a crucial role in many markets, which are not necessarily related to ICT; many commercial agreements impose switching costs in the case of the premature ending of a contract. They also arise when a consumer makes investments specific to buying from a given firm; the cost of time spent due to the necessary paperwork when changing electricity provider is an example of such switching costs. Large switching costs imply that the consumer is, to a great extent, "captured" by her/his current provider: cheaper and better opportunities are not seized in order to avoid the cost of switching supplier; in the economics jargon, this is known as the "lock-in" effect.

In some cases, switching costs cannot be avoided. Think, for example, of the transition from vinyl long-playing records to music CDs during the late 80s. This transition implied a large switching cost for the many music lovers who had to upgrade their collection of vinyl LPs to the new technology. In other cases, firms intentionally create switching costs in order to strengthen customers' lock-in, thus dissuading them from shifting to a competitor's product, brand or service. For example, mobile phone carriers often charge an early termination fee to customers who have signed multi-year contracts; likewise, loyalty programs which reward customers in case of repeated purchases are another example of intentionally created switching costs.[25]

---

[25]See Varian and Shapiro (1999) for a detailed analysis on how firms may artificially generate switching costs to lock-in their customers.

Switching costs are particularly severe in high-tech industries. Take software applications: once a consumer has got the hang of a given application, then moving to a new one with, let's say, a different user interface may imply a significant cost related to learning how to use the new application. Switching costs are even more relevant in the case of customised software, namely software which is specifically tailored to certain customers' needs. Mobile telephony is another good example: until a few years ago, in many European countries, consumers who were willing to change operator had to change their phone number; this represented a substantial switching cost for individuals who in case of a change of operator had to inform all their friends and relatives about the new number. In Italy, things changed only in 2002, when the national regulatory authority in telecommunications mandated operators to provide the so-called "mobile number portability", that is, to allow users to keep the old phone number when switching operator. The aim of the regulator's intervention was clear: imposing number portability was a way to reduce switching costs, to stimulate customers' mobility and to improve market competitiveness.

There is a large economic literature on the effects of switching costs on market equilibrium and efficiency. As mentioned above, as an obstacle to consumers' mobility, switching costs tend primarily to affect negatively market's efficiency: they reduce the competitive pressure among firms and drive prices up. In the presence of switching costs, firms do not have incentives to behave aggressively against rivals, because they know that this may not be enough to steal customers from competitors. On the contrary, firms may be induced to raise their prices to increase their revenues, as they are aware that they do not risk losing customers. Economic theory has shown that, in extreme cases, switching costs may allow firms to charge monopoly prices, thus completely eliminating the effects of competition. On top of that, in the presence of switching costs, it is more difficult for a new firm to enter the market and to steal customers from competitors; in this sense, switching costs represent a barrier to entry. Also this effect, just as those above, is likely to have a negative impact on market efficiency.

The presence of locked-in customers encourages firms to set relatively high prices; nonetheless, there is also a countervailing effect of switching costs that must be mentioned. When customers are locked-in to a given supplier, they represent a valuable source of revenues; hence, anticipating this, the firm may be willing to behave more aggressively in the first place, that is, it may be induced to set low prices to build up a installed base of locked-in customers.

Hence, switching costs have two opposing effects on market efficiency: on the one hand they increase firms' market power and their ability to raise prices but, on the other, they induce firms to price more aggressively in the first place. The overall price effects of switching costs in oligopoly are ambiguous.

In high-tech sectors switching costs come in combination with network externalities and this makes things even more complicated. Interestingly, in fact, network effects may actually be a source of switching costs. With network effects, the value attached by an individual to a given technology is influenced by its customer base; in this context, it is clear that when switching to an alternative technology, the individual will also take into account the different network effects she/he will enjoy with the new technology. Suppose a new, qualitatively better and incompatible technology has become available and consider a customer who is thinking about adopting it. In case of adoption, she/he will incur several switching costs (i.e. the monetary cost of buying the product, the cost of learning how to use the new technology, etc.); on top of that, the customer incurs also "network-related" costs of switching: by shifting from a widespread technology to a new one (namely without a customer base), the individual incurs a loss due to the smaller network effects. If network effects are particularly relevant, the typical inertia of high tech markets emerges, with individuals preferring to stay with the old/obsolete but widespread technology even if a better one is available.

We have already discussed these issues in the previous sections of this chapter and, in particular, we know that a crucial role for the functioning of high-tech markets is played by technology compatibility/standardisation. When technologies adhere to a common standard (they are compatible), the "network-related" costs of switching are negligible: with compatible technologies the individual enjoys the same network effects both in the case she/he stays with the old technology and in the case she/he switches to the new one. Therefore, we can say that compatibility tends to reduce customers' switching costs; with smaller switching costs, customers' mobility is higher and firms are induced to compete more effectively. In a word, compatibility increases competition and makes markets more efficient.

The fact that often firms want to keep their products incompatible, even if compatibility would be easily achievable, supports these arguments; as stated by Paul Klemperer:

> switching costs often damage competition, and firms may therefore also dissipate further resources creating and defending incompatibilities [...] Because switching costs very often make competition, and especially entry, less effective, I (and others) favor cautiously pro-compatibility public policy. (Klemperer, 2008)

Chapter 4

Two-Sided Networks

4.1 Introduction

Paying by credit card, searching for information in Yellow Pages, or even playing with a PlayStation or listening to music with an iPod are very common activities in our everyday lives. Despite being apparently unrelated, credit cards, phone directories, MP3 players and video game consoles are all examples of what we call, in economics jargon, two-sided markets/networks. There are two main features which characterise two-sided markets. First is the existence of two separate groups of agents (the two sides of the market) which interact with one another by means of a platform or intermediary. Secondly, decisions taken by the agents belonging to one side of the market affect the benefits enjoyed by the agents on the other side; in other words, a two-sided market is characterised by the presence of so-called cross-side network effects.[1]

Take Yellow Pages for example. The publisher of the phone directory acts as a platform intermediating between two groups of users: companies and consumers. The former advertise their businesses in the directory while the latter can easily find information (phone numbers, addresses, etc.) on the companies they are looking for. Clearly, a company is willing to advertise its business in Yellow Pages only if the directory is widely used by consumers; in turn, a consumer is keen to look for information in the directory (and, possibly, even to pay a price for it) provided that a large number of companies advertise their products and services in it. Therefore, a phone directory provides an intermediation service which is more valuable for users belonging to one side of the market, the more users there are on the other side. As in Chapter 3, users benefit from network externalities but unlike in the previous case, what matters here is the number of users

---

[1]In the economics literature, there is no agreed-upon definition of two-sided markets. In this chapter we take the definition provided by Rysman (2009).

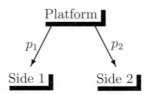

Figure 4.1: representation of a two-sided platform

on the other side of the market, and not the number of users on the same side. For this reason, in the case of two-sided markets, we talk about cross-side network effects. As we shall see in the next pages, given the two-sided nature of the market, the publisher of Yellow Pages needs to select an appropriate pricing strategy in order to stimulate the diffusion of the phone directory on both sides of the market; only in this case, in fact, each side can benefit from substantial network effects stemming from the other group of users.

The popular MP3 player iPod is another example of a two-sided platform. Apple both produces the digital media player and manages the iTunes website where music can be downloaded. Record labels and music listeners represent the two sides of the market in this case. Apple needs to sell iPods to many consumers so that record labels are induced to let their songs be downloaded from iTunes. At the same time, music listeners are willing to purchase an iPod only if a great variety of music is available on-line. Therefore, also in this case cross-side network externalities are crucial.

Yellow Pages and iPod represent only two examples of a more widespread phenomenon. An increasing number of companies, so-called digital intermediaries, have emerged during recent years following the ICT revolution. Not only iTunes but also several well-known dotcoms such as `Amazon.com` (books and music), `eBay.com` (on-line auctions), `AutoScout24.com` (new and second hand cars) provide intermediation services to thousands of sellers and millions of buyers all around the world.

However, two-sided markets also include more traditional activities such as Yellow Pages, real estate agencies or payment systems. Many are the examples of two-sided markets and their number is growing day-by-day. Particularly relevant are the following:[2]

- **software: text readers and writers.** Many programs, such as Adobe Acrobat, are designed for two separate groups of users: those who create text-content and those who want to read it. It is interesting to note that the software interface to read PDF files is normally available as freeware, while one needs to purchase a license for the text writer required to generate PDF documents;

---

[2]For a comprehensive list of two-sided markets see Armstrong (2002) and Rochet and Tirole (2001).

- **software: operating systems.** Operating systems, such as Microsoft Windows, are another example of platforms that intermediate between two sides of the market: software programmers who are willing to develop new applications that run on very popular operating systems and consumers who are willing to install operating systems that have a great availability of programs. It is worthwhile mentioning that most of Microsoft's profits come from the Windows licenses purchased by consumers;

- **payment systems: credit and debit cards.** When a consumer purchases a product she can pay in cash or by means of an electronic payment system such as a credit or debit card. Credit and debit cards are another example of platforms affected by cross-side network effects. Consumers' benefits of holding a credit card increase with the number of shopkeepers who accept it as a means of payment; in turn, shopkeepers are more willing to join the electronic payment system the greater the number of cardholders. As in the previous two examples, normally only one side of the market is charged a fee for the intermediation service: the shopkeeper pays the electronic payment system provider an amount of money proportional to the value of the transaction, while the service is usually free of charge for the consumer;

- **television and advertising.** Traditional tv channels earn most of their revenues from advertising fees; they offer services to two separate groups of agents. Viewers receive entertainment and news, while companies advertise their products during breaks;[3]

- **video game consoles.** A producer of video game consoles interacts with two types of agents: video game players, who are interested in purchasing the consoles, and developers of video games. The wider the range of video games available for the console, the greater the benefit for players. At the same time, developers are more willing to create new video games if the console is very popular among consumers.

Several interesting observations can be derived from these examples. In some cases the platform provides only an intermediation service which allows the two sides of the market

---

[3]Note that in this case cross-side network effects are both positive and negative. Companies benefit from an increase in the number of viewers which, in turn, increases their willingness to advertise. However, an increase in advertising tends to reduce the benefits enjoyed by viewers, thus generating a negative cross-side effect. In this chapter we limit ourselves to the case of positive cross-side externalities.

to "meet" and then, eventually, complete transactions. eBay is a typical example of a "pure intermediary": buyers and sellers make transactions through the on-line auction site and pay eBay a fee for the intermediation service. Similar cases are Yellow Pages, real estate agencies and other digital intermediaries.

In other cases the platform itself directly completes transactions with one or both sides of the market. Sony, for example, sells PlayStations to consumers and provides programmers with the technical specifications needed to develop new games. Similarly, Adobe releases for free the software Reader but sells the software Writer to generate PDF documents. The model we present in this chapter is very stylised and applies to both the case of a pure intermediary as well as to the case of a platform making direct transactions with the user.

The second interesting observation concerns the pricing strategies adopted by intermediaries. Figure 4.1 represents a two-sided platform where p_1 and p_2 denote the prices set for the two sides of the market.[4] In the previous examples we have seen that one side of the market often obtains the service for free. This means that the platform is subsidising consumption on one side of the market by setting a price below production costs, while the other side is charged a high price. In other words, the firm balances the prices of the two sides of the market so that one side is subsidised and the other represents the only source of revenues for the firm.[5]

Table 4.1 summarises some relevant examples of two-sided markets; for each case we highlight which side generates revenues for the platform and which one obtains the service for free and, therefore, is subsidised.

In the next section, we present a theoretical model to analyse the pricing strategy of a platform; in particular, we derive the conditions under which it is optimal for the firm to subsidise one of the two sides, i.e. to charge a price below production costs. Following this analysis, we discuss efficiency of two-sided markets.

---

[4]As discussed previously, p_1 and p_2 represent either the prices for the intermediation services (as in the example of eBay) or the prices for the products offered by the platform (the licensing fees for the software in the example of Adobe).

[5]As mentioned in a previous footnote, the definition of two-sided markets is still debated in the literature. According to Rochet and Tirole (2006), a market is said to be two-sided when, for a fixed level of the aggregate price $P = p_1 + p_2$, the overall number of transactions changes with p_1 and p_2. Following this definition, what matters is not only the aggregate price level but also how P is shared between the two sides of the market. In other words, in a two-sided market the price structure is "non-neutral", since for a given P different combinations of p_1 and p_2 generate a different number of transactions, and therefore a different level of profits for the platform.

Industry	Two-sided platform	Side 1	Side 2	Subsidised side	Source of revenue
real estate	real estate agency	buyer	seller	none	sales commissions
software	operating system	user	developer	side 2	licensing; e.g. Microsoft earns nearly 70% of revenues from licensing to end-users
video game	console	player	game developer	none	games sales to players and licensing to developers generate substantial revenues
payment card system	credit card	card holder	merchant	side 1	commissions; e.g. in 2001 American Express earned 82% of its revenues from merchants
media	TV network	viewer	advertiser	side 1	most of the revenues of commercial TV networks come from ads

Table 4.1: examples of two-sided markets

4.2 Pricing strategies in two-sided markets

The aim of this section is to determine the optimal pricing strategy of a platform acting as a monopolist in a two-sided market.[6] Take a monopolistic real estate agency as an example; the agency offers intermediation services to real estate buyers and sellers. Both sides pay a fee for the intermediation service.

In order to analyse the optimal pricing strategy of the platform, we need to determine the demand function for the intermediation services on both sides of the market. Suppose that each side is made up of a mass equal to 1 of potential users. Similarly to Chapter 3, we assume that a consumer belonging to side $i = 1, 2$ enjoys a utility from the intermediation service which depends on: i) the stand-alone benefit derived from the intermediation service, denoted by k_i and uniformly distributed over $[0, 1]$;[7] and ii) the number of users belonging to the other side of the market, y_j, with $j = 1, 2$ and $j \neq i$. This latter effect represents the so-called cross-side network externality: the

---

[6]This section is based on the work by Parker and Van Alstyne (2005).

[7]In the case of real estate agencies, k_i may be related to the time that parties save by consulting the agency rather than looking for buyers or sellers on their own. Alternatively, buyers and sellers may benefit from the agency dealing with all the legal and formal aspects of the transaction.

more popular the service is on side j of the market, the greater the value for each single consumer on side i.[8]

Formally, let $U(k_i, y_j)$ denote the gross utility enjoyed by the representative consumer belonging to side i when she joins the platform; following the above discussion, utility is increasing in k_i, the stand-alone utility, and in y_j, the number of consumers belonging to the other side of the market. Formally:

$$\frac{\partial U}{\partial k_i} > 0, \quad \text{and} \quad \frac{\partial U}{\partial y_j} > 0, \quad \text{with } i \neq j, \text{ and } i, j = 1, 2.$$

For simplicity, we assume that the utility function is separable in its two arguments and takes the following functional form:

$$U(k_i, y_j) = k_i + \theta_{ji} y_j,$$

where $\theta_{ji} > 0$ represents the intensity of the externality operating from side j to side i, that is, it measures how the willingness to pay of users on side i is affected by an increase in the number of consumers belonging to side j.[9] Finally, we assume that cross-side network externalities are not very large; formally, $\theta_{12} + \theta_{21} < 2$;[10] note that this assumption implies that $\theta_{21}\theta_{12} < 1$.

Let us now determine the demand function for the intermediation services on both sides of the market. Given the prices charged by the monopolist (p_1 and p_2) and the number of consumers belonging to the other side of the market, each user decides whether or not to access the intermediation service. For each side of the market we can identify a consumer who is indifferent between accessing the service or not; formally the indifferent consumers are characterised by stand-alone utilities $\tilde{k}_i$, $i = 1, 2$, which are determined by the following conditions:

$$\tilde{k}_1 + \theta_{21} y_2 - p_1 = 0 \quad \Rightarrow \quad \tilde{k}_1 = p_1 - \theta_{21} y_2,$$

$$\tilde{k}_2 + \theta_{12} y_1 - p_2 = 0 \quad \Rightarrow \quad \tilde{k}_2 = p_2 - \theta_{12} y_1.$$

---

[8]Note that, unlike in Chapter 3, in this section, we assume that the externality is based on the actual network size rather than on the expected one. In the literature, this case is referred to as *responsive* expectations (see Hagiu and Halaburda, 2013). We chose this approach to make the model more tractable.

[9]Note that we have implicitly assumed that consumers belonging to the same side of the market have homogeneous preferences with respect to the cross-side network externality: formally θ_{ji} is the same for all consumers on side i.

[10]If network effects are very large, $\theta_{12} + \theta_{21} > 2$, the model does not admit meaningful solutions; on top of that, the existence of very large network effects is not supported by empirical evidence; therefore, we believe that the assumption $\theta_{12} + \theta_{21} < 2$ represents a good description of two-sided markets.

All consumers with a stand-alone utility greater than or equal to $\tilde{k}_i$ access the service on side i; recalling that consumers are uniformly distributed over $[0, 1]$, the overall number of users accessing the service on side i of the market equals $y_i = 1 - \tilde{k}_i$. Therefore:

$$y_1 = 1 + \theta_{21} y_2 - p_1, \quad \text{and} \quad y_2 = 1 + \theta_{12} y_1 - p_2.$$

These two equations represent the number of users joining the platform as a function of the number of consumers on the other side of the market. In order to determine the demand functions, we need to solve the system of the above equations; after some algebraic manipulation it follows that the demand functions are:

$$y_1(p_1, p_2) = \frac{1 - p_1 + \theta_{21}(1 - p_2)}{1 - \theta_{21}\theta_{12}}, \tag{4.1}$$

$$y_2(p_1, p_2) = \frac{1 - p_2 + \theta_{12}(1 - p_1)}{1 - \theta_{21}\theta_{12}}. \tag{4.2}$$

Figure 4.2 plots the demand function for side 1 of the market;[11] note that as the intensity of the network externality operating from side 2 to side 1 increases, $y_1(p_1, p_2)$ shifts outwards: *ceteris paribus* the larger θ_{21}, the more consumers on side 1 are willing to access the platform. Finally, it is interesting to note that the demand function on side i decreases with both prices:

$i)$ $\dfrac{\partial y_i}{\partial p_i} = -\dfrac{1}{1 - \theta_{12}\theta_{21}} < 0$, and $ii)$ $\dfrac{\partial y_i}{\partial p_j} = -\dfrac{\theta_{ji}}{1 - \theta_{12}\theta_{21}} < 0$, with $i \neq j$, and $i, j = 1, 2$.

Expression $i)$ highlights the standard negative relationship between quantity and price. Expression $ii)$ shows the cross-side network effect: an increase in p_j reduces y_j, the number of consumers on side j of the market, and, due to the cross-side network effect, this is translated into a reduction of the number of consumers on side i of the market, y_i.

4.2.1 The benchmark: two independent monopolists

Before analysing the case of a platform serving both sides of the market, let us consider a benchmark where the two sides are served by separate monopolists.[12] Suppose that firm 1 operates on side 1 and firm 2 on side 2. For simplicity, we assume that the production costs of both firms equal zero; therefore, given the demand functions defined

---

[11] The figure representing the demand for side 2 is analogous.

[12] Note that this benchmark also represents the real-world case of credit card associations discussed in the final part of this chapter.

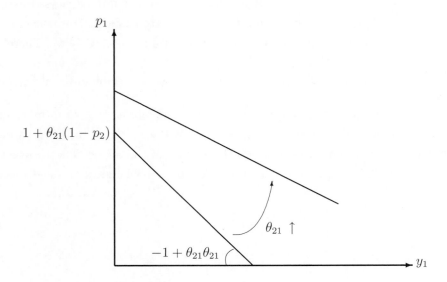

Figure 4.2: demand function with cross-network externalities

in expressions (4.1) and (4.2), the profit maximisation problems of the two firms are as follows:

$$\max_{p_1} \pi_1(p_1, p_2) = p_1 \frac{1 - p_1 + \theta_{21}(1 - p_2)}{1 - \theta_{21}\theta_{12}}, \qquad \max_{p_2} \pi_2(p_1, p_2) = p_2 \frac{1 - p_2 + \theta_{12}(1 - p_1)}{1 - \theta_{21}\theta_{12}}.$$

The prices charged by the firms are obtained by solving the system of the two first order conditions:

$$p_1^{ind} = \frac{2 + \theta_{21}(1 - \theta_{12})}{4 - \theta_{21}\theta_{12}} \quad \text{and} \quad p_2^{ind} = \frac{2 + \theta_{12}(1 - \theta_{21})}{4 - \theta_{12}\theta_{21}}.$$

Following the assumption $\theta_{12}\theta_{21} < 1$, both prices are positive; by substituting p_1^{ind} and p_2^{ind} into the profit functions, it is possible to determine the equilibrium profits of the two firms:

$$\pi_1^{ind} = \frac{(2 + \theta_{21}(1 - \theta_{12}))^2}{(1 - \theta_{12}\theta_{21})(4 - \theta_{12}\theta_{21})^2}, \qquad \pi_2^{ind} = \frac{(2 + \theta_{12}(1 - \theta_{21}))^2}{(1 - \theta_{12}\theta_{21})(4 - \theta_{12}\theta_{21})^2}.$$

4.2.2   A platform serving both sides of the market

Let us now move to the more interesting case of a single platform operating on both sides of the market. In this case, the firm sets p_1 and p_2 in order to maximise the sum of the profits obtained on both sides of the market; formally:

$$\max_{p_1,p_2} \Pi(p_1,p_2) = p_1\,y_1(p_1,p_2) + p_2\,y_2(p_1,p_2)$$

$$= p_1\frac{1 - p_1 + \theta_{21}(1 - p_2)}{1 - \theta_{21}\theta_{12}} + p_2\frac{1 - p_2 + \theta_{12}(1 - p_1)}{1 - \theta_{21}\theta_{12}}.$$

From the first order conditions we derive the "optimal pricing correspondences", $p_1(p_2)$ and $p_2(p_1)$, namely the two functions which define the optimal price on side i for each price charged on side j. These functions illustrate the interaction between the prices charged by the platform on the two sides of the market.

From the derivatives of Π with respect to p_1 and p_2, one can determine the optimal pricing correspondences:

$$p_1(p_2) = \frac{1 + \theta_{21} - (\theta_{12} + \theta_{21})\,p_2}{2} \quad \text{and} \quad p_2(p_1) = \frac{1 + \theta_{12} - (\theta_{12} + \theta_{21})\,p_1}{2}. \tag{4.3}$$

The two functions are negatively sloped and this fact highlights the strategic complementarity between p_1 and p_2. Consider, for instance, what happens when the platform increases p_2. This leads to a reduction of y_2 which, in turn, due to the effect of cross-side network externalities, is translated into a lower consumer willingness to pay on side 1. Therefore, as p_2 increases, the platform is induced to reduce p_1, and this explains the negative slope of expressions (4.3).

The optimal pricing strategy

The examples provided at the beginning of this chapter suggest that it is often profitable for a platform to subsidise access on one side of the market by charging a very low price, even below production costs. In our framework, where production costs are assumed to be zero, subsidising access is equivalent to setting a negative price.

By solving the system of the optimal pricing correspondences in expressions (4.3), we determine the equilibrium prices charged by the platform:

$$p_1^* = \frac{1 - \theta_{12}}{2 - \theta_{12} - \theta_{21}}, \quad \text{and} \quad p_2^* = \frac{1 - \theta_{21}}{2 - \theta_{12} - \theta_{21}}. \tag{4.4}$$

The above expressions show that the equilibrium prices depend on the intensity of cross-side externalities; in particular, three scenarios are possible: a) the intensity of network externalities from side 1 to side 2 and that from 2 to 1 are not too large and of similar magnitude, (formally: $\theta_{12} < 1$ and $\theta_{21} < 1$), b) the intensity of network externalities from side 2 to 1 is much larger than the one from side 1 to side 2 ($\theta_{12} < 1$ and $\theta_{21} > 1$) and c) the intensity of externalities from side 1 to side 2 is much larger than that from 2 to 1 ($\theta_{12} > 1$ and $\theta_{21} < 1$).

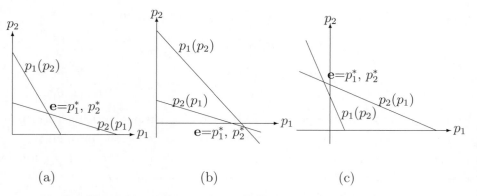

(a)   (b)   (c)

Figure 4.3: pricing strategies in two-sided markets

These scenarios are represented in the three panels of Figure 4.3 where the optimal pricing correspondences have been plotted according to the different degrees of intensity of the cross-side network externalities. The equilibrium prices given in expressions (4.4) are identified by the intersection of the two optimal pricing correspondences.

Case a) is characterised by intermediate and almost symmetric values of θ_{12} and θ_{21}. In this case, the intersection of the two optimal pricing correspondences lies in the upper-right section of the diagram (p_1, p_2); therefore, both prices are positive and no side of the market is subsidised (panel (a) of Figure 4.3). In case b), the intensity of network externalities from side 2 to side 1 is stronger than that going in the opposite direction; as shown in the second panel of Figure 4.3, the two optimal pricing correspondences intersect in the lower-right section, where $p_1 > 0$ and $p_2 < 0$. In this case, on side 2 of the market, the platform sets the price below production costs; this fact stimulates sales on this side of the market and, due to the strong intensity of the cross-side network externalities, it leads to a significant increase in the willingness to pay of consumers belonging to side 1. The platform then raises p_1 and the associated increase in profits more than compensates the losses from side 2. Similarly, in case c) it is profitable for the platform to set $p_1 < 0$ and $p_2 > 0$, thus subsidising side 1 and earning large profits from side 2 (panel (c) of Figure 4.3). In other words, in cases b) and c), the platform optimally subsidises the side of the market which generates larger externalities. The following result summarises the above discussion:

Result 1 (Pricing strategies in two-sided markets). *In a two-sided market, it is profitable for a platform to subsidise the side of the market which generates greater externalities: if $\theta_{ij} > 1$ and $\theta_{ji} < 1$, then $p_i^* < 0$ and $p_j^* > 0$.*

According to this result, when the intensities of network externalities are very asymmetric, it is profitable for the platform to subsidise the side which generates more value.

The platform chooses the optimal price pair by balancing cross-side network effects; in this way, the firm internalises part of the value generated by network externalities.

Finally, by substituting the equilibrium prices into the function $\Pi(p_1, p_2)$, we determine the equilibrium profits:

$$\Pi^* = \frac{1}{2 - \theta_{12} - \theta_{21}}.$$

4.2.3   Single platform *vs* independent firms

The presence of a monopoly platform serving both sides of the market may generate efficiency concerns; the argument goes as follows: when the platform has full control over p_1 and p_2, it may use its market power to the detriment of consumers and this may, eventually, harm social welfare.

A comparison with the benchmark reveals that these concerns are not justified. By looking at the equilibrium prices and profits in the cases of two independent monopolists and of a single platform serving both sides, we derive the following result:

Result 2. *Consider the case of symmetric network externalities, $\theta_{12} = \theta_{21}$. In comparison to the case of two independent monopolists, when the two sides are served by a single platform:*

1. *the prices on both sides of the market are lower, $p_1^* < p_1^{ind}$ and $p_2^* < p_2^{ind}$; therefore consumer surplus is larger;*

2. *industry profits are larger: $\Pi(p_1^*, p_2^*) > \pi_1(p_1^{ind}, p_2^{ind}) + \pi_2(p_1^{ind}, p_2^{ind})$.*

This result is of great interest because it shows that the market is more efficient when only one platform serves both sides rather than when there are two independent monopolists: both producer and consumer surpluses are larger in the former case.

The platform serving both sides of the market exploits the strategic complementarities between p_1 and p_2 and takes into account the fact that a change in the price charged on one side affects the demand of the other side. On the contrary, independent firms do not internalise the complementarities between the two sides and they end up charging their customers too high prices.

Result 2 holds when the intensities of cross-side network externalities are equal but it can also be extended to the asymmetric case. As discussed previously, a platform operating on both sides of the market coordinates prices according to the intensity of cross-side network effects: the price is lowered on the side of the market which generates larger externalities. This fact suggests that when network effects are asymmetric, what matters is not the price on one side of the market but, rather, the "total price level", $P = p_1 + p_2$, that is the amount paid by a pair of consumers who get in touch through the platform. Following the previous analysis, when there is only one platform operating on both sides, the price level equals $p_1^* + p_2^* = 1$ while in the case of independent firms:

$$P^{ind} = p_1^{ind} + p_2^{ind} = 1 + \frac{\theta_{12} + \theta_{21}(1 - \theta_{12})}{4 - \theta_{12}\theta_{21}}.$$

It is straightforward to check that $P^{ind} > 1$. Regardless of the intensities of network externalities, the price level in the case of independent firms is larger than with a single platform. This fact suggests that the overall surplus enjoyed by consumers on the two sides is larger with a single platform.[13] This discussion clearly shows that the ability of the platform to set the prices on the two sides of the market yields both larger industry profits and consumer surplus, thus increasing market efficiency.

Competition among agents on one side of the market

So far we have assumed that the utility of users on one side of the market depends only on the number of users belonging to the other side. This setting applies to many markets but it does not fit those where one side is made up of competing firms. For example, AutoScout24 is an intermediary between car dealers, on the one side, and buyers on the other; car dealers compete against each other to sell cars to final users (see Box 2.3). In this case, the utility enjoyed by each dealer depends not only on the number of consumers belonging to the other side of the market, but also on the number of dealers operating on the same side, i.e. the degree of competition.

The model by Baye and Morgan (2001) on infomediaries (gatekeepers) presented in Chapter 2 examines exactly this case. The utility which each firm derives from accessing the gatekeeper's site increases with the number of subscribing consumers and decreases with the probability of the rival firm being on-line, a measure of competitive pressure. In this context the platform's pricing decision is more articulated than the one discussed in Section 4.2.2.

Baye and Morgan show that it is profitable for the gatekeeper to set p_1 and p_2 to induce full participation only on the consumer side; with full consumer participation the externalities operating from the consumer to the firm side are maximum. However, it is not optimal for the platform to stimulate full firm participation. A decrease in the price charged to firms reduces the cost of their participation but, at the same time, it increases competitive pressure and this fact reduces firms' willingness to join the platform. Baye and Morgan show that this second effect makes partial participation on the firm side desirable for the gatekeeper.

---

[13] The proof of this result is algebraically complex and it has been omitted for the sake of brevity. Instead, it is straightforward to check that even when the intensities of the cross-side network externalities are asymmetric, industry profits are larger when the market is served by a single platform.

Box 4.1 – Cross-side network externalities: the case of Yellow Pages[a]

In a recent work, Marc Rysman has empirically investigated the market for Yellow Pages, a typical two-sided market, where the two sides are represented by consumers and advertisers. The aim of Rysman's research was to verify whether in the market for Yellow Pages cross-side externalities are as relevant as predicted by economic theory; in other words, the author wanted to assess empirically: *i*) whether and how much a greater consumer usage of a given directory is translated into a larger retailer willingness to pay for an ad and *ii*) if and how much a greater number of advertisements is valued by individuals.

Rysman used data on the distribution and the quantity of ads of nearly 500 different volumes of Yellow Pages in the U.S.A. in 1996.

The author simultaneously estimated the demand functions on the two sides of the market; formally, with regard to the user side, the estimated demand was:

$$\log (x_j) = \alpha_1 \log (y_j) + \mathbf{Z}_j^x \beta^x + \xi_j,$$

where x_j and y_j represent, respectively, the diffusion among individuals of the volume j of Yellow Pages and the number of ads published in it and where parameter α_1 represents the intensity of the cross-side externality, i.e. in what way and how much the number of ads published in a given directory affects diffusion among individuals. $\mathbf{Z}_j^x$ is a vector of several control variables, including data on the population of the area where a given directory is distributed and various other characteristics (level of education, income, etc.).

With regard to the demand for advertising, Rysman estimated the following relationship:

$$\log (p_j) = \gamma \log (y_j) + \alpha_2 \log (x_j) + \mathbf{Z}_j^p \beta^p + \nu_j,$$

where p_j is the price to publish an ad on volume j, and $\mathbf{Z}_j^p$ includes a set of control variables. Parameter α_2 represents the intensity of the cross-side externality generated by the consumer side, i.e. in what way and how much the diffusion of volume j affects the price for an advertisement on the same volume.

The results of the estimations are consistent with what has been discussed throughout this chapter; in particular, the estimated parameters α_1 and α_2 concerning the two cross-network externalities are both positive and statistically significant.

More specifically, Rysman found that the intensity of the externality going from individuals to advertisers is almost four times stronger than the one going in the opposite direction ($\alpha_1 = 0.154$ and $\alpha_2 = 0.565$).

Following the above discussion, this result justifies the typical pricing strategy observed in the market for Yellow Pages, which usually consists in giving directories away for free to consumers.

[a]Taken from Rysman (2004).

4.2.4 Platform competition and efficiency

In the previous sections of the chapter we assumed that the intermediation services are offered by a single platform acting as a monopolist. At this point it is interesting to examine what happens to social welfare when more than one platform operates in the market. In other words, we now focus on the effect of competition among platforms providing intermediation services on market efficiency.

From basic microeconomics we know that competition reduces prices and enhances social welfare. However, as shown in Result 2, in the case of two-sided markets the presence of a single platform exploiting complementarities between the two sides of the market may be socially desirable. It is, therefore, interesting to investigate the effects of platform competition on social welfare.

Unfortunately, the formal analysis of competition among platforms in two-sided markets is extremely complicated. In this section, we limit our ourselves to a comparison between the two most extreme scenarios: monopoly and perfect competition; moreover, for the sake of simplicity, we assume that, in the case of perfect competition, platforms are fully compatible. Compatibility implies that the utility of users on side i depends on the overall number of users belonging to side j, regardless of the platform providing them access; therefore, with full compatibility, competing platforms have networks of the same size. The market for Internet access can be seen as an example of a two-sided market characterised by competition between compatible platforms; Internet service providers (ISPs) compete on the two sides of the market: on the one side, they sell broadband Internet access services to consumers and, on the other, they charge fees to content and application providers. ISPs adhere to a common standard (based on HTML and TCP/IP protocol) so that each individual can reach any on-line content, regardless of which ISP provides access to websites and portals and vice versa.

With full compatibility, platforms services are perfectly homogeneous and consumers select the platform only on the basis of the access price they are charged; competition drives prices on both sides of the market down to the marginal cost and industry profits go to zero. As expected, with perfect competition industry profits are smaller than Π^*, the profits of the platform acting as a monopolist. But what about consumers? Are consumers better off under perfect competition than under monopoly?

To address these questions, we need to compare the surplus enjoyed by consumers in the two cases. In Figure 4.2, consumer surplus is represented by the area lying below the demand function and above the equilibrium price; formally, letting CS_i denote the consumer surplus on side i, it follows that:

$$CS_1 = \int_{p_1}^{1+\theta_{21}(1-p_2)} y_1(p_1, p_2)\mathrm{d}p_1 = \frac{(1 - p_1 + \theta_{21}(1 - p_2))^2}{1 - \theta_{21}\theta_{12}},$$

$$CS_2 = \int_{p_2}^{1+\theta_{12}(1-p_1)} y_2(p_1, p_2)\mathrm{d}p_2 = \frac{(1 - p_2 + \theta_{12}(1 - p_1))^2}{1 - \theta_{21}\theta_{12}}.$$

The overall consumer surplus is the sum of the surpluses on the two sides of the market: $CS = CS_1 + CS_2$.

With perfect competition, equilibrium prices equal zero, the marginal cost of production; by substituting $p_1 = 0$ and $p_2 = 0$ into CS_1 and CS_2, we determine, after some simple algebraic manipulation, the overall consumer surplus in the perfectly competitive

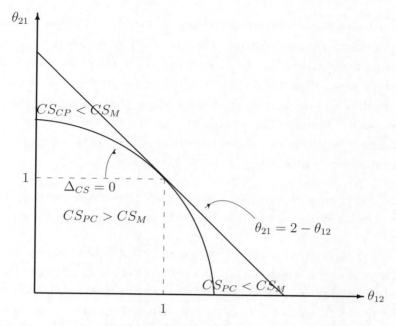

Figure 4.4: consumer surplus: perfect competition *vs* monopoly

scenario:

$$CS_{PC} = \frac{1}{2} \frac{(1+\theta_{21})^2 + (1+\theta_{12})^2}{1 - \theta_{12}\theta_{21}}.$$

In the case of a monopolistic platform, equilibrium prices are defined in expressions (4.4); by substituting these prices into CS_1 and CS_2 we determine the overall consumer surplus for this case:

$$CS_M = \frac{1 - \theta_{12}\theta_{21}}{(2 - \theta_{21} - \theta_{12})^2}.$$

In order to compare the surpluses in the two cases let us define the following function:[14]

$$\Delta_{CS} = CS_M - CS_{PC}.$$

Δ_{CS} depends on the intensities of cross-side network effects and it can be represented in the $(\theta_{12}, \theta_{21})$ plane. Following the assumption $\theta_{21} + \theta_{12} < 2$, we limit our attention to the area of the plane below the $\theta_{21} = 2 - \theta_{12}$ line. The contour line $\Delta_{CS} = 0$ in Figure 4.4 represents all the pairs $(\theta_{12}, \theta_{21})$ such that $\Delta_{CS} = 0$, that is, the intensities of network externalities such that consumer surpluses are the same under monopoly and under perfect competition. The set of points $(\theta_{12}, \theta_{21})$ lying below (respectively above) the line $\Delta_{CS} = 0$, are such that consumer surplus under perfect competition is larger (respectively smaller) than under monopoly.

---

[14]Formally, $\Delta_{CS} = \frac{1}{2} \frac{\theta_{12}^4 + \theta_{21}^4 - 2(\theta_{12}^3 + \theta_{21}^3) - 2(\theta_{12}^2 + \theta_{21}^2)(1 - \theta_{21}\theta_{12}) + 2\theta_{21}\theta_{12}(\theta_{21} + \theta_{12} - 4) + 6}{(\theta_{21} + \theta_{12} - 2)^2(\theta_{21}\theta_{12} - 1)}$.

Figure 4.4 shows an extremely interesting result. When the intensities of the cross-side network effects are highly asymmetric, consumer surplus is larger under monopoly than under perfect competition. There are two areas of the plane where this occurs: the first one is the top-left hand region of the diagram (where θ_{21} is large and θ_{12} is small) and the second one is the bottom-right hand region of the diagram (where θ_{12} is large and θ_{21} is small). Therefore, in a two-sided market, the standard result according to which consumers benefit from a more competitive market may not apply. The following result summarises our discussion:

Result 3. *With highly asymmetric intensities of cross-side network effects, consumer surplus under monopoly is larger than under perfect competition.*

An increase in competitive pressure has two effects. On the one hand, it induces firms to decrease prices, which consumers clearly benefit from. On the other hand, firms cannot balance the prices charged on the two sides of the market appropriately; more specifically, platforms cannot price below the marginal cost on one side and compensate losses by increasing the price charged on the other side. When cross-side network effects are symmetric, the first (competitive) effect dominates and therefore consumer surplus is larger under perfect competition. Vice versa, with asymmetric cross-side network effects, the possibility of balancing prices on the two sides of the market becomes crucial; in this case, it is socially efficient to subsidise the side of the market which generates more value. This strategy can be implemented by a monopolist but not by a firm operating under perfect competition; in the latter case, competitive pressure induces platforms to charge both sides of the market a price equal to the marginal cost, thus preventing them from subsidising the side that generates larger externalities.

Result 3 holds provided that the intensities of the cross-side network effects are asymmetric enough and such that the monopolist subsidises one side of the market; Figure 4.4 shows that a necessary condition for consumer surplus to be larger under monopoly is that either $\theta_{12} > 1$ (side 1 of the market should be subsidised) or $\theta_{21} > 1$ (side 2 of the market should be subsidised).

Results 1 to 3 raise a series of controversial antitrust issues. In recent years, antitrust authorities have ruled on several cases involving two-sided markets, such as the mergers between America Online (AOL) and Time Warner (Internet portals and broadband access) and between HotJobs and Monster.com (on-line employment agencies) or the well known Microsoft case. Consider two standard arguments commonly supported by antitrust authorities: *i*) competition increases market efficiency, *ii*) very low prices (prices below the marginal cost of production) may signal a predatory intent by a dominant firm.

These arguments may not apply to two-sided markets. From Result 3 we know that, under some circumstances, fiercer competition may actually harm consumers. On top of that, an appropriate balance between prices charged to the two sides of the market is a typical strategy for a profit maximising platform and, therefore, a price below the marginal cost may not necessarily imply any predatory intent.

The above considerations highlight the need for antitrust authorities to consider carefully the peculiarities of two-sided markets in order to take correct decisions. We will discuss these issues in greater detail in Chapter 8.

Box 4.2 – Dominant positions and *multihoming*[a]

As discussed in Chapter 3, network externalities induce markets to *tip* towards highly concentrated configurations characterised by one large firm dominating the market. *Market tipping* may occur also in two-sided markets due to the presence of cross-side network externalities.

Rysman (2009) highlights the two crucial elements that affect the likelihood of market tipping. On the one hand, it is more likely for different standards to coexist in the long run (and, in this case, tipping does not occur) if competing platforms find a way to differentiate from each other. For example, Microsoft and Apple have differentiated their operating systems. Windows and Mac OS X are incompatible; PCs are mainly intended for business and gaming while Macs have a lot of entertaining and powerful media features such as iMovie and iTunes.

On the other hand, Rysman shows that tipping is less likely to occur when individuals may adhere simultaneously to more than one platform, the so-called *multihoming*. For example, in the case of credit cards, merchants often accept payments with different cards (VISA or American Express); similarly, in the market for video game consoles, developers often write games for more than one platform, thus avoiding the need to sign exclusive contracts with only one of them. It is clear that in those markets where multihoming is a widespread practice on at least one side of the market, it is easier for incompatible platforms to coexist.

---

[a]Taken from Rysman (2009).

4.3   A case study: the credit card industry

We conclude this chapter by presenting one of the most interesting examples of two-sided markets, namely credit card payment systems.[15] Payment systems have been at the centre of a lively debate in recent years especially following a series of investigations conducted by competition authorities both in Europe and in the U.S.A.

Credit card payment systems are made up of banks and financial institutions which offer intermediation services to merchants, on the one side, and to consumers, on the

---

[15]Besides credit cards, the arguments presented in this section can be applied to payment systems in general.

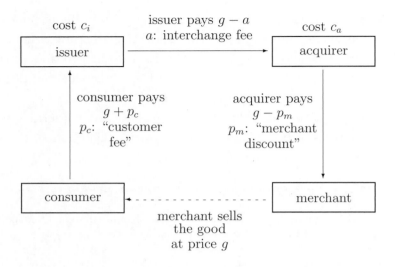

Figure 4.5: credit card association

other. Consumers benefit from holding a certain credit card only if they can use it in a large number of shops, i.e. if it is widely accepted by merchants; similarly, for a merchant it is profitable to join the credit card system provided that many individuals use the card to purchase goods and services. The credit card payment system aims at balancing the effects of cross-side network externalities by appropriately setting the prices for the intermediation service on the two sides of the market.

Before presenting a simple model of a credit card platform, it is worthwhile spending a few words to describe the main features of payment systems. These systems are rather complex because they involve several agents at the same time. In particular, there are two main types of payment systems, credit card associations, such as VISA or Mastercard, and proprietary systems, such as American Express or Diners.

Credit card associations operate on the basis of an agreement among banks or financial institutions. Each transaction by credit card involves several agents: the merchant, who accepts credit card payments for the purchases of products, the acquiring bank which accepts and processes payments on behalf of the merchant, the cardholder who pays her purchases by credit card and, finally, the issuing bank which issues the credit card to the individual consumer. In a credit card association, the two sides of the market are served by separate agents: the acquiring bank that provides intermediation services to merchants and the issuing bank that serves consumers. Instead, in proprietary systems, the tasks of acquiring and issuing banks are performed internally by the system which, therefore, directly deals with the two sides of the market.

Interestingly, the distinction between card associations and proprietary systems re-

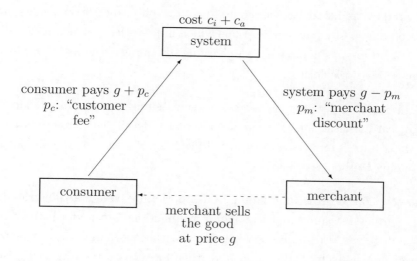

Figure 4.6: proprietary system

calls the one made in the first part of this chapter, namely the benchmark case of separate firms serving the two sides and of an integrated platform operating on both sides of the market. As we see later, this distinction is important to interpret the main findings of the theoretical analysis that we present.

In order to work properly, credit card associations require some form of coordination among member banks. In particular, such coordination is obtained through the so-called interchange fee. In order to have a clear picture of how a credit card association works, it is useful to look at Figure 4.5. Suppose that a consumer purchases by credit card a product priced at g. The consumer pays the issuing bank $g + p_c$, the price of the good plus the so-called customer fee (p_c), the fee paid by the consumer for the intermediation service. In turn, the issuing bank pays the acquiring bank $g - a$, i.e. the price of the good net of the interchange fee a. Finally, the acquiring bank pays the merchant $g - p_m$, that is the price of the good net of the so-called merchant discount, the fee paid by the merchant for the intermediation service (p_m).

Three aspects of a credit card association deserve to be highlighted:

- for each transaction, p_c and p_m are the prices paid by the two sides of the market for the intermediation service; they are the equivalent of p_1 and p_2 in our basic set-up. In credit card associations these two prices are set independently by the issuing and the acquiring bank;

- the merchant may shift the discount p_m to consumers by charging those who pay the good by credit card a price equal to $g+p_m$. This practice, known as *surcharging*, is often banned by payment systems which impose the so-called no surcharge rule; the reason for this is obvious: surcharging discourages the use of credit cards and damages card platforms;

- the interchange fee is a payment between issuing and acquiring banks for each credit card transaction. We analyse in greater detail the characteristics of a later on; it is important to say, for now, that a is set cooperatively by all the banks belonging to the association.

Let us now consider the functioning of a proprietary system as illustrated in Figure 4.6. Here, both the issuing and the acquiring functions are performed by the system itself. This fact has two main consequences; on the one hand, the entire transaction is processed internally by the system and, therefore, there is no need to establish an interchange fee. On the other hand, both sides of the market are directly served by the system of payments which sets both p_c and p_m in order to maximise its overall profits. As discussed in the previous section, the ability to control the two prices is particularly relevant since it allows the system to balance the two fees appropriately in order to exploit cross-side network effects. Clearly, in a credit card association where fees are set independently by issuing and acquiring banks, the complementarities between the two sides of the market may not be fully exploited. As we see in the next section, the interchange fee is the device which associations may use to balance prices on the two sides of the market.

A thorough understanding of the role of the interchange fee in payment associations is important also to evaluate several antitrust cases concerning the credit card industry. The way the fee is determined has been investigated by several competition authorities in Europe, in the U.S.A. and in Australia too. This issue dates back to 1984 when VISA was alleged of anticompetitive practices by the National Bancard Association (NaBanco) in relation to the interchange fee. More recently, in December 2007, also Mastercard has been accused of anticompetitive behaviour by the European Commission with regard to the interchange fee.[16]

4.3.1   The interchange fee

The interchange fee is a payment which goes from acquiring to issuing banks; issuers, in fact, generally incur higher costs than acquirers and, for this reason, they need to be compensated. Issuers not only bear the costs of processing card transactions, but also

---

[16]For further details on the Mastercard case see Bolt (2008).

those associated with the risk of providing credit to customers; on top of that, issuers usually insure customers against fraudulent uses of the card.

Besides compensating issuers for their services, the interchange fee plays an important role in relation to the two-sided nature of the market. Suppose that a credit card association increases a. This decision has two effects: on the one hand, the acquiring bank incurs in larger per transaction costs which are then reflected in a higher merchant discount, p_m; on the other hand, the increase in a reduces the marginal cost of the issuing bank, which reacts by reducing p_c. Therefore, an increase of the interchange fee has two consequences: it induces the acquiring bank to raise p_m and the issuing bank to decrease p_c.

In order to understand better the role of the interchange fee, we present a simplified version of the model by Schmalensee (2002); as we shall see, this model is similar to the benchmark case with independent firms serving the two sides of the market, here represented by merchants (side m) and consumers (side c).

As mentioned previously, a credit card association is based on an agreement among banks. For simplicity, we focus our attention on the case of two banks which have agreed to offer payment services: one bank acts as the acquirer and interacts with merchants while the other is the issuer offering payment cards to consumers.[17]

The interchange fee is chosen cooperatively by the two banks; in the model, we assume that a is chosen to maximise the overall number of credit card transactions.

Formally, the timing of the game is as follows:

t=1: the banks set the interchange fee, a. They make this choice cooperatively with the aim of maximising the overall number of transactions;

t=2: given a, the acquiring and the issuing bank determine p_c and p_m independently one from another. The issuer and the acquirer incur costs for each transaction, respectively denoted by c_i and c_a;[18]

t=3: merchants and consumers decide whether or not to join the credit card association;

t=4: cardholders purchase from merchants.

---

[17]Actually, banks belonging to credit card associations act both as acquiring and issuing banks. In case of "on-us" transactions (consumer and merchant are clients of the same bank) the issuer and the acquirer are the same bank which processes internally the entire transaction; clearly, in this case, no interchange fee is due. However, since the number of banks is extremely large, the probability of "on-us" transactions is very low and it is customarily assumed that issuing and acquiring banks are independent entities. We adhere to this assumption in this section.

[18]The cost of managing the payment system along with other expenses, such as insurance against fraud or consumer default, are included in c_i and c_a.

Box 4.3 – VISA credit card network: how many transactions?[a]

Evans (2003) estimated the determinants of the number of VISA card transactions. Formally, letting Y denote the total amount of transactions processed by the VISA network, and y_c and y_m the number of individuals who have joined the network and the number of merchants accepting VISA cards as a means of payment, respectively, Evans estimated the following function:

$$Y(y_m, y_c) = y_c^{\alpha} y_m^{\beta}, \quad \alpha, \beta > 0.$$

According to this relationship, Y increases with the number of merchants who accept VISA cards and with the number of individuals who hold the same type of card. Parameters α and β represent the elasticities of the number of credit card transactions with respect to y_c and y_m, respectively
The aim of the analysis was to estimate the magnitude of the elasticities α and β.
The period examined went from 1981 to 2001 and data refers to the U.S. market. The author estimated a log-linear functional specification of $Y(\cdot)$ and obtained the following result:

$$\log Y = -8.49 + 0.84 \log y_c + 1.73 \log y_m.$$

The estimated values of the two parameters of interest are $\alpha = 0.84$ and $\beta = 1.73$; these coefficients take the expected sign, thus confirming that the number of transactions processed via VISA grows with both y_c and y_m. It is interesting to note that the estimated value of β is more than the double of the value estimated for α; this implies that in comparison to an increase in the number of individuals, a greater number of merchants accepting VISA has a much larger impact on the number of transactions.

[a]Taken from Evans (2003).

As usual, we solve the model by backward induction. Starting from the last stage of the game, let us determine the number of credit card transactions given p_c and p_m. By using data provided by the VISA payment system, Evans (2003) studied the relationship between the number of merchants and of consumers who joined the VISA system and the amount of transactions paid by credit card. Box 4.3 summarises the main results of Evan's research; following this analysis, we assume that the number of credit card transactions, denoted by Y, is increasing in the number of credit card owners (y_c) and in the number of merchants who accept payments by credit card (y_m); formally, we assume that:

$$Y = y_c^{\alpha} y_m^{\beta}, \quad \text{with} \quad \alpha, \beta > 0,$$

where α and β denote the elasticities of the number of transactions with respect to the number of consumers and merchants, respectively.[19] In other words, these parameters describe how a change in y_c (respectively y_m) affects the total number of transactions

---

[19]Formally, $\frac{\partial Y}{\partial y_c} \frac{y_c}{Y} = \alpha$ and $\frac{\partial Y}{\partial y_m} \frac{y_m}{Y} = \beta$.

processed by credit card. These elasticities can be interpreted as the intensities of the cross-side network effects and they play a central role in our analysis, as it will be made clearer later on.

According to Evans' estimates the parameter β is more than twice α; in other words, an increase in the number of merchants is found to have a much greater impact on the overall number of transactions than an increase in the number of consumers; this fact implies that the merchant side of the market is the one which generates more value for VISA.

Let's consider now stage $t = 3$, where both consumers and merchants decide whether or not to join the credit card network. As in Schmalensee (2002), we assume that this decision is taken on the basis of the per transaction prices, p_c and p_m. For the sake of simplicity, we assume that the number of consumers and merchants who join the credit card system depends linearly on the per transaction prices:

$$y_c(p_c) = A_c - p_c \quad \text{and} \quad y_m(p_m) = A_m - p_m, \tag{4.5}$$

where A_i measures the size of demand on side $i = c, m$.

Consider now the two banks playing at stage $t = 2$ of the game; following the above arguments and recalling the fact that the acquiring bank pays the issuing bank the interchange fee,[20] it follows that the profit maximisation problems for the two banks are:

$$\max_{p_c} \ \pi_i(p_c) = (p_c - c_i + a) \, y_c(p_c)^\alpha y_m^\beta(p_m) \quad \text{and} \quad \max_{p_m} \ \pi_a(p_m) = (p_m - c_a - a) \, y_c(p_c)^\alpha y_m^\beta(p_m),$$

where $y_c(p_c)^\alpha y_m(p_m)^\beta$ represents the number of credit card transactions as a function of the number of consumers and merchants who join the payment system. From the first order conditions, we determine the optimal prices charged by the two banks given a:

$$p_c(a) = \frac{A_c - \alpha(a - c_i)}{1 + \alpha} \quad \text{and} \quad p_m(a) = \frac{A_m + \beta(a + c_a)}{1 + \beta}.$$

As expected, since the interchange fee represents a cost for the acquiring bank and a revenue for the issuer, p_m is increasing in a, while p_c is decreasing in a: $p'_m(a) > 0$ and $p'_c(a) < 0$.

Proceeding backwards to the first stage of the model, now we determine the interchange fee. As explained previously, we assume that the two banks choose a cooperatively in order to maximise the number of credit card transactions; by substituting $p_c(a)$

---

[20]Which of the two banks pays the interchange fee actually depends on whether a takes a positive or negative value. In principle, it may occur that banks set $a < 0$; in this case, the issuer pays the acquirer.

and $p_m(a)$ into (4.5), we determine the overall number of transactions as a function of the interchange fee; formally:

$$Y(a) = \left(\frac{\alpha\,(A_c - c_i + a)}{1 + \alpha} \right)^{\alpha} \left(\frac{\beta\,(A_m - c_a - a)}{1 + \beta} \right)^{\beta}.$$

It can be shown that this function is concave. By differentiating it with respect to a and then by solving the first order condition, the interchange fee which maximises the number of transactions is:

$$a^* = \frac{(A_m - c_a)\,\alpha - (A_c - c_i)\,\beta}{\alpha + \beta}. \tag{4.6}$$

This expression highlights the role of the interchange fee in balancing the effects on the overall number of transactions deriving from the two sides of the market: a^* depends on the intensities of cross-side network effects (here measured by parameters α and β), on the size of demands (A_m and A_c) and on the costs incurred by the banks (c_a and c_i).

Let's consider the relationship between the optimal interchange fee and the intensities of the cross-side network effects; taking the derivatives of a^*, we can see that the interchange fee is increasing in α and decreasing in β, formally:

$$\frac{\partial a^*}{\partial \alpha} = \frac{\beta((A_c - c_i) + (A_m - c_a))}{(\alpha + \beta)^2} > 0 \quad \text{and} \quad \frac{\partial a^*}{\partial \beta} = -\frac{\alpha((A_c - c_i) + (A_m - c_a))}{(\alpha + \beta)^2} < 0.$$

The sign of the two derivatives can be easily interpreted on the basis of the arguments discussed previously. An increase in α means that consumers have a greater impact on $Y(a)$. In this case, the two banks benefit from agreeing on an increase in a^* in order to stimulate transactions. Following the increase in the interchange fee, the issuing bank lowers p_c and this, in turn, induces more consumers to join the credit card network. Similar arguments explain why a^* increases with β.

As mentioned above, the interchange fee is used not only to balance the intensities of the cross-side network effects; from expression (4.6), it is straightforward to observe that a^* is adjusted to compensate for differences in cost and demand conditions on the two sides of the market. To see this, let us assume, for the sake of simplicity, that $\alpha = \beta = 1$; in this case, the optimal interchange fee is:

$$a^* \mid_{\alpha=1,\beta=1} = \frac{(A_m - A_c) + (c_i - c_a)}{2}.$$

From this expression it follows that:[21]

1. the interchange fee is an increasing function of the difference in the demand size on the two sides of the market ($A_m - A_c$). For instance, if only a small number of

---

[21] The discussion presented holds also for the general case of $\alpha > 0$ and $\beta > 0$.

consumers is willing to join the credit card system (A_c is small in comparison to A_m), banks are better off by setting a large a^*; in this way, the issuing bank lowers p_c, thus inducing the largest possible number of consumers to join the network and, consequently, stimulating the overall number of credit card transactions;

2. a^* is chosen in order to compensate for cost asymmetries between issuing and acquiring banks. Suppose that c_i is much greater than c_a which, *ceteris paribus*, implies that p_c is much larger than p_m. By increasing the interchange fee, banks align their marginal costs; prices are then more similar to each other and this fact, in turn, is translated into a larger number of credit card transactions.

These arguments highlight the crucial role played by the interchange fee in the credit card system; it is important to note that, similarly to Result 2, also consumers may benefit from balancing prices on the basis of the different cross-side network externalities and on the asymmetries of demand sizes and production costs. Therefore, an appropriate choice of the interchange fee may be Pareto efficient.

Going back to the antitrust issues mentioned previously, what does this model suggest? As discussed earlier, since a^* is set collectively by the banks belonging to the credit card system, strong concerns have been raised both in Europe and in the U.S.A. with regard to a possible anticompetitive use of the interchange fee. The economics literature has not come to a definite conclusion on this topic yet.[22] The model we have presented does not address the issue directly and we do not intend to use it to derive excessively general prescriptions; nevertheless, it suggests the importance of the interchange fee as a means of balancing prices on the two sides of the market; on the basis of the results shown in Sections 4.2.3 and 4.2.4, the opportunity of balancing prices may lead to an improvement in social welfare.

---

[22]Manenti and Somma (2011) show that in the presence of competition between a credit card association and a proprietary system, the former does not use the interchange fee anticompetitively against the latter neither. For a summary of the main contributions on the role of the interchange fee and the related antitrust issues see Verdier (2009).

Chapter 5

Access and Interconnection in Telecommunications

5.1 Introduction

Telecommunications (TLC) is certainly one of the most important high-tech industrial sectors. Recent data show that, on average, 70% of the economic value generated in high-tech markets can be traced back to telecommunication services, including voice telephony (both fixed-line and mobile), radio and television broadcasting, as well as Internet services.[1] Moreover, telecommunications is one of the fastest developing and most dynamic high-tech sectors. The liberalisation processes which have taken place in Europe during the last twenty years in fixed-line telecommunications are clear evidence of the technological advances sweeping over this industry; these advances have, in fact, led to remarkable reductions in the costs of providing telecommunications services, thus making it possible for certain industry segments to be opened up to competition.

To get a rough idea of the importance of deregulation processes, take a look at Figure 5.1. In all the countries taken into consideration, the number of firms offering fixed-line telecommunications services is quite large; in some cases, such as Germany, Austria and the U.K., more than a hundred TLC companies have entered the market in recent years. These figures are quite impressive if one considers that up to a few years ago fixed-line telephone services were provided by monopolists only, in most cases state-owned companies.

---

[1]Data taken from the AssInform Report 2010 on ICT.

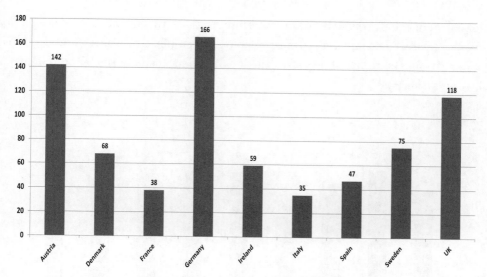

Figure 5.1: the number of fixed-line operators in Europe – 2008[2]

However, these numbers must be interpreted with caution; in fact, as shown in Figure 5.2, the massive entry of new TLC operators has not led to a substantial erosion of the incumbents' market share. In all countries considered, the market share of former monopolists is still above 50% and, in some cases, it is even close to 70%. To summarise, while Figure 5.1 suggests that deregulation has been successful in terms of stimulating market entry, from Figure 5.2 it appears that competition has not significantly reduced the dominant position of incumbent firms.

In order to reconcile these contrasting observations, we need to go a bit more into the details of the telecommunications industry. The major obstacle to liberalisation is, in fact, related to the physical structure of the telecommunications network; in particular, a crucial role is played by the so-called *local loop*, i.e. the wired connection from customers' premises to the telephone company's backbone network.

The local loop is both non duplicable and essential. It is non duplicable due to the enormous costs required to develop an alternative infrastructure; it is essential because new entrants need access to the existing local infrastructure to reach final users. In most countries, the local loop is still under the incumbent's control, who competes against entrant companies (the so-called OLOs, other licensed operators) in the provision of telecommunications services. The most critical aspect is given by the fact that the

---

[2]All the data presented in this Chapter are taken from *Progress Report on the Single European Electronic Communications Market – 2008/2009* by the European Commission. The reports are available on-line at ec.europa.eu/information_society/policy/ecomm/doc/implementation _enforcement/annualreports/15threport/comm_en.pdf.

incumbent may act strategically when determining the terms of access to the local loop. In order to protect new entrants from possible anticompetitive conducts and to ensure fair competition, the terms of access to the local loop are usually set by an independent regulatory authority.[3]

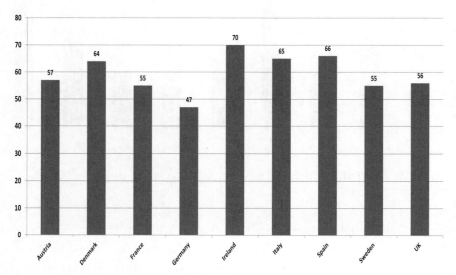

Figure 5.2: incumbents' market shares (%) – 2008

It is now possible to provide an explanation for the contradictory scenario emerging from Figures 5.1 and 5.2. On the one side, the fact that new operators had been granted access to the existing local loop without the need to develop their own infrastructure has stimulated market entry. At the same time, though, entrant firms have not succeeded in gaining significant market shares: incumbents have managed to fix the terms of access to the local loop directly, or indirectly by influencing the regulatory process, at conditions which are rather unfavourable for new entrants.

This scenario, characterised by the central role of the incumbent's local loop for the provision of TLC services, is radically changing during the last few years. Recent technological advances, especially the advent of wireless telecommunications and the deployment of alternative access technologies, are totally re-shaping the structure of the industry. Wireless technologies allow OLOs to provide telecommunications services

---

[3]This scenario is similar to other network markets, such as electricity, gas and water industries. As in the case of telecommunications, also these industries have been deregulated and opened up to competition throughout Europe; typically, incumbents own the physical infrastructure (transportation/transmission network) that competitors need to access in order to provide their services and the terms of access are crucial for the effectiveness of deregulation.

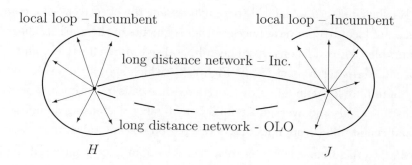

Figure 5.3: one-way access

without needing to access the local loop. Take mobile telephony for instance; each operator can roll out its own network, made up of radio towers and antennas, at a far lower cost than that for an alternative wired network. Unlike fixed-line communications where there is only one local infrastructure, in mobile telephony operators control their own network; therefore, competition is much more effective since it takes place among "infrastructured operators". In this completely different scenario, the key issue is no longer given by access to the incumbent's local loop, but by interconnection among the networks of the various operators. Mobile phone networks must be interconnected in order to allow customers of different operators to call each other; in technical jargon, we move from a scenario dominated by the so-called one-way access problem (namely, access to the incumbent's local loop) to one based on two-way access (namely, interconnection among competing networks).

5.2   One-way access

Telecommunications services, both voice and data communication, can be seen as a combination of several elements. Take, for instance, a fixed-line long-distance call between user h, living in town H, and user j, living in town J as shown in Figure 5.3. In order for this call to be placed, the two users need to be connected through a dedicated line involving several physical network elements: a line in the local loop of both towns, a line in the long-distance network which connects the two local loops and various telephone exchanges involved in the connection. All these elements are complementary one to another and are necessary to place the call between h and j.

As discussed above, the non-duplicability of the local loop is the main reason why in most countries liberalisation has not produced the expected results. Almost everywhere in Europe, the local infrastructure has been kept under the control of the former monopolist and this has de facto weakened to a great extent the effectiveness of competition in the provision of local telephone services. Other segments of the market, characterised by more favourable cost conditions, have been liberalised more effectively and competition has had a much greater impact. Take Figure 5.4 which shows the evolution of average fees for a ten minute local and long-distance fixed-line calls in European countries. While for long-distance calls the average fee follows a steadily decreasing trend, for local calls the fee has been stable throughout the entire period of time taken into consideration.

According to this figure, while for local calls the dominant position of the incumbent based on its control of the local loop has substantially prevented liberalisation from having a relevant impact on prices, for long distance calls, competition seems to have played a much more significant role. To understand this trend better, let us now go back to Figure 5.3 which illustrates the market for a typical long-distance call between towns H and J. The service is provided by the incumbent firm and by an OLO. The incumbent owns not only the local loop in towns H and J but also a long distance infrastructure. The OLO, instead, owns only a long distance network that connects the two local loops; hence, in order to provide the service to end users, the alternative operator needs access to the incumbent's local loop.

The determination of the terms of access to the incumbent's network (so-called one-way access) is crucial in order to have effective competition. The incumbent may deny access to the infrastructure, or, in less extreme cases, charge a very high access fee to substantially increase the rival's cost. In other words, the incumbent may strategically use the terms of access to the local loop against competitors.[4] For this reason in most European countries the determination of the terms of access is left to regulatory authorities. The refusal to grant access to infrastructures that are deemed to be *essential* for the provision of the service and *non duplicable* under sustainable economic conditions, is considered a case of abuse of dominant position and it is banned by competition laws (art. 102 of the Treaty on the Functioning of the European Union). An extensive economic literature has focused on the determination of the terms of access to the local loop by regulatory authorities, the so-called *access pricing* problem;[5] in the next section, we use a simple theoretical model to capture the most relevant aspects related to access pricing.

---

[4]In some cases, such as in the U.S.A., in order to reduce incentives towards anticompetitive conducts, the owner of the local infrastructure is prevented from providing long distance services (so-called break up). In Europe, instead, a different approach has been adopted. Incumbents have been kept vertically integrated in order to fully exploit the efficiency gains accruing from the complementarities between services along the value chain. To prevent incumbents from using access services strategically, independent regulators have been put in charge of the determination of the access fees.

[5]For a comprehensive review of the literature on the determination of the access fee in telecommunications see Laffont and Tirole (2000) and Vogelsang (2003).

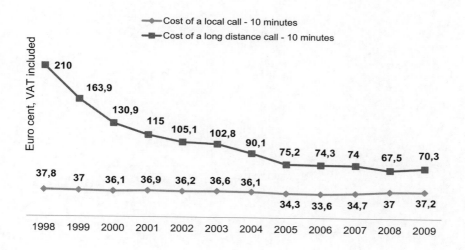

Figure 5.4: trend in fixed line fees in Europe[6]

5.2.1 Access pricing with imperfect downstream competition

Consider an industry made up of two vertically related segments, as illustrated in Figure 5.5.[7] In the upstream segment there is a monopolist, the incumbent, denoted by M; firm M is also active in the downstream segment where it faces competition from n operators, the so-called OLOs; hence, in the downstream segment $n+1$ firms compete against each other.

For the sake of simplicity, we assume that the demand for telecommunications services (measured, for instance, by minutes of conversation) is linear:

$$P = 1 - q_M - \sum_{i=1}^{n} q_{O,i},$$

where q_M denotes the quantity produced by the incumbent and $q_{O,i}$ is the quantity offered by the alternative operator $i = 1, .., n$. Throughout this section we assume that firms compete *à la Cournot*, in other words they choose the quantity to be produced.

In telecommunications, the upstream segment is represented by the local loop, owned and managed by firm M, that the OLOs need to access in order to provide their services.

---

[6]Weighted average of the prices charged in the 27 countries of the European Union.

[7]The analysis presented in this section is based on Vickers (1995); we refer the reader to the original work for further details on the relationship between the regulation of the access fee and the vertical structure of the industry in the presence of asymmetric information.

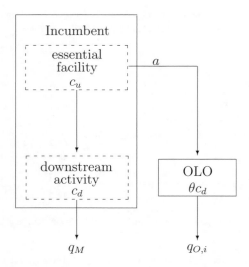

Figure 5.5: the vertical structure of the industry

We assume that for each unit of product (i.e. for each minute of conversation) a single unit of access is needed. Let a denote the access price, that is how much the OLO owes the monopolist for each unit of access to the local network; therefore, $a\,q_{O,i}$ is the total amount which the downstream operator i pays M in order to access the local loop and to provide customers with $q_{O,i}$ minutes of conversation. The overall cost incurred by the incumbent to provide one minute of conversation is $c_u + c_d$: the upstream cost, c_u, related to the management of the local network, plus the downstream cost, c_d, related to the provision of telecommunications services to final users; henceforth we assume that $c_u + c_d < 1$.[8]

In turn, the marginal cost of each OLO is given by a, the per-minute access price paid to the incumbent, plus the cost related to the downstream activity. We assume that OLOs are more efficient than the incumbent: the OLOs' marginal cost for the downstream activity is θc_d, with $\theta \leq 1$.

Assumption. *The OLOs are more efficient than the incumbent: their marginal cost for the downstream activity is θc_d, with $\theta \leq 1$.*

Parameter θ measures the efficiency of the alternative operators: the lower θ, the more efficient the OLOs are in comparison to the incumbent. Therefore, the overall

---

[8]The case of $c_u + c_d > 1$ is not interesting; in this case, the incumbent's marginal cost is larger than the intercept of the demand function and, therefore, it is not profitable for the incumbent to operate in the market.

marginal cost of each rival operator equals $a + \theta c_d$. The assumption of more efficient OLOs is based on a practical observation: one of the main reasons why policy makers have deregulated telecommunications markets has been to stimulate the entry of more efficient firms.

Finally, we assume that all firms incur a fixed cost of production F; this cost may be related to the cost of equipment and infrastructures needed to operate, or even to expenditures for marketing and advertisement. On the basis of all these arguments, we can write the monopolist's and the OLOs' profits as follows:

$$\pi_M(a, q_M) = \underbrace{(P - c_u - c_d)q_M}_{\text{downstream profits}} + \underbrace{(a - c_u)\sum_{i=1}^{n} q_{O,i}}_{\text{access profits}} - F \text{ and } \pi_{O,i}(q_{O,i}) = (P - a - \theta c_d)q_{O,i} - F.$$

Note that firm M benefits from selling access to the local network when the per-minute access fee a is larger than the marginal cost of running the upstream network, c_u; clearly, "access profits" are proportional to the overall minutes of conversation generated by the OLOs' customers: $\sum_{i=1}^{n} q_{O,i}$.

Non-regulated access fee. As anticipated above, the terms of access are generally set by an independent regulatory authority. Nonetheless, it is interesting to consider first the case of an unregulated incumbent; in other words, we begin our analysis by presenting a benchmark where we assume that firm M is free to choose the access terms. This benchmark is extremely important since it helps us understand how the incumbent may strategically use the access price. We start with a short-term analysis, where the number n of downstream firms is exogenously given. We then extend the model by considering a long-term perspective where n is endogenous and varies with market conditions.

As a reference, let us first consider what happens when firm M operates as a monopoly also in the downstream segment of the market (non access is provided). This is the case of a standard monopoly with marginal cost $c_u + c_d$; equilibrium price and profits are equal to:

$$P_{mon} = \frac{1 + c_u + c_d}{2} \quad \text{and} \quad \pi_{mon} = \frac{(1 - c_u - c_d)^2}{4} - F.$$

Consider now n alternative operators competing downstream against the incumbent. As mentioned previously, we assume that firms compete in quantities. In order to characterise the equilibrium we proceed by backward induction: first, given the access price a, we determine the equilibrium in the downstream segment; then, going backwards, we define the value of a which maximises the incumbent's profits.

By differentiating $\pi_M(a, q_M)$ and $\pi_{O,i}(q_{O,i})$ with respect to the output, and thereby solving the system of first order conditions, we determine the quantity produced by each firm and the equilibrium price charged to final users, given a:[9]

$$q_M(a) = \frac{1-(n+1)(c_u+c_d)+n(a+\theta c_d)}{n+2},$$

$$q_O(a) = \frac{1+c_u+c_d(1-2\theta)-2a}{n+2}, \qquad\qquad (5.1)$$

$$P(a) = \frac{1+c_u+c_d+n(a+\theta\, c_d)}{n+2}.$$

Note that the quantity produced by firm M is increasing in a; instead, the output of the OLOs is decreasing in the access price. This is not surprising if we consider that the access price is a cost component for each alternative operator: as a increases, the OLOs are induced to reduce their production, and this is translated into a larger incumbent's market share. It is possible to show that total output $q_M(a) + n q_O(a)$ decreases with the access fee and this explains why $P(a)$ is increasing in a.

By substituting expressions (5.1) into the incumbent's profit function, we can rewrite $\pi_M(a, q_M)$ as a function of the access price a only:

$$\pi_M(a) = (P(a) - c_u - c_d)q_M(a) + n(a - c_u)q_O(a) - F.$$

This function is concave in a and it has a maximum in:

$$a^* = \frac{1 + c_u}{2} - \frac{(n + 4\,\theta)}{2\,(n + 4)}\, c_d.$$

This expression represents the non-regulated access price that the incumbent sets when left free to choose the terms of access to the local network. The following result highlights two interesting features of a^*:

Result 1. *When the terms of access to the local network are not regulated: i) the incumbent chooses an access fee above the marginal cost of running the upstream infrastructure, $a^* > c_u$,[10] and ii) the more efficient the OLOs the larger the access fee, $da^*/d\theta < 0$.*

Result 1 highlights the strategic role of the access fee. It shows that it is optimal for the incumbent to increase rivals' cost by setting a^* above c_u, the cost of providing upstream services; this clearly puts the OLOs in a disadvantageous position in comparison to M. On top of that, the incumbent sets the access fee at a higher level the more efficient the OLOs are (the smaller θ).

---

[9]The equilibrium quantities are determined following the fact that the n alternative operators are symmetric; this implies that they produce the same quantity, that is $q_{O,i} = q_O$, $\forall i$.

[10]One can check that $a^* > c_u$ if condition $(1 - c_u)/2 > c_d(n + 4\,\theta)/(2\,(n + 4))$ holds. Note that the right hand side of this inequality is increasing in θ; therefore if the inequality holds under $\theta = 1$, then it holds for any value of θ. When $\theta = 1$, the condition can be rewritten as $(1 - c_u)/2 > c_d/2$, which is always true for $c_u + c_d < 1$.

By substituting a^* into $P(a)$, we determine the equilibrium price and profits of the incumbent:

$$P^* = \frac{1 + c_u + c_d}{2} - \frac{n(1 - \theta)}{n + 4} c_d \quad \text{and} \quad \pi_M^* = \frac{(1 - c_u - c_d)^2}{4} + \frac{n(1 - \theta)^2}{n + 4} c_d^2 - F.$$

The comparison between π_M^* and π_{mon} yields a surprising result: the incumbent benefits from competition in the downstream segment of the market. Even though this seems to be paradoxical, it can be easily explained. On the one hand, downstream competition tends to reduce incumbent's profits. On the other hand, however, since rivals are more efficient than the incumbent in serving final users ($\theta \leq 1$), it is profitable for firm M to partially "delegate" the provision of long distance services to rivals and then to extract the surplus that they generate through an appropriate choice of the access fee. In other words, it is as if firm M out-sources production to the more efficient OLOs and then taxes them through a. This second (positive) effect more than offsets the negative effect of competition. Clearly, when $\theta = 1$, that is, when OLOs are as efficient as the incumbent, for the incumbent it is optimal to foreclose the downstream market; formally, one can check that a^* is such that $q_{O,i}(a^*) = 0$ when $\theta = 1$. The incumbent benefits from competition in the downstream segment only if it can "delegate" the production to more efficient firms.

Finally, consumers do not benefit greatly from downstream competition; P^* is only slightly lower than P_{mon} and the two prices become closer and closer the less efficient alternative operators are, i.e. as θ increases. Therefore, the message which emerges from the analysis of the unregulated access case is the following: the incumbent uses the access terms strategically in order to exploit the higher efficiency of OLOs; competitors and consumers enjoy the benefits of liberalisation only marginally.

Regulated access fee and competition. The analysis presented in the previous section suggests that the incumbent may use the access fee strategically in order to extract profits from the OLOs or, in the most extreme case, to foreclose the downstream market. This is the reason why in several countries the terms of access to the local loop are set by regulatory authorities.

Therefore, in this section we extend the previous model to consider the case of a regulated access fee. In the analysis, we assume that the regulatory authority sets a with the aim of maximising social welfare (the sum of consumer and producer surpluses). Let us start by considering a short-term perspective where the number of OLOs is fixed. For a given n, the only effect from lowering a is the reduction of the OLOs' marginal cost. In this case, it is optimal for the regulatory authority to set a so that $P^* = c_u + \theta c_d$; in other words, the socially optimal access fee is such that the downstream market price equals the lowest marginal cost of providing telecommunications services.[11]

Let us now move to the more interesting long-term scenario where n is exogenous. As time passes by, firms enter and exit the downstream market and n is endogenously determined by the so-called *free entry* condition: the number of downstream firms is such that their profits equal zero. In this case, when determining a, the regulatory authority faces a more complicated trade-off than in the short-term since a also affects the number of entrants. By setting a low access fee, the authority reduces the OLOs marginal cost and this stimulates entry in the downstream market. In this way, the lower a the more firms enter, the lower the price and the more efficient the market. Nonetheless, a larger number of firms also implies an inefficient duplication of fixed costs F incurred by each single entrant.

Expressions (5.1) still represent the equilibrium quantities and price given n and a; in the long run, the number of firms operating in the downstream market is determined by the free entry condition: as long as profits are positive (negative), new OLOs enter (exit) the market. The entry/exit process continues until the active firms obtain zero profits: when this occurs, there is no room for additional firms in the market and the process comes to an end. Therefore, by combining expressions (5.1) with the free entry condition $\pi_{O,i} = 0$, we determine the long run equilibrium quantities, the price and the number of OLOs as a function of a:

$$q_M(a) = f + a - (1 - \theta)c_d - c_u, \quad q_O = f, \quad P(a) = a + f + \theta c_d,$$

$$\text{(5.2)}$$

$$n^{fe}(a) = \frac{1 - 2(f+a) + (1 - 2\theta)c_d + c_u}{f},$$

where $f \equiv \sqrt{F}$. Note that, as argued previously, $n^{fe}(a)$ is decreasing in a: the larger the access fee, the larger the OLOs' marginal costs and, therefore, all other things equal, the smaller the number of market entrants.

Let us now determine the socially optimal value of a. The regulatory authority chooses the access fee in order to maximise the social welfare, $W(a)$, defined as the sum of consumer and producer surpluses. Formally, $W(a) = CS(a) + \pi_M(a) + \sum_{i=1}^{n^{fe}(a)} \pi_{O,i}(a)$, where $CS(a)$ denotes consumer surplus, which corresponds to the area below the demand

---

[11]Note that in our analysis, we do not take into account the fact that the regulated access fee must guarantee non negative profits for the incumbent. In order to induce $P^* = c_u + \theta c_d$, the regulatory authority sets a below c_u; at this level of the access fee, M incurs losses when providing access services. Moreover, the downstream market price ($P^* = c_u + \theta c_d$) is smaller than the overall marginal cost of the incumbent ($c_u + c_d$) and therefore, firm M is not willing to serve any consumers. We assume that the losses incurred by the incumbent are covered by non-distortionary subsidies.

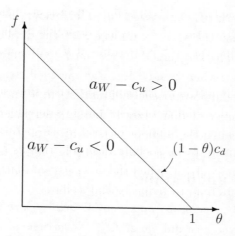

Figure 5.6: the socially optimal access fee (with free entry)

function $P = 1 - q_M(a) - \sum_{i=1}^{n} q_{O,i}$ and above the equilibrium price:

$$CS(a) = \frac{(1 - P(a)) \left(q_M(a) + \sum_{i=1}^{n^{fe}(a)} q_{O,i}(a) \right)}{2}.$$

By maximising the social welfare function with respect to a, we derive the following result:[12]

Result 2. *When there is free entry in the downstream market, the socially optimal access fee is:*

$$a_W = c_u + f - (1 - \theta)c_d.$$

As argued previously, the access fee affects entry in the downstream market which, in turn, has opposite effects on social welfare. A lower a induces more OLOs to enter the market thus increasing social welfare for two reasons: $i)$ the downstream market becomes more competitive and, $ii)$ downstream costs are lower since OLOs are more efficient than the incumbent. This latter effect is stronger the smaller θ (that is, the more efficient OLOs are in comparison to the incumbent). The downside of increasing entry is related to the inefficient duplication of fixed costs F incurred by each entrant.

Figure 5.6 illustrates the socially optimal access fee in a (θ, f) space; for small values of f and of θ, it is optimal for the regulatory authority to stimulate entry by subsidising

---

[12]The social welfare function is computed by substituting expressions (5.2) into $W(a)$; formally:

$$W(a) = \frac{f^2}{2} + (a - 1 - 2c_d + 3\theta c_d)f + \frac{3\theta^2 c_d^2}{2} + (a - 1 - 2c_d) c_d\theta + \frac{1 - a^2}{2} - c_u(1 - a)c_d(c_u + c_d - a).$$

One can check that $W(a)$ is concave.

access to the local network (the access fee a_W is set below the upstream marginal cost, $a_W - c_u < 0$). In this case, the negative effect due to the duplication of fixed costs is of little magnitude (f is small) and the OLOs are much more efficient than the incumbent (θ is small).[13] By contrast, when f and θ are large, the inefficiency due to the duplication of fixed costs dominates the positive effect of market entry and the regulatory authority prefers to limit the number of downstream firms by setting the access fee above the upstream marginal cost ($a_W - c_u > 0$).

5.2.2   Local loop unbundling

As mentioned previously, access to an essential facility is a relevant issue in several network industries such as gas and electricity. Nevertheless, in telecommunications it plays an even more crucial role; due to the rapid technological progress characterising telecommunications, access to the local infrastructure is central for the provision of new and advanced services. For example, in recent years the development of new data transmission technologies, such as xDSL, has made it possible to provide broadband services through the incumbent's local loop. In other words, thanks to new technologies, the traditional copper network, originally designed to transmit fixed-line telephony only, can now be used for more advanced services.[14]

For this reason, it is worthwhile focusing more closely on some technical aspects related to access to the local loop in telecommunications. Technically speaking, access to the local network, *local loop unbundling* in the industry jargon, means that the incumbent rents to the OLOs the copper cables running from customers' premises to local telephone exchanges. Initially, local loop unbundling was a tool which enabled OLOs to offer voice telephony services to their customers; then, due to technological developments, local loop unbundling enabled entrants to offer more advanced services such as DSL-based Internet access. The type of services which OLOs can offer (voice telephony, broadband Internet access, Voice over IP telephony, etc.) depends on the entrants' degree of control over the leased line; for this reason, it is customary to distinguish among different types of unbundling according to the entrant's degree of control over the unbundled copper line:

1. bitstream access;

---

[13] Also in this case, as in the short term analysis, we assume that any losses incurred by the incumbent are covered by non-distortionary subsidies.

[14] More recently, a new technology called "vectoring" allows to upgrade the copper network so drastically that it is possible to provide Internet access services on the traditional telecommunications network at a speed comparable to that of fibre network. For a theoretical analysis of vectoring and its impact on the deployment of new infrastructures, see Bourreau et al. (2013).

2. shared access;

3. full unbundling.

Bitstream is the least advanced form of access. The incumbent keeps full control over the copper line; entrants are not allowed to add any additional equipment to the incumbent's DSL and are restricted to supplying the services designated by the incumbent. With this type of access OLOs essentially commercialise the incumbent's DSL services; OLOs may enter the market without having to develop any facilities or infrastructures but they are unable to differentiate their services from those offered by the incumbent.

A slightly more advanced form of local loop unbundling is given by shared access. In this case, the incumbent and the OLO share the copper line; usually, with shared access consumers can acquire data/Internet services from an alternative operator while retaining the incumbents' voice services. With shared access, the entrant needs to invest in its own infrastructure in order to supply services; in particular, the OLO must install devices (splitters) to separate voice from data traffic.

Finally, full unbundling is the most advanced form of access to the local loop. Entrant firms lease the entire copper cable of the incumbent, thus acquiring full control over the line; with full unbundling, the OLOs supply both voice and Internet services to final users who, therefore, deal with only one operator. Full unbundling gives the entrant complete control over the local line but it requires substantial investments to be implemented; the OLOs, in fact, must own a sufficiently widespread backbone infrastructure connecting the incumbent's local exchanges. Moreover, in order to transmit voice and data packages over the local line, OLOs must invest in additional equipment. Since OLOs have full control over the line, they can greatly differentiate their services from those supplied by the incumbent.

According to several commentators, full unbundling is the preferable form of access to the local loop since it provides the OLOs with the appropriate incentives to build their own infrastructures and, at the same time, it enables them to differentiate their services from the incumbent's. Instead, less advanced forms of unbundling, in particular bitstream access, are particularly effective during the early stages of liberalisation processes since they enable OLOs without any infrastructure to enter the market.

Figure 5.7 shows the number of bitstream and fully unbundled lines leased by the incumbents in Europe. The figure shows a clear pattern: while the number of bitstream lines is stable over time, the trend of fully unbundled lines is steadily increasing. This pattern has an interesting interpretation which we discuss in the following paragraph.

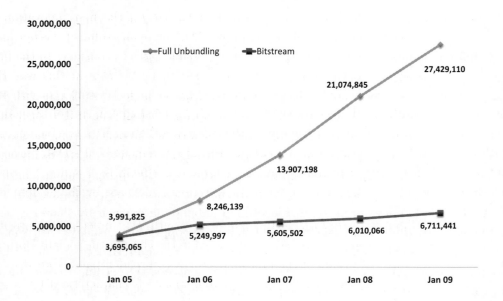

Figure 5.7: bitstream and fully unbundled lines in Europe

Access and investments: the ladder of investment theory

The liberalisation processes which have taken place in the European telecommunications industry during the last twenty years have had both short-term and long-term goals. In the short-term, the aim of liberalisation was to stimulate competition and to reduce prices for final users. In this perspective, as suggested by the previous analysis, an appropriate regulation of the terms of access to the local loop is essential to enable entrants to compete effectively. Figure 5.4, which we have previously discussed, actually suggests that some noteworthy results have been achieved with regard to the short-term goal of liberalisation.

In a longer term perspective, the aim of liberalisation has been to stimulate entrants to invest in order to build up their own infrastructure. As long as entrants rely on incumbent's network to provide their services, they cannot compete on an equal footing with incumbents; effective competition may emerge only between infrastructured operators. On top of that, the development of alternative networks (e.g. fibre optical networks) is often seen as the best way to accelerate the creation of innovative/advanced Internet services. With regard to this latter point, empirical evidence suggests that broadband Internet access is indeed more widespread in countries where alternative transmission networks are available.[15]

---

[15]For further details see Distaso et al. (2006) and Maldoom et al. (2003).

The issue, hence, is how can entrants be stimulated to invest in infrastructures? From our previous discussion on the various forms of local loop unbundling it emerges that entry may occur without relevant investments via bitstream access, it may occur after having undertaken a certain amount of investment, via full unbundling or, in the more extreme case, OLOs may enter with their own infrastructure. Clearly, this latter option requires huge investments and it is unlikely to occur in the short run. Therefore, entry may take place gradually: initially via bitstream access, then by moving to full unbundling in order to allow the entrant to supply differentiated services; at later stages, the entrant firm may eventually opt for building its own physical local network.

These considerations shed new light on the role of local loop unbundling which can be considered as a bridge towards the so-called "facility based" competition, namely competition among infrastructured operators. In this direction, a recent theoretical approach to local loop unbundling, known as the *ladder of investment* theory, has been proposed by Professor Martin Cave (see Cave, 2004); this approach has gained popularity among European regulators and policy makers and deserves a brief discussion.[16]

In short, according to Cave's theory, regulation of the terms of access to the local loop should evolve over time and be designed in order to provide the OLOs with the appropriate incentives to build-up their own network infrastructures. The mechanism underlying the ladder of investments is extremely simple. At the early stages of market liberalisation, the regulatory authority should encourage entry by fixing very low access prices for the network elements that are too expensive for new entrants to replicate. As soon as new entrants consolidate their market positions and gain brand recognition and customer base, regulatory authorities should increase access prices, starting from the network elements that are easier to duplicate (i.e. by raising the price of bitstream access). The increase in the price of these network elements should encourage new entrants to invest in order to migrate towards higher levels of the investment ladder, thus shifting from bitstream access to more advanced forms of unbundling. Ultimately, as soon as entrant operators have gained sufficient revenues and technological know-how, they can climb the last step of the ladder, i.e. they can invest in their own infrastructure.

Figure 5.7 seems to support the ladder of investment theory. It shows that in Europe, as time passed by, the number of bitstream access has been stable while that of fully unbundled lines has substantially increased; consistently with Cave's theory, this suggests that, indeed, entrant firms have been climbing the ladder of investments moving from bitstream to full unbundling.

With regard to the price of access to the local loop, the ladder of investment theory recommends to adopt a dynamic and differentiated approach. More specifically, as ar-

---

[16]For further details on the topic and on the empirical validity of the ladder of investment theory, see Distaso et al. (2009), Cave (2006) and Cave and Vogelsang (2003).

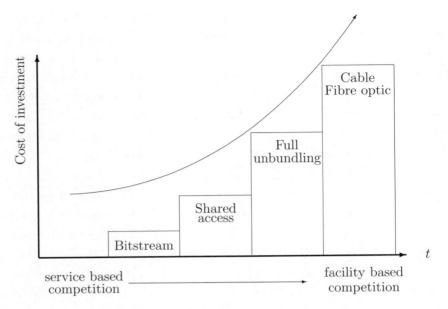

Figure 5.8: the ladder of investments

gued by Professor Cave, prices for the least advanced forms of unbundling (i.e. bitstream and shared access) should *a*) increase over time and *b*) be negatively correlated with the price of full unbundling. In this way, OLOs are provided with the correct incentives to develop their own facilities: as long as the price of bitstream access increases and that of full unbundling decreases, firms are clearly induced to invest in order to move from the former type of access to the latter.

Figure 5.8 provides a simple graphical representation of the ladder of investments. As one may note, full unbundling is not the last step of the ladder. The ultimate goal for regulatory authorities is to induce OLOs to deploy their own access network to achieve complete independence from the incumbent. This is, for instance, the case of OLOs which provide communications services through alternative platforms such as optical fibre or cable.

The emergence of a variety of competing platforms for the provision of telecommunications services represents a radical change in the structure of the industry and it has important effects on the behaviour of operators. When competition takes place between infrastructured operators, the scenario shifts from the one dominated by the one-way access problem (access to the incumbent's network) that we have discussed so far, to a different one dominated by the so-called two-way access problem (when independent networks need to be interconnected with each other). Two-way access is the topic we are going to discuss in the next section.

Box 5.1 – Why do firms interconnect their networks?

An interesting question to ask ourselves is the following: why do telecom companies that often compete fiercely in the market for the provision of communications services collaborate to interconnect their networks? Why do firms benefit from an interconnection agreement? The answer to this question lies in one of the main features of a physical communication network, i.e. the presence of strong network externalities.

The role of network externalities in communications networks is well-known since the formulation of the famous Metcalfe Law, named after the electrical engineer who co-invented Ethernet. According to this law, the value/benefit v^i which individual i enjoys from joining a network which enables n individuals to communicate with each other (the willingness to pay to enter a network) increases with the number of individuals who can be reached through the network (i.e. the network size). For simplicity, we assume that the benefit which individual i derives from joining the network depends only on network externalities; formally:

$$v^i = n.$$

Suppose that two networks operate on the market: one belongs to firm A and is of size n_a while the other belongs to firm B and is of size n_b. The question we want to answer is the following: what incentives do the two firms have to let users belonging to different networks communicate with each other? Or, in other words, what is the incentive for interconnection?

If the two networks are not interconnected then each individual can only communicate with the users belonging to the same network; therefore the benefit which individual i derives from belonging to network A equals $v_a^i = n_a$,

while it equals $v_b^i = n_b$ if individual i belongs to network B. This means that the overall value of the two networks (the sum of the individual benefits of all the users) is:

$$V_a^N = \sum_{i=1}^{n_a} v_a^i = n_a^2, \text{ and } V_b^N = \sum_{i=1}^{n_b} v_b^i = n_b^2.$$

The above expressions show the mathematical formulation of the Metcalfe Law: the overall value of a telecommunications network is proportional to the square of the number of individuals joining the network.

Consider now the case of interconnected networks: each user can communicate with all the others, regardless of which network they belong to; therefore, the benefit that a user derives from joining one of the two interconnected networks is:

$$v_a^i = n_a + n_b, \text{ and } v_b^i = n_a + n_b,$$

thus, the overall value of the two networks when they are interconnected is:

$$V_a^I = \sum_{i=1}^{n_a} v_a^i = n_a^2 + n_a n_b,$$

$$V_b^I = \sum_{i=1}^{n_b} v_b^i = n_b^2 + n_b n_a.$$

By observing V_a^I and V_b^I, we can see that with interconnection the overall value is increasing for both networks; formally: $V_a^I - V_a^N = n_a n_b$ and $V_b^I - V_b^N = n_a n_b$.

In the presence of network externalities, both firms benefit from interconnection. Both networks grow in size thanks to interconnection: individuals belonging to network i can communicate with those belonging to network j and this leads to an increase in value for all users.

5.3   Two-way access and interconnection

As mentioned previously, the basic idea of the ladder of investment theory is that regulatory authorities in telecommunications should stimulate firms' investments in network infrastructures; as time goes by, competition should take place among infrastructured operators. This already occurs in mobile telephony, where several operators with their own infrastructures, made of antennas and radio stations, compete against each other.

The presence of several infrastructured operators changes the market structure substantially. Unlike in fixed-line telephony where OLOs need to "buy" access from the incumbent firm in order to reach final users, in the case of competition among operators owning an infrastructure, each of them buys and sells access at the same time. The strategic interdependence among firms moves from a one-way access problem to a two-way access problem. This happens whenever consumers belonging to different networks call each other: the operator of the calling party needs to access the network of the receiving party operator to allow users to communicate; hence, each operator buys access to the network of the rival firms and sells access to its own network depending on whether its subscriber places or receives a call. This form of access which goes in both directions is also known as interconnection.

As highlighted in Box 5.1, due to the presence of network externalities, operators benefit from interconnecting their infrastructures. This means that it is profitable for them to reach an agreement that guarantees mutual access to their networks. In the next section, we specifically focus on the determination of the interconnection fee, namely the fee that operators pay each other to interconnect.[17]

5.3.1   Interconnection fee and collusion

With two-way access each operator both pays (when needing access to a competitor's network) and receives (when providing access to its network) a payment for interconnection services. In this section, we present a simple theoretical model of competition and interconnection among telecommunications networks, based on the work by Laffont et al. (1998a).[18]

---

[17]It is important to stress that there are many cases of interconnection which do not involve competition among operators. Take, for example, international telecommunications. If someone in France (a subscriber of France Telecom) wants to call someone, let's say, in Italy (a subscriber of Telecom Italia) France Telecom needs to access Telecom Italia's network; at the same time, the Italian operator pays to access to the French network in the case of a call in the opposite direction. This is a case of two-way access where the operators do not compete against each other. For further details on this topic, see Carter and Wright (1994), Wright (1999) and Manenti (2001).

[18]For a review of the literature on interconnection, see Laffont and Tirole (2000).

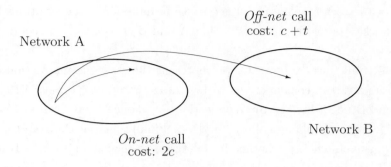

Figure 5.9: *on-net* and *off-net* calls

For the sake of simplicity, let us consider a duopoly: we assume that there are two firms in the market, A and B, both endowed with their own infrastructure. The two firms compete in prices and offer differentiated services; product differentiation could be related for example to the quality of the supplied services, to customer support or to contractual arrangements with subscribers. Formally, we represent competition through a standard Hotelling model with firms located at the extreme points of a unit-length segment.

Each phone call is a combination of two separate services: "origination" and "termination"; therefore we distinguish between two different types of calls, as illustrated in Figure 5.9: *on-net* calls which occur between subscribers belonging to the same network (origination and termination on the same network) and *off-net* calls which involve subscribers of different networks (origination and termination on different networks).

We assume that the price of the phone call is set by the calling party's operator and that the firm cannot price discriminate between on- and off-net calls (same price for both types of calls).

Clearly, on-net and off-net calls entail different cost for the calling party's operator. In the case of on-net calls, the firm incurs both the origination and termination costs; we assume, for simplicity, that the two services have the same marginal cost c, so the overall cost of an on-net call is $2c$. In the case of off-net calls, the firm incurs the origination cost and pays the interconnection fee, denoted by t, to access the competitor's network. Therefore, the overall cost of an off-net call is $c + t$.

In order to prevent market leaders from adopting anticompetitive practices, many regulatory authorities (such as Ofcom in Great Britain, FCC in the U.S.A. and AgCom in Italy) impose the so-called "reciprocity rule": two operators are obliged to charge each other the same fee for termination services regardless of the direction of the call. For this reason, in what follows, we assume that access fees are reciprocal. Moreover, the determination of the reciprocal terms of access are usually left to negotiations between competing networks; therefore, we assume that A and B choose the interconnection fee cooperatively.

On the basis of all these arguments, we represent the strategic interaction between the two operators and the consumers as a three-stage game (see Figure 5.10): in the first stage, A and B negotiate the interconnection fee t; once t has been set, each firm decides the price for each phone call: p_a and p_b. Finally, in the third and last stage of the game, consumers choose whether to subscribe to firm A or to firm B and how many phone calls to place. For the sake of simplicity, we assume that consumers follow a two-step decision process: they first choose their network on the basis of firms' prices p_a and p_b and, then, they decide how many phone calls to place.

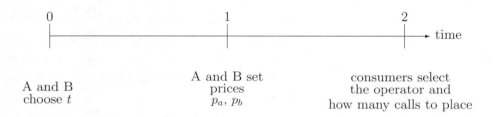

Figure 5.10: the timing of the interconnection game

First we determine how many consumers subscribe to either A or B for given p_a and p_b. As mentioned previously, we represent the duopolistic competition as a Hotelling model of product differentiation; we assume that the two firms are located at the extremes of the segment $[0, 1]$ (firm A in 0 and firm B in 1). Consumer preferences are heterogeneous with respect to the services provided by the two firms; the exact location of each consumer on the segment represents her preferences: consumers located near the origin prefer the services provided by firm A, while those who are located near 1 have a preference for firm B. We assume that consumers are of mass 1 and are uniformly distributed over the $[0, 1]$ interval.

Let $\tilde{x}$ denote the location of the consumer who is indifferent between buying from A or from B; formally for this consumer the following condition must hold:

$$p_a + d\tilde{x} = p_b + d(1 - \tilde{x}), \tag{5.3}$$

where $d\tilde{x}$ and $d(1 - \tilde{x})$ represent the disutilities incurred by the consumer who has to choose between the services offered by A and B while her ideal product is $\tilde{x}$;[19] parameter d measures how costly it is for a consumer to join a network which is not the ideal one.

[19]We also assume that the market is "fully covered", so that $\alpha_a + \alpha_b = 1$.

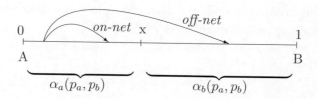

Figure 5.11: interconnection and market shares

Clearly, all consumers located on the left of $\tilde{x}$ prefer to subscribe to firm A, while all those located on the right of $\tilde{x}$ prefer firm B. Therefore, we calculate the demand for subscriptions:

$$\alpha_a(p_a, p_b) = \frac{1}{2} - \frac{p_a - p_b}{2d}, \quad \text{and} \quad \alpha_b(p_a, p_b) = 1 - \alpha_a(p_a, p_b) = \frac{1}{2} - \frac{p_b - p_a}{2d}. \quad (5.4)$$

Once we have derived the demand for subscriptions, the next step is to define the firms' profits; in order to do this, we need to determine the number of phone calls placed by each consumer once she has taken her subscription decision. Two further simplifying assumptions are needed:

1. *linear demand function:* once a consumer has chosen to subscribe to firm i =A, B, she makes $q(p_i) = 1 - p_i$ phone calls, where p_i denotes the price set by firm i;

2. *balanced calling pattern:* the probability of having an on-net or off-net phone call is proportional to the network size (the number of subscribers): for instance, if the user making the call belongs to the network of firm A, then the probability of the call being on-net or off-net equals α_a and α_b, respectively (see Figure 5.11).[20]

On the basis of assumptions 1 and 2, it follows that the profit function of firm A (and likewise of B) is:

$$\pi_a(p_a, t) = \underbrace{\alpha_a q_a(p_a)\alpha_a(p_a - 2c)}_{\text{on-net profits}} + \underbrace{\alpha_a q_a(p_a)\alpha_b(p_a - c - t)}_{\text{off-net profits}} + \underbrace{\alpha_b q(p_b)\alpha_a(t - c)}_{\text{interconnection profits}}.$$

The interpretation of this expression is straightforward. The number of calls originated from the subscribers of firm A is $\alpha_a q_a(p_a)$; a share α_a of these calls are directed to subscribers of the same network (on-net) and each one generates a per unit profit $p_a - 2c$; a share α_b of the calls is directed to subscribers of firm B (off-net), and each one generates a per unit profit equal to $p_a - c - t$. Finally, A terminates a fraction α_a

---

[20]This last assumption, which is widely used in the literature, greatly simplifies the analysis; see Laffont and Tirole (2000). Nevertheless, it is not without loss of generality: see Armstrong (2004) and Dessein (2004).

of the $\alpha_b q_b(p_b)$ calls originated from B's network; from these incoming calls, A enjoys a per call interconnection profit equal to $t - c$.

By substituting expressions (5.4) into $\pi_a(p_a, t)$ (and likewise into $\pi_b(p_b, t)$), we can rewrite firm A's profit function as:

$$\pi_a(p_a, t) = \left(\frac{1}{2} - \frac{p_a - p_b}{2d} \right) (1 - p_a) (p_a - 2c) + \left(\frac{1}{2} - \frac{p_a - p_b}{2d} \right) \left(\frac{1}{2} + \frac{p_a - p_b}{2d} \right) (t - c) (p_a - p_b).$$

According to the timing of the game, we proceed by backward induction in order to determine the prices charged by A and B, given the interconnection fee t. By differentiating the profit functions $\pi_a(p_a, t)$ and $\pi_b(p_b, t)$ with respect to p_a and p_b respectively and then by solving the system of first order conditions, we obtain the equilibrium prices as a function of the interconnection fee t:[21]

$$p_a(t) = p_b(t) = p(t) = \frac{1}{2} + c + d - \frac{1}{2}\sqrt{(1 - 2c)^2 + 2t(c + 2d - t)}. \tag{5.5}$$

As one may expect, the equilibrium prices depend on the interconnection fee, t, on the cost of the service, c, and also on d, the parameter representing consumer preferences. In particular, note that $dp(t)/dt > 0$: the larger the interconnection fee, the higher the equilibrium price. This consideration is of crucial importance: the interconnection fee is one of the components of the marginal cost, therefore the larger t, the greater the cost incurred by the two firms and the higher the prices that they charge.

Once we have derived the equilibrium prices in the second stage of the game, we proceed to the first stage where firms jointly determine the interconnection fee. We assume that t is set in order to maximise joint profits; formally, by substituting $p_a(t)$ and $p_b(t)$ into $\pi_a(p_a, t)$ and $\pi_b(p_a, t)$, it follows that the two firms choose t to maximise:

$$\pi_a(t) + \pi_b(t) = \frac{d \left(2\sqrt{1 - 4c + 4(d^2 + c^2)} - 2d(t - c) - 4d - c + t \right)^2}{2}.$$

Note that this function is concave in t; by solving the first order condition we derive the optimal interconnection fee:

$$t^* = c + \frac{(1 - 2c)^2}{2d}. \tag{5.6}$$

According to expression (5.6), the two firms set t^* above the termination cost. Firms choose a large interconnection fee to reduce their incentives to price aggressively in order to attract consumers (we have just argued that $p(t)$ is increasing in t): if an operator lowers its price to attract new subscribers, also the number of off-net calls increases, which obviously requires the firm to pay larger interconnection fees. For this reason,

---

[21] Since firms are symmetric, they charge the same price in equilibrium.

a large t reduces the incentive to compete fiercely in order to increase the number of subscribers. In other words, this means that the interconnection fee represents a collusive device used by firms to keep prices high.

Result 3. *The interconnection fee is a collusive device: by setting $t^* > c$, firms compete less aggressively.*

5.3.2 Interconnection and calling rates

The analysis of the previous section is based on the assumption that firms charge linear and not discriminatory prices. At this point, however, it is interesting to extend our discussion to answer the following question: what happens when firms adopt more sophisticated pricing strategies? In the case of mobile services, it is very common for firms to use nonlinear prices or to discriminate customers according to phone call destination. It is, therefore, interesting to examine whether the interconnection fee may still be used as a collusive device also in these cases.

Nonlinear pricing. Nonlinear pricing is a widely used strategy for phone calls. A simple form of nonlinear pricing is the so-called two-part tariff where users are charged a per minute rate p and a fixed rate, F, which is paid regardless of the amount of calls. From standard industrial organisation models, we know that the optimal two-part tariff for a monopolist is as follows: the per minute rate p is set equal to the marginal cost of production, in order to stimulate users to place phone calls; the fixed part of the tariff, F, is then used to extract consumer surplus associated with price p. Laffont et al. (1998a) prove that also in an oligopolistic setting with firms charging nonlinear prices, in equilibrium the per minute rate equals the marginal cost. This fact implies that: i) firms derive profits from the fixed part of the tariff only, ii) firms compete against each other by lowering F. This last observation has interesting consequences on the role of the interconnection fee. As argued in Result 3, when firms charge linear prices, t represents a collusive device which reduces the incentives to compete aggressively on p. Instead, in the case of two-part tariffs, firms compete on F; as a consequence, with nonlinear prices, the interconnection fee, which affects the per minute price but not the fixed part, does not have a collusive role anymore.

On-net/off-net price discrimination. Phone companies frequently charge different prices depending on whether a call is on-net or off-net; in the economic jargon, this means that they price discriminate according to phone call destination.

The question is the following: do firms that price discriminate according to the destination of the call still collude tacitly through the joint determination of the interconnection fee? Laffont et al. (1998b) prove that also in this case the interconnection fee is no longer a collusive device. To understand their arguments, it is important to note that the interconnection fee affects only the price of off-net calls: since on-net calls are placed among subscribers of the same operator a firm does not need access to the rival's network to terminate them.

Box 5.2 – Internet telephony

Internet telephony, commonly known as VoIP (*Voice over Internet Protocol*), is considered by many as the *killer application* in telecommunications. VoIP is a technology which enables the user to make phone calls over the Internet, without necessarily accessing the traditional telephone network. VoIP has become very popular thanks to the diffusion of high-speed broadband Internet access, such as xDSL. Thanks to VoIP, nowadays, we can make calls anywhere in the world at very low rates, in comparison to those charged by traditional operators.

VoIP technology involves the digitisation of voice signals, which are then encoded, packetised and transmitted as IP packets over the Internet. Similar steps (in the reverse order) are followed on the receiving side: IP packets are received, decoded and converted from digital to analog to reproduce the original voice stream. Nowadays, thanks to broadband Internet connections enabling IP packets to be sent without delays, the quality of VoIP has reached a standard comparable to that of fixed-line phone calls.

The use of Internet telephony has increased rapidly also thanks to the availability of new technologies which allow VoIP transmission through broadband Internet connections without the need of a computer. Figure 5.12 shows the share of VoIP phone traffic in some European countries. We can see that in countries such as France, Denmark or Germany the penetration of VoIP is rather impressive; in 2008, according to data collected by the European Commission, the average amount of VoIP traffic in Europe was well above 14%.

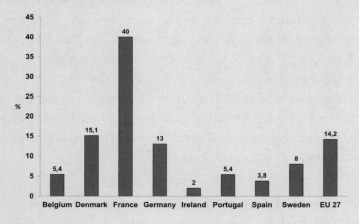

Figure 5.12: share of VoIP traffic – 2008

However, the most effective way of competing against each other is by lowering the price of on-net calls. On the contrary, attracting subscribers by reducing the price of off-net calls stimulates the amount of these calls and, consequently, the payments owed for the termination service. On-net prices, instead, can be reduced to attract new subscribers without incurring larger costs for interconnection.

Therefore, even though firms collude tacitly on t, that is, they increase the interconnection fee to compete less aggressively on the price of off-net calls, the benefits from collusion are eroded by competition on the price of on-net calls. In other words, any possible gain deriving from collusion in the off-net segment through an increased interconnection fee is swept away by fiercer competition in the on-net call segment. Hence, when firms discriminate according to phone call destination, they do not have incentives to collude on t.[22]

5.3.3   Interconnection and the "receiving party pays" regime

In the model presented in the previous section, we assumed that the entire cost of a phone call is borne by the calling party, i.e. the caller pays a price which covers the cost of both the origination and the termination services. This payment regime, known as "calling party pays" (CPP), is commonly used by many European telecommunications companies. It is important to note that the CPP regime is strictly related to the two-way access issue discussed in this section. In the case of an off-net call, the operator of the calling party incurs the cost of termination by paying the interconnection fee to the receiving party's network; in turn, this operator charges the caller a price which also covers the interconnection fee. As suggested by the model presented in the previous pages, the CPP regime based on bilateral interconnection implies the risk of collusion inflating the prices of calls.[23]

---

[22]Notably, Gabrielsen and Vagstad (2008) prove that in some specific circumstances the interconnection fee may be used once again as a collusive device also in the case of price discrimination between on-net and off-net calls. The result is based on the fact that users tend to call mostly a limited number of people (friends and relatives); this generates club effects and transaction costs (switching costs when changing network) which determine the possibility of colluding on the interconnection fee. See the original paper for further details.

[23]Even in those cases where regulatory agencies decided to take action against collusion, such as in the U.K. where interconnection fees between mobile operators have been capped, further difficulties emerged. As argued in Littlechild (2006), the introduction of cost-oriented caps to interconnection fees requires regulatory authorities to keep on monitoring firms' activities. This may represent an extremely expensive task; Littlechild estimated that in the U.K. the introduction of cost-oriented price caps for mobile termination services has led to an additional burden for the Authority amounting to more than 25 million British pounds.

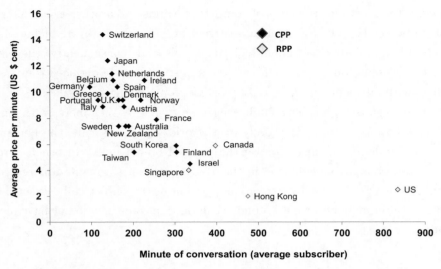

Figure 5.13: calling party pays *vs* receiver party pays – 2007[24]

CPP, however, is not the only possible payment regime for telecommunications services. In the U.S.A. and Canada, telecom operators adopt the so-called "receiving party pays" (RPP) regime, where also the receiver contributes to the payment of the call. The underlying economic principle of RPP is that the receiver derives a benefit from being called and, for this reason, she should be willing to pay for the service.

Unlike the CPP regime, in the case of RPP the cost of the termination service is not covered by the interconnection fee but it is incurred by the receiving party. Therefore, under the RPP regime, the scenario shifts from bilateral to the so-called "bill and keep" (BAK) interconnection: each operator (both calling and receiving) bills the service it provides (the origination and the termination service, respectively), keeps the whole payment made by its customer (calling party and receiving party, respectively) and no interconnection fee is due.

Clearly, the absence of interconnection fees eliminates the possibility of colluding on t. As a consequence, market prices are expected to be lower in those countries where RPP in place. Figure 5.13 seems to support this hypothesis; in the case of mobile telecommunications. It illustrates for several countries the relationship between the average per minute price and the average length of a call. We can see that the countries with lower prices and longer calls are those where the RPP regime is in place, such as U.S.A., Canada, Hong Kong and Singapore.

---

[24]Data taken from *Merrill Lynch – Global Wireless Matrix – June 2007.*

Chapter 6

Cumulative Innovation in Dynamic Industries

6.1 Introduction

Typically, ICT products and technologies are extremely complex since they combine several technological components. Take mobile phones or the MPEG format (Motion Picture Expert Group), the well-known data compression technology for audio and digital video files, for example. A mobile phone allows us not only to place calls but also to take photos, listen to music or, just like a personal digital assistant (PDA), to schedule meetings; modern smartphones feature advanced computing capabilities which allow high-speed Internet access. Thanks to technological progress, the convergence of communication services and the digitisation of information, it is now possible to bring together in a single product, the mobile phone, a whole range of services that had been developed in the past for a number of different technological platforms (PDAs, cameras, MP3 players and so on). Likewise, MPEG is actually a combination of several innovations; the basic version of MPEG is covered by a series of patents belonging to more than 20 companies and institutions ranging from the Columbia University to large corporations such as LG Electronics and Philips.

These two simple examples are representative of how the innovation process develops in modern economies and in Information & Communication Technologies in particular. In these industries, follow-on inventions build on earlier innovations and, therefore, the whole process is characterised by a sequence of incremental steps where later innovations represent improvements of previous inventions.

The cumulativeness of the innovation process has important consequences on market efficiency. Initial inventions, namely those which take place during the early stages of the sequence, are highly desirable: they contribute to social welfare not only directly but also indirectly by fostering the emergence of follow-on inventions whose development, in their absence, may be delayed or may even not be possible at all.

Moreover, another feature of cumulativeness is given by the fact that by building on previous innovations follow-on inventors often need to negotiate licensing agreements in order to access relevant technologies. This is particularly evident in the case of electronics and other IT sectors where products often embed a wide range of technological components developed by other companies. Going back to our first example, it is highly unlikely for the smartphone producer to be the owner of patents protecting, for instance, the PDA, the photo camera and the data transmission protocol technologies at the same time. In this case, the producer can operate only once it has signed licensing agreements with all the companies owning the relevant technologies.

This chapter and the next one are devoted to the discussion of some of the major aspects related to the cumulativeness of innovation processes. In particular, in this chapter, we focus on the role of patenting. As we illustrate in the following sections, in modern economies, companies use patents not only to protect their innovations and to appropriate the returns of their R&D investments but also for strategic reasons. The strategic role of patents is of crucial importance in industries where innovation is highly cumulative. As mentioned above, in these industries companies often need to negotiate licensing agreements in order to access relevant technologies; in such circumstances, the ownership of sizable patent portfolios increases their bargaining power and their chances of closing "good deals". According to several commentators, the strategic use of patents is the most likely explanation for the surge in patent applications observed all over the world since the 80s.

In the following sections, after presenting some data on patenting, we proceed with a formal analysis of the optimal patent policy in the case of cumulative innovation; the remaining sections are devoted to investigating some of the most interesting issues related to licensing negotiations among different generations of inventors. In Chapter 7, we go even further by focusing on *open innovation*, an alternative approach to innovation which is becoming increasingly popular in several frontier industries. Firms adopting this approach aim at involving third parties (customers, suppliers, rival firms and research institutions) in the innovation process in order to improve it, make it faster and more fruitful.

6.2   Patents and other appropriability mechanisms

Before examining the most relevant aspects related to cumulative innovation processes, we start this chapter by discussing the alternative mechanisms which firms may use in order to appropriate the returns of their R&D investments. The main focus of this chapter is on patents; therefore, it is useful to begin our analysis by briefly reviewing the basic legal and economic aspects of patenting.

6.2.1 A guided tour through the patent office

Let's start with a brief description of the main legal features of patents. Rather than providing a comprehensive discussion on the patent system we restrict our attention to those aspects which are useful for the analysis presented in the following sections of the chapter.

A patent grants its holder a temporary monopoly position on the exploitation of an invention. In particular, the patent-holder acquires the exclusive right to prevent other parties from using, commercialising or importing the patented product or process. Therefore, thanks to patent protection, the holder can impede third parties from making an unauthorised use of the invention; for this reason patents are often said to represent a "negative right". This aspect is particularly important in the case of ICT sectors. As mentioned previously, ICT products and technologies are extremely complex and in several cases they are covered by a large number of overlapping patents. Each patent-holder has a veto power: by denying access to the single component under his control, he may prevent the use of the technology altogether; therefore, a follow-on inventor interested in accessing the various relevant technologies needs to sign licensing agreements with all the different patent-holders.

Before examining these strategic aspects related to patents, let us start by reviewing what an innovator should do in order to obtain patent protection for her invention. The first step is to file an application at the patent and trademark office (PTO). The application document contains a series of information and, in particular, the description of the invention (the so-called specification) and its claims. The specification illustrates how the invention works; it has to be detailed enough to allow an expert in the relevant technological field to replicate the invention. Patent claims, instead, determine the scope of protection granted to the patent-holder; claims are, therefore, of the utmost importance since they define patent breadth, i.e. the extent of the protection granted by the patent.

The PTO assesses whether or not the invention satisfies the requirements for patentability. In particular, PTO examiners check if the invention complies with the following requirements:

- subject-matter eligibility;

- novelty;

- non-obviousness;

- industrial applicability.

According to international patent laws, not all subject-matters can be patented. In particular, discoveries, scientific theories and mathematical methods are typically not eligible for patentability.[1] Novelty and non-obviousness are the most difficult requirements to assess. An invention is considered novel/new if it represents an advance over existing knowledge. In order to check for this requirement, examiners proceed to the so-called *prior-art search*; they examine the existing stock of knowledge by reviewing all the information available on the subject which may be contained in patents, in patent applications or in scientific and technical publications. In turn, an invention is viewed as non-obvious when it meets the so-called inventive-step standard which requires the innovation not to be a mere extension of the prior art. Finally, industrial applicability simply requires the invention to be susceptible of use in some kind of industry, broadly defined to include agriculture as well.

The review process at the PTO is usually rather long and it can take up to three years from the filing date of an application to the final decision (patent granted or rejected).[2] During this period of time, the PTO examiners may decide to meet the inventor, to ask her to modify the application and, in particular, to alter the patent claims.[3] Once the patent has been granted, the invention is protected for twenty years from the filing date of the application, provided that the patentee pays the renewal fees. As mentioned above, the patent confers the right to prevent unauthorised use of the invention. If the inventor believes that her patent has been infringed, she can go to Court in order to put the illegal use of the invention to an end and ask for damages. The lawsuit can be rather lengthy and the patentee can also ask the Court for a preliminary injunction in order to immediately restrain the third party from continuing with patent infringement. The Court may decide that there has been patent infringement (and in this case the payment of damages is imposed) or it may conclude that the patent has not been violated. It is interesting to notice, however, that the Court can go beyond the simple infringement/non-infringement decision; it can also overrule the PTO decision and invalidate the patent when it assesses that the invention does not meet the patentability requirements.

---

[1] Other subject-matters that, according to the European patent law, are excluded from patentability are software, methods for the treatment of humans and animals, plant or animal varieties and the biological processes for their production.

[2] See Harhoff and Wagner (2009) for a thorough description of the review process at the European patent office.

[3] A patent application may confer significant economic value to the holder also during the long review phase at the PTO; see Peitz and Koenen (2012) for a recent contribution on the economics of "pending patents".

Box 6.1 – The market for ideas in Europe

As highlighted by Athreye and Cantwell (2005), technology licensing has greatly increased since the 90s. In a recent work published in *Research Policy*, Gambardella et al. (2007) analyse the licensing agreements negotiated by European firms. The work is based on data taken from a survey administered to a sample of firms located in France, Germany, Great Britain, Italy, the Netherlands and Spain (the so-called PatVal-EU survey). The work is divided into two parts; in the first the authors estimate a probit model in order to establish which are the main determinants of patents being actually licensed. The results obtained are in line with the theoretical predictions and highlight the fact that the likelihood of licensing is increasing in patent breadth (proxied by the number of claims listed in each patent) and decreasing in the size of the patent-holder (therefore, larger-sized firms are less likely to license their technologies). Moreover, the authors show that there is a positive correlation between the economic value of the patent (measured in different ways such as the number of countries where the patent-holder has applied for IP protection) and the probability of the technology being traded.

The second part of the work is probably the most interesting one. The authors observe that about 11% of the patents is actually licensed while another 7% is not, even though the owners are willing to do so. Why aren't these technologies traded? There are two possible explanations: *i*) the patents protect technologies which are not very attractive and so there is no actual demand for them, *ii*) negotiations of licensing agreements are hampered by the presence of transaction costs due to the difficulty of finding licensees or due to possible information asymmetries. To identify which is the most reasonable explanation, the authors investigate the determinants of patent-holders' willingness to license. The authors do not find significant difference between the determinants of the firms' willingness to license and the actual occurrence of the licensing event. This result suggests that the characteristics of the patents which innovators are willing to license are not significantly different from those of the patents which are actually traded; the authors interpret this result as evidence of the fact that the failure to license patents is not due to their quality but instead to the presence of significant transaction costs. The authors conclude that, absent these market frictions, the market for ideas could be almost 70% larger, thus increasing the share of licensed patents from 11% to around 18%.

6.2.2 The role of patents

Patent protection grants the patent-holder a monopoly position for twenty years; in this manner, the inventor is able to collect profits to reward her investment in R&D activities. The traditional view suggests that, absent patent protection, an invention can be easily imitated by competitors; this fact inevitably reduces the profits the inventor is able to appropriate thus lowering her incentives to invest in research projects. According to the traditional view, therefore, the existence of a patent regime increases social welfare since it induces firms to invest in R&D.

Still from the society standpoint, patents may be beneficial also for another reason: they favour the diffusion of relevant information concerning the innovation. As a matter of fact, when filing the patent application the inventor has to describe her innovation accurately; she has to explain what the innovation is, how it works, what its possible uses are. This information is potentially very meaningful since it can inspire the creation of follow-on products or processes. On top of that, once the patent has expired, the innovation falls into the public domain and it can be exploited by anyone.

Patents, however, may be useful for other reasons as well. A patent is a proprietary right on an invention and, as such, it can be transferred to other firms or individuals. Clearly, in principle, even non-patented inventions may be sold or licensed. However, as observed by Arrow (1962), selling inventions is a rather complex matter. Before making the purchase, the potential buyer wants to know exactly what the innovation is and how it works. Nonetheless, the inventor may be reluctant to provide such information in great detail. If she does so, there is the risk of imitation: once the potential buyer has learned about the innovation, he can easily reproduce it without paying anything to the inventor. Patents may actually represent a solution to Arrow's appropriability problem. The inventor can describe her patented innovation in detail without fearing imitation which is prevented by the law. Therefore, according to several commentators, patents favour the emergence of the so-called "market for ideas" where innovations and technologies are traded.

The existence of a thriving market for ideas is important also because it enhances the possibility of a more efficient division of labour. Firms can specialise in the development of research projects and then sell or license their inventions to others dealing with the production and commercialisation phases. This is the case of the so-called "fabless" firms – literally firms without fabrication plants – which, for instance, operate in the chemical and semiconductor industries and deal only with the development of innovations to be sold or licensed in the market (see Arora and Fosfuri, 2000 and Hall and Ziedonis, 2001).

Finally, patents may be useful also for signalling purposes. As discussed in a recent work by Pluvia Zuniga and Guellec (2009), the ownership of a sizable patent portfolio enhances the probability of firms receiving credit from banks. In other words, in the presence of information asymmetry, patents may be useful in order to signal the creditworthiness of firms. This is especially the case of start-up firms in ICT whose reputation is unknown and whose profitability is hard to assess (see, also, Cockburn and MacGarview, 2009).

6.2.3   Other appropriability mechanisms

Even though in this chapter we focus mainly on patents, it is important to highlight that there are other mechanisms that firms may use in order to appropriate the returns of their investments in R&D.

	Secrecy	Patents	Other legal	Lead time	Comp. Sales services	Comp. Sales production
Food	58.54	18.26	21.18	53.37	39.83	51.18
Textiles	63.7	20	25.87	58.26	55.22	58.26
Paper	55	36.94	26.45	47.1	40	39.84
Printing/Publishing	32.5	12.08	21.67	48.33	66.25	60.42
Petroleum	62	33.33	6.33	48.67	40.33	35.67
Chemicals. nec	52.77	37.46	21.62	48.62	44.92	41.31
Basic Chemicals	48	38.86	11.57	38.29	45.86	44.71
Plastic Resins	55.93	32.96	18.15	38.33	44.63	46.11
Drugs	53.57	50.2	20.82	50.1	33.37	49.39
Miscellaneous Chemicals	70.69	39.66	25.52	55.52	55.17	48.97
Rubber/Plastic	56.86	32.71	10.14	40.86	34.29	37.71
Mineral Products	46.11	21.11	12.22	39.72	37.78	40
Glass	46.67	30.83	11.67	50	62.5	70
Concrete. Cement. Lime	45	30	17.5	38	45.5	40
Metal.nec	65.83	20	5	50.83	58.33	61.67
Steel	37	22	11.5	61.5	34.5	42
Metal Products	43.07	39.43	18.18	48.18	37.05	40.11
General Purp. Machinery. nec	49.19	38.78	20.88	52.23	41.15	43.65
Special Purp. Machinery. nec	45.08	48.83	23.05	59.69	46.33	51.09
Machine Tools	61.5	36	9	61	43	34.5
Computers	44.2	41	27.2	61.4	40.2	38
Electrical Equipment	39.09	34.55	15	33.41	32.27	31.82
Motor/Generator	50.91	25.23	19.09	48.86	47.27	45.23
Electronic Components	34.04	21.35	20.19	45.58	50	51.15
Semiconductors	60	26.67	22.5	53.33	42.22	47.5
Communications Equip.	47.21	25.74	20.15	65.59	42.06	41.18
TV/Radio	50	38.75	35.63	53.75	24.38	38.75
Medical Equipment	50.97	54.7	29.03	58.06	52.31	49.25
Precision Instruments	47.29	25.86	20.86	54.14	49.57	45.57
Search/Navigational Equip.	48.95	28.68	24.08	46.84	32.89	40.53
Car/Truck	42.22	38.89	19.44	65.56	41.67	42.22
Autoparts	50.83	44.35	15.65	64.35	44.84	53.06
Aerospace	55.1	32.92	16.15	58.02	34.58	46.88
Other Manufacturing	49.29	33.81	26.61	63.51	42.56	45.3
ALL	51	34.83	20.71	52.76	42.74	45.61

Table 6.1: effectiveness of appropriability mechanisms – product innovation[4]

With regard to this point it is of great interest to discuss the work by Cohen et al. (2000). The study is based on a survey questionnaire administered to 1,478 R&D labs in the U.S. manufacturing sector. The most striking result that emerges from the analysis

---

[4]Source Cohen et al. (2000).

is that the managers of the R&D labs do not consider patents as the most effective mechanism in order to profit from their innovation.

In particular, Cohen et al. (2000) examine six possible mechanisms which firms may use to appropriate the results of their R&D activities: secrecy, patents, other legal mechanisms, lead time and sales of complementary services (Comp. Sales/serv) or products (Comp. Sales/prod). The managers of the R&D labs were asked "to report the percentage of their product and process innovations for which each appropriability mechanism had been effective in protecting the firm's competitive advantage".

Table 6.1 shows the findings of the survey, where firms are grouped according to their industrial sector; the table suggests some interesting considerations. The cross-column sums add up to more than 100% and this fact suggests that firms rely on more than one mechanism to protect the same innovation. Moreover, considering all sectors together (the last row of the table, ALL), patents are the second to last mechanism with regard to appropriability effectiveness. Lead time, i.e. the fact that the inventor is the first firm able to commercialise the innovation, along with secrecy appear to be the most effective in order to benefit from the results of the R&D activities; sales of complementary products or services follow closely behind. Data at the sector level show that patents are considered to be effective for more than 50% of innovations only in the case of pharmaceutical products (Drugs) and medical equipment.[5]

6.2.4   The strategic role of patents

Figure 6.1 depicts the long-run trend in patent applications filed at the USPTO. As shown by the data, there has been a remarkable growth in the number of patents requested since the 80s. Even though the increase in patenting is common to many sectors, it is particularly strong in emerging industries such as ICT and pharmaceuticals. For instance, in the early 80s the number of patent applications filed at the USPTO in the field of *Computer and Communication Technology* represented just 5% of the total; by the late 90s this number increased to 20% (see Hall et al., 2001).

The boom in the number of applications seems to contradict the evidence illustrated in the work by Cohen et al. (2000); as discussed above, managers consider secrecy, lead time and the sales of complementary products and services more effective than patents in order to appropriate the returns from innovation. However, according to Cohen et al. (2000), this contradiction is only apparent and can be explained by the strategic role

---

[5]In a recent article focusing on registered companies in the U.K., Hall et al. (2013) report that just 4% of the firms engaged in some form of R&D have filed a patent application (at the U.K. or at the European patent office) during the period 1998–2006; the percentage reaches 16% when considering only companies in high-tech sectors.

which patents play in modern economies. As mentioned in the Introduction, technological complexity implies that in several sectors firms do not have proprietary control on all the components of the relevant technologies they need. In these cases, in order to operate, firms must negotiate licensing agreements with the owners of such technologies. A large patent portfolio is an important asset that firms may use in order to increase their bargaining power in negotiations. In many cases, firms resort to cross-licensing agreements according to which parties guarantee reciprocal access to their patented technologies;[6] the ownership of a sizable patent portfolio may be a strategic device used to reach a favourable agreement.

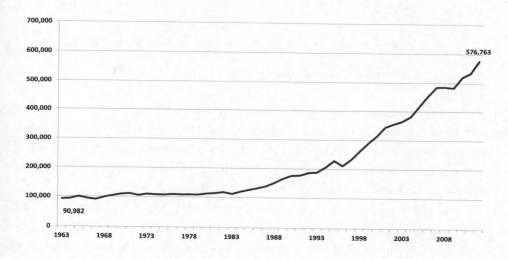

Figure 6.1: number of applications filed at the USPTO[7]

Besides enhancing bargaining power in cross-licensing negotiations, firms may stock up on patents for either defensive or aggressive motives. A large patent portfolio may represent an important defensive safeguard against the possibility of rival firms taking legal action for patent infringement; moreover, patents can also be used aggressively in order to foreclose competitors or, more generally, to hamper rival firms.[8]

---

[6]See Chapter 8, for an economic analysis of cross-licensing agreements.

[7]See www.uspto.gov.

[8]A recent article published in *The Wall Street Journal* announces a series of actions that the Obama administration plans to take against patent-holding firms which strategically abuse of the patent system and disrupt competition. In a public speech in February 2013, President Obama warned against so-called "patent trolls" and said that these firms "don't actually produce anything themselves. They're just trying to essentially leverage and hijack somebody else's idea to see if they can extort some money out of them" (Obama to move against "Patent Trolls", *The Wall Street Journal*, 4 June 2013).

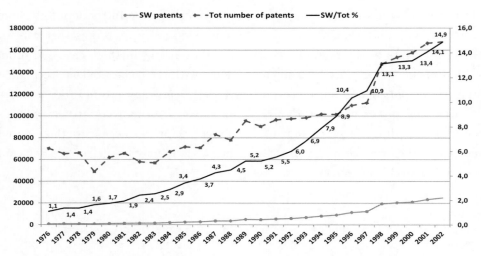

Figure 6.2: software patents granted by the USPTO[9]

The idea that patents have an increasingly important strategic role is supported by a number of empirical contributions. Among these, the work by Bessen and Hunt on software patents granted by the USPTO is particularly interesting. Figure 6.2 shows the spectacular growth in software patenting from 1976 to 2002. In 1976, 1.1% of patents were related to software; this figure increased up to 14.9% in 2002.

Table 6.2 shows the distribution of software patents per industry. Three out of four software patents belong to firms operating in manufacturing industries (28% in electronics and 24% in machinery); software publishers, namely those companies that are most likely to be involved in the development of software programs, account for only 5% of the overall number of software patents. By contrast, the share of programmers and engineers, i.e. those involved in the writing of software code, is much larger in software publishers and, more generally, in non-manufacturing sectors. Only 11% of the overall programmers and 32% of the total number of programmers and engineers are employed in the manufacturing sector. These figures suggest that there is little correspondence between software development and patent ownership. Table 6.2, therefore, confirms the relevant strategic role of patents: companies in electronics and machinery have greater propensity to patent and amass large portfolios of intellectual property rights despite employing only a small fraction of programmers and engineers.[10]

---

[9]Taken from Bessen and Hunt (2007).

[10]The relevance of the strategic role of patents is further supported by a thorough econometric analysis presented in Bessen and Hunt (2007). The two authors show that the increase in R&D investments and in the number of programmers and engineers employed offer only a partial explanation to the boom in software patenting. The greatest part of this growth can be explained by strategic motives.

	Software Patents	Programmers	Programmers and Engineers
	(a)	(b)	(c)
Manufacturing	75%	11%	32%
Chemicals	5%	1%	2%
Machinery	24%	3%	7%
Electronics	28%	2%	7%
Instruments	9%	1%	4%
Non-manufacturing	25%	89%	68%
Software Publishers and other software	7%	33%	18%

Table 6.2: the distribution of software patents[11]

According to several authors, there are other possible explanations to the boom in patenting. For instance, in the U.S. there has been an extension of the admissible subject matters: besides software, bio-tech and even business method inventions are also eligible for patenting.[12] In addition to that, a series of new procedures and institutional changes have made patenting more convenient.[13] Indeed, PTOs are now more likely to grant patents; moreover, patent protection and enforcement have become stronger during recent years. To summarise, nowadays, it is more profitable for firms to patent their inventions.

A natural question arises: what are the consequences of such growth in patenting? Some authors suggest that the quality of granted patents has seriously dropped during recent years; as we see later on in Section 6.5, many believe that patents are often granted to inventions which the PTO should immediately reject without further review. The major concern is that the strengthening of patent protection combined with the lower quality of granted patents may actually decrease incentives to invest in R&D activities. The underlying reasoning is straightforward: nowadays, due to the great number of patents in circulation, the likelihood of a firm violating one of them has increased substantially; therefore, the risk of either having to pay large licensing fees or being involved in lengthy and expensive lawsuits has now become a tangible possibility. Paradoxically, rather than stimulating innovation, in modern economies, patents may actually undermine the incentives to invest in R&D projects.

---

[11]Source Bessen and Hunt (2007).

[12]One of the most striking examples of patents covering a business method is Amazon's "one click shopping" (see Box 6.4).

[13]We refer in particular to the creation of the Court of Appeals for the Federal Circuit that in the U.S. handles appeals on patent lawsuits. See Gallini (2002) for further details.

Box 6.2 – The strategic role of patenting

The strategic role of patents in ICT is supported by a large anecdotal evidence.

Apple's Risk games.   Apple has been long known as a very tough fighter in legal battles. Since 2011, it engaged a dispute with Samsung, its main competitor in the tablet and smartphones segments. Everything began on 15 April 2011 when Samsung was sued in the U.S. District Court of California for violating Apple's IP rights on the touch screen technology and for alleged similarities in packaging and icons for apps. Samsung's reaction was immediate. Seven days later, the Korean-based company countersued Apple by filing complaints in Seoul, Tokyo and Mannheim alleging Apple's infringement of Samsung's patents for mobile communication technologies. Since then the saga continued with the two companies carrying out legal battles in more than fifty lawsuits all around the globe with billions of dollars in damages claimed between them. The ultimate costs of this legal war and how these affect consumers are at the moment unknown as the battle is still ongoing. The only thing which is certain is that these costs are not going to be negligible neither for the companies nor for consumers.

Less recently, in October 2009, Apple has been the protagonist of another famous legal battle against Nokia, the major competitor in the smartphone segment at that time. The company from Espoo sued Apple for the infringement of ten Nokia patents protecting some of the most essential aspects of Gsm, Umts and Wifi protocols. Apple immediately took counteraction against Nokia. Within a couple of months, Apple filed a lawsuit accusing Nokia of 13 patent infringements. The two companies engaged in a nearly two-year litigation in several courts before finally settling in June 2011 with a cross-licensing agreement and with Apple paying an undisclosed amount of royalties based on iPhone sales (taken from Wikipedia).

IBM vs Sun Microsystems. Gary Reback in an article published by *Forbes* in 2002 reports how patents may be used to blackmail rivals. The story goes back to the 80s and features Sun Microsystems – then a small firm – and IBM. According to Reback, IBM accused Sun of violating seven patents; in response to Sun's ar-

guments according to which the accusation was false, IBM argued: "OK, maybe you don't infringe these seven patents. But we have 10,000 U.S. patents. Do you really want us to go back to Armonk [IBM headquarters in New York] and find seven patents you do infringe? Or do you want to make this easy and just pay us $20 million? After a modest bit of negotiation, Sun cut IBM a check, and the blue suits went to the next company on their hit list." (see Patently Absurd, *Forbes* magazine, 24 June 2002).

Rembrandts in the Attic. According to Jaffe and Lerner (2004), following a series of pro-patent policies adopted in the U.S.A., companies are now much more aggressive in protecting their intellectual property. Firms file patent infringement lawsuits also for technologies they have never used. In 2000, British Telecom (BT) found out that it owned a U.S. patent concerning cross-referencing in hypertexts. Even though BT did not actually use this technology, it decided to exploit it by suing Prodigy, an Internet Service Provider, for patent infringement. Likewise, Texas Instruments has repeatedly taken legal action against several firms for the infringement of some patents protecting its integrated circuit designs. These cases of companies trying to profit from technologies which they have never used are referred to as attempts to make money out of their "Rembrandts gathering dust in the attic".

Oracle's strategy. According to Oracle's vice president Jerry Baker, it is virtually impossible to develop software products without risking patent infringement; this is the reason why Oracle is very careful in designing its patenting strategy. Baker describes the company's strategy as follows: "As a defensive strategy, Oracle has expended substantial money and effort to protect itself by selectively applying for patents which will present the best opportunities for cross-licensing between Oracle and other companies who may allege patent infringement. If such a claimant is also a software developer and marketer, we would hope to be able to use our pending patent applications to cross-license and leave our business unchanged" (taken from Boldrin and Levine, 2008).

6.3 Standing on the shoulders of giants

Traditionally, innovation has been analysed in the literature as something that takes place once and for all: an isolated event, unrelated to any innovation that may have occurred in the past and bearing no effect on possible future inventions. This approach is certainly a convenient starting point for our analysis; however, it does not capture a couple of relevant features characterising the dynamics of innovation in frontier industries.

In high-tech industries, indeed, the innovation process is highly cumulative and different generations of innovators contribute to knowledge creation. Typically, innovation in ICT proceeds along incremental steps: inventors improve technologies developed by others or modify them to allow for new applications or uses. Take the computer industry for instance. A new software application often needs functionalities which are provided in existing software packages; in these cases programmers may avoid inefficient duplications by "re-using"/incorporating pieces of the already existing source code into the new program. Likewise, as mentioned in the Introduction, due to increasing technological complexity, firms in electronics and semiconductors need to negotiate licensing agreement with the owners of the essential technologies that they use.

The cumulativeness of innovation processes combined with the complexity of modern technologies make it extremely difficult to design industrial policies aimed at stimulating R&D investments. The different generations of inventors may have conflicting interests. Consider, for instance, a policy strengthening patent rights (for example, an increase in patent length): while early inventors benefit from stronger protection of their innovations, follow-on innovators, i.e. those that use the patented technologies, may be seriously impaired by such a policy.

Let's go into greater detail. In the case of isolated innovation, patent protection stimulates R&D investments on the one hand, but it grants monopoly power to the innovator on the other; hence, the socially optimal patent policy needs to balance the (positive) effect of increased R&D incentives with the (negative) effect accruing from the deadweight loss. When innovation is cumulative, two additional effects need to be taken into account.

Early inventions create the basis for further technological improvements. Using Sir Isaac Newton's words, if we can see further "it is by standing on the shoulders of giants"; in other words, the fortunes of follow-on innovators are, to a large extent, attributable to earlier inventors.[14] Therefore the social benefit of an innovation is not only represented by its stand-alone value but it also depends on the contribution it provides to

---

[14]We can say that also this section and the following ones are de facto the result of a cumulative innovation process; the shoulders of the giants we are standing on are actually very broad. See Scotchmer (2004) for a thorough discussion on these topics.

future innovations. When the innovation process is cumulative, the R&D efforts of early inventors generate a positive externality that goes to the benefit of follow-on innovators.

One way to compensate early innovators for their contributions is by means of a stronger patent protection. In this way, in order to access the essential technologies, future inventors are required to negotiate licensing agreements with the patent-holders, thus rewarding them for the externality that they have generated. Going back to the MPEG example mentioned in the Introduction, firms that embed this data-compression technology into their products must reach an agreement with the patent-holders for the use of the underlying technological components.

This example introduces the second important aspect of the cumulative innovation process. Patent protection on initial innovations may undermine the R&D incentives of follow-on innovators: taking into account the licensing fees owed to patent-holders, follow-on inventors may not be left with enough incentives to invest. In the economics jargon, this phenomenon is known as the *hold-up* of future innovations. As we see in the next sections, the optimal patent policy crucially depends on the likelihood of future innovations being held-up. In what follows, we provide a formal analysis of the optimal patent policy; we start with the case of isolated invention and then we move to the more interesting scenario of cumulative innovation.

6.3.1 Patent policy in the case of isolated innovation

Consider a firm which is deciding whether or not to invest in a research project. The project is identified by two parameters $\{v, c\}$ which have the following interpretation: by investing an amount c in R&D the firm obtains an innovation valued at v.[15] We assume that the innovation is patentable and "isolated", namely, it is neither based on previous inventions nor is it a basis for future improvements or innovations.

After the innovation has been realised, the production/commercialisation phase takes place: the innovation is used to produce a new good to be sold to consumers. Figure 6.3 represents the market for the new product; the MC line is the marginal (and average) production cost and D is the demand function of consumers. For the sake of simplicity, we normalise to 1 the length of the commercialisation phase i.e. the life cycle of the new product.

The first step to define the optimal patent policy is to determine the social welfare generated by the innovation. We need to distinguish between two phases of the life cycle of the product depending on whether the innovation is protected by a patent or not (i.e. depending on whether the patent is still valid or has expired). Suppose that the

---

[15]As we clarify later, v is the social value of the innovation when production takes place under perfect competition.

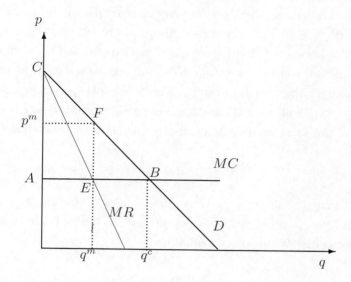

Figure 6.3: profits and social welfare – isolated innovation

innovation is not protected by a patent. In this case, competitors imitate the product and, therefore, the market becomes perfectly competitive with the equilibrium price and quantity being MC and q^c respectively. In equilibrium, all firms, including the innovator, obtain zero profits and social welfare (the sum of consumer and producer surpluses) is maximised. In Figure 6.3, social welfare equals the area of the triangle ABC; this area represents v, one of the two parameters identifying the characteristics of the research project.

Consider now what happens when the innovation is protected by a patent. Imitation cannot occur and so the innovator is the market monopolist: it produces q^m (the quantity such that the marginal production cost equals the marginal revenue, MR) and charges p^m. Therefore, as shown in Figure 6.3, the innovator's profits correspond to the area of the rectangle $AEFp^m$. The presence of a sole producer reduces social welfare down to the area $AEFC$ and so the area of the triangle EBF corresponds to the deadweight loss.

To simplify our analysis it is useful to introduce the following notation. The profits obtained by the innovator when the patent is valid can be seen as a fraction $x \in [0, 1]$ of the overall value v; therefore vx corresponds to the area of the rectangle $AEFp^m$. Similarly, the deadweight loss can be interpreted as a fraction $d \in [0, 1]$ of v; therefore, vd corresponds to the area of the triangle EBF.

Let's now determine the social welfare associated with the innovation protected by a patent of length $T \in [0, 1]$.[16] As argued above, there are two separate phases of the product life cycle: between T and 1, the patent has expired and the invention is publicly available; the market is perfectly competitive and social welfare is at its highest level, v. Between 0 and T, the patent is valid, there is only one producer and social welfare is reduced to $v - vd$. Following these arguments and recalling that the innovator bears the R&D cost c, the social welfare associated with the innovation equals:

$$T\left(v - vd\right) + (1 - T)v - c = v\left(1 - dT\right) - c. \tag{6.1}$$

The firm obtains revenues vx until instant T, namely during the period of time in which the innovation is protected by a patent and it obtains 0 afterwards. Therefore, the research project generates profits equal to:[17]

$$vxT - c. \tag{6.2}$$

How long should the patent last? In order to determine the socially optimal patent length, we need to look for the value of T which maximises social welfare (expression (6.1)) subject to the constraint according to which the R&D project is profitable (expression (6.2) greater than or equal to zero).[18]

Expressions (6.1) and (6.2) highlight that the relevant trade-off in the case of isolated innovation is between deadweight loss and R&D incentives. An increase in T extends the period of time in which the deadweight loss reduces social welfare, on the one hand, and in which the innovator collects revenues, on the other. Formally, the determination of the socially optimal patent policy (the optimal patent length) is straightforward. From the social point of view it is optimal to set T such that the revenues collected by the innovator, vxT, equal the R&D cost c. Smaller values of T are not optimal since they are not enough to stimulate the R&D investment; neither are larger values of T

---

[16]As mentioned previously, when there is no patent protection, imitation occurs and the innovator obtains zero profits. Therefore the existence of a patenting system is a necessary condition to stimulate the innovator to invest in R&D. Consequently, we determine the social value of the innovation conditional upon the presence of a patent.

[17]For the sake of simplicity, we assume that future values are not discounted.

[18]In what follows, we derive the socially optimal value of T under the assumptions that: *i)* the realisation of the project is socially desirable (i.e. expression (6.1) is positive for any patent length T), and *ii)* given a sufficiently large patent length, the revenues that the innovator is able to collect are enough to cover the initial investment c (formally, we assume that expression (6.2) is positive for some values of $T \in [0,1]$). Note that this is the most interesting case to focus on. For instance, if the innovation were not profitable, regardless of patent length, we would reach the following trivial conclusion: the innovator does not invest in R&D at all.

desirable since they increase the length of the "monopoly phase" without affecting the R&D investment decision.

The following result summarises the above arguments:

Result 1. *In the case of isolated innovation, the socially optimal patent length equals* $\overline{T} = c/vx$, *i.e. it is the value of T such that $vxT - c = 0$.*

Box 6.3 – Cumulative innovations

Innovation processes are characterised by a high level of cumulativeness in many high-tech sectors. A typical example is Microsoft Excel, the most popular spreadsheet application. Excel is based on its predecessor, Lotus 1-2-3, which, in turn, drew heavily from Visi-Calc, the first spreadsheet for personal computers (see Box 8.2 for details on the history of VisiCalc). Undoubtedly, Excel is a much more powerful application than VisiCalc; nevertheless, several functionalities available in Microsoft's product had already been developed in the late 70s by the creators of Visi-Calc.

Another relevant example of cumulative innovation is the laser, probably one of the most important discoveries of the twentieth century (see Scotchmer, 2004, for a brief history of laser). The laser was invented in the 50s by Charles Townes and his colleagues; its theoretical foundations date back to 1917, when Albert Einstein published a famous article on the quantum theory of radiation and were complemented by a series of studies on the radar technology that had been carried out during the Second World War. Townes and his team of scientists discovered a way to create energy thanks to "atom-stimulation"; initially, they invented the maser, the predecessor of the laser. After solving a series of technical difficulties and thanks to the availability of new materials, it was finally possible to develop the laser.

As reported in Scotchmer (2004), both the laser and the maser were "discoveries in search for an application": even though the inventors were aware of the potential of these new technologies, they were not able to identify an immediate application. Nowadays, laser technology is used in many fields, ranging from medicine to telecommunications, from audio (CDs) to video systems (DVDs). As documented by the site www.patentweb.de/laser/, several patent applications filed in recent years are based on laser technology; this occurred for over 1,000 patents granted by the US Patent and Trademark Office in the period 1997–2002.

6.3.2 The case of cumulative innovation

In this section, we extend the previous analysis by considering a cumulative innovation process.[19] Suppose that there are two innovators, firm A and firm B, which are deciding whether or not to undertake a research project. The two firms make their choices sequentially. Firm A is the first to choose; if it invests then firm B has the opportunity to undertake its project. On the contrary, if A does not invest then neither can B.

---

[19]We present a simplified version of the model by Green and Scotchmer published in *The RAND Journal of Economics* in 1995.

Therefore, the two projects are sequentially tied one to the other: the investment of firm A is essential for firm B to develop the second-generation project.

The two research projects have the same features as the ones described in the case of isolated innovation. Each project is identified by a pair of parameters $\{v_i, c_i\}$, with subscript $i = A, B$ denoting whether it refers to firm A's or B's project. After innovation i has been developed, the production/commercialisation phase starts, i.e. the innovation is used to realise a new product. We assume that innovation i is patentable and that, once the patent has expired, imitation occurs and commercialisation takes place in a perfectly competitive environment. Finally, we assume that product i's life cycle is normalised to 1.

For the sake of simplicity, we assume that the new products are commercialised in different markets or in different countries. This amounts to saying that firms A and B are not competing against each other.[20]

Besides patent length $T \in [0, 1]$, when innovation is cumulative also patent breadth plays a relevant role. Breadth identifies the extent to which a given patent covers the field to which it pertains; in other words, it defines the minimum size of improvements that another inventor has to make in order to develop a non-infringing innovation. Henceforth, we denote breadth by β, and we interpret it as the probability of the second innovation infringing the patent protecting the first invention; the larger β, the greater the likelihood of infringement.

In the case of infringement, firm B needs to sign a licensing agreement with the first innovator in order to sell its product.[21] If the parties do not reach an agreement then the case is brought before a Court which determines the licensing fee; we assume that the Court sets a fee equal to half of the revenues collected by the second innovator.

As in the case of isolated innovation, the inventor is able to collect revenues during the period of validity of the patent only (between times 0 and T). Once the patent has expired (between times T and 1) imitation occurs and the market becomes perfectly competitive. To sum up, the overall amount of revenues obtained by firm $i = A, B$ equals $v_i x T$.

Social value of the two innovations. The social value of the second innovation is determined in the same way as in the case of isolated invention. We distinguish between

---

[20]The results we are about to show can be extended to the case of competition between firms; see Green and Scotchmer (1995).

[21]Note that we are assuming that both innovations are patentable and that, with probability β, the second innovation violates the patent protecting the first one; in this case, the second innovation cannot be commercialised without the first innovator's permission. This scenario is usually referred to as *blocking patents*.

two phases depending on whether the patent protecting firm B's innovation is valid or it has expired. In the case the patent has expired, production is realised by a perfectly competitive industry and social welfare equals v_B; during patent validity, production is realised by the monopolistic firm B and the associated deadweight loss reduces social welfare to $v_B - dv_B$. Therefore, the social value of the second innovation equals:

$$T\,(v_B - dv_B) + (1 - T)v_B - c_B = v_B\,(1 - dT) - c_B. \tag{6.3}$$

Consider now the first innovation. As shown in expression (6.4), the social value of A's innovation is made up of two separate components: a stand-alone social value, as for the second innovation, and an "externality". This latter component accounts for the fact that the first innovation "paves the way" for the second inventor: firm B has the opportunity to undertake its R&D project only if the first innovation has been developed. Therefore, the externality component in expression (6.4) equals the social value of the second-generation invention.[22] Formally:

$$\underbrace{v_A\,(1 - dT) - c_A}_{\text{stand-alone value}} + \underbrace{v_B\,(1 - dT) - c_B}_{\text{externality}}. \tag{6.4}$$

Timing of the game. By putting all the previous arguments together, we can summarise the dynamics of the game played by the two firms as follows:

$t = 1$: the first firm to move is A which decides whether or not to realise the research project $\{v_A, c_A\}$. If the project is developed, then firm A applies for patent protection; if the project is not undertaken the game ends;

$t = 2$: if firm A realises its invention, then firm B moves and decides about its project $\{v_B, c_B\}$. Firm B takes its decision knowing whether or not its innovation violates A's patent. In the former case, before investing c_B, the second innovator negotiates a licensing agreement and pays firm A the licensing fee $L(T)$ as specified below. Once it has developed its invention, firm B applies for patent protection.

Following Green and Scotchmer (1995), we assume that licensing negotiations occur under symmetric information: the values and costs of both projects, $\{v_A, c_A\}$ and

---

[22]In the setting we are considering, the value of the externality is the highest possible: the second innovation cannot be realised without the first one. More generally, the realisation of the first innovation may simply increase the probability of the second-generation invention being developed, or it may decrease the required R&D expenditures. In these cases, the externality component equals the increase in the probability of the second innovation taking place or the reduction in R&D costs.

$\{v_B, c_B\}$, are common knowledge.[23] If parties do not reach an agreement, the dispute is settled before a Court; we assume that the Court imposes firm B a payment $L(T) = v_B xT/2$, that is, half of the revenues obtained from commercialisation.

The aim of the following pages is to determine the socially optimal patent policy in terms of patent length, T, and breadth, β.[24]

Patent policy under symmetric information

The first step to determine the socially optimal values of T and β is to characterise the behaviour of the two firms.

Let's consider what happens once the first innovation has been developed. Result 2 illustrates the conditions under which firm B invests in R&D and it also shows the licensing fee paid to the first innovator in case of infringement; Figure 6.4 provides a graphical representation of this result.[25]

Result 2. *Firm B invests in R&D if and only if the revenues from commercialisation are larger than (or equal to) the costs of the research project: $v_B xT \geq c_B$; in case of patent infringement, firm B pays firm A a licensing fee equal to:*

$$ L(T) = \begin{cases} \frac{v_B xT - c_B}{2} & if & c_B \leq v_B xT < 2c_B, \\ \frac{v_B xT}{2} & if & v_B xT \geq 2c_B. \end{cases} $$

According to Result 2, firm B undertakes its project if and only if the overall revenues generated during the commercialisation phase are larger than (or equal to) the R&D costs, $v_B xT \geq c_B$. This result is straightforward in the case of no patent infringement: firm B benefits from the overall revenues from commercialisation and, therefore, it undertakes the project provided that they are no less than c_B. More interestingly, according to Result 2, the condition $v_B xT \geq c_B$ ensures the profitability of the follow-on project also in the case of infringement, when firm B earns $v_B xT - L(T)$, i.e. the revenues from commercialisation net of the licensing fee owed to firm A. The intuition for this result is given by the fact that the failure to reach a licensing agreement corresponds to the worst possible scenario for both firms. On the one hand, firm B does not realise its innovation and it obtains zero profits; on the other hand, the first innovator does not receive any licensing fee. This implies that as long as $v_B xT \geq c_B$, the two firms

---

[23] As we clarify later on in Section 6.3.3, the assumption of symmetric information is crucial for the results of the model.

[24] As in the case of isolated invention, in our analysis we assume that the realisation of both innovations is socially desirable and that it is possible to determine T and β so that both projects are profitable.

[25] See the Mathematical Appendix for a formal proof.

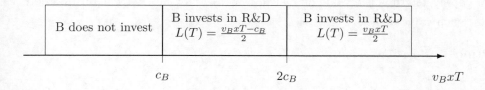

Figure 6.4: firm B's decision

benefit from agreeing on a sufficiently low licensing fee which makes the realisation of the follow-on project profitable.

Result 2 is extremely important. As mentioned at the beginning of the section, one of the most relevant aspects of the cumulative innovation process is that excessively strong patents may jeopardise future innovations, thus generating the so-called hold-up problem. Result 2 implies that, in the setting we are examining, licensing negotiations are efficient and they eliminate the risk of hold-up altogether. The condition needed to make the follow-on project profitable simply requires commercialisation revenues to cover R&D costs. The following corollary summarises this discussion:

Corollary 1. *Licensing negotiations are efficient and there is no risk of holding up the follow-on innovation.*

Result 2 is relevant also because it highlights the distinct roles played by patent length and breadth. Condition $v_B x T \geq c_B$ is necessary and sufficient to guarantee the development of the second innovation; therefore, B's decision to invest is influenced only by patent length. Patent breadth, instead, only affects how firms A and B share the revenues generated by the second innovation: a larger β increases the likelihood of infringement and, therefore, firm A's licensing fee. The following corollary summarises the above considerations:

Corollary 2. *Patent breadth affects the division of profits between the two firms but not the decision to develop the follow-on innovation.*

The previous results also have some interesting implications for the socially optimal patent policy. First of all, patent breadth does not affect the realisation of firm B's project (Corollary 2); this means that, if we focus only on the second innovation, any value of β is socially optimal. Secondly, patent length T plays a crucial role for the development of the second innovation: firm B undertakes its research project only when T is large enough to ensure that $v_B x T \geq c_B$; following the same arguments used in the case of isolated innovation, when we focus on the second innovation only, the socially optimal patent length is the value of T such that $v_B x T$ equals c_B. For future reference, we define such value of T as $\overline{T}_B$:

Definition 1. $\overline{T}_B$ *is the patent length T such that $v_B x T - c_B = 0$.*

The first innovator's decision and the socially optimal patent policy. Consider now the first innovator. Firm A collects revenues from two sources: i) it benefits from commercialising its innovation – "direct profits" in expression (6.5); ii) if the second project is developed, firm A obtains the payment of the licensing fee in the case of patent infringement – "licensing profits" in expression (6.5). Therefore, the overall profits of the first innovator are:

$$\underbrace{v_A x T}_{\text{direct profits}} + \underbrace{\beta L(T)}_{\text{licensing profits}} - c_A. \tag{6.5}$$

Clearly, expression (6.5) is increasing both in patent length, T, and breadth, β. As discussed previously, when innovation is cumulative, the realisation of the first invention is extremely desirable from the social welfare perspective. The sequence of innovations takes place if and only if firm A undertakes its project. In other words, besides its stand-alone value, the first innovation generates a positive externality which enables firm B to develop its own project. Therefore, patent length and breadth need to be defined such that firm A's research project is profitable.

In order to determine the socially optimal patent policy, we need to consider two cases: I) the first innovation generates small direct profits (v_A is small) and II) the first innovation generates large direct profits (v_A is large). Figure 6.5 provides a graphical representation of the socially optimal patent policy.[26]

Case I) The first innovation generates small direct profits. Suppose that the first innovation has little stand-alone value thus generating small direct profits (v_A small and such that $v_A x \overline{T}_B < c_A$); its value lies primarily in the fact that it paves the way for further innovations.[27] With little direct profits, firm A is willing to undertake its research project only if it benefits from substantial licensing fees, $\beta L(T)$. Licensing fees, in turn, depend on patent breadth and length; the question is, therefore, the following: from the social welfare perspective, which of the two patent dimensions is it best to manipulate in order to increase $\beta L(T)$ and to induce firm A to invest?

Patent breadth affects how the two firms share the revenues generated by the second innovation, but it does not influence neither the extent of the deadweight loss nor the

---

[26] The formal proof of the socially optimal patent policy is presented in the Mathematical Appendix.

[27] For example the first innovation may be a basic research tool which is useful to develop follow-on innovations only and which generates small direct revenues from commercialisation.

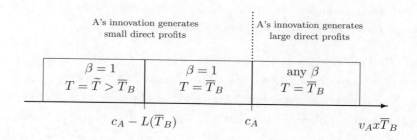

Figure 6.5: socially optimal patent policy

realisation of B's innovation (see Corollary 2). In other words, an increase in β only has the (beneficial) effect of enlarging $\beta L(T)$. Consequently, it is socially optimal to set β at the highest level as possible (i.e. $\beta = 1$) in order to stimulate the realisation of the first project. Extending patent length, instead, entails the standard trade-off between incentives to invest in R&D and deadweight loss, as described in the case of isolated innovation. Therefore, similarly to what we have seen in the previous section, it is socially optimal to set T at the minimum level that induces the first innovator to invest in R&D.

As shown in Figure 6.5, there are two possible subcases which need to be considered: a) direct profits are "very small" and b) direct profits are only "small". Consider subcase a) which emerges when the first innovation is not profitable even though patent protection is very strong, formally even though $\beta = 1$, and $T = \overline{T}_B$ (namely, patent length is sufficient to stimulate the follow-on innovation). In this case, the only way to induce firm A to invest is to increase patent length above $\overline{T}_B$; as shown in the figure, the optimal patent length is $\widetilde{T}$, defined as the value of T which allows firm A to cover its R&D costs: $v_A x \widetilde{T} + L(\widetilde{T}) - c_A = 0$, with $\widetilde{T} > \overline{T}_B$.

Consider now subcase b): direct profits are "small" but not "very small". Formally, this case emerges when the first innovation is profitable provided that $\beta = 1$ and $T = \overline{T}_B$. It is easy to see that, in this case, $\overline{T}_B$ is the socially optimal patent length. If $T < \overline{T}_B$, firm B does not invest and, consequently, the first innovator does obtain any licensing fee; clearly, neither $T > \overline{T}_B$ is desirable: under this condition the deadweight loss associated with the monopolistic position of both innovators would last longer without increasing R&D incentives (both firms invest even when $T = \overline{T}_B$). The following observation summarises these considerations:

Observation 3. *When the first innovation generates small direct profits the patent policy needs to be designed in order to guarantee large licensing profits. The socially optimal* *patent policy is such that: patent breadth is maximum ($\beta = 1$) and patent length is large enough to induce the first innovator to invest.*

Case II) The first innovation generates large direct profits. Suppose that the first project generates large direct profits: v_A large and such that $v_A x \overline{T}_B \geq c_A$; in this case, when $T \geq \overline{T}_B$, both firms invest in R&D regardless of patent breadth. Therefore, the socially optimal patent policy is easily determined: $T = \overline{T}_B$ (both firms invest) and β can take any value since it affects only the division of profits between the two innovators without any welfare effect.

Observation 4. *When direct profits are large, the first innovator invests in R&D regardless of the amount of licensing revenues. Any patent breadth is socially optimal while patent length balances research incentives with deadweight losses.*

Optimal patent length: isolated and cumulative innovation. Before concluding this section, it is interesting to examine how the cumulative nature of the R&D process affects the socially optimal patent length.

In other words, we now investigate whether cumulativeness calls for longer or shorter-lived patents in comparison to the case of isolated (non-cumulative) innovation. In order to address this issue, we compare the socially optimal patent length derived in the previous section with the socially optimal value taken by T when the two research projects are carried out by the same firm; this latter case resembles the isolated innovation scenario: it is "as if" the single inventor had the possibility of realising a research project with value $v_A + v_B$ and cost $c_A + c_B$. The main result derived from this comparison is the following:

Result 3. *The socially optimal patent length is larger when the research projects are developed by two different firms rather than in the case of a single innovator.*

The intuition underlying Result 3 goes as follows: consider the case of a single innovator; clearly, the firm can realise the second innovation without paying any licensing fee (it owns the first innovation). The overall amount of profits collected by the firm equals $v_A x T - c_A + v_B x T - c_B$. Hence, by applying Result 1, when the two research projects are carried out by the same innovator, the socially optimal patent length is the value of T such that $v_A x T - c_A + v_B x T - c_B = 0$.

If the research projects are carried out by two different firms, instead, part of the profits generated by the second innovation are enjoyed by the follow-on inventor. Consequently, firm A's profits are smaller than $v_A x T - c_A + v_B x T - c_B$; hence, if patent length T is such that $v_A x T - c_A + v_B x T - c_B = 0$, firm A's project is no longer profitable.

This observation is sufficient to say that, if the projects are carried out by two different firms, patent length needs to be larger than in the case of a single innovator in order to induce firm A to innovate. The implication of Result 3 is, therefore, of great interest: when the innovation process has a cumulative nature, patents should live longer than in the case of isolated innovation.

6.3.3 Information asymmetry and the *hold-up* problem

According to the previous model based on Green and Scotchmer (1995), when the innovation process is cumulative, patents should be broad in order to compensate early innovators for the externality they generate. A large β does not imply a deadweight loss and, as shown in Corollary 1, it does not hold future innovations up.

In their analysis, Green and Scotchmer assume that licensing negotiations occur in a context of symmetric information: both firms know costs and values of the two innovations, $\{c_i, v_i\}$, $i =$A,B. However, there are actually many factors which may complicate licensing negotiations. For instance, firms may be asymmetrically informed about costs and revenues generated by the two projects or they may have opposing views about the likelihood of patent infringement occurring. In these cases, licensing negotiations may not be as smooth as in Green and Scotchmer (1995) and parties may fail to reach a mutually profitable agreement.[28] In what follows, we extend the analysis of the previous section in order to account for the presence of asymmetric information;[29] in particular, we assume that the R&D cost of each project is private information of the innovator. As we shall see, information asymmetry may lead to inefficient licensing agreements and, therefore, the optimal patent policy derived in the previous section needs to be reconsidered.

Formally, we assume that the R&D cost of firm i, c_i, with $i=$A,B, is uniformly distributed over the interval $[0, 1]$; firm i privately observes the realisation of c_i before deciding whether or not to undertake the research project. Moreover, we assume that the realisations of c_A and c_B are statistically independent one from another; this assumption implies that by observing the realisation of the cost of its project, firm A cannot infer any information about the cost incurred by firm B and vice versa.

For the sake of simplicity, we assume that, when the patent is valid, the inventor is able to appropriate the whole social value of the innovation. Formally, the profits enjoyed by the firm until instant T equal v_i; in line with the previous notation, we are

---

[28]In a recent paper, Comino et al. (2011) show that parties do not manage to sign efficient licensing contracts simply because the first innovator is unable to observe the timing of the investment of the follow-on inventor.

[29]The following analysis is based on Bessen (2004).

considering the case where $x = 1$ and $d = 0$ (zero deadweight loss).[30] This assumption has an important consequence for the socially optimal patent policy. Since there is no deadweight loss associated with the patent, then any length T which induces firms to invest in R&D is optimal from the social welfare point of view. Therefore, without loss of generality, in what follows we assume that patent length is maximum, $T = 1$ and we focus our attention on the role of patent breadth. Note that with $T = 1$, the commercialisation of firm i's product generates profits equal to v_i.

Lastly, in the case of patent infringement, we assume that licensing negotiations are as follows: firm A makes a take-it-or-leave-it proposal and if firm B rejects it, then the Court sets a licensing fee equal to $v_B/2$, similarly to the previous section.

Negotiations and the hold-up problem. We start this section by examining whether licensing negotiations are efficient thus inducing firm B to invest. As mentioned above, we assume that the first innovator makes a take-it-or-leave-it proposal which the follow-on inventor may either accept or reject; firm A's proposal can be based only on the value v_B of the follow-on innovation and not on the cost c_B whose realisation is privately observed by firm B. In particular, in case of infringement, firm A proposes to firm B the payment of sv_B, with $s \in (0, 1)$. Clearly, since the Court imposes the payment $v_B/2$ in the case of rejection, firm B never accepts proposals characterised by $s > 1/2$; therefore, the first innovator is forced to propose $s \leq 1/2$.

Let us go into the details of the licensing negotiations. The first innovator knows that firm B accepts proposals $s \leq 1/2$ only if $(1 - s) v_B \geq c_B$, that is, only if the revenues generated by the second innovation, net of the licensing fees, are greater than (or equal to) the cost of the investment. Therefore, following the assumption that c_B is uniformly distributed over $[0, 1]$, firm A anticipates that:

- the proposal is accepted with probability $(1 - s)v_B$ (namely, the probability of the event $c_B \leq (1 - s)v_B$). In this case, firm B develops its project and pays sv_B to firm A;

- the proposal is rejected with probability $1 - (1 - s)v_B$ (namely, the probability of the event $c_B > (1 - s)v_B$). In this case, firm B does not undertake the research project and firm A does not obtain any licensing revenues.

Summing up, the licensing profits that the first innovator expects to obtain when proposing $s \leq 1/2$ are $(1 - s) sv_B^2$. By solving a simple maximisation problem, it is straightforward to check that it is optimal for the first innovator to set $s = 1/2$.

---

[30]For instance, this scenario occurs when the innovator discriminates perfectly among consumers, thus extracting the overall social welfare associated with the innovation.

This result has a couple of relevant implications. First of all, A's proposal corresponds to the payment imposed by the Court in case of disagreement. Moreover, it is straightforward to check that licensing negotiations are not efficient and do not eliminate the hold-up problem. In particular, when $c_B \in (v_B/2, 1]$, the realisation of the second innovation is socially desirable but not profitable. The following result summarises this discussion:

Result 4. *With asymmetric information about R&D costs, licensing negotiations are inefficient. If the patent owned by firm A is violated and if $c_B \in (v_B/2, 1]$, the follow-on innovation is held-up: even if socially desirable, firm B does not develop its innovation.*

Unlike the case of symmetric information, when R&D costs are privately observed, patent breadth plays a critical role in determining the likelihood of the second innovation being developed. A larger β increases the probability of the second innovation violating the patent protecting the first one; since licensing negotiations are inefficient (Result 4), a larger β increases the probability of hold-up:

Corollary 3. *With asymmetric information about R&D costs, patent breadth affects firm B's decision of developing its research project. An increase in β makes the hold-up problem more likely to occur.*

With asymmetric information, patent breadth has contrasting effects on innovation. In principle, a larger β increases the licensing revenues of firm A thus stimulating its investment; at the same time, however, it also reduces firm B's profits and, therefore, it weakens its incentives to undertake the R&D project. We discuss the role of patent breadth in greater details in the next section.

Optimal patent breadth. In order to define the socially optimal patent breadth, we need to take a closer look at the first inventor's behaviour. Firm A collects profits from two sources: direct profits from the commercialisation of its invention (these profits amount to v_A) and licensing profits in the case of patent infringement; in particular, firm A obtains licensing profits $v_B/2$ with probability $\beta v_B/2$, i.e. the probability of infringement multiplied by the probability of firm B actually undertaking its research project. It follows that firm A undertakes its project when:

$$\underbrace{v_A}_{\text{direct profits}} + \underbrace{\beta \left(\frac{v_B}{2}\right)^2}_{\text{licensing profits}} - c_A \geq 0. \tag{6.6}$$

Expression (6.6) and Corollary 3 highlight the contrasting welfare effects due to a greater patent breadth. On the one hand, an increase in β stimulates firm A's innovation:

the wider the breadth, the greater the likelihood of patent infringement and the larger the licensing profits which the first innovator expects to obtain. On the other hand, however, a wider breadth also exacerbates the hold-up problem due to the inefficient licensing negotiations (Corollary 3). The socially optimal patent breadth is obtained by appropriately balancing these two opposing effects; a simple numerical example can help us to understand better these arguments.

A simple numerical example. Consider a policy maker who sets patent breadth in order to maximise social welfare $W(\beta)$. Consistently with the assumptions of the model, we consider the case of a policy maker who does not observe the realisations of the R&D costs of the two firms; the only information available is that c_A and c_B are uniformly distributed over the interval $[0, 1]$. Therefore, the social welfare function which the policy maker maximises is as follows:

$$W(\beta) = I(II + III + IV),$$

where:

$$I = pr\left(v_A - c_A + \beta\left(\frac{v_B}{2}\right)^2 \geq 0\right), \qquad II = v_A - E\left[c_A | v_A - c_A + \beta\left(\frac{v_B}{2}\right)^2 \geq 0\right],$$

$$III = \beta pr\left(c_B \leq \frac{v_B}{2}\right)\left(v_B - E\left[c_B | c_B \leq \frac{v_B}{2}\right]\right), \qquad IV = (1 - \beta)(v_B - E[c_B]).$$

Term I denotes the probability of firm A developing its own research project; as discussed above, this event occurs when condition (6.6) holds. Term II represents the social welfare derived from the realisation of the first innovation: v_A net of the expected R&D costs of the first project, conditional on the fact that inequality (6.6) is satisfied. Finally, terms III and IV represent the social benefits associated with the realisation of the second innovation in the case of patent infringement and no patent infringement, respectively. When there is patent infringement (event which occurs with probability β), the second innovation is developed if $c_B \leq v_B/2$ and social welfare equals $v_B - E[c_B | c_B \leq v_B/2]$; if there is no patent infringement, the second innovation is always developed and social welfare equals $v_B - E[c_B]$.

Let us now determine the socially optimal value of β. For the sake of simplicity, we assume that $v_B = 1$. Since the R&D costs are uniformly distributed over $[0, 1]$, we can prove that the patent breadth which maximises $W(\beta)$ corresponds to:

$$\beta^W = \begin{cases} 1 - v_A & \text{if } v_A \leq 1, \\ 0 & \text{if } v_A > 1. \end{cases}$$

This expression shows that the socially optimal patent breadth is decreasing in the amount of direct profits of the first innovator (v_A); this result can be easily interpreted in light of what we have already discussed. Since there is no deadweight loss associated with patents ($d = 0$), the relevant trade-off which the policy maker needs to balance is the one highlighted above. As β increases there are two contrasting welfare effects: the first innovator has more incentives to invest in R&D but the probability of the second innovation being held-up increases. The socially optimal patent breadth, therefore, depends on the amount of direct profits enjoyed by the first innovator; when v_A is small, i.e. when firm A is involved in basic research activities which generate little direct profits, then β should be large enough to guarantee a sufficient amount of licensing profits in order to induce the first innovator to invest. As v_A increases, the socially optimal patent breadth reduces: the direct profits the first innovator obtains get larger and larger and this allows the policy maker to lower β in order to reduce the hold-up risk. When $v_A \geq 1$ firm A's direct profits are greater than c_A. Therefore, firm A undertakes its project no matter how much licensing profits are collected. In this case, it is socially optimal to set $\beta = 0$ in order to eliminate the hold-up problem altogether.

Before concluding the presentation of this model, it is worthwhile highlighting an important implication of our discussion. When innovation is cumulative and licensing negotiations are inefficient, it does not necessarily follow that stronger patent protection leads to larger investments in research activities. To understand this point, consider the case where v_A is large enough to guarantee the profitability of the first research project ($v_A \geq 1$); by strengthening patent protection (namely by setting a larger patent breadth) the policy maker clearly reduces the overall level of R&D activities: a larger β reduces the likelihood of developing the second innovation without increasing the first innovator's incentives.

6.4   Patent thickets and anticommons

As discussed in Section 6.2, the number of applications and patents granted by the various Patent and Trademark Offices around the world has substantially increased during recent years. This phenomenon is common to many sectors but it is particularly evident in those industries which produce technologically complex products, such as software, electronics and semiconductors. We have already mentioned in the Introduction to this chapter the MPEG technology which is covered by a large number of patents owned by different operators. Another interesting example is the technology for third generation mobile phones. As reported by Goodman and Myers (2005), the number of patents that are considered to be essential for this technology amounts to 7,796! The phenomenon of technologies protected by a large number of overlapping intellectual property rights owned by different operators is so significant that a specific expression has been coined to describe it: *patent thicket.*

The existence of numerous patent-holders may prevent the achievement of socially desirable outcomes. In a well-known study on biomedical research published in 1998 in *Science*, Michael Heller and Rebecca Eisenberg highlight the possible risks associated with patent thickets (see Heller and Eisenberg, 1998). Even though the authors do not argue against patents altogether, they suggest that overlapping property rights could seriously undermine R&D incentives. Innovators interested in using a technology covered by several patents need to negotiate licensing agreements with all the different right-holders. Time and resources needed to complete all the transactions may exponentially increase with the size of the patent thicket; as a result, access to the technology may be delayed, or even prevented and the innovation process may considerably be slowed down. This is what Heller and Eisenberg define as the *tragedy of the anticommons.*[31]

An alternative theory concerning the consequences of patent thickets has been proposed by Lichtman (2006). As opposed to Heller and Eisenberg (1998), the author argues that property right fragmentation makes licensing agreements easier to negotiate. His argument goes as follows. When ownership is highly fragmented, each patent-holder controls only a tiny part of the whole technology; therefore, the value of each single patent is smaller and this fact induces patent-holders to negotiate less aggressively (i.e they are more willing to sign licensing agreements). For this reason, a more fragmented ownership implies faster negotiations and smaller licensing payments.

At this point the following question arises: who is right? Heller and Eisenberg or Lichtman? In other words, do patent thickets slow licensing negotiations down or do they speed them up? And further, do they depress or stimulate firms' incentives to invest in R&D? These issues are extremely relevant in ICT sectors where patent thickets are very common; in order to address these topics, in the next pages we present a simplified version of the model by Galasso and Shankerman (2010).

---

[31]The tragedy of the anticommons is the mirror-image of the tragedy of the commons, and older expression used to describe the phenomenon according to which the absence of an owner regulating access to an economic resource leads to the overuse and, therefore, depletion of the resource itself. The expression was introduced by Garrett Hardin in an article published in *Science* at the end of the 60s. The commons were parcels of land in pre-industrial England which herders were entitled to let their cows graze on. The absence of an owner regulating access to the commons caused an excessive exploitation of the land which ended up being completely depleted. The tragedy of the anticommons is the opposite phenomenon which occurs when excessive ownership fragmentation leads to the underutilisation of resources/technologies.

6.4.1 Licensing agreements and patent thickets

The setting proposed by Galasso and Shankerman is as follows. There is an innovator who wants to undertake a research project based on an existing technology. The technology is covered by n patents and each patent is owned by a different firm. In order to carry out her project, the innovator needs to negotiate a licensing agreement with each of the n patent-holders. Therefore n represents the fragmentation of ownership rights: the larger n, the more fragmented the relevant technology. Galasso and Shankerman study how fragmentation affects the time the innovator needs to sign the licensing agreements.

Formally, let us assume that if the innovator reaches an agreement with all the n patentees, the research project generates profits equal to v. If licensing agreements are signed only with $m < n$ patentees, the research project can still be developed by using alternative (less efficient) technologies. Even though the innovator does not have the permission to use those parts of the technology for which agreements have not been signed, she can, in their stead, employ more obsolete technologies which are available in the public domain.[32] In this case, however, the profits generated by the innovation are lower than those enjoyed with the full set of licensing agreements. More specifically, the profits generated by the innovation are:

$$
\begin{cases}
v & \text{if } n \text{ licensing agreements have been signed,} \\
v\frac{m}{n} & \text{if } m < n \text{ licensing agreements have been signed.}
\end{cases}
\tag{6.7}
$$

These expressions show that profits are increasing in m, the number of licensing agreements which have been signed. Following the original model, we assume that there are no other costs associated with the development of the innovation, besides those related to licensing.

Fragmentation and negotiation of a single licensing agreement. Let us focus, for the moment, on the negotiations between one of the n patentees and the innovator. The two parties do not know whether the innovation violates the patent or not; nonetheless, we assume that the innovator has some kind of informative advantage in comparison to the patent-holder. In particular, we assume that the innovator privately observes the exact probability $p \in [0, 1]$ of the innovation infringing the patent; the patent-holder, instead, only knows that p is drawn from a uniform distribution over the interval $[0, 1]$.

The timing of the negotiations between the innovator and the patentee is the following:

---

[32] Alternatively, we may think that the innovator carries out some (costly) inventing-around activities in order to develop the required technologies on her own.

$t = 1$: the patent-holder makes the following take-it-or-leave-it proposal: in exchange for the payment of L the innovator is allowed to use the patented technology;

$t = 2$: the innovator decides whether or not to accept the proposal. If she accepts, the technology is licensed at L. Otherwise, the case is brought before the Court which verifies whether or not the innovator is violating the patent; in the case of infringement, the Court determines the licensing fee. When the parties go to Court, they both incur legal costs denoted by S.

According to our assumption, when parties do not reach an agreement (when the innovator rejects the patent-holder's proposal), the probability of the Court verifying that the innovation does not violate the patent is $1 - p$; in this case, the innovator is allowed to use the fraction of the technology for free. Instead, with probability p, the Court finds the innovator liable for infringement and awards damages to the patentee. Following Galasso and Shankerman, we assume that the Court determines the amount of damages on the basis of the *unjust enrichment principle*: the innovator is required to pay the difference between the profits that she obtains by using the fraction of the technology and those obtained without it. Formally, following expression (6.7), the Court establishes damages equal to $v - v(n-1)/n = v/n$; this expression represents the value of the fraction of the technology. Note that this value is decreasing in n; in other words, the more fragmented the technology, the smaller the value of each of the n parts.

As mentioned previously, the aim of the model by Galasso and Shankerman is to determine the impact of fragmentation on the total time needed to conclude licensing negotiations. Consider the single negotiation between the innovator and one patent-holder and let δ denote the time needed to sign a licensing agreement. If the innovator accepts the proposal of the patent-holder, then negotiations are very fast; in what follows we normalise to zero the time needed to sign the agreement in this case ($\delta = 0$). If the case is brought before the Court, negotiations last longer and $\delta = 1$.

Let us start with the second stage of the negotiation game ($t = 2$), when the innovator decides whether or not to accept the take-it-or-leave-it proposal. The decision is taken by comparing the expected payments in the two cases. If the proposal is accepted, the innovator pays L. If the proposal is rejected, the case is brought before the Court; with probability p the innovator is found liable of patent infringement and the Court imposes a licensing fee equal to v/n. With probability $1 - p$, according to the Court there is no patent infringement and the innovator is allowed to use the fraction of the technology for free. As mentioned above, when the case is settled by the Court the innovator incurs legal expenses S. Therefore, the innovator accepts the proposal made by the patentee if $L \leq pv/n + S$, that is:

$$p \geq (L - S)n/v; \tag{6.8}$$

clearly, the innovator accepts the proposal if the probability of the Court verifying patent infringement is high.

Let us now move back to the first stage of the negotiation game $(t = 1)$. The patent-holder only knows that the probability of patent infringement, p, is drawn from a uniform distribution over the interval $[0, 1]$; therefore, when proposing the payment L, the patent-holder expects to obtain:

$$\pi(L) = \underbrace{\left(1 - (L - S)\frac{n}{v}\right) L}_{\text{expected licensing revenues}} + \underbrace{\int_{0}^{(L-S)\frac{n}{v}} \left(p\frac{v}{n} - S\right) p.}_{\text{expected revenues with the Court's intervention}}$$

With probability $(1 - (L - S)\, n/v)$, namely the probability of condition (6.8) being satisfied, the innovator accepts the proposal and pays L. With complementary probability, when p falls between 0 and $(L - S)\, n/v$, the innovator rejects the proposal, the case is brought before the Court and the patentee obtains pv/n net of the legal expenses S.

By differentiating $\pi(L)$ with respect to L, after some algebraic manipulation, we determine the licensing proposal of the patent-holder: $L^* = v/n - S$. Note that the proposal depends on the degree of ownership fragmentation of the technology (namely it depends on n); the following result highlights the effect of fragmentation on L^*:

Result 5. *The higher the degree of ownership fragmentation of the technology, the lower the licensing payment proposed by the patent-holder; formally L^* is decreasing in n.*

The patent-holder knows that if the proposal is rejected, then the case is brought before the Court; the patent-holder incurs the legal expenses S and, with probability p, he receives v/n as compensation damages for patent infringement. Consequently, the greater the fragmentation the smaller the amount of damages he receives. For this reason, the benefit deriving from "going to Court" reduces with fragmentation; hence, as n gets larger, the patentee lowers L^* in order to reduce the likelihood of the innovator rejecting the proposal. In other words, the patent-holder becomes less aggressive during negotiations as n increases.

Once L^* has been determined, we can calculate the probability of the proposal being accepted and, therefore, the expected length of negotiations between the innovator and the patent-holder. More specifically, by substituting L^* into (6.8), it follows that parties reach an agreement provided that $p \geq p^* = 1 - 2Sn/v$; in this case, the length of the negotiations between the innovator and one patent-holder is $\delta = 0$. When $p < p^*$, the innovator rejects the proposal, parties go to Court and licensing negotiations last $\delta = 1$. Consequently, the expected length of negotiations is:

$$E\left[\delta\right] = 1 \int_{0}^{p^*} 1 dp + 0 \int_{p^*}^{1} 1 dp = 1 - 2S\frac{n}{v}. \tag{6.9}$$

From expression (6.9), we derive the following result:

Result 6. *The higher the degree of ownership fragmentation of the technology, the shorter the expected length of negotiations between the innovator and each single patent-holder; formally, $E[\delta]$ is decreasing in n.*

The interpretation of this result is straightforward. From Result 5, we know that the higher n the smaller the value of each single negotiation. As a consequence, the patent-holder behaves less aggressively in order to reduce the probability of a legal dispute; this explains why greater fragmentation speeds negotiations up.

Galasso and Schankerman (2010) test Result 6 by using U.S. data on patent litigations. For each patent which has been litigated before Court, the two authors calculate the length of negotiations as the difference between the date in which the case is brought in front of the Court and the date in which the dispute is actually settled; this difference is the dependent variable in their analysis. Among the various regressors, the one which is of greatest interest is related to ownership fragmentation of the relevant technology; Galasso and Shankerman measure this variable on the basis of a careful examination of patent documents. Interestingly, the authors find support for Result 6: negotiations are faster when the ownership of the technology is highly fragmented.

Fragmentation and total negotiation time. The previous arguments seem to support Lichtman's conjecture: the more fragmented the ownership of the technology, the faster the negotiations between the innovator and a patent-holder. However, so far, we have considered one licensing negotiation only; in order to determine which view, Lichtman's or the anticommons, is the correct one, we need to consider the total negotiation time. An increase in n means that the number of licensing agreements which an innovator needs to sign becomes larger. This implies that even if negotiations for a single licensing agreement do not last very long, the total time spent by the innovator to negotiate with the entire range of patent-holders may increase with n.

In order to compute the total negotiation time, we need to make some additional assumptions concerning how negotiations proceed. More specifically, we consider the two following polar scenarios: i) the innovator negotiates all the n licensing agreements at the same time (minimum length of negotiations) and ii) negotiations are sequential, that is, they are completed one at a time (maximum length of negotiations).

In the first scenario, total negotiation time corresponds to expression (6.9). Therefore, in this case Lichtman's conjecture is confirmed. Consider now scenario ii), where negotiations are sequential; in this case, negotiations last n times the length of each single negotiation: $nE[\delta]$. Therefore, by simply differentiating $nE[\delta]$ with respect to n, we can compute the effect of fragmentation on the total negotiation time:

$$\frac{\partial \left(nE[\delta]\right)}{\partial n} = \underbrace{E[\delta]}_{\text{thicket effect} >0} + \underbrace{n\frac{\partial E[\delta]}{\partial n}}_{\text{Lichtman effect} <0}. \tag{6.10}$$

The first term of the derivative is positive and represents the so-called "thicket effect": as n increases, so does the number of negotiations, thus augmenting total negotiation time. The second term, instead, is negative and corresponds to the so-called "Lichtman effect", as highlighted in Result 6. Which effect dominates is a priori not clear; with sequential negotiations the impact of technology fragmentation is, therefore, ambiguous. The dispute between the supporters of Lichtman's conjecture and the "fans" of the anticommons remains still unsettled.[33]

6.5   How strong are weak patents?

Several commentators argue that the surge in the number of patents granted in recent years by PTOs has led to a substantial decrease in the quality of protected inventions. A prime example of the decrease in the quality of patented technologies is the U.S. patent no. 5.443.036, entitled "Method of exercising a cat", issued in August 1995; Figure 6.6, taken from the original patent file, shows how the invention works. According to the abstract, the invention consists in:

> a method for inducing cats to exercise consisting of directing a beam of invisible light produced by a hand-held laser apparatus onto the floor or wall or other opaque surface in the vicinity of the cat, then moving the laser so as to cause the bright pattern of light to move in an irregular way fascinating to cats, and to any other animal with a chase instinct.

This patent is rather odd, to say the least. However, it is not the only example of "naive" patents. Among the many examples, we can also find patents protecting peanut-butter sandwiches or others concerning anti-gravity machines and technologies which allow you to travel faster than the speed of light![34]

These examples are all signals of a rather worrying phenomenon: more and more often patent protection is granted to obvious and useless technologies which PTOs, instead,

---

[33]Galasso and Shankerman's estimations are based on data concerning single licensing negotiations; for this reason, these data are not completely appropriate to fully evaluate the sign of expression (6.10). Nonetheless, according to their understanding based on some indirect assessments of the phenomenon, they believe that the Lichtman effect dominates; consequently, ownership fragmentation seems to speed negotiations up. See Galasso and Shankerman (2010) for greater details.

[34]See Jaffe and Lerner (2004) and Lemley et al. (2005).

should reject immediately. Joseph Farrell and Carl Shapiro, two eminent scholars in the field, refer to *weak patents* in these cases.

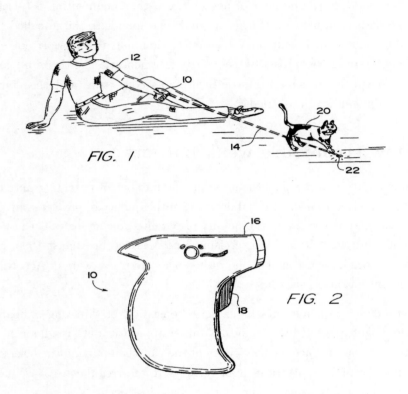

U.S. Patent   Aug. 22, 1995   5,443,036

FIG. 1

FIG. 2

Figure 6.6: United States Patent n.5.443.036

What is going wrong with the current patent system? Many authors have stressed that, in recent years, the number of patent applications has boomed. The workload of Patent Offices has substantially increased and the amount of time PTO examiners devote to reviewing each application has been greatly reduced.[35] According to Lemley and Shapiro (2005), even if it usually takes from two to three years for a patent to be

---

[35] Caillaud and Duchene (2011) study the overload problem at the PTO and show that, for a large set of parameter values, multiple equilibria co-exist. In particular, the two authors prove the existence of a low-R&D equilibrium where: firms invest little in research activities, they file patent applications also in the case of obvious innovations and the (congested) PTO grants weak patents with large probability.

granted or rejected, on average, a patent examiner spends only 18 hours per application to search for prior art, to conduct interviews with the applicant's attorney, to write reports, and so on. This time is clearly not enough for the application to be examined in detail.

Another reason why the figures of granted patents has soared is due to the fact that patent offices are financed through application and renewal fees; clearly, this way of financing induces PTOs to increase the number of examined applications and to reduce the time devoted to the review process. Finally, according to some commentators, weak patents are also granted because of the remarkable technological complexity of many frontier industries; in these cases, it may be extremely difficult for the examiners to assess whether an innovation is truly new and non-obvious.

In any case, regardless of which explanation is the most reasonable, it is a fact that an increasing number of patents can be classified as weak. It is therefore interesting to study the effects and the implications of the presence of weak patents and, eventually, to find out how to limit this phenomenon.

Following Lemley et al. (2005), patents protecting absurd technologies, such as those described above, do not have any practical effect: these technologies will never be used nor embedded in follow-on innovations. According to this argument, we could simply ignore weak patents. However, this view is probably too optimistic. Leaving the most extreme cases aside, weak patents protecting useless/absurd technologies might entail significant consequences for the functioning of markets.

Consider, for instance, the relationship between the holder of a weak patent and a (potential) innovator willing to use the patented technology. Both parties are aware that, in case of litigation before Court, the review process is very thorough and, therefore, the patent is likely to be invalidated. According to some observers, the fact that licensing negotiations occur in the shadow of litigation implies that the patent-holder cannot demand large fees for the use of his technology. As a consequence, it is true that weak patents entail very little effects and we should not be too concerned with their existence. Moreover, in order to reduce the number of weak patents, PTOs should spend much more time and resources in order to improve the entire screening process; the increase in costs deriving from closer scrutiny is likely to exceed the benefits of mitigating the problem generated by weak patents. However, this encouraging view of weak patents may fail in many realistic contexts. This seems to be the case, for instance, of the long-lasting legal dispute between Amazon and Barnes & Noble briefly described in Box 6.4: a patent protecting a barely innovative business method has generated large inefficiencies related to the huge litigation costs incurred by the two firms.

Box 6.4 – 1-Click shopping *vs* Express Lane

In the Autumn of 1997, Amazon filed a patent application to protect the invention known as *1-Click shopping*. The invention consists in a method for placing instant on-line purchases by storing customer information, including a unique ID number, within a cookie. Users are then able to purchase by associating their ID with their credit card information that has already been stored on Amazon's server; customers need to enter their credit card and address information only once and when they return to the website, only a single mouse-click is needed to make purchases. This was considered a controversial business method right from the very beginning; according to many experts and commentators, the invention was very similar to other on-line payment methods and, in any case, it was of limited technical content.

Nonetheless, on the 28 September 1999, two years and one week after the application was filed, Amazon was granted U.S. patent n. 5,960,411. Just twenty-three days after the 1-Click patent was issued, Amazon filed a lawsuit in the Federal District Court of Seat-tle against Barnesandnoble.com (B&N here-after), a rival on-line bookseller and its largest competitor. Amazon's goal was to stop B&N from using its *Express Lane* shopping process on the grounds of patent infringement. At that time, B&N offered its customers two purchasing options. The first was a virtual *Shopping Cart* and the second was Express Lane. This latter option allowed pre-registered customers to purchase a book via a single click of the mouse. The key enabler was a cookie that allowed B&N's server to recognise purchasers and relate their orders to specific credit and shipping information previously stored on the company's server. According to Amazon, this violated its 1-Click patent. On the 1 December 1999 the Court sided with Amazon and granted a preliminary injunction against B&N which was ordered to remove Express Lane from the company website. Not surprisingly, B&N appealed and a long and heated legal battle began.

The case was settled two years later when Amazon and B&N reached an undisclosed agreement.

The whole picture concerning the effects of weak patents is very complex. It is undoubtedly true that patents protecting useless or absurd inventions do not have any practical consequences; clearly, for these cases, it is neither desirable nor convenient to enhance the examination process. The crucial issue is, therefore, to determine which applications need to be carefully examined by the patent offices. A promising way of improving the review process is by means of a greater involvement of those subjects who are more likely to have relevant information concerning the invention. One of the proposals which is currently being discussed is a two-tiered patent system in which two patent regimes coexist: *i*) a gold-plated patent regime in which the application is examined with closer scrutiny by the PTO and which guarantees stronger rights in the case of acceptance, and *ii*) a second, "regular", patent regime, where applications are more summarily reviewed and provided with weaker patent protection. In such a two-tiered patent regime, it is the inventor herself that reveals relevant information when selecting which patent regime to opt for; for instance, when she believes that her invention is highly valuable, then she probably applies for a gold-plated patent.[36]

Another proposal aimed at involving third parties in the review process is to establish a more effective opposition system. For example, in Europe, within the nine months after grant, other parties (for instance competitors) can challenge the validity of the patent on the basis of some evidence that they provide; the patent office evaluates the opponents' arguments and then decides whether to confirm or to revoke the validity of the patent.

Recently, Joseph Farrell and Carl Shapiro have presented an interesting theoretical analysis concerning the effects of weak patents; in the following section, we present a simplified version of their work. The main question which the two authors address is the following: when (i.e. for what kind of innovations) is a more meticulous examination of patent applications desirable?

6.5.1   The model by Farrell and Shapiro

Farrell and Shapiro (2008) present a model which moves from the two stylised facts emerging from our previous discussion. The first concerns the behaviour of the PTO. Examiners devote a limited amount of time to reviewing each application; as a consequence, the risk of granting patents to obvious applications is high. More specifically, a technology may be granted patent protection under two different circumstances:

1. the technology is a "true innovation" that fulfils the novelty and non-obviousness requirements. Clearly, since no similar inventions actually exist, the application makes it through the PTO screening process;

2. the technology does not meet the novelty or the non-obviousness standards and, therefore, it is a "false innovation". The PTO does not find any similar inventions due to the poor accuracy in the prior art search; therefore, the patent is erroneously granted.

The second stylised fact which Farrell and Shapiro take into account concerns the review process in the case of patent litigation. When opponents challenge the validity of the patent, the Court proceeds with a very thorough examination in order to decide whether to confirm or to revoke the patent. Consequently, the decision taken by the Court is much more accurate than the one taken by the PTO.

---

[36] Atal and Bar (2013) present a theoretical model to investigate the consequences of a two-tiered patent system. The authors show that the introduction of a second patent tier reduces the incidence of weak patents; however, inventors of economically more significant innovations do not necessarily apply for gold-plated patents.

True innovations, false innovations and PTO scrutiny. Let us now move to the model by Farrell and Shapiro and consider the case of a technology which may be granted patent protection. Suppose that the probability of the technology being a "true innovation" is $\theta \in (0,1)$. With probability $1 - \theta$, the technology replicates the same/similar functionalities of some existing technology and it is, therefore, a "false" innovation.

The PTO review process is not perfect. True innovations are always granted patent protection; however, in some cases, also false innovations are erroneously approved by the PTO. Hereafter, the probability of the PTO correctly deciding to reject an application for a false innovation is denoted by $\alpha \in [0,1]$; hence, $1 - \alpha$ represents the probability of the office making mistakes and erroneously granting patent protection to a false innovation. The parameter α measures the scrutiny of the PTO's examination process: the higher α, the more thorough the process. Note that since $1 - \theta$ is the probability of the technology being a false innovation, then $(1 - \theta)(1 - \alpha)$ represents the probability of the PTO granting a patent to a false innovation.

Following our previous arguments, perfect screening by the PTO should result in patents granted with probability θ (the probability of a technology being a true innovation); however, since the PTO's examination process is imperfect, the actual probability of a patent being granted is larger and equal to $\theta + (1 - \theta)(1 - \alpha)$. Therefore, by applying Bayes' rule, we can determine the probability of a patented technology being a true innovation:

$$\tilde{\theta} \equiv \frac{\theta}{\theta + (1 - \theta)(1 - \alpha)}.$$

In what follows, we refer to $\tilde{\theta}$ as the "quality" of the patent, that is the probability of it protecting a true innovation. Clearly, the closer the scrutiny of the PTO, the higher the quality of the patent: as α increases so does $\tilde{\theta}$; furthermore, when $\alpha = 1$, then the patented technology is certainly a true innovation, $\tilde{\theta} = 1$.

Consider now the Court which decides on patent validity in case of litigation; its review process is much more accurate than that of the PTO. For the sake of simplicity, we assume that the Court's examination process is perfect so that it always assesses correctly whether the patented technology is a true or a false innovation. Therefore, the probability of the Court confirming patent validity equals $\tilde{\theta}$, the quality of the patent; on the contrary, $1 - \tilde{\theta}$ is the probability of the Court ruling the patent invalid and, hence, overturning the PTO's decision.

When $\alpha < 1$, we say that the patent is weak: the PTO grants protection also to false innovations and, therefore, in case of litigation, the Court rules the patent invalid with probability $1 - \tilde{\theta} > 0$. If $\alpha = 1$, we say that the patent is "strong": it protects a true innovation and it is never ruled invalid by the Court.

The model. We can now analyse in greater detail the model by Farrell and Shapiro. Consider an industry made up of a research laboratory, denoted by R, and $n \geq 1$ downstream firms. The lab owns a patented technology which the downstream firms need to use in order to produce; the patent protecting the technology is of quality $\tilde{\theta} \leq 1$.

For the sake of simplicity, we assume that the lab does not operate in the downstream market; its only revenues accrue from the fees obtained by licensing the technology to the n firms. We also assume that the only costs incurred by the downstream firms are the licensing fees paid to the lab. Finally, demand in the downstream market is linear, $p = a - bQ$, with p denoting the price and Q the total quantity produced by the n firms.

The timing of the game is the following:

$t = 1$: the lab proposes a non-exclusive licensing contract to each of the n firms. The contract takes the form of a two-part tariff, $L(q) = F + rq$, where F is a fixed payment and r is a per-unit royalty; therefore, when producing a quantity q, the total amount of royalties a firm owes the lab equals rq. We also assume that the lab cannot discriminate among firms; in other words, it has to offer the technology to all the n firms under the same contractual conditions;

$t = 2$: each firm decides whether or not to accept the proposal of the laboratory. In case of acceptance, the firm sells its product to consumers and pays $L(q)$ to the lab. The firm may still decide to use the technology even after rejecting the licensing proposal; in this case, the lab may bring the firm before the Court for alleged patent infringement. In line with the previous discussion, the Court confirms patent validity with probability $\tilde{\theta}$; in this case, the firm cannot use the technology and, as a consequence, it must stop production. With probability $1 - \tilde{\theta}$, the Court rules the patent invalid and, therefore, the n firms are allowed to use the technology for free;

$t = 3$: firms decide how much to produce. When $n \geq 2$, firms compete *à la Cournot*.

We assume that the probability $\tilde{\theta}$ is common knowledge: both the lab and the firms observe patent quality. Moreover, we also assume that litigation before the Court is costless (legal expenses are normalised to zero). This second assumption has two relevant consequences. First, if there is alleged patent infringement, the lab always brings the case before the Court. Second, after rejecting the licensing proposal, it is optimal for a downstream firm to use the technology anyway. The firm cannot produce if it does not use the technology; alternatively, by employing the lab's technology the firm earns positive expected profits: the Court may rule the patent invalid thus making the technology freely available.

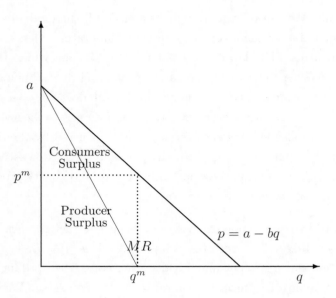

Figure 6.7: vertically integrated monopoly

As mentioned previously, the aim of Farrell and Shapiro is to analyse the economic consequences of weak patents and, in particular, to determine whether or not a more thorough examination process by the PTO is socially desirable. In order to do so, we start by presenting the benchmark case of a vertically integrated monopoly; in other words, we consider a single firm which both owns the patented technology and is the only operator in the downstream market.

Benchmark: vertically integrated monopoly.   Being the vertically integrated monopolist the owner of the technology, it operates with zero (marginal and total) costs. Therefore, its profits equal $(a - bq)q$. Figure 6.7 illustrates the profit maximisation problem of the monopolist: the firm produces the quantity q^m such that the marginal revenues MR equals the (zero) marginal costs of production.

After some algebraic manipulation it is straightforward to check that the optimal monopoly quantity and price are:

$$q^m = \frac{a}{2b}, \quad \text{and} \quad p^m = \frac{a}{2}.$$

Producer surplus (i.e. monopoly profits) equals $PS^m = a^2/4b$, while consumer surplus is $CS^m = a^2/8b$. Therefore, social welfare in the case of a vertically integrated monopoly is:

$$W^m = CS^m + PS^m = \frac{3a^2}{8b}.$$

Market equilibrium and social welfare. Let's consider now the case of n downstream firms and one upstream lab, R. The first step to determine the market equilibrium is to define under which conditions a downstream firm accepts the lab's proposal, provided that all the other $n - 1$ firms have accepted it; clearly, the firm decides whether to accept or reject the proposed licensing contract by comparing the profits it obtains in the two cases.

If the firm accepts the proposal, provided that all the remaining firms do the same, then competition takes place between n identical firms characterised by the same marginal cost, r, the royalty charged by the lab for each unit of output. Therefore, in this case, the firm chooses the quantity q which maximises its profits, $(a - b(q + Q_{-i}))q - rq - F$, where Q_{-i} denotes the total quantity produced by the other $(n - 1)$ firms.

Since firms are symmetric, the quantity produced by each of them, as well as the market price, can be easily determined:[37]

$$q(r) = \frac{a - r}{b(n + 1)}, \qquad p(r) = \frac{a + nr}{n + 1}. \tag{6.11}$$

Clearly, these expressions depend on the royalty rate r. By substituting $q(r)$ and $p(r)$ into the profit function, we derive the profits of a downstream firm when it accepts the contract proposed by the laboratory:

$$\pi(r) - F, \quad \text{where} \quad \pi(r) \equiv \frac{1}{b}\left(\frac{a - r}{n + 1}\right)^2.$$

Suppose the firm rejects the licensing proposal. As explained previously, the firm uses the technology without the lab's permission; consequently, the lab brings the case before the Court for alleged patent infringement. With probability $\tilde{\theta}$ the Court confirms the validity of the patent and imposes the downstream firm to stop production; in this case the firm earns zero profits. With probability $(1 - \tilde{\theta})$, the Court rules the patent invalid and, therefore, the technology becomes publicly available and can be used for free by any firm. Formally, patent invalidation is equivalent to a zero-fee licensing contract ($r = 0$ and $F = 0$) and, therefore, firm's net profits equal $\pi(0)$. Summing up, if the firm rejects the licensing proposal, its expected profits are $\tilde{\theta}0 + (1 - \tilde{\theta})\pi(0)$.

Now we can determine whether or not the downstream firm accepts the labs' proposal; by using the expressions derived above, it follows that the firm accepts the proposal if:

$$\pi(r) - F \geq (1 - \tilde{\theta})\pi(0). \tag{6.12}$$

---

[37]Expressions (6.11) are the standard output and the equilibrium market price for the firms in the case of a Cournot oligopoly with n active firms producing with marginal cost r.

Consider now the laboratory deciding which licensing contract to propose to the n firms. R chooses the royalty rate and the fixed part of the tariff in order to maximise licensing revenues, under the constraint according to which each downstream firm is induced to accept the proposal (formally condition (6.12) must be satisfied). Therefore the maximisation problem of the lab is as follows:

$$\max_{r,F} \quad n\left(rq\left(r\right)+F\right)$$

$$s.t. \quad \pi\left(r\right)-F \geq (1-\tilde{\theta})\pi\left(0\right).$$

The laboratory knows that once the contract has been signed, a downstream firm produces $q(r)$; therefore, the licensing revenues collected from each downstream firm equal $rq(r) + F$. This expression is increasing in the fixed part of the tariff; as a consequence, the laboratory optimally sets F at the largest possible level, that is the level such that each downstream firm is indifferent between accepting or rejecting its proposal. Formally:

$$F = \pi\left(r\right) - (1-\tilde{\theta})\pi\left(0\right). \tag{6.13}$$

Following expression (6.13), the maximisation problem of the lab becomes:

$$\max_{r} \quad n\left(rq\left(r\right) + \pi\left(r\right) - (1-\tilde{\theta})\pi\left(0\right)\right).$$

The optimal royalty r^* is obtained by solving the first order condition of the above maximisation problem:

$$r^* = \frac{a}{2} - \frac{a}{2n}.$$

By substituting r^* into expression (6.13), we determine the optimal value of F:

$$F^* = \frac{a^2}{4} \frac{1 + n\left(2 + n(4\tilde{\theta} - 3)\right)}{n^2\left(1+n\right)^2 b}.$$

Moreover, by plugging r^* into expressions (6.11) we find the equilibrium price and quantity in the downstream market:

$$p^* = \frac{a}{2}, \quad \text{and} \quad Q^* = \frac{a}{2b}.$$

Quite interestingly, these expressions correspond to the ones in the benchmark. This fact implies that, by appropriately setting r and F, the lab is able to replicate the same outcome of a vertically integrated monopolist. It is important to stress that this result has been obtained regardless of patent quality: the vertically integrated monopoly outcome emerges also when patents are very weak (α close to 0 and $\tilde{\theta}$ approaching θ).

Clearly, since the equilibrium prices and quantities coincide, then also consumer and producer surpluses, as well as social welfare, are the same as in the benchmark; therefore, they are given by expressions CS^m, PS^m and W^m, respectively.

Result 7. *Regardless of patent quality (no matter what values α and $\tilde{\theta}$ take), the lab sets r and F in order to replicate the market equilibrium of the vertically integrated monopoly; equilibrium price, quantity and social welfare are p^m, q^m and W^m, respectively.*

Result 7 can be interpreted on the basis of the standard theory of two-part tariffs in vertically related markets. According to this theory, the two parts of the nonlinear price serve different purposes. The variable (per-unit) part is used to manipulate the marginal cost of the downstream firms and, therefore, it is employed in order to affect the equilibrium price. The fixed part of the tariff, instead, is used to extract profits from the downstream firms without affecting market equilibrium. More specifically, in the setting we are examining:

i) R sets the royalty at a level such that the equilibrium price in the downstream market corresponds to the one which emerges in the case of a vertically integrated monopoly; in this way, the lab maximises producer surplus. This can be observed in expression r^*: the optimal royalty is 0 if $n = 1$ and it increases with the number of downstream firms. With only one downstream firm the market is monopolised; by setting $r^* = 0$, R induces the downstream firm to set a price equal to p^m. As n increases, the market becomes more and more competitive and, consequently, the equilibrium price lowers beneath p^m. In order to compensate the effect of fiercer competition, the lab increases r^*; in this way, downstream firms face a larger marginal cost and they are induced to charge a higher price. In equilibrium, the increase in r^* exactly compensates the effect of fiercer competition and the market price is still p^m;

ii) once producer surplus has been maximised through the royalty, the lab uses the fixed part F in order to extract the largest possible amount of rents from the downstream firms. One can note that F^* is increasing in the probability of the patent being ruled valid by the Court, $\tilde{\theta}$ (i.e. patent quality). A large $\tilde{\theta}$ reduces the expected profits that downstream firms obtain when rejecting the proposal, $(1 - \tilde{\theta})\pi(0)$; hence, in this case, firms are more willing to pay a larger F^* to use the technology. It is also interesting to note that, in some circumstances, it may be optimal for the lab to propose a contract with $F^* < 0$; in other words, in some cases, the lab may propose to pay a fixed amount of money to each downstream firm. The reason for this is the following. As highlighted in point i), with many downstream firms, the laboratory chooses a very large royalty in order to induce them to charge p^m; clearly, the downstream firms are willing to accept a contract specifying substantial royalties only if they are compensated through negative fixed payment, $F^* < 0$.

We can now address the central issue tackled by Farrell and Shapiro (2008): is it socially desirable to have the PTO examining patent applications with greater scrutiny? In what follows, we analyse this question from two perspectives: an *ex post* perspective according to which the lab has already developed the technology and an *ex ante* perspective where we consider the incentives to develop the technology.

PTO scrutiny and social welfare

What is the effect of a closer PTO scrutiny when reviewing patent applications? As discussed above, as α increases, the probability of the PTO erroneously granting patents to false innovations lowers. Therefore, to answer the question we need to compare social welfare when the patent is granted and when it is not.

Suppose that the laboratory has already developed its technology and it has filed a patent application; the probability of the technology being a true innovation is θ. As explained at the beginning of this section, with probability $\theta + (1 - \theta)(1 - \alpha) = 1 - \alpha(1 - \theta)$ the PTO grants patent protection; in this case, from Result 7, we know that social welfare equals W^m. When the patent application is rejected (event occurring with probability $\alpha(1 - \theta)$) the technology becomes publicly available and it can be used for free by any of the downstream firms. Following expressions (6.11), we know that, absent patent protection, each firm produces $q(0) = a/b(n + 1)$ at $p(0) = a/(n + 1)$; the total quantity produced by the n firms amounts to $na/b(n+1)$ and social welfare is $\overline{W}(n) = [na^2 (2 + n)]/[2 (1 + n)^2 b]$. It is straightforward to check that:

- $\overline{W}(1) = W^m$: when there is only one downstream firm, social welfare is the same as in the case of a vertically integrated monopolist;

- $\overline{W}(n)$ increases in n: the more competitive the market, the larger the social welfare.

Given α, which measures the scrutiny of the PTO's examination process, the expected social welfare is a weighted sum of W^m and $\overline{W}$:

$$E[W] = (1 - \alpha(1 - \theta))W^m + \alpha(1 - \theta)\overline{W}(n),$$

with probability $1 - \alpha(1 - \theta)$ the patent is granted and, therefore, social welfare is W^m, while it equals $W(n)$ in case of rejection (event which occurs with probability $\alpha(1 - \theta)$).

By differentiating $E[W]$ with respect to α we determine the welfare effect of a closer scrutiny by the PTO:

$$\frac{dE[W]}{d\alpha} = (1 - \theta) \left(\overline{W}(n) - W^m\right).$$

Clearly a larger α increases social welfare if $\overline{W}(n) > W^m$. A more thorough examination by the PTO increases the probability of rejection; therefore, it becomes more likely for social welfare to equal $\overline{W}(n)$ rather than W^m.

By comparing $\overline{W}(n)$ and W^m, we derive the following result:

Result 8. *When the PTO reviews patent applications more thoroughly, expected social welfare: a) does not change if $n = 1$ ($\overline{W}(1) = W^m$); b) increases when $n > 1$, (as $\overline{W}(n) > W^m$, when $n > 1$).*

According to Result 8, the social desirability of a more rigorous examination by the PTO crucially depends on the number of downstream firms. In particular, if $n = 1$ an increase in α does not affect $E[W]$.

This result has greater relevance than what it may seem at a first glance. It actually applies to all the cases where there are several downstream firms which operate in separate markets and, therefore, do not compete against each other. In this case, each single relationship between the laboratory and a downstream firm is independent from the others. This implies that the case of $n \geq 1$ non-rival firms corresponds to a simple n-times replication of the $n = 1$ scenario analysed previously. The following corollary summarises this point:

Corollary 4. *If the downstream firms do not compete against each other, a more thorough examination process by the PTO does not have any effect on expected social welfare.*

Note that our analysis does not take into account the fact that greater scrutiny entails larger examination costs borne by the PTO. Once these costs are taken into account, Corollary 4 implies that, when there is no competition in the downstream market, a more thorough examination by the PTO actually decreases social welfare.

With downstream competition, according to part b) of Result 8, a more rigorous examination by the PTO is socially desirable. The reason for this is related to the different equilibria which emerge when the laboratory is granted a patent and when it is not. If the lab holds a patent, then, as shown in Result 7, regardless of the number of downstream firms, the equilibrium replicates the one of a vertically integrated monopolist. On the contrary, in the case the lab is not granted the patent, downstream firms may use the technology for free and, therefore, a standard n-firm oligopoly equilibrium arises: competition drives the equilibrium price down and increases social welfare. These arguments also imply that the benefit from a more thorough examination by the PTO increases with the number of downstream firms; when n is large and the patent is not granted, then the downstream market is highly competitive and generates a considerable social welfare. The following corollary summarises these observations:

Corollary 5. *The social desirability of a more rigorous examination by the PTO is increasing in the number of firms competing in the downstream market.*

The analysis by Farrell and Shapiro contributes to the discussion on the consequences of weak patents. The "optimistic" view according to which weak patents entail only marginal effects on social welfare is supported when the lab's technology is used by firms which are not competing against each other; in this case, the market equilibrium is the same with or without patent protection and, therefore, a more thorough examination simply implies larger costs for the review of applications. On the contrary, when the technology is employed by competing firms, the analysis by Farrell and Shapiro suggests that a closer scrutiny in the review process is likely to increase social welfare, thus supporting the more "pessimistic" view on weak patents. A larger α decreases the probability of the vertically integrated monopoly equilibrium emerging.

Weak patents and innovation incentives

The previous analysis has been carried out according to an *ex post* perspective: we have analysed the welfare effects of a more rigorous examination of patent applications under the assumption according to which the lab had already developed the technology. Nonetheless, since the main aim of patenting is to stimulate R&D activities, it is interesting to extend the previous discussion and consider an *ex ante* perspective. In other words, now we investigate the effects of a closer scrutiny by the PTO on innovation incentives.

More specifically, consider the lab choosing whether or not to invest in a research project. If R invests, then with probability θ it obtains a true innovation, while with probability $1 - \theta$ the innovation simply replicates existing technologies (it is a false innovation). If, on the contrary, the lab does not invest in the project then it obtains no innovation at all.

As in Farrell and Shapiro (2008), we analyse the effects of weak patents by comparing the expected social welfare in the following two scenarios: *i*) patents are weak (weak-patent regime) and *ii*) there is no patent protection whatsoever (no-patent regime). Furthermore, for the sake of simplicity, we assume that in scenario *i*) the PTO does not carry out any screening activity and grants patent protection to all the applications it receives; according to our notation this amounts to assuming that $\alpha = 1$. Note that this last assumption implies that we are considering the worst possible scenario for weak patents, i.e. the case where there is no scrutiny by the PTO.

On the basis of these assumptions, in scenario i) the lab invests in the research project,[38] it obtains the patent with probability 1 and expected social welfare equals W^m (see Result 7).

Let us now consider the no-patent regime. Absent patent protection, the lab does not invest in the research project. In order to determine the expected social welfare in this case, we need to distinguish between two scenarios. With probability θ the lab's technology would have been a true innovation; since the lab does not invest in R&D, the innovation is not developed and social welfare is zero. With probability $1 - \theta$ the lab would have developed a false innovation. This implies that there already is a technology performing the same tasks even without the lab developing its project. In this case, since all the n firms can freely access the existing technology, then social welfare equals $\overline{W}(n)$, as defined previously. On the basis of these arguments, when there is no patent protection (case ii)), expected social welfare equals $(1 - \theta)\overline{W}(n)$.

We can now compare expected social welfare obtained in the two regimes. The weak-patent regime is preferred to the no-patent regime when $W^m \geq (1 - \theta)\overline{W}(n)$. After some simple algebraic manipulation we derive the following result:

Result 9. *If the lab invests in the research project only when patent protection is available and assuming $\alpha = 0$ (the PTO approves any application), the weak-patent regime is socially preferred to the no-patent regime if $\theta \geq [2n + n^2 - 3]/[4n(2 + n)]$.*

This result has a straightforward interpretation. If the probability θ of the lab developing a true innovation is large enough, then the weak-patent regime is socially preferred to the no-patent regime. If, on the contrary, it is likely for the lab to develop a false innovation, then weak patents are not desirable.

From this result, we derive the following corollary:

Corollary 6. *The threshold value $[2n + n^2 - 3]/[4n(2 + n)]$ highlighted in Result 9:*

i) equals 0 when $n = 1$;

ii) is increasing in n.

When there is no competition among downstream firms, the threshold value for θ is 0: the weak-patent regime is always preferred to the no-patent regime (part i) of Corollary 6). As discussed previously, when $n = 1$ the market equilibrium is the same as in the vertically integrated monopoly, regardless of whether the lab has been granted the patent or not. In this case, patents are desirable since they stimulate R&D investments. With at least two rival firms, patent protection eliminates the social benefit accruing from

---

[38]We are implicitly assuming that R&D costs are lower than the revenues accruing from the innovation.

downstream competition. This negative welfare effect is stronger as n gets larger; this is the reason why patent protection becomes less desirable as the number of downstream firms gets larger; formally, the threshold value of θ is increasing in n (part ii) of the corollary).

Summarising, similarly to the *ex post* analysis, when innovation incentives are taken into account, the social desirability of weak patents depends on how competitive the downstream market is; when the number of rival firms operating downstream is small, then weak patents are likely to be socially desirable thanks to their positive effect on innovation incentives. By contrast, when the downstream market is (potentially) highly competitive, weak patents tend to reduce social welfare.

6.6　Mathematical appendix

Proof of Result 2. If the second innovation does not infringe firm A's patent, then condition $v_B xT \geq c_B$ ensures that firm B invests in its project. Suppose now that the second innovation violates A's patent. Two are the possible subcases which need to be examined: $i)$ $c_B \leq v_B xT < 2c_B$ and $ii)$ $v_B xT \geq 2c_B$. In the first case, firm B invests in the R&D project only in case the two firms sign a licensing agreement. When they fail to reach an agreement, then the Court establishes a licensing fee equal $L(T) = v_B xT/2$ which makes B's investment not profitable. Clearly, if B does not invest then A does not gain any licensing profits. Following these argumentations, it is profitable for both firms to agree on a licensing contract such that each party obtains half of the profits generated by the second innovation, $v_B xT - c_B$; in this way it is profitable for firm B to invest in the project and firm A obtains licensing fees $L(T) = (v_B xT - c_B)/2$.

Consider case $ii)$ where $v_B xT \geq 2c_B$. If parties do not reach any agreement, then the Court imposes $L(T) = v_B xT/2$ and firm B invests in the R&D project. Since B develops its project even in the absence of a licensing agreement, then firm A is not willing to accept any amount of money smaller than that established by the Court; B is not willing to pay more. Therefore, firm B develops the project and pays $L(T) = v_B xT/2$ to firm A.　　　　　　　　　　　　　　　　　　　　　　　　　　　　　　　　□

The optimal patent policy in Green and Scotchmer's model (Section 6.3.2). The aim of the patent policy is to reduce patent length in order to minimise the negative effects of deadweight loss, conditional on inducing firms to invest in research and development. Recalling that $\overline{T}_B$ is the length such that the revenues associated with the second innovation equal the R&D costs, in this section, we define the optimal patent policy by focusing our attention on the three separate areas shown in Figure 6.5:

a) $v_A x \overline{T}_B \geq c_A$; in this case, with a patent of length $\overline{T}_B$ the first innovation is profitable even if there are no licensing profits. Therefore any value of β is optimal. With regard to patent length, there are two possible cases to consider. In the first case, it is socially optimal to reduce patent length below $\overline{T}_B$: in this way the second innovation is not developed but the deadweight loss associated with the first innovation is reduced. In this case the optimal patent length is T such that $v_A x T - c_A = 0$. The second possible case is when the social benefit from the second innovation is larger than the gains derived from the reduction of the deadweight loss associated with the first innovation; in this case the optimal patent length is $\overline{T}_B$ and both innovations are developed (this is the case shown in Figure 6.5).

b) $c_A > v_A x \overline{T}_B \geq c_A - L(\overline{T}_B)$; with a patent of length $\overline{T}_B$, direct profits are not enough to induce firm A to invest. As discussed in the chapter the socially optimal way to increase the profits of the first innovator is to broaden patent breadth. In this case, therefore, the socially optimal patent policy is characterised by $\beta = 1$ and length $T = \overline{T}_B$.

c) $v_A x \overline{T}_B < c_A - L(\overline{T}_B)$; even with maximum breadth ($\beta = 1$) and length $\overline{T}_B$ the first innovation is not profitable: $v_A x \overline{T}_B + L(\overline{T}_B) - c_A < 0$. Therefore, in order to induce firm A to invest, patent length needs to be extended beyond $\overline{T}_B$. The socially optimal patent policy is: $\beta = 1$ and length $\tilde{T}$, which is defined as the value of T such that $v_A x T + L(T) - c_A = 0$.

$\square$

Chapter 7

Imitation, Open Source and File Sharing

7.1 Introduction

In modern economies, the role of patents has substantially changed from the one for which they were originally intended. As discussed in Chapter 6, firms often employ patents strategically in order to improve their bargaining position vis -à- vis other companies or, even worse, they use them as "legal weapons" towards competitors. According to some commentators, this evidence alone is enough to justify the request for an urgent and thorough revision of the patent and copyright systems. However, the strategic (mis)use of patents is not the only argument supporting such a request. In recent years, various high-tech sectors have experienced striking innovation rates despite the low propensity of companies towards patenting; in other words, in several sectors, patent protection does not seem to be a necessary condition for the flourishing of innovation.

Such criticisms are, however, not completely new. Similar arguments had already been put forward by Fritz Machlup and Edith Penrose in a 1950 article in *The Journal of Economic History* (see Machlup and Penrose, 1950). Already in those days, the role of the patent system had sparked a fierce debate at the U.S. Congress. Moreover, in the same article, the two authors recall that this was not the first time in history that the role of the IP system had been challenged. A lively discussion on the same issues dates back to the mid–late nineteenth century when the opponents to the IP system did not simply demand a reform but the complete abolishment of patent and copyright protection. Edith Penrose, in the famous book *The Economics of the International Patent System*, summarises all her doubts questioning the desirability of patent laws as follows:

If national patent laws did not exist, it would be difficult to make a conclusive case for introducing them; but the fact that they do exist shifts the burden of proof and it is equally difficult to make a really conclusive case for abolishing them. (see Penrose, 1951)

The literature on the pros and cons of intellectual property rights is extremely rich. In this chapter we limit the discussion to some of the most relevant theoretical contributions challenging the desirability of the current IP legislation; we then proceed by presenting some examples of remarkably innovative industries which have employed IP laws in a rather non-traditional way.[1] Careful readers may have noted that we have already partially addressed these issues in Chapter 6 when we presented the article by Cohen et al. (2000) on U.S. manufacturing companies. This study suggests that, besides patents and copyright, other mechanisms, such as lead time or sales of complementary products or services, can be used by firms to appropriate the returns of their R&D investments. The authors actually show that, in most industrial sectors, companies perceive these alternative mechanisms to be much more effective than patents and copyright.

Recently, many firms, especially those operating in high-tech industries, have substantially modified their innovation strategies, by shifting from a "closed" to an "open" approach. With a closed approach to innovation, firms keep strict control over their intellectual property in order to tightly supervise the creation and the management of their own ideas; research activities are carried out within the boundaries of the firm, in proprietary research laboratories. Alternatively, firms may adopt an open innovation approach characterised by the use of external as well as internal ideas; firms conduct research in collaboration with partners and this allows them to share risks and rewards. With open innovation, the boundaries between a firm and its environment are much more blurred as innovations can be easily transferred inwards and outwards. In modern economies, and in particular in high-tech sectors, open innovation is rather popular; in highly innovative industries firms need to follow an open innovation approach if they want to keep pace with the fast technological progress which, to a large extent, takes place outside their boundaries. Open innovation requires a different way of managing intellectual property; rather than excluding third parties from using their inventions, firms use patents and copyright to stimulate contributions to the innovation process from the largest possible pool of agents. A common practice in today's industries is technology licensing, a typical open strategy to innovation aimed at establishing research collaborations and partnerships; internal inventions which are not used in a firm's business are taken outside the company, through licensing (or joint ventures).

---

[1] A thorough discussion about the current IP system can be found in Jaffe (2000) and Bessen and Meurer (2008).

One of the most relevant examples of open innovation is open source software, which we will discuss in greater detail later on in this chapter; open source software is computer software whose source code is available and released under a license that permits third parties to study, modify and improve the code and, eventually, also to distribute it. Unlike proprietary/closed source licenses that are intended to exclude third parties from the innovation process, open source licenses are specifically designed to attract external contributions to innovation.

Another valuable aspect of open innovation is the "creative re-use" of inventions. Companies often share ideas and research activities thus saving time and efforts by relying on innovations developed by others. According to Foray (2006), the most important benefit of open innovation lies in the possibility of taking advantage of heterogeneous abilities and experiences; the more an innovative idea is spread among researchers and entrepreneurs with different attitudes and backgrounds, the more likely it is for this idea to generate further innovation in different environments. Following Chesbrough (2003), the benefits of opening the creative process up to external parties derive from the fact that "not all smart people work for us. We need to work with smart people inside and outside our company".

Box 7.1 – Creative ideas from customers and suppliers

Nowadays, the open approach to innovation is popular also among firms operating in traditional sectors. For example, Procter & Gamble has drastically changed its way of dealing with innovation; from a closed approach exclusively oriented towards its own research labs, P&G has embraced a new philosophy aimed at involving external contributors such as universities and suppliers in the development of new products. According to Alan George Lafley, the former company's Chief Executive Officer, around half of P&G ideas for new products have been developed outside the boundaries of the company.

Likewise, an increasing number of firms is attempting to involve customers in the development of new ideas and products. This is, for instance, the case of the *Mindstorms* project launched by LEGO, the producer of the famous interlocking plastic bricks, and of IBM's *On-line jam sessions*. It is worthwhile mentioning also StataCorp, the producer of Stata, the well known software for statistical analyses; at the meetings of Stata users, StataCorp organises the *wishes and grumbles* sessions where participants have the opportunity to highlight any problems or limitations of the software, and to suggest possible improvements.

History abounds of examples of manufacturing sectors which have been organised according to the principles of open innovation, even though these experiences were limited in time and space. This was the case of the *fabrique lyonnaise*, the silk industry in the Lyons of the eighteenth century and the British iron industry of the nineteenth century.[2] A more recent example of open innovation takes us back to ICT; as documented

---

[2]See Foray (2006) for further details of these historical examples of open innovation.

by Meyer (2007), from 1975 to 1986, the *Homebrew Computer Club*, an informal group of expert programmers and hobbyists with an electronic engineering background, represented one of the most influential forces contributing to the development of modern PCs. Occasionally, at meetings, the members of the club shared their ideas and experiences in their attempt to create innovative computing devices. Communication among members was further enhanced through a newsletter and several workshops. From the ranks of the club came some successful entrepreneurs of the PC industry such as Steve Wozniak and Steve Jobs, the co-founders of Apple.

Besides all these potential benefits, open innovation entails a series of risks too. By relying heavily on external contributions, a company may lose control over its business. Moreover, the competitive advantage of a firm may be eroded; by opening up its innovation process, a firm faces the risk of collaborators and contributors transforming into competitors. In addition, the involvement in the innovation process of third parties characterised by heterogeneous experiences and attitudes may turn out to be a daunting task.[3] Therefore, the open innovation approach may also imply substantial coordination costs for the firm. Another relevant issue concerns the incentives for companies to maintain an open approach to innovation in the long-run. With the exception of open source software, the examples that we have mentioned so far seem to suggest that the open approach is limited in time and space. For instance, even though the computer industry was highly cooperative in its early days, as time passed by it became more and more influenced by a commercial logic with firms increasingly exploiting IP rights strategically against competitors. Some scholars, indeed, argue that open innovation represents a valuable business model only for non-core activities or as a rearguard strategy that firms may adopt when lagging behind.[4]

The final section of this chapter shifts attention to another aspect which is somehow related to open innovation, that is the management of intellectual property rights in the age of the Internet. The digital revolution has made it easier to transfer information of any kind through the Internet; this represents both a threat and an opportunity for ICT firms. On the one hand, it is easier for them to reach consumers (take software,

---

[3]Whelan et al. (2011) report that while companies such as Procter & Gamble, Cisco Systems, Genzyme, General Electric and Intel have attained market leadership thanks to open innovation strategies, others "are failing because they neglect to ensure that the outside ideas reach the people best equipped to exploit them". For this reason, the authors highlight the importance of creating a network of so-called innovation brokers who contribute to the matching of outside ideas and opportunities with internal resources.

[4]For instance, according to Kenneth Morse, the head of the *Entrepreneurship Center* at MIT, IBM uses an open innovation approach only for software, a non-core activity for the company. By contrast, in the hardware part of its business the company adopts an extremely closed approach to innovation; see *The Economist*, 13 October 2007.

music or films for example) but on the other hand digital piracy may erode the ability of firms to generate profits. Similarly to firms adopting an open approach to innovation, digital content producers must be careful when releasing and distributing their products on-line as well as when managing their intellectual property rights.

7.2   The case against intellectual monopoly

Several scholars strongly disagree with the current intellectual property rights system. Among these, two of the most critical are certainly Michele Boldrin and David Levine who recently wrote the book entitled *Against Intellectual Monopoly* (see Boldrin and Levine, 2008); the two authors argue that IP laws provide inventors and authors with an excessively strong protection with the consequence that patents and copyright hamper innovation and technological progress, rather than promoting it.

IP laws grant inventors two fundamental rights. The first is the "right to sell the first copy", that is the inventor's right to sell her innovation. The second, which Boldrin and Levine critically define as "intellectual monopoly", refers to the inventor's right to regulate the use which can be made of the innovation. Intellectual monopoly establishes a fundamental difference between "traditional goods" and those protected by IP rights. For instance, the buyer of a potato is completely free to decide what to do with it: he can "eat it, throw it away, plant it or make it into a sculpture". On the contrary, the uses of a good protected by intellectual property are much more limited as they are narrowly defined by IP laws and by the innovator's will. According to Boldrin and Levine, the right to sell the first copy is sufficient to compensate the inventor for her R&D efforts and investments. On the contrary, intellectual monopoly guarantees the inventor excessively large profits and it enables her to thwart competitors' innovations.

An example taken from Boldrin and Levine's book helps us understand better their arguments. Consider an author who has just finished writing a novel. Without intellectual monopoly protecting the manuscript, anyone who purchases a copy of the novel can do whatever he wants with it: he can read it, give it away, leave it on the shelf of his library and so on; moreover, the purchaser can also make copies of the novel and sell them. Boldrin and Levine ask themselves the following question: what is the value of the manuscript when there is no intellectual monopoly? Or, in other words, how much is a publisher willing to pay for the manuscript when purchasers can make and sell copies of the book? Clearly, the value attached to the manuscript depends on the amount of profits the publisher is able to obtain from printing and distributing it.

According to the traditional view, in the absence of intellectual monopoly the manuscript is worth zero for the publisher. The underlying reasoning goes as follows: when it is possible for the buyers of a book to become producers (by making and selling copies of it) the market becomes perfectly competitive; the price decreases down to the marginal cost of copying the book and profits go to zero. Therefore, nobody (neither the publisher nor the buyers) is willing to pay for the novel a price above the marginal cost of copying it. Consequently, the author cannot compensate the costs of writing the manuscript (the cost of the first copy) and if she takes this fact into account, it is likely that she will choose to spend her time on more enjoyable/profitable activities rather than writing the novel. Without property rights, no one is willing to "create" artistic works; in other words, no one would innovate.

According to Boldrin and Levine, the traditional view is not correct from a logical point of view and it is also contradicted by empirical evidence. The argument according to which the price equals the marginal cost of copying mixes up short-run and long-run perspectives. It is not possible to copy books instantly, so in the short-run the overall capacity of producing books is limited. Clearly, with capacity constraints, even in a perfectly competitive setting the equilibrium price is larger than the marginal cost. Figure 7.1 provides a graphical representation of this argument; the overall production capacity is limited to $\bar{q}$ which is smaller than $\tilde{q}$, the quantity demanded when the price equals the marginal cost of copying (MC). Therefore, in the short-run, consumers are rationed, the equilibrium price p_{SR} is above MC and each copy sold generates a positive margin. Therefore, as long as the production capacity is limited with respect to demand, the author collects profits (the so-called competitive rent) even in absence of intellectual monopoly.

Moreover, the competitive rent is likely to be only a fraction of the author's actual profits. As mentioned in Chapter 6 when we presented the research conducted by Cohen et al. (2000), the inventor enjoys the so-called *first mover advantage*; the inventor is aware of all the possible uses of her innovation and, therefore, she is in the best position to exploit it commercially: imitation cannot occur instantly and in the meantime the innovator can collect revenues which increase her profits well above the competitive rent.

The traditional view of intellectual property is also contradicted by empirical evidence; Boldrin and Levine argue that in industries such as agriculture, traditional manufacturing and finance innovation has flourished even in the presence of weak intellectual property protection. According to the two authors, the case of software describes the controversial role played by IP rights; in the early days of this industry, many seminal inventions were developed within an extremely cooperative environment where program-

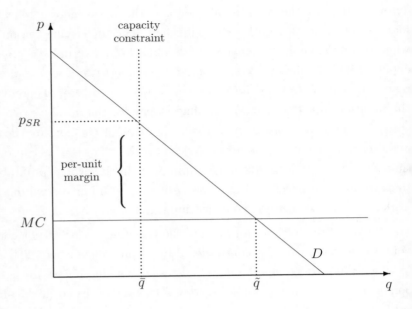

Figure 7.1: competitive equilibrium with capacity constraints

mers used to freely exchange parts of software code among each other; during this early period, patents and copyright played a very limited role. In the current (maturity) phase things have changed radically: the primary goal of companies has shifted from innovation and growth to protection of market shares and profits; during this stage, patent have become more important as they represent strategic weapons to be used agains competitors. According to Boldrin and Levine, patents are no longer contributing to spurring further innovation but, rather, they hamper it.

7.3 Imitation and incentives for innovation

In 1981, IBM officially announced the launch of its first personal computer. A few day later, Apple, the market leader at that time, responded with a full-page ad on the *Wa Street Journal* headlined: *Welcome IBM. Seriously* (see Figure 7.2).

According to Bessen and Maskin (2009), Apple was right in welcoming the entry c such a strong competitor. In those days the computer sector was extremely dynami and Apple realised that IBM's entry would have made the industry much more livel and innovative. Apple would have benefited from IBM's R&D investments by imitatin or, simply, by drawing inspiration from the competitor's blockbuster products.

From the Apple–IBM episode, Bessen and Maskin argue that weak IP rights ar better suited to industries where innovation is sequential and companies invest in different/complementary R&D projects. Weak intellectual property rights affect firm's profitability in two ways; on the one hand, a firm's innovation can be easily imitated by competitors and this, in the short-run, reduces its profits. However, in the long-run, when innovation is cumulative, imitation may also have positive effects: the firm which was previously imitated may, in turn, "copy" competitors to provide consumers with more innovative and technologically advanced products. In dynamic industries, there are good reasons to believe that long-run effects overturn the short-run ones; innovation is fostered by imitation and this goes to the benefit of both consumers and firms. To support this idea, Bessen and Maskin mention the performance of several industries such as software, personal computers and semiconductors. These industries have been extremely dynamic despite firms' low propensity to patent combined with a significant rate of product imitation.

Welcome, IBM.
Seriously.

Welcome to the most exciting and important marketplace since the computer revolution began 35 years ago.

And congratulations on your first personal computer.

Putting real computer power in the hands of the individual is already improving the way people work, think, learn, communicate and spend their leisure hours.

Computer literacy is fast becoming as fundamental a skill as reading or writing.

When we invented the first personal computer system, we estimated that over 140,000,000 people worldwide could justify the purchase of one, if only they understood its benefits.

Next year alone, we project that well over 1,000,000 will come to that understanding. Over the next decade, the growth of the personal computer will continue in logarithmic leaps.

We look forward to responsible competition in the massive effort to distribute this American technology to the world. And we appreciate the magnitude of your commitment.

Because what we are doing is increasing social capital by enhancing individual productivity.

Welcome to the task. **apple**

Figure 7.2: Apple welcomes IBM

More specifically, Bessen and Maskin show that the positive long-term effects of weak patent protection and imitation emerge if the industry satisfies the following conditions:

- **the innovation process is cumulative:** each successive invention builds on the preceding one. Examples of cumulative innovation abound; for instance, just to take a relevant case, Microsoft's Excel builds on Lotus 1-2-3 which, in turn, was an evolution of VisiCalc (see Box 8.2 for details). Cumulativeness of innovation is a crucial condition; if innovation is isolated, imitation simply reduces current profits and it frustrates firm's innovative efforts. On the contrary, when innovation spurs further innovation, the possibility of being imitated may lead to a long-term positive effect: in the future, a firm which has been imitated may in turn imitate competitors;

- **complementarity of research projects:** each research idea is developed by several innovators who follow different (complementary) research lines. The overall probability of the idea being actually developed increases with the number of complementary research lines;

- **imperfect competition:** an innovation can be imitated by a limited number of firms; hence, imitation reduces profits without eliminating them altogether.

In the next section, we present a simplified version of the Bessen and Maskin model published in the *RAND Journal of Economics* in 2009; we focus on the case where innovation is not protected by patents, namely the case of the weakest possible IP rights.

7.3.1   The model by Bessen and Maskin

Consider two firms, A and B, simultaneously deciding whether or not to invest in a research project which may result in an innovation with social value $v > 0$. Each project may or may not succeed and we assume that the innovation is actually developed (the value v is realized) if at least one research project is successful.

If only one of the two firms invests in the research project, then the probability of developing the innovation is $p \in (0,1)$. Instead, if both firms undertake the research project, then the probability of the innovation being developed (i.e. the probability of at least one of the projects being successful) increases to $P \in (0,1)$, with $P > p$. Using the same terminology as in Bessen and Maskin (2009), when $P > p$ the two research projects are said to be complementary.

We assume that no intellectual property protection is available; hence imitation occurs: the firm which has not succeeded in developing the innovation copies the successful competitor. Imitation implies lower profits for the innovator; following Bessen and Maskin, we assume that each firm obtains a share s of the value v, with $0 < s \le 1/2$, regardless of which of the two firms has developed the innovation. The assumption $s > 0$ is in line with the third condition listed above: competition is imperfect so that imitation reduces the innovator's profits but does not eliminate them altogether.

For the sake of simplicity, we assume that the cost of the research project is zero for firm A and it is $c > 0$ for firm B. Following these assumptions: *i*) the investment is always profitable for firm A and, *ii*) A's decision to invest is also socially desirable.

Henceforth, we assume that v is uniformly distributed over $[0, 1]$ and that both firms know the realisation of v before taking their investment decision. The timing of the game is as follows:

t_1 - the value v is drawn from a uniform distribution function over the interval $[0, 1]$ and is observed by both firms;

t_2 - once v has been observed, each firm decides whether or not to undertake the research project. The two firms take their decisions simultaneously.

The static case: isolated innovation

We begin the analysis by considering the static case of isolated innovation. Our aim is to examine whether or not the two firms have the appropriate incentives to undertake their research projects in the presence of imitation (absent patent protection).

The socially optimal investment level. Let's start by determining the socially optimal conditions for the two firms to undertake their research projects. We know that the investment by A is always desirable; therefore, we need only determine the socially optimal behaviour of firm B. In order to find out when it is socially desirable to have also firm B investing, we need to compare social welfare with and without B's investment.

Suppose that only firm A invests in the project; since the innovation can be obtained without cost, then the expected social welfare equals pv, where p is the probability of the innovation being developed. By contrast, when both firms invest in the project, the expected social welfare equals $Pv - c$: in this case, the likelihood of v being realized increases from p to P and the R&D costs increase from 0 to c. Therefore, it is socially preferable to have both firms investing in their research projects when $Pv - c \geq pv$, that is when:[5]

$$v \geq \frac{c}{P - p} \equiv v_S^I.$$

This condition shows that it is socially desirable to have both firms investing in research and development if the value of the innovation is well above c. The benefit deriving from B's investment is related to the increase in the probability of the innovation being developed and is proportional to its social value; formally, the social benefit from firm B's investment is $v(P - p)$.

---

[5]We assume that v_S^I as well as all the various cut-off values of v that we are going to derive in the analysis belong to the interval $[0, 1]$.

The market equilibrium.   Let us now determine the market equilibrium. As mentioned previously, we assume that the innovation cannot be patented and therefore can be imitated: even a firm which has not invested in the research project or which has failed to develop the innovation can capture part of v. Formally, if at least one of the two firms succeeds in the research project, then both firms obtains sv.

Since firm A's project is always profitable, we need only consider firm B's decision; the question, therefore, is: when does firm B invest, rather than just imitate the competitor? Suppose that firm B does not invest in R&D and imitates A's innovation. In this case, the probability of the innovation being developed equals p and the expected profits of firm B are psv. Instead, if B undertakes the research project, then its expected profits are $Psv - c$: when both firms invest, the likelihood of obtaining the innovation rises to P and, regardless of which firm has developed the innovation, they both obtain sv. Clearly, when investing in the project, firm B incurs cost c. Therefore, it is profitable for firm B to invest in the research project when $Psv - c \geq psv$, that is when:

$$v \geq \frac{c}{s(P - p)} \equiv v_{Eq}^I.$$

Underinvestment.   Now we can compare the socially optimal outcome with the market equilibrium. As mentioned previously, since firm A incurs zero R&D costs, it always invests and this decision is also socially optimal. In the case of firm B, an underinvestment problem may arise. It is socially optimal for firm B to invest when v is larger than v_S^I; however, due to the fact that it captures only a share s of the social value of the innovation, firm B invests only when $v \geq v_{Eq}^I$, with $v_S^I < v_{Eq}^I$. Following these arguments, when $v \in \left(v_S^I, v_{Eq}^I\right)$, firm B does not invest despite its investment being socially desirable; this fact implies that the market fails to induce the socially optimal amount of research and development:

Result 1. *In the case of isolated innovation and no intellectual property protection, there is underinvestment in R&D activities. Formally, the probability of underinvestment is* $c(1 - s)/\left(s(P - p)\right) \equiv \Delta^I$.

Proof. The social value of the innovation is randomly drawn from a uniform distribution over the interval $[0, 1]$; hence, the probability of underinvestment equals $v_{Eq}^I - v_S^I = c(1 - s)/(s(P - p))$. $\qquad\square$

This analysis supports the traditional view favouring patent protection: when firms cannot protect their inventions, they invest too little in research activities in comparison to the social optimum (underinvestment). Result 1, however, has been obtained in the case of isolated innovation; the key issue, now, is to analyse what happens if innovation is cumulative. As we shall see in the following paragraph, in a dynamic context the results of the model change substantially.

The dynamic case: sequential innovation

Let's now shift to the case of sequential innovation. We consider a game with an infinite time horizon; in each period t, with $t = 1, 2...\infty$, the two firms decide whether or not to undertake the research project. The innovation process is cumulative in the following sense: if in period t the innovation is developed, then the process carries on to the next period; in $t + 1$, once again, each firm decides whether or not to undertake a research project. Instead, if in t neither of the firms develops the innovation, then the process comes to a halt and none of the firms can invest in research projects anymore. In other words, with cumulative innovation, future inventions may occur only if today's innovation has been developed.

Formally, the two firms are involved in an infinitely repeated game, where the stage game corresponds to the one described previously for the case of isolated innovation. In other words, in a generic t, provided that the innovation has been developed in all the previous periods, firms A and B decide whether to invest in the research project with value v, thus incurring costs 0 for firm A and c for firm B. If only one of the two firms undertakes the project, then the probability of obtaining v and continuing the sequence of innovations equals p; if both firms invest, the probability of success increases up to $P > p$. For the sake of simplicity, following Bessen and Maskin (2009), we assume that the various innovations which are developed over time have the same social value, which is determined once and for all in $t = 1$ by randomly drawing v from the uniform distribution over $[0, 1]$.

The socially optimal investment level.

As in the case of isolated innovation, we start the analysis by determining the socially optimal outcome. Therefore, we compare the social welfare that can be obtained in the two possible scenarios: in each period t either only firm A invests in the research project or both firms invest.[6] When only firm A invests in the research project, the expected social welfare is:

$$pv + p(pv) + p\left[p(pv)\right] + ... = \sum_{t=1}^{\infty} p^t v = \frac{pv}{1 - p}.$$

---

[6]Note that in each period of time t, the stage game is the same. Therefore, if firm B's investment in $t = 1$ is socially desirable, it will still be so in any other future period of time. This means that we need to consider only two alternative scenarios: i) at each period t only firm A invests; ii) at each period t both firms invest.

The first term, pv, represents the expected social welfare of the first innovation, the one in period $t = 1$: it has a social value of v and the probability of being developed is p. The second term, $p(pv)$, represents the expected social value of the second innovation: in $t = 2$, firm A can undertake its project only if the previous innovation has been developed (event which occurs with probability p) and the probability of success of this project equals p. The third term refers to the project in $t = 3$ which can be undertaken only if the first two innovations have been developed, event which occurs with probability p^2. By proceeding in this way, we calculate the overall expected social value of the sequence of innovations, which turns out to be $pv/(1 - p)$.

If in each period t, both firms invest in the research projects, we know that the probability of the innovation being developed increases and equals P. Since firm B incurs cost c in each period, the expected social welfare in this case is:

$$Pv - c + P(Pv - c) + P[P(Pv - c)] + ... = \left(\sum_{t=1}^{\infty} P^t (v - c) \right) - c = \frac{Pv - c}{1 - P}.$$

The interpretation to the terms of this expression is similar to the one provided above for the case of only firm A investing at each period t; when both firms undertake the research project, the probability of developing an innovation equals P and the overall R&D costs are c.

By looking at the two levels of expected social welfare we have just derived it is possible to verify that it is socially optimal to have both firms investing in their research projects if:

$$v \geq \frac{c(1 - p)}{P - p} \equiv v_S^S.$$

A comparison between the two scenarios of isolated and sequential innovation is useful to derive an interesting observation: it is easy to check that when innovation is sequential, the threshold value of v from which firm B's investment is socially optimal is lower than in the case of isolated innovation; formally, $v_S^S < v_S^I$. In other words, when innovation is sequential it is more desirable to have firm B investing in each period. This is in line with Green and Scotchmer's model presented in Chapter 6. When innovation is cumulative, the social value of the current innovation is also related to its contribution to future inventions. In the model by Bessen and Maskin, the development of the innovation at time t is essential to guarantee the opportunity of investing in future research projects; this gives rise to a positive externality and it explains why firm B's investment is more desirable in the case of sequential innovation.

The market equilibrium.   Let us now focus on the firms' investments decisions. As in the case of isolated innovation, given that firm A always invests, we need only consider firm B. If B decides not to invest and to imitate A's innovation, it obtains $psv + p(psv) + p[p(psv)] + \dots$ which can be rewritten as $psv/(1-p)$.[7] Instead, if firm B invests in research activities, then the expected profits are $Psv - c + P(Psv - c) + P[P(Psv - c)] + \dots$, that is $(Psv - c)/(1 - P)$.

By comparing these two expressions, we can easily check that it is profitable for firm B to invest in each period when:

$$v \geq \frac{c(1-p)}{s(P-p)} \equiv v_{Eq}^S.$$

As in the case of the social optimum, the incentives to invest in R&D are higher when innovation is sequential: in this case, the threshold value from which firm B invests, v_{Eq}^S, is lower than the corresponding threshold when innovation is isolated, v_{Eq}^I (firm B invests in a larger number of cases). This result is particularly interesting and sheds new light on the Apple–IBM episode, mentioned at the beginning of the section.

When innovation is sequential, firm B has greater incentives to invest in research activities. By undertaking its research project, B reduces the probability of the sequence of innovations coming to a halt; by investing today, the firm increases its chances of imitating A's future innovations. In other words, when innovation is sequential, investment incentives at t are greater since the firm benefits from the competitor's future R&D only by developing its own current innovation.

To convince the reader that the larger incentives to invest actually depend on the possibility of imitating A's innovations in the future, let us consider what happens if B is the only firm in the market. In this case there are no competitors to imitate and firm B derives zero profits if it does not invest. On the contrary, B's expected profits in the case of investment in R&D are $pv - c$ (with isolated innovation) and $pv - c + p(pv - c) + \dots = (pv - c)/(1 - p)$ (with sequential innovation). In both cases, it is profitable for B to invest when $v \geq c/p$. Therefore, if there is no possibility of imitating competitors, then the incentives to invest in the case of isolated innovation are the same as those with sequential innovation.

Underinvestment: isolated and sequential innovation. One may wonder whether underinvestment occurs also with sequential innovation. By comparing social incentives with private ones, we can check that underinvestment arises also in the case of sequential innovation although with smaller intensity. Firm B invests if $v \geq v_{Eq}^S$, but in order to maximise social welfare, investment should occur when $v \geq v_S^S$, with $v_S^S < v_{Eq}^S$;

---

[7] The interpretation of this expression is similar to the one provided for the expected social welfare, given that B captures a fraction s of the entire social value of the innovation.

therefore, for $v \in (v_S^S, v_{Eq}^S)$, there is underinvestment, as highlighted in the following result:

Result 2. *When innovation is sequential and there is no intellectual property protection, there is underinvestment in R&D activities. Formally, the probability of underinvestment equals $c(1 - s)(1 - p)/ (s(P - p)) \equiv \Delta^S$.*

Proof. Given that v is randomly drawn from a uniform distribution over the interval $[0, 1]$, the probability of underinvestment is $v_{Eq}^S - v_S^S = c(1 - s)(1 - p)/ (s(P - p))$. □

A comparison between Result 1 and Result 2 reveals that underinvestment is less likely to occur in the case of sequential innovation than when innovation is isolated.

Corollary 7. *When there is no intellectual property protection, the probability of underinvestment is lower in the case of sequential innovation than in the case of isolated innovation. Formally, $\Delta^S < \Delta^I$.*

The above corollary summarises the main idea presented in Bessen and Maskin's work: when innovation is sequential, firms' R&D investment incentives are greater and therefore underinvestment is less likely to occur in equilibrium.

The underlying intuition of this result is in line with the explanation provided to interpret the inequality $v_{Eq}^S < v_{Eq}^I$. When innovation is cumulative, the possibility of imitating the competitor's innovations in the future represents a further incentive to undertake R&D investments today; this reduces the market inefficiency.

This consideration is of fundamental importance for policy makers. When innovation is sequential, there is less need to stimulate firms to invest in R&D. Therefore, the role of patents in providing incentives to invest turns out to be less relevant in the case of industries characterised by cumulative innovation processes, such as software or computer industries.

To complete our analysis we should determine the market equilibrium when innovations can be patented. The formal analysis of this case is rather complex and for reasons of space we shall not include it in this section. However, we can get a rough idea of the inefficiencies which may arise when innovations are patentable by recalling the results obtained in Chapter 6. When firms can protect their innovations, future innovators need to negotiate licensing agreements with patent-holders in order to use their inventions. From Chapter 6, we know that if information among parties is asymmetric, licensing negotiations between subsequent generations of inventors turn out to be inefficient: in some cases, the follow-on innovator does not obtain the license to use earlier inventions and cannot undertake her R&D activity even though the investment may be socially desirable. Therefore, when innovations are protected by patents, the inefficiency of licensing negotiations may lead to a lower number of firms involved in research activities: following the same line of arguments of Bessen and Maskin, this inefficiency may further reduce R&D incentives and therefore it may exacerbate the underinvestment problem.

7.4 Open source software

The model by Bessen and Maskin supports the idea that in those industries where innovation is highly cumulative, weak intellectual property rights provide a "nourishing environment" for the development of innovations. This perspective is shared by several scholars and seems to be confirmed by the experience of open source, one of the most important phenomena characterising the software industry in recent years. As discussed below, open source is computer software whose source code has been made available and licensed in order to allow anyone to study, change and distribute the software to others.

As in other examples of open innovation, the basic idea of open source software is to involve as many people as possible in the development and distribution of new programs. This means that other actors besides the initial developers of the software contribute in various ways to the improvement of the product. The involvement of third parties occurs thanks to open source licenses, a collection of rules which establish how a certain software may be used and distributed. The relevance of these licenses is so crucial that a software is defined as open source only when it is released through a specifically approved open source license.

Before focusing our attention on some key issues related to open source software, it is useful to spend some words to clarify the meaning of "open source code" and briefly illustrate the history of open source.[8]

7.4.1 A brief history of open source

Open source software is a relatively old phenomenon, much older than what we may think. Actually, in the early days of the software industry, programs were developed according to an open source approach. Software was not a product per se but it was sold bundled together with hardware. In order to avoid costly duplications, programmers and engineers used to freely exchange lines of code among each other and the practice of software re-use was very common among developers.[9] In other words, developers

---

[8]The history of open source is based on Lerner and Tirole (2002).

[9]It is interesting to note that during the 70s there were several organisations which were expressively aimed at exchanging software codes; for example, one of the most relevant was *SHARE*, the Society to Help Avoid Redundant Efforts.

frequently re-used lines of code written by others, possibly after some adjustments to adapt the code to their needs, thus speeding-up the process of software development.

With the advent of personal computers in the mid-70s, software development was gradually divided from hardware production; in subsequent years, separate markets for games, applications and utilities developed quickly. Since then, commercial software vendors started to play a key role in the market and this, in turn, introduced major changes in the software development process. The common practice of software re-use was slowly abandoned and programs started to be distributed only in the so-called "executable" format, a binary code including a collection of instructions that only computers can read.

The shift from source code to executable code represents a turning point in the history of software; the main difference between the two codes lies in the format which they are written in. Usually, a developer writes the source code of a software in a programming language such as C++, Pascal or Java. Once the source code has been completed, it is compiled and converted to binary code. The difference between executable and source code is of fundamental importance: while the source code is written in a language which is readable by people, the executable format is a sequence of 0–1 digits which can be read by computers only. As a consequence, a programmer receiving the binary code cannot understand the functioning of the software and the structure of the code; therefore, with the binary format programmers are no longer able to modify/adapt the software and they are prevented from re-using it. The software industry abandoned the collaborative approach which characterised its early days and evolved towards a closed/proprietary approach.

To curb this trend, in the early 80s, Richard Stallman, a computer programmer working at the MIT artificial intelligence laboratory, founded the *Free software foundation*. The aim of the foundation was to re-establish the practice of releasing the source code of the software and to make it legally binding. One of the most important achievements of the foundation has certainly been the creation of the General Public License (GPL), the prototypical open source license detailing how the software and its accompanying source code can be copied, distributed and modified.

With Richard Stallman and his foundation a new era in the software industry began. The term "open source" was adopted for the first time in 1998 by a group of people belonging to the free software movement; they chose this label specifically to emphasise the fact that software development should be open and based on the sharing and collaboration among developers. Another important milestone in the history of open source goes back to 1991 when the Finnish–American student Linus Torvalds started developing what is probably the best known open source software: the Linux operating system.

From the late 90s onwards, the diffusion of the Internet has led to an astonishing growth of open source software; thanks to the Internet, programmers located around the world can easily share the code and collaborate in the development of the software.

Soon after the GPL, other open source licenses were created; some of them became very popular, while other licenses were seldom, never, or no longer used by any active projects; furthermore, many of the licenses were legally incompatible with each other, seriously restricting the ways in which developers could combine source codes. In order to bring order to this intricate issue, at the end of the 90s, the open source definition (the so-called OSI, open source initiative, definition) was formulated to establish which requirements an open source license needs to fulfil. Nowadays there are more than 60 OSI approved open source licenses.

Open source licenses

The license establishes the rules and regulations governing use, distribution and sales of a software product. According to the OSI definition, a license is open source if it meets the following requirements:[10]

1. **source code:** the program must include the source code of the software;

2. **derived works:** the license must allow the licensee to modify the code and to develop derived works;

3. **free redistribution:** the license shall not restrict any party from selling or giving the software away. The license shall not require the licensee to pay royalties, namely payments for each unit of distributed product.

The aim of these conditions is to keep the software source code open, thus promoting access, diffusion and collaborative development (sharing and re-use) of programs.[11] Take condition 3, for example; the fact that the licensee is allowed to redistribute the source code without having to pay any royalty spurs the diffusion of the program. Conditions 1 and 2 promote software re-use; the availability of the source code allows expert users to modify the software and, possibly, even to develop a derived product which may be drastically different from the original one.

It is important to note that the three conditions described above do not necessarily imply that the software needs to be released for free. As mentioned previously, according

---

[10]In this section, we focus on the most important requirements imposed by the OSI definition. For further details on the other conditions which need to be satisfied by open source licenses, see http://www.opensource.org/docs/osd.

[11]Careful readers will surely have noted that these conditions resemble Boldrin and Levine's arguments presented at the beginning of the chapter. Conditions 1–3 exclude the possibility of intellectual monopoly.

to condition 3, the developer/licensor cannot limit the licensee's freedom to redistribute the software through payment schemes such as royalties. However, the developer is free to charge the licensee a price for the code.[12]

Today there are more than 60 licenses which satisfy the OSI definition. The main difference among them is related to the restrictions imposed on derived software. The GPL, often considered the most restrictive license, establishes that a software derived from a GPL-ed code must be licensed under GPL too;[13] this requirement is known as *inheritance* or *copyleft provision*. Licenses such as the LGPL (Lesser General Public License), instead, allow developers to re-use some parts of the code without imposing the derived software to be distributed under the same licensing terms as the original program. Finally, the BSD (Berkeley Software Distribution) and all the other so-called *artistic licenses* do not impose any regulations on derived software. This implies that a software derived from a source code released under BSD license, can eventually be distributed under a "traditional" proprietary (i.e. non-open source) licensing scheme.

Open source today

Open source is no longer a phenomenon restricted to hackers or computer experts. The widespread diffusion of the Internet has led to the emergence of a very large open source community; in particular, the Internet has facilitated the development of software programs among a great number of dispersed user-programmers who coordinate their activities and share their efforts on-line.

It is interesting to know how many programmers are involved into open source software development, or how many individuals make daily use of an open source application; unfortunately, it is not easy to estimate the extent of the open source movement. Believe it or not, to a certain extent we are all open source users; for instance, each time we access the Internet we use an open source software since the operating systems managing many Web servers are open source. Google itself, just to take a very relevant example, employs Linux and, hence, any time we run a query we become open source users; moreover, Google Chrome, the world famous browser is a spin-off of the open source project called Chromium.

Nonetheless, even if precise figures on the diffusion of open source software are not available, there is no doubt that in several market segments open source products have

---

[12]To stress the fact that what is important is the openness of the software code and not its availability free of charge, the open source community argues that the word free, in the expression *free software*, must be intended in the sense of *free as in free speech, not as in free beer*.

[13]According to some scholars, the GPL is the only "true" open source license. The literature often distinguishes between free software and open source software. The first expression identifies software which is licensed under the GPL. The second refers to programs distributed under other open source licenses. In this chapter, for the sake of simplicity, we use the expression open source for both cases.

gained a leading position. The Linux counter website (linuxcounter.net) estimates that in June 2013 Linux users were around 66 million. According to other specialised websites, Apache in the Web server segment and Chrome and Firefox in the browser segment are the market leaders.[14] Further data on the diffusion of open source can be found on SourceForge.net, the most important Web-based open source projects repository. SourceForge acts as a centralised location for software developers to control and manage open source software development. Anyone who wants to develop a new software can use the services provided on SourceForge.net; for example, it is possible to launch a new project by opening a dedicated website on the platform. Here developers are free to provide all the information on the project and, possibly, the first lines of code in the attempt to attract other developers and obtain their contributions.

The figures of SourceForge.net are impressive: as of May 2013, the repository hosts more than 324,000 projects and has more than 3.4 million registered developers.[15] Table 7.1 contains some information on the open source projects hosted on SourceForge.net in December 2004. On the basis of these data, we can say that:

Development phase		Number of developers		Content		License	
early stage	56.7 %	one	66.9 %	communications	7.7 %	GPL	66.5 %
advanced	43.3 %	two	15.7 %	database	2.5 %	LGPL or similar	14 %
		three or four	10 %	desktop	1.5 %	BSD or similar	17.1 %
		five or six	3.5 %	education	1.5 %	other	2.4 %
		more than six	3.9 %	games	10.9 %		
				Internet	11.6 %		
				multimedia	8.6 %		
				office	4.2 %		
				science	7.5 %		
				security	1.8 %		
				software tools	22.4 %		
				systems	15.6 %		
				text editors	3.2 %		
				other	0.8 %		

Table 7.1: characteristics of open source projects[16]

---

[14]According to netcraft.com, in June 2013 Apache's market share was 53.3%; the site www.w3schools.com estimated that in May 2013 Chrome and Firefox market shares were 52.9% and 27.7% respectively.

[15]A large number of projects hosted on SourceForge.net are, however, inactive; therefore, these data inevitably overestimate the extent of the open source phenomenon. Nevertheless, the figures remain certainly impressive and confirm that open source represents one of the main actors in the software industry.

[16]Data taken from Comino et al. (2007) based on around 88,000 projects.

- more than half of the projects are at an early stage of development. This confirms that the site is essentially used by project leaders as an instrument to attract other developers in the attempt to involve them in the development and improvement of the project;

- the distribution of projects in terms of the number of developers is highly skewed. Projects with just one developer account for 66.9% of the whole sample, and more than 80% of the projects have at most two active developers. There are, however, also a few projects involving a great number of developers. Nearly 600 projects are quite large and involve more than 16 developers;

- there is a great variety in terms of software content. The most popular categories are: software tools to develop other programs, games, Internet applications, communication programs and multimedia applications;

- the most popular license is GPL, which is employed in about two-thirds of the projects.

7.4.2   Secrets to success

The high quality and the enormous popularity of several open source software projects has attracted the attention of many scholars interested in understanding the "secrets to success"; this issue is particularly relevant when attempting to assess the possibility of extending the open source approach to other industries besides software. In what follows, we focus on four separate aspects related to open source success; we then complete this overview in Section 7.4.3 where we explore the relationship between open source and commercial/for-profit activities.

Cumulativeness of innovation processes.   Innovation in the software industry is highly cumulative. As mentioned previously, in fact, software re-use is common practice for the development of a new program. A couple of examples are illustrative with regard to this point.[17] The first one is Internet Tablet, an operating system for mobile phones developed by Nokia and installed in the N800 series. Internet Tablet includes lines of code of several open source programs such as Linux, X-Window, GNOME, and BlueZ. It has been estimated that its source code is made up of more than ten million lines and that about 85% are taken from existing open source software programs while only 15% have been actually developed or modified by Nokia.

The second interesting example is Darwin, the core program of Apple's MAC OS X operating system. Based on NeXTSTEP, a software that Apple bought from NeXT

---

[17]The examples are taken from Anttila (2006).

Software, Darwin has been developed by combining several components taken from open source applications such as NetBSD, OpenBSD, FreeBSD; as in the case of Internet Tablet, most of the seventeen million lines of code included in Darwin come from existing open source software and only a small fraction of them has actually been written by Apple (80% and 20% respectively). Following the model by Bessen and Maskin, we can say that the cumulativeness of innovation characterising the software industry combined with the practice of software re-use (actually a form of product imitation) are the two crucial ingredients which determine the success of the open source approach.

External contributions. Open source inherently implies collaborative innovation. As argued in the introduction, one of the main advantages of the open source approach is related to the opportunity of receiving external contributions in the process of software development. In some cases, these contributions become so relevant and frequent that a proper community of developers (the so-called open source community) actually emerges; members of the community interact with one another in order to improve software projects. External contributions can take different forms such as simple suggestions for improvements of the software, advice on testing beta-versions of the programs, reporting bugs, editing of user's manuals, or even writing lines of code.

Box 7.2 – Cooperative development on SourceForge: the case of Freenet

In an article published in *Research Policy*, von Krogh et al. (2003) study the case of Freenet, a software which enables anonymous peer-to-peer communication. The Freenet project was founded in 1999 by Ian Clarke who in those days was a student at the University of Edinburgh; after completing the software design (made up of a series of independent modules), Clarke uploaded it on SourceForge.net in order to stimulate contributions from other programmers. In March 2000, the first beta version of the software was released for free. In the same year, 8 new versions of the software were released and the total number of downloads amounted to more than 650,000. Interactions among software developers were organised through a mailing list which involved more than 350 people. The turnover rate of programmers was very high: during the period of time investigated by the authors, an average of 45 programmers were contributing to software development each week. During the entire period of observation there were a total of 11,210 emails and 1,714 threads (sequences of mails on the same topic). Software contributions were highly concentrated: 53% of all the lines of code were written by four programmers only.

Leadership, modularity and other organisational aspects. As illustrated by the case of Freenet in Box 7.2, in many cases open source software is developed by one or more expert users, who start writing lines of code for the software programs they are interested in. Usually, once a beta version of the software is ready, developers release it via the Internet, for example on sites such as SourceForge.net, in order to attract other developers and to increase the number of users.

Usually, initial developers and new users who contribute to software development are not organised within a formal structure; the absence of hierarchical relationships in the community of users/developers is probably one of the most striking aspects of the open source development model. For this reason it is interesting to focus our attention on some organisational issues. Firstly, even though there is no formal authority, open source projects usually have a leader (in most cases one of the initial developers or those programmers who have provided significant contributions to the project) who coordinates activities during the entire development process and whose leadership is recognised by the whole community of users/developers.

Another important organisational aspect relates to the modularity of software programs; a software is often made up by several independent modules, each of which contains all the lines of code necessary to execute a particular functionality. Once they have been developed, the modules are combined together to form the final software application. The advantage of modularity is that complex programming activities can be broken down into simpler tasks; each developer is then responsible only for a single part of the entire program and this enables a more efficient division of labour. According to Linus Torvalds, one of the secrets to Linux success lies in its modularity.[18] Moreover, another advantage of modularity is that it favours software re-use: the functionality executed by a single module can be rather easily embedded in other software applications.

Finally, coordination among developers requires a continuous exchange of information; this may be obtained, for instance, via email or newsgroups. An important tool to coordinate developers' activities is the CVS, *Concurrent Versioning System*, a software control system which allows developers to access the most recent version of the program and keep track of its development.

Motivations to contribute. One of the key questions which has fascinated open source scholars during the last ten years is the following: why do bright, skilled, in many cases unpaid, developers contribute to open source projects? Several empirical studies have investigated the motivations of developers to contribute to open source projects. Lakhani and Wolf (2005) present an interesting analysis based on a survey administered to approximately 700 software developers involved in nearly 300 open source projects. A

---

[18]See Narduzzo and Rossi (2005) for a thorough discussion on modularity in open source.

first interesting finding of the two authors is that 40% of the interviewed programmers
were paid by their employers to join an open source project; for them, being involved in
the development of a project was not a matter of free personal choice. The remaining
60% of programmers took part in projects of their own free will.

Motivations	All	Volunteer programmers	Paid programmers
Enjoyment-based intrinsic motivations			
Programming is intellectually stimulating	44.9%	46.1%	43.1%
Like working with this team	20.3%	21.5%	18.5%
Economic/extrinsic motivations			
Improve programming skills	41.3%	45.8%	33.2%
Software needed (work or personal use)	58.7%	.	.
Enhance professional status	17.5%	13.9%	22.8%
Other intrinsic motivations (obligation/community based)			
Belief that source code should be open	33.1%	34.8%	30.6%
Feel personal obligation to contribute	28.6%	29.6%	29.6%
Dislike proprietary software	11.3%	11.5%	11.1%
Enhance reputation of open source	11.0%	12.0%	9.5%

Table 7.2: motivations to contribute to open source projects[19]

The interviewees were then asked to select which was the motivation behind their
involvement in open source projects. As shown in Table 7.2, the authors identify three
different types of motivations: *i*) extrinsic motivations, related to the immediate or delayed benefits accruing to the individual generally through the direct use of the software
or through monetary compensations (e.g. better jobs or career advancement); *ii*) intrinsic motivations, associated with the pleasure enjoyed when involved in programming
activities; *iii*) other kinds of intrinsic motivations, related to a strong sense of identification with the open source movement and adherence to its norms of behaviour and
philosophy. The second column of Table 7.2 contains the percentage of programmers
who selected a specific motivation; the third and fourth columns distinguish between
the voluntary contributors and the paid ones respectively.

The most common motivation to contribute was extrinsic: 58.7% of the developers
were actually users of the software. The second most common motivation was intrinsic:
44.9% of the interviewed programmers found it intellectually stimulating to participate
in the project. The third most popular motivation to contribute was, again, extrinsic
and it referred to the opportunity of learning from expert users thus improving one's
programming abilities (selected by 41.3% of the sample). Other important motivations
belonged to the third category: one third of the programmers claimed to be involved in

---

[19]Taken from Lakhani and Wolf (2005).

open source projects because they agreed with the norms of the movement and believed that all software should be released under open source licenses; others, instead, felt an obligation to contribute to open source projects.

Lakhani and Wolf did not find significant differences in motivations between paid and unpaid developers; more specifically, the only two differences worth mentioning are: volunteers selected more frequently the item "Improve programming skills" (45.8% compared to 33.2%), while paid programmers reported more often "Enhance professional status" (22.8% compared to 13.9%).

7.4.3   Open source and business

Until recently, open source was perceived as a threat by software businesses. Nowadays, things have changed substantially and both large established incumbents such as IBM, Sun Microsystems, HP, Nokia, Siemens as well as start-ups are increasingly embracing open source strategies.

Take IBM for example; according to the company website, the firm has been involved in the open source movement for more than ten years; it has invested more than a billion dollars in the development of Linux and it is currently taking part in about 150 open source projects. Moreover, it has also released into the public domain more than 500 patents which were in its portfolio. Finally, IBM has also founded the *Eclipse* project, an integrated software development environment; the company has released the source code of Eclipse to the *Eclipse Foundation*, an organisation made up of more than 120 members, which are in many cases large commercial firms.

Many are the reasons why companies adopt open source strategies. As in the examples of Nokia and Apple discussed in the previous section, the decision of developing an open source software may be based on the possibility of re-using existing lines of code, thus substantially reducing the time and costs required for software completion. Network externalities may be another explanation for the adoption of open source strategies; as argued in Chapter 3, network externalities, very common in the case of software products, play a crucial role in the spreading of ICT products and in the building-up of a large installed base of users. In particular, a firm may choose an open source strategy in order to stimulate the adoption of its software product so that it becomes the industry standard; the firm can then derive profits by selling other (hardware or software) products which are compatible with the industry standard. Another advantage of open source is that a firm may benefit from third parties' contributions which improve the software product. As mentioned previously, external contributions may take different forms from code development to the writing or translation of a user's manual.

Box 7.3 – Creative Commons: some rights reserved

The advent of the Internet has jeopardised the traditional model of IP protection based on copyright; the Web has made it easier to copy and distribute digital content. Following this evolution a new model of collaborative creation has recently acquired increasing popularity. We are referring to the so-called *Creative Commons*, a phenomenon which first appeared in the U.S.A. at the beginning of this century, thanks to Professor Lawrence Lessig.

Creative Commons licenses enable an artist or, more generally, any creator of content to open up her work and distribute it according to the "some rights reserved model". As in the case of open source, Creative Commons licenses grant some rights also to others than the author in order to encourage the diffusion and circulation of works.

More specifically, an author can decide: *i*) to authorise/not to authorise commercial uses of the work; *ii*) to authorise/not to authorise the creation of derivative works and, in the case of authorisation she can *iii*) impose such works to be released under the same licensing scheme as the original work; finally, *iv*) the author can also demand authorship attribution, i.e. to be mentioned as the author of the original work. By combining these clauses in various ways, different Creative Commons licenses with various degrees of restrictions can be obtained (they differ according to what can be legally done with the original work).

Nowadays, an increasing number of contents and artistic works are released under Creative Commons licenses. For instance, since 2007 the BBC has started to distribute all its multimedia content under Creative Commons licenses, thus allowing anyone to re-use and publish them.

Creative Commons is a signal of the fact that IP management is deemed to change; maybe we will need to wait some years to see if David Bowie's forecasts are correct. In a 2002 interview to *The New York Times*, the White Duke prophesised "I don't think [the music industry] is going to work by labels and by distribution systems in the same way. The absolute transformation of everything that we ever thought about music will take place within 10 years, and nothing is going to be able to stop it. I see absolutely no point in pretending that it's not going to happen. I'm fully confident that copyright, for instance, will no longer exist in 10 years, and authorship and intellectual property is in for such a bashing".

Another important issue which has been widely discussed in the literature concerns the business models which can be applied to open source. The crucial point is the following: even though open source does not necessarily mean software for free, it is true that some of the clauses imposed by open source licenses significantly reduce the possibility of exploiting it commercially. We know that open source licenses guarantee that any licensee can re-distribute the product without paying any additional fees to the vendor; therefore, the acquirer can potentially become a competitor of the firm which originally developed the program.

With regard to this issue, it is interesting to mention the work by Daffara (2009), which describes the major business models adopted by software houses. Daffara examines over 200 software houses which adopt open source strategies and investigates which business models are the most common.[20] As shown in Table 7.3, selling complemen-

---

[20]The author selected firms that obtained at least 25% of their revenues (directly or indirectly) from

tary services is the business model adopted by 131 firms in the sample; in most cases, firms create the software, release it under open source licenses and profit from selling training, consulting and customisation services. Another popular business model is the sale of complementary products: 44 firms in the sample earn profits by selling hardware products which make use of the open source software.

Business model	Number of firms
Sale of complementary services	131
Open core	52
Sale of complementary products	44
Dual licensing	19
Other business model	29

Table 7.3: open source business models[21]

Other common open source business models are open core and dual licensing, two forms of versioning strategies. In the first case, the firm releases the core version of the program for free and under an open source license and profits from the sales of upgraded versions of the software combining the core program and some additional functionalities. In the case of dual licensing, there is only one version of the software which is distributed under two different licensing schemes: an open source and a proprietary one. The open source version is available for free unlike the proprietary one. As shown by Comino and Manenti (2011), dual licensing is an appropriate strategy when most of the demand is made up of commercial users who need the software to embed it into their derived products. Embedders prefer to have proprietary control on their products and, therefore, dislike the restrictions typically imposed by open source licenses. As a consequence, some of them are willing to pay in order to obtain the proprietary version of the software: proprietary licenses give full control on the code to the licensees who are then free to embed it into their own applications without fear of infringing copyleft provisions. Instead, users who adopt the open source version are those who are not particularly affected by the restrictions imposed by the license; these users contribute to improving the code and this allows the software vendor to sell upgraded versions of the product at a higher price.

In order to understand better how these versioning strategies work, we present a formal analysis of the open core business model.

---

open source activities.

[21]Taken from Daffara (2009).

Box 7.4 – Open source firms? Better young and small

A recent study by Bonaccorsi et al. (2006) examines the main characteristics of open source software firms. The authors collected data on 769 software firms operating in Finland, Germany, Italy, Portugal and Spain; all data refer to year 2004. Nineteen firms in the sample offered open source software only ("Only OS" in Table 7.4); instead, in 514 cases software products were released under proprietary licensing agreements ("Only proprietary"). The remaining 236 firms adopted "hybrid models": some software programs were available as open source while others were distributed under proprietary licensing schemes. Following a cluster analysis, the authors classified these latter 236 firms in two separate categories: those which were more oriented towards open source (characterised by a greater number of open source products and often adopting GPL licensing schemes, "More OS oriented" in the table) and those which were less oriented towards open source ("Less OS oriented").

Table 7.4 shows the main characteristics of the four categories of firms in terms of size (number of employees) and start-up year. The data show that the firms which were more OS oriented were smaller sized and relatively younger.

Category	N. of firms	Employees (average)	Employees (std. dev.)	Start-up year (min)	Start-up year (max)
Only OS	19	5,74	5,21	1991	2004
More OS oriented	70	9,83	11,6	1979	2004
Less OS oriented	166	63,41	210,44	1968	2004
Only proprietary	514	32,83	84,29	1968	2004

Table 7.4: software firms adopting open source strategies[a]

[a]Taken from Bonaccorsi et al. (2006).

The open core model

Suppose a commercial software house is selling a software made up of two separate components: i) the core program which provides the basic functionalities and ii) a plug-in, an extension of the program, namely a set of software components which add specific features to the core application. Let $s \geq 0$ denote the quality of the core program and sb that of the plug-in; in other words, we assume that the quality of the additional features depends on the intrinsic quality of the plug-in, b, and on that of the core program: if the core program is of low quality then also the additional features provided by the plug-in are of little use. Accordingly, when the two components are used together, the software is of quality $s(1 + b)$.

The software house can choose between two alternative strategies for the development and distribution of its product. The first strategy is in-house development; in this case, all the components (core and plug-in) are developed internally by the software house and are distributed under a proprietary licensing scheme. The quality of the core program equals s_{IH}, where subscript IH stands for in-house development. The alternative for

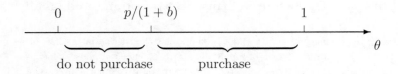

Figure 7.3: purchasing decision with in-house development

the software house is to adopt an open core strategy: besides distributing the two components jointly under a proprietary licensing scheme (we refer to this version of the software as the "proprietary" one), the software house releases the core of the program as open source (we refer to this one as the "open source", OS, version). In this case, consumers have two options to choose from: the open source version, which consists only of the core program or the proprietary version which includes also the plug-in. If consumers adopt the open source version, they contribute to improving the software, thus increasing the quality of the core up until s_{OC} which is larger than s_{IH}.[22] We also assume that the open source version is released for free (e.g. it is freely downloadable from the Internet). Finally, for the sake of simplicity, we normalise the quality of the core program in the case of in-house development to one: $s_{IH} = 1$.

In-house development. Suppose that the software house decides to develop the software internally. We assume that consumer reservation utility equals zero and that their preferences with respect to software quality are heterogeneous. Formally, let parameter θ measure consumer evaluation of quality; we assume that θ is uniformly distributed over the interval $[0, 1]$: consumers characterised by a small value of θ care little about the quality of the software while those with a larger θ are more sensitive.

Let's determine the demand for software, that is the number of consumers who decide to purchase the software at a given price. In the case of in-house development, the quality of the two components equals $s_{IH}(1 + b)$; since $s_{IH} = 1$, then the quality is equal to $(1 + b)$. Accordingly, the net utility which the consumer of type θ enjoys when purchasing the software at price p is:

$$U(\theta) = \theta\,(1 + b) - p.$$

Clearly, consumer of type θ decides to purchase the product if $U(\theta) \geq 0$, that is when the net utility derived from the purchase is larger than the reservation utility. After some simple algebraic manipulation we can check that a consumer buys the product if

---

[22]The subscript OC in the expression s_{OC} denotes that fact that we are considering the quality of the core program in the case of open core strategy.

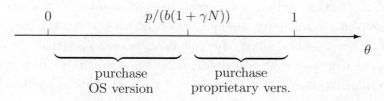

Figure 7.4: purchasing decision with open-core

$\theta \geq p/(1+b)$; this means that, given p, only those consumers who are sensitive enough to software quality purchase the product. As highlighted by Figure 7.3, consumers characterised by a θ between $p/(1+b)$ and 1 purchase the software, while those with θ between 0 and $p/(1+b)$ do not purchase. Recalling that θ is uniformly distributed over $[0,1]$, the demand function is $D(p) = (1 - p/(1+b))$. We assume that production and development costs are zero and therefore the firm chooses the price which maximises the following profit function:

$$\pi_{IH}(p) = p\left(1 - \frac{p}{(1+b)}\right).$$

From the first order condition, it is straightforward to check that the optimal price is $p_{IH}^* = (1+b)/2$; by substituting this expression into $\pi_{IH}(p)$ we obtain the equilibrium profits in the case of in-house development:

$$\pi_{IH}^* = \frac{1+b}{4}.$$

Open core strategy. Let's now consider the case of open core strategy. The firm sells the proprietary version of the software (core and plug-in) at price p; moreover, it also releases for free the core program under an open source license. Consumers, therefore, can choose between the two versions of the product, proprietary and open source. Following the empirical evidence presented in this chapter, we assume that the benefits which the software house enjoys from releasing the open source version derive from the contributions received by the community of users; in other words, we assume that the consumers who choose the open source version contribute to improving the core program by writing lines of code, by fixing bugs or by suggesting possible enhancements of the product.[23]

---

[23]Note that, for the sake of simplicity, we are not taking into consideration other possible advantages deriving from open source. In particular, in this model we assume that there are no network externalities, which are another typical reason why firms release software as open source. Moreover, since we are assuming that the open source version is available for free, this model neither takes into account the other typical advantage of adopting versioning strategies, namely the possibility of selling the "low"

Formally, let N denote the mass of consumers who adopt the open source version, that is the size of the community; the quality of the core program increases with N: $s_{OC} = 1 + \gamma N$, where 1 is the quality generated by software house (that is s_{IH}), and γN is the improvement derived from contributions by the community. In particular, γ is the parameter which measures the importance of the contributions by the community: when γ is high, then the community of users contributes greatly to the improvement of the program while when γ is small then the community of users does not contribute very much.

We can now determine how many users decide to download the open source version of the core program for free and how many prefer to purchase the proprietary version at p; in order to do this, we need to compare the net utility of the consumer of type θ in both cases:[24]

$$
\begin{aligned}
U_{OS}(\theta, N) &= \theta (1 + \gamma N); \\
U_P(\theta, N) &= \theta (1 + \gamma N)(1 + b) - p.
\end{aligned}
$$

The comparison between $U_{OS}(\theta, N)$ and $U_P(\theta, N)$ sheds light on the trade-off which consumers face when deciding between the two products: the open source version is free but it has no plug-in while the proprietary version is fully featured but requires the payment of the price p.

Note that the open source version of the software guarantees consumers a utility larger than the reservation value: $U_{OS}(\theta, N) \geq 0$ for each θ. This fact implies that all consumers adopt one of the two versions and therefore, unlike in the case of in-house development, the market is fully covered.

Now we can determine the number of consumers adopting the open source version or the proprietary one. In order to do so, we proceed by determining the indifferent consumer, that is the consumer identified by a taste parameter $\theta = \tilde{\theta}$ such that $U_P(\tilde{\theta}, N) = U_{OS}(\tilde{\theta}, N)$; after some simple algebraic manipulation, we have $\tilde{\theta} = p/(b(1 + \gamma N))$. As shown in Figure 7.4, all consumers whose sensitivity to quality is larger than $p/(b(1 + \gamma N))$ purchase the proprietary version; all those with a smaller θ prefer the open source version. Following the assumption on the distribution of θ, we can now determine the mass of consumers adopting the open source version, that is the size of the community, as a function of the price: $N = p/(b(1 + \gamma N))$.

For the sake of simplicity, rather than looking for the profit maximising price, we determine the optimal value of N, that is the size of the open source community that

quality product to consumers with a reduced willingness to pay, that is to segment the market (see Chapter 2).

[24]The subscripts OS and P denote which version the consumer selects: the open source version or the proprietary one, respectively.

maximises the profits of the software house. Following the expression of N that we have just derived, we can write the market price as a function of the community size: $p = Nb(1 + \gamma N)$. Therefore, we can now define the profits of the firm as a function of N:

$$\pi_{OC}(N) = Nb(1 + \gamma N)(1 - N),$$

where $(1 - N)$ is the mass of consumers who purchase the proprietary version. From the first order condition with respect to N we determine the optimal size of the open source community:

$$N^* = \frac{\gamma - 1 + G}{3\gamma},$$

where $G \equiv \sqrt{1 + \gamma + \gamma^2}$. By substituting N^* in the function $\pi_{OC}(N)$ we derive the equilibrium profits in the case of open core strategy:

$$\pi_{OC}^* = \frac{b(2\gamma + 1 - G)(\gamma - 1 + G)(2 + \gamma + G)}{27\gamma^2}.$$

The optimal strategy. By comparing π_{OC}^* with π_{IH}^*, we can determine under which conditions it is optimal for the firm to choose the open core strategy.

Result 3. *The firm chooses the open core strategy when the plug-in's quality is high enough; formally, when $b \geq \bar{b}$, with $\bar{b} \equiv 27\gamma^2/(8G^3 - 8 + 8\gamma^3 - 12\gamma - 15\gamma^2)$.*

This result has a straightforward interpretation. In the case of the open core strategy, the software house makes profits from the sale of the plug-in only, given that the core program is available for free as open source.[25] The benefit of the open core strategy is due to the fact that the contributions of the open source community increase the quality of the core program, s, and, as a consequence, that of the plug-in, sb. Therefore, the firm benefits substantially from the external contributions of the community only when b is large enough; consequently, the open core strategy is more profitable than in-house development when b is above the threshold value $\bar{b}$.[26]

By differentiating $\bar{b}$ with respect to γ we derive the following corollary:[27]

---

[25]Note that the open core strategy can also be interpreted as follows: the software house releases the core program into the public domain and deals only with the sale of the plug-in. Consumers who are interested in the complete software download the core program for free and buy the plug-in separately. In this case, it is clear that no profits are derived from the core program.

[26]Our analysis does not take into account a potential risk of the open core strategy. When the software is released as open source, it may occur that a programmer develops a competing plug-in and then sells it on the market. This fact reduces the profits that the software house can capture.

[27]Even if the result stated in this corollary is quite intuitive its proof involves a series of algebraic manipulation which we do not include for reasons of space.

Corollary 8. *The larger* γ, *the more profitable for the software house to adopt the open core strategy; formally,* $\bar{b}$ *is decreasing in* γ.

The underlying intuition of this corollary is rather straightforward: the more valuable the contributions of the open source community (the higher γ), the more profitable the open core strategy.

Summing up, open core is a profitable strategy when either the plug-in is of sufficiently high quality or the open source community largely contributes to the development of the core. But what about social welfare? It is possible to check (even though the formal proof is rather cumbersome) that social welfare is larger in the case of open core strategy; this fact occurs because of two reasons. The first one is related to the fact that all consumers adopt one of the two versions of the software while in case of in-house development some consumers do not buy the program at all; this fact clearly reduces the typical deadweight loss associated to the smaller monopoly quantity. The second positive welfare effect, is due to the fact that when the open core strategy is adopted the quality of the core program increases thanks to the contributions by the community of users. By combining the two positive effects, it follows that an open core strategy positively affects social welfare

7.4.4   OScar and Free Beer: open source beyond software

One of the most debated issues in the economics literature on open source concerns the possibility of applying the open source approach to other sectors besides the software industry. There are many examples of open content projects which aim at spreading culture and sharing knowledge with the same approach of open source software. A couple of well-known cases are, for instance, open science, extensively discussed by Dasgupta and David (1994), and Wikipedia, the on-line encyclopedia which some scholars believe to be as accurate as the Encyclopedia Britannica (Giles, 2005).

These are not the only cases of open content. For instance, a recent study carried out by OECD describes several projects aimed at sharing teaching materials (see OECD, 2007). Moreover, as argued by Raasch et al. (2009), important and successful cases of open content can be found not only in the film and music industry, but also in the creation of geographical maps and bioinformatics databases.

In the case of production of physical goods, the open source approach appears to be less common. Nevertheless, there are some examples of development of prototypes based on the open innovation model. The following table taken from Raasch et al. (2009) presents six significant examples (Table 7.5). In two cases (Free Beer and Neuros OSD, a device which stores different types of audio and video content) a prototype was successfully developed and production and commercialisation have already started. In other cases (RedRap, a 3D photocopying machine and Openmoko, a mobile phone) the products have been developed and are currently being tested. OScar and OSGV (two projects for the development of an open source car), instead, are still in the planning phase of the process.

Project name	Product	Development phase	Community size
Free Beer	beer	production	15
Neuros OSD	media centre	production	30,000
Openmoko	mobile phone	beta version	2,000
RedRap	3D photocopier	beta version	1,500
OScar	car	planning	3,000
OSGV	car	planning	250

Table 7.5: open design projects[28]

7.5 Intellectual property in the Internet age

One of the distinguishing features of open source lies in the way the owner (the original developer) of the software handles the intellectual property rights protecting the software. This issue allows us to introduce another important topic in ICT, namely the management of intellectual property in the Internet age. The digital revolution along with the popularity of the Internet has made it easier to copy, duplicate, and exchange information goods such as software, music, films and books. This has had a great impact on the behaviour of both consumers and content producers.

Moreover, in recent years, this technological progress has greatly increased public awareness towards a renovated system of IP laws that favour/stimulate access to information to promote knowledge sharing. Open source software can be viewed as a signal of this mounting awareness; in open source, the management of IP rights is crucial to stimulate code re-use and contributions from third parties. Open source programs are distributed with the so-called *copyleft provision*; copyleft is a play on the word copyright to describe the practice of using copyright law to offer the right to distribute copies and modified versions of a work and requiring that the same rights be preserved in modified versions of the work. This is a novel practice of exploiting intellectual property rights aimed at including third parties in the creation and distribution of the software rather than excluding them. This idea of including third parties in the innovation process is

---

[28]Taken from Raasch et al. (2009).

also common to other sectors besides software. This is, for instance, the case of the *Creative Commons* project described in Box 7.3. Authors who release their artistic product under a Creative Commons license can decide which rights to reserve themselves and which ones to guarantee to the users of the product.

Box 7.5 – An instructive story: the case of Napster[a]

Napster represented the first example of a successful peer-to-peer system. In 2000, just one year after its launch, there were already about 20 million Napster users around the world.

Technically speaking, Napster was not a pure peer-to-peer system (i.e. a network made up of peer computers organised in a non-hierarchical way) but it operated in a more centralised manner: a system of central servers represented the higher hierarchical level which dealt with coordination tasks while the actual file sharing took place directly through users' PCs (the lower hierarchical level). This centralised/hierarchical structure was also the main weakness of this file sharing network; when a series of lawsuits were filed by different record labels, it was relatively easy for Courts to determine Napster's liabilities for repeated copyright infringements.

Following these lawsuits, in July 2001, a Court injunction imposed Napster to stop operating. A couple of months later, Napster signed a licensing agreement with several record labels. The agreement stipulated the payment of 26 million dollars as compensatory damages and a further 10 million dollars for the possibility to continue operating. Napster was then transformed from a free to a fee-based service in order to recover, at least partially, the licensing payments owed to the record labels. This attempt failed and Napster was forced to shut down. On 17 May 2002, Napster was acquired by Bertelsmann AG for 8 million dollars.

File sharing did not end with Napster, however. Peer-to-peer networks have learned the lesson quite well. Nowadays file sharing is organised through pure peer-to-peer systems; for instance, Morpheus and LimeWire, both based on the Gnutella protocol, are completely decentralised systems which are much less exposed to lawsuits.

---

[a]Taken from Wikipedia.

Open source software and Creative Commons are two important phenomena of the information society we are living in. Access to information and content have acquired a strategic role in today's economy. Policy makers acknowledge the importance of these issues; for example, the Digital Agenda of the European Commission suggests which strategies and best practices should be adopted by EU national governments in order to take advantage of the growing opportunities emerging from the digital revolution. The most important area on which the Digital Agenda focuses on is precisely the promotion of access to information and content.[29]

---

[29]For further details on the European Digital Agenda see `ec.europa.eu/digital-agenda/`.

7.5.1 Intellectual property and digital piracy

Nowadays, the ease with which we can copy, duplicate and distribute information goods poses serious challenges for intellectual property protection.[30]

Peer-to-peer networks (P2P), for example, allow users to share files and exchange content. At the end of the 90s there was only Napster; today several P2P sites, such as Gnutella, eMule, OpenNap, Bittorrent or Frostwire, are available on the Internet. Major record labels and film studios have taken legal actions against the unauthorised sharing of their copyrighted content. After the legal dispute lost by Napster, file sharing networks have reorganised themselves to become less exposed to lawsuits (see Box 7.5) and the ever increasing number of P2P networks and users are clear evidence of the fact that legal actions have not been the appropriate way to deal with this phenomenon.

For this reason, several record labels, film studios, publishers and copyright holders in general are looking for other ways to defend their rights; one way is through the adoption of Digital Rights Management (DRM), i.e. a class of access control technologies aimed at limiting the use of digital content after sale. In software, a typical DRM technology is on-line activation; software houses use this technology to limit the number of systems the software can be installed on by requiring authentication with an on-line server. An early example of DRM is the *Content Scrambling System* (CSS) employed by the DVD Forum on DVDs; CSS uses an algorithm to encrypt content on the DVD disc. Manufacturers of DVD players must implement it in their devices so that they can decrypt the encrypted content to play DVDs. The CSS includes restrictions on how the DVD content is played, including what outputs are permitted and how such outputs are made available.

DRM technologies are still quite popular among content producers; however, some of the biggest content and hardware providers, such as Apple, Amazon and Walmart among others, have announced that they will stop using DRM. These technologies may pose severe limitations to the use of the product; for example, in the case of music files, they may limit the number or type of devices where the music can be played, thus decreasing the quality of the product perceived by consumers.

7.5.2 The potential benefits of digital piracy

So far, we have stuck to the traditional view according to which piracy reduces firms' profits. However, it is also possible for an holder of intellectual property rights to benefit

---

[30]On-line piracy certainly represents a major source of concern for the cultural industry. According to a recent analysis by Tera consultants, illegal downloads have doubled in the last ten years; estimated losses for 2011 in the European culture industry amount to 19 billion euros.

from piracy. According to Belleflamme and Peitz (2010), there are three possible reasons why piracy may be beneficial:

1. **network effects**. Many digital products are characterised by the existence of significant network effects; in these cases, the presence of a file sharing site may be beneficial for the firm since it increases its installed base of users. This argument resembles the Paradox of Economides discussed in Chapter 3. The negative effect due to the increased competition from the P2P site may be more than compensated by the value deriving from network effects. According to Conner and Rumelt (1991), a certain level of digital piracy can enhance not only firms' profits but also social welfare. Clearly, the firm can also attempt to reduce the competitive pressure from the P2P site by, for instance, increasing the quality of the original (not the pirated) version of the product or by offering additional functionalities or services, such as better customer care services;

2. **indirect appropriability**. The possibility of duplicating a product, for example by photocopying a book, represents certainly a positive and valuable aspect for consumers. The key point here is that duplicability may be positive also for the copyright holder when she can, partially or entirely, appropriate this greater value. This is the idea at the basis of the so-called "indirect appropriability", introduced by Liebowitz (1985) in a study on scientific journals. The author argued that the ability to make copies may increase consumer willingness to pay for originals and, thereby, allows producers to earn greater profits. Indirect appropriability may be possible when the publisher is able to discriminate between users who are interested in duplicating the original and those who are not, thus charging a higher price to the former set of users. As just mentioned, Liebowitz (1985) applied his theory having essentially in mind the case of scientific journals. For this reason, even though many further contributions in the literature have been based on Liebowitz's concept of indirect appropriability, it seems difficult to apply it to digital markets where products can be easily and costlessly duplicated;

3. **sampling strategies**. Many digital products are actually experience goods; in other words, their quality can be assessed only after the purchase or once the product has been used. For instance, the features and the functionalities of a software are known only after it has been installed and used. The same thing occurs in the case of music and films. Producers of experience goods often distribute trials for free-testing; in this way, consumers experience the quality of the product and, if satisfied, they purchase it. The same idea can be used to explain how a producer can benefit from the presence of a P2P website: consumers may obtain a copy of

the product from the website and, once they have experienced its quality, they can decide to buy the original. Clearly, in order for the presence of a P2P network to be beneficial for the firm, the pirated copy must be of a lower quality than the original version, in order to avoid the risk of product cannibalisation.

A simple model of sampling. Suppose that a digital product is supplied by a single firm; for simplicity, we normalise the marginal cost of production to 0. The product may be of high or low quality; we also assume that the quality of the product is private information of the firm. More specifically, before deciding whether or not to purchase the product, consumers only know that the probability of the product being of high quality (normalised to 1 for simplicity) equals $\phi \in (0, 1)$ while the probability of the product being of low quality (normalised to 0 for simplicity) equals $1 - \phi$. Therefore, before the purchase, expected product quality is $\phi \times 1 + (1 - \phi) \times 0 = \phi$.

Besides purchasing the original version from the firm, consumers may also download for free a pirated version of the product from a peer-to-peer website. The P2P network plays a double role; on the one hand, it competes with the firm and, on the other, it works as a "sampling device": once obtained the product from the P2P network, a consumer realises the quality of the product and if the quality is high she may decide to buy the original version. P2P consumers may be willing to pay for the original version because, for example, they are afraid of being caught with the illegal copy of the product and do not want to run the risk of being sanctioned.

The firm and the P2P network compete in prices "à la Hotelling": the firm and the website are located at the extremes of a unit-length segment (the firm at point 0 and the P2P website at point 1) while consumers are assumed to have mass 1 and to be distributed uniformly over the segment; the location of each consumer represents her preferences towards the two versions of the product. Consumers who are located near 0 (near 1) have a preference towards the original (pirated) version.

On the basis of the previous considerations, the expected utility of a consumer located in $x \in [0, 1]$ who purchases the original version is:

$$U_{OR}(\phi, x) = \phi - x - p,$$

where x represents the transportation cost and p is the price charged by the firm. At the same time, the expected utility derived from downloading for free the pirated version is:

$$U_{P2P}(\phi, x) = \phi - (1 - x).$$

Before determining the market equilibrium when the firm competes against the P2P website, it is useful to derive the equilibrium price and profits in the benchmark case where the product is supplied by the firm only (monopoly – no P2P). In this case, only the consumers who enjoy a non-negative net utility buy the digital product from the firm; formally, consumers such that $U_{OR}(\phi, x) \geq 0$. Therefore, for a given price p, the number of consumers who actually purchase the product is $\phi - p$ and, consequently, the profit function is:

$$\pi^m(p) = p(\phi - p).$$

By solving the first order condition, it follows that the equilibrium price and profits when there is no P2P website are:

$$p^m = \frac{\phi}{2} \quad \text{and} \quad \pi^m = \frac{\phi^2}{4}.$$

Note that the equilibrium price and profits are the same regardless of whether the product supplied by the firm is of high or low quality; moreover, p^m and π^m depend positively on probability ϕ: the lower the expected quality, the lower the price and profits.

Consider, now, what happens when the firm competes with the P2P website. In what follows, we assume that $\phi \geq 3/4$; this condition guarantees that the market is fully covered and, therefore, that, in equilibrium, all consumers adopt one of the two products: some buy the original version while others download the pirated one from the website. It is straightforward to check that in comparison to the monopoly case the firm offering a low quality product obtains smaller profits; this is due to the fact that when the firm sells a low quality product and competes with the P2P network, the number of consumers who purchase the original version is lower than in the monopoly case. This result may change in the event of a high-quality product. Let's consider this case in greater detail.

Each consumer decides which version to adopt by comparing the utility derived from the original version and from the pirated one. The indifferent consumer is located at x such that $U_{OR}(\phi, x) = U_{P2P}(\phi, x)$; formally, the indifferent consumer is positioned in:

$$\tilde{x}(p) = \frac{1 - p}{2}.$$

Given p, all those consumers located to the left of $\tilde{x}(p)$ purchase the original version, while the others download the pirated one. Following the assumption of uniform distribution, the mass of consumers purchasing the original version equals $\tilde{x}(p)$, while $1 - \tilde{x}(p)$ is the mass of consumers who download for free the pirated version.

Box 7.6 – File sharing and legal sales

Several empirical papers investigate the effects of a peer-to-peer network on firm sales. In what follows, we summarise the results shown in a couple of the most significant contributions in the literature, namely those by Fukugwa (2011) and Tanaka (2004).

The first study focuses on the video games market and is based on a questionnaire sent in 2009 to 10,000 Japanese users of two of the most popular game consoles, Nintendo DS and Sony PSP. According to this data, a significant share of about 40% of users stated that they were able to download and install pirated video games. The study by Tanaka (2004), instead, analyses the effect of P2P networks on the sales of music CDs in Japan. The two studies find no evidence of a significant impact of file sharing networks on market sales.

However, an interesting result emerges from Tanaka's article. The fact that P2P networks do not affect sales is due to two contrasting effects which balance each other. In particular, Tanaka shows that the presence of a P2P network increases the sales of high quality music, while it tends to reduce those of low quality music. Therefore Tanaka suggests that file sharing websites can be a powerful channel which drives consumers to search for better quality music.

This result is in line with the sampling model we present in this Chapter. The presence of a P2P network has two contrasting effects on firm profits. It lowers them, since the P2P network actually is a competitor of the firm; however, there is also a positive effect. The P2P network represents a promotional channel: first consumers test the product by downloading the pirated copy and then, if they are satisfied with its quality, some of them proceed to buying the original version.

Clearly, only producers of high quality goods can actually benefit from the presence of a P2P website. A file sharing network, by contrast, damages firms which produce low quality goods since they are affected only by the negative impact of file sharing systems.

Consider the firm that is deciding which price to charge. The firm knows that its product is of high quality and it anticipates that some P2P consumers, once they have realised the high quality of the product, buy the original version. More specifically, the firm sells to two categories of consumers: those who since the very beginning purchase the original product (of mass $\tilde{x}(p)$) and those who purchase the product after having obtained it from the P2P website. We assume that a fraction μ of consumers who have downloaded the pirated version are afraid of being caught with the illegal copy of the product and therefore decide to destroy it. Since they have verified that the product is of high quality, some of these "frightened" consumers may decide to purchase the original version; in particular, this occurs to all those consumers for whom $U_{OR}(1,x) = 1 - x - p \geq 0$.[31] Therefore, a fraction μ of consumers located on the $(\tilde{x}(p), \bar{x}(p))$ segment purchases the original version after having tried the pirated one, where $\bar{x}(p)$ is the value of x such that

---

[31]Note that we are implicitly assuming that P2P consumers are myopic: utility U_{P2P} does not take into account that once verified the high quality of the product, the consumer may actually decide to purchase the original version.

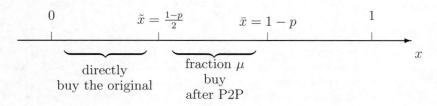

Figure 7.5: consumers' choice with a P2P network

$U_{OR}(1, x) = 0$, that is $\bar{x}(p) = 1 - p$.[32]

The firm's profits are, therefore, the sum of two separate components (see Figure 7.5): the profits which come from consumers who directly buy the original version (direct profits) and those deriving from the consumers who buy the product after having tried the pirated version (P2P derived profits). Formally:

$$\pi(p) = \underbrace{\tilde{x}(p)\,p}_{\text{direct profits}} + \underbrace{\mu\,(\bar{x}(p) - \tilde{x}(p))\,p}_{\text{P2P derived profits}} = p\left(\frac{1-p}{2}\right)(1+\mu).$$

It is easy to check that $\pi(p)$ is a concave function; by solving the first order condition, we determine the equilibrium price and profits:

$$p^* = \frac{1}{2} \quad \text{and} \quad \pi^* = \frac{1+\mu}{8}.$$

It is interesting to note that, unlike the case of monopoly, the profits of the high quality firm do not depend on ϕ, the expected quality of the product. This happens because the marginal consumer $\bar{x}(p)$ purchases the original version only after having verified that the product is of high quality.

By comparing the market equilibria with and without the P2P website, it follows that piracy is beneficial for the firm when $\mu > 2\phi^2 - 1$. The following result sums up this consideration:

Result 4. *Consider an experience good whose quality is unknown to consumers. If the good is of high quality, then the producer benefits from the presence of a peer-to-peer network provided that the fraction of consumers who purchase the original version once they have tried the pirated one is large enough; formally, $\mu > 2\phi^2 - 1$.*

The above result is extremely interesting because it proves that if the fraction of "pirates" who decide to purchase the original version is large enough then the producer

---

[32] $\bar{x}(p)$ identifies the consumer who is indifferent between buying from the firm a high quality copy of the product and not buying anything at all. One can easily check that $\bar{x}(p) > \tilde{x}(p)$.

of the high quality good obtains greater profits when competing against a P2P website rather than when it acts as a monopoly. When μ is large, in fact, the P2P website is a powerful "advertising" channel which informs consumers about the quality of the product. Finally, let us note that μ can be naturally interpreted as the strength of the legal system against piracy; therefore, our result suggests that if the enforcement against piracy is tight enough, then consumers are induced to purchase the original version once they have tried the pirated one and this goes to the benefit of firms selling high quality products.

Chapter 8

Antitrust in High-Tech Sectors

8.1 Introduction

Careful readers will have surely noticed that market efficiency in ICT sectors is a topic that has emerged throughout all the chapters of this book. The interest towards this issue lies not only in the increasing importance of digital markets in modern societies, but also in some of the peculiarities characterising these sectors. As argued in the previous chapters, the presence of substantial economies of scale combined with the effect of network externalities and the high innovation rates along with the common practice of filing several patent applications and of using them as a strategic weapon, are all features which typically characterise digital markets and which are likely to favour the emergence of dominant firms.

The main aim of policy makers and antitrust authorities is to increase and preserve all dimensions of the economic efficiency of markets: allocative (social welfare maximisation), productive (minimisation of production costs) and dynamic (stimulus to research and development). According to the traditional view, these goals are best achieved by promoting competition among firms; competitive pressure induces companies to cut their production costs and to reduce market prices, thus increasing both allocative and productive efficiency; moreover, the presence of competitors forces firms to increase efforts in R&D in order to develop new goods and services or to improve production processes (dynamic efficiency).

For these reasons, in order to promote fair competition, several countries have adopted antitrust regulations aimed at preventing and eventually punishing anti-competitive practices; the two main areas of intervention of antitrust laws are the abuse of market power by dominant firms and collusion.[1] A firm is said to be dominant when

---

[1]Besides the abuse of dominant position and collusion, antitrust authorities are also active in re-

it behaves "to an appreciable extent independently of its competitors";[2] abuse of dominance takes place, for instance, when such a firm adopts strategies aimed at forcing rivals to exit the market. Collusion, instead, occurs when firms form a cartel or when they find a way to coordinate their strategies in order to keep prices above the competitive level to extract monopoly rents.

Due to the characteristics of ICT sectors, the emergence of abuse of dominance and collusion are a concrete possibility; for this reason, antitrust authorities must pay particular attention to the functioning of these markets. Even though a comprehensive discussion of the full range of antitrust issues in ICT is beyond the scope of this chapter, in the following sections we present some prime examples which highlight the peculiarities of the enforcement of antitrust laws in these markets. We also introduce a couple of theoretical models which we believe can contribute greatly to the understanding of some specific issues related to competition policy in high-tech sectors.

8.2 Collusion in digital markets

In Chapter 2, we thoroughly discussed the efficiency of on-line markets in comparison to brick-and-mortar ones. In particular, we showed that firms can benefit from the Internet by adopting specific commercial strategies, such as versioning or bundling; we argued that firms operating on-line are able to design articulated strategies and set prices that are very close to consumer willingness to pay.

In this section, we focus on the on-line book retailing and we present the work by Latcovich and Smith (2001). As we shall argue, on-line retailers are able to closely monitor competitors' pricing strategies; this feature of digital markets enables firms to adopt commercial strategies which weaken competitive pressure.

The on-line book market is one of the most mature retail sectors on the Internet featuring several conditions that should make it highly competitive, with cost-oriented prices and little dispersion. Books are homogenous goods; retailers can, at most, differentiate their services on the basis of delivery time and shipping fees. Moreover, no

---

viewing mergers and acquisitions and in controlling state aids to companies. Mergers and acquisitions, in fact, increase market concentration and may, in some cases, substantially reduce the effectiveness of competition; for this reason, mergers and acquisitions among large companies need to be approved by antitrust authorities. State aid legislation lays down a general rule according to which the state should not aid or subsidise private companies in distortion of free competition; exceptions are admitted in the case of natural disasters or to help regional development.

[2]European Court of Justice, case 27/76 United Brands Co. and United Brands Continental BV *vs* European Commission.

substantial investments are required to operate and this implies that barriers to entry are negligible.

Latcovich and Smith focus on the U.S. market by examining the on-line price trend of 12 books selected among the top positions of the "bestseller lists" of *The New York Times* and of *The Times*. The authors collected data on the prices charged by several Internet retailers from August 1999 to February 2000.[3] During this period of time, the U.S. on-line book retailing was characterised by the presence of two dominant companies (Amazon.com and Barnes & Noble) and a competitive fringe of smaller retailers. The two authors collected data for the two market leaders and for three smaller operators, Fatbrain, Buy.com and A1books.com.

Data	Rank	Amazon.com	Bn.com	A1 Books	Fatbrain	Buy.com
30 Aug 99	5	13,90	13,97	18,25	19,95	n.d.
06 Sept 99	5	13,98	13,97	18,25	13,95	n.d.
. . .	. . .	. . .	. . .	. . .	. . .	. . .
18 Oct 99	12	13,98	13,97	18,25	13,95	n.d.
25 Oct 99	*18*	*19,57*	*19,56*	18,25	13,95	n.d.
1 Nov 99	20	19,57	19,56	18,25	13,95	n.d.
8 Nov 99	20	19,57	19,56	18,25	13,95	n.d.
15 Nov 99	24	19,57	19,56	18,25	19,55	n.d.
22 Nov 99	23	19,57	19,56	19,50	19,55	n.d.
29 Nov 99	25	19,57	19,56	19,50	19,55	16,77
06 Dec 99	24	19,57	19,56	19,50	19,55	16,77
13 Dec 99	17	19,57	19,56	19,50	19,55	18,77
20 Dec 99	21	19,57	19,56	19,00	19,55	18,77
27 Dec 99	22	19,57	19,56	19,00	19,55	18,77
3 Jan 00	20	19,57	19,56	19,00	19,55	18,77
10 Jan 00	*15*	*13,98*	*13,97*	19,00	19,55	18,77
17 Jan 00	*23*	*19,57*	*19,56*	19,00	19,55	18,77
24 Jan 00	32	19,57	19,56	18,25	19,55	18,77
. . .	. . .	. . .	. . .	. . .	. . .	. . .
21 Feb 00	40	19,57	19,56	18,25	19,55	18,77

Table 8.1: on-line retailing prices of Hannibal by T. Harris[4]

---

[3]More precisely, the prices of six books were collected starting from August 1999 while the prices of the remaining titles were gathered from November 1999.

[4]Data taken from Latcovich and Smith (2001).

The tables show the prices charged by the five retailers for two of the twelve titles examined:[5] *Hannibal* by Thomas Harris, the third novel of the famous Hannibal Lecter series and *Pop Goes the Weasel* by James Patterson, a crime novel featuring detective Alex Cross.[6] For reasons which will soon be clear, in the second column (labelled by "Rank") we show the ranking of the book in the bestseller list of *The New York Times* at the beginning of each week.

In both cases, the tables show that during the first weeks of observation, prices set by the two market leaders, Amazon and Barnes & Noble, were substantially lower than those of the competitive fringe; in some cases, the difference in prices was around 30–40%. Therefore, our first consideration is that prices were highly dispersed; for instance, in the first week, the price of Hannibal ranged from 13.90$ to 19.95$.

A more interesting observation can be made by looking at the dynamic pattern of the pricing strategies of the two market leaders. As long as the book is included in the top 15 selling titles of the NYT list of bestsellers, Amazon.com and Barnes & Noble charge a price lower than competitors. As time passes by and the book exits the top selling positions, the prices charged by the two dominant companies soar above those of the competitive fringe. In other words, unlike what one might expect, the prices charged by Amazon.com and Barnes & Noble show an anti-cyclical pattern: the two firms increase their prices when demand shrinks!

Date	Rank	Amazon.com	Bn.com	A1 Books	Fatbrain	Buy.com
8 Nov 99	3	13,48	13,47	17,75	18,85	n.d.
15 Nov 99	3	13,48	13,47	17,75	18,85	n.d.
22 Nov 99	4	13,48	13,47	18,75	18,85	n.d.
29 Nov 99	5	13,48	13,47	18,75	18,85	12,94
6 Dec 99	8	13,48	13,47	18,75	18,85	13,47
...	...	...	...	...	...	...
24 Jan 00	12	13,48	13,47	17,75	18,85	13,47
31 Jan 00	*18*	*18,87*	*18,86*	17,75	18,85	13,47
7 Feb 00	19	18,87	18,86	17,75	18,85	13,47
14 Feb 00	20	18,87	18,86	17,75	18,85	15,00
21 Feb 00	29	18,87	18,86	17,75	18,85	18,17

Table 8.2: on-line retailing prices of *Pop Goes the Weasel* by J. Patterson[7]

---

[5]Data on the hardcover price of each book were taken directly from the websites of the retailers; shipping costs are not included, since they are almost identical across firms.

[6]For reasons of space, we present the observations of two books only. In the other cases price trends are very similar to those presented in Tables 8.1 and 8.2.

[7]Data taken from Latcovich and Smith (2001).

The pricing strategy adopted by the two market leaders seems quite odd. Typically, when a bestseller is launched, book retailers charge high prices in order to sell the product to those (impatient) consumers who want to purchase it at once. Afterwards, as time passes by, prices are reduced to attract those consumers with a lower willingness to pay for the product. However, the evidence shown in the tables suggests that the two market leaders coordinated on the opposite pricing behaviour.

The fact that Amazon.com and Barnes & Noble coordinated on different pricing strategies emerges clearly when looking at the prices charged when a book re-entered the top 15 selling titles. This was the case of Hannibal: on 10 January 2000, after a couple of months in position 20 of the bestseller list, the book re-entered the top 15, probably due to an increase in sales during Christmas holidays; immediately, Amazon.com and Barnes & Noble lowered prices to the level charged some months earlier (respectively, 13.98$ and 13.97$). A week later, the book exited the top positions of the list and the two market leaders raised prices back to 19.57$ and to 19.56$, respectively.

How can we explain this puzzling pricing strategy? The most convincing explanation proposed by Latcovich and Smith is collusion. The two authors interpret the behaviour of Amazon.com and Barnes & Noble in light of the work by Rotenberg and Saloner (1986). The authors prove that when demand is high, collusion is difficult to sustain, especially when demand is expected to decrease over time; in other words, when demand is high, firms are tempted to break the cartel, cutting prices in order to expand their market shares. Clearly, if firms act in this way, the cartel collapses and firms end up engaging in a price war.[8] The actual behaviour of Amazon.com and Barnes & Noble fits the arguments discussed by Rotenberg and Saloner (1986). When demand is high, the two leading firms coordinate on a low price in order to reduce the incentives to break the cartel. Once the book exits the top selling positions (i.e. when demand shrinks), Amazon.com and Barnes & Noble coordinate on a higher price.

The collusive hypothesis is also supported by the fact that the prices charged by the two firms were extremely close to each other and, in some cases, even identical. It is important to note that collusion between these two operators was favoured by the possibility for each firm to closely monitor the price charged by the competitor. In digital markets, companies can observe rivals' prices easily and quickly via a simple click of the mouse. As argued by the traditional industrial organisation literature, cartels are likely to be long-lasting when firms are able to check each others' behaviour and thus to

---

[8] Alternatively, one may think that the two market leaders adopted a bait-and-switch pricing strategy, namely they decided to reduce their profit margin from bestsellers in order to attract customers and sell them other products too. However, this argument is not completely convincing because it does not explain the perfect matching between the prices of Amazon.com and Barnes & Noble, that were equal down to a single cent.

respond quickly in case someone breaks the collusive agreement.

This simple example shows that in digital markets not only consumers but also firms can benefit from greater information on the commercial strategies adopted by rivals; companies can monitor competitors' behaviour, thus favouring collusive practices. Long term relations and repeated interactions among on-line retailers along with the greater ease with which firms can obtain information about each other may substantially contribute to cartel sustainability.

8.3   Network effects and compatibility: the Microsoft case

In Chapter 3, we presented the main economic and strategic aspects of network markets; we showed that these markets are known as *winner takes all*, since, typically, the presence of network externalities enables a certain technology to impose itself as the standard. We also argued that when different technologies compete in the market, compatibility is one of the most relevant strategic levers. In some cases, compatibility may be convenient for all firms, while in others firms may be involved in battles for the standard; these battles frequently end up with one firm imposing its technology as the standard. In these circumstances, antitrust authorities need to continuously monitor market dynamics in order to avoid the abuse of the dominant position by market leaders.

The well-known "Microsoft case" exemplifies the importance of these features. Specifically, the European Commission, the antitrust authority at the EU level, accused Microsoft of violating article 82 of the EC competition law (now article 102 of the Treaty on the Functioning of the European Union).[9] According to the European Commission, Microsoft abused its dominant position through two distinct strategies:

1. by deliberately restricting interoperability between Windows PCs and non-Microsoft work-group servers;

2. by tying its Windows Media Player (WMP) to the Windows operating system.

The case was raised in December 1998 when Sun Microsystems, a rival of Microsoft, sued Bill Gates' company for anticompetitive conduct. The complaint concerned the lack of disclosure of some technical information on Windows interfaces which Sun needed in order to develop products for computers running Windows operating system (OS); in other words, Microsoft's behaviour hampered the possibility for Sun to develop software

---

[9]This section is based on the brief review of the case provided by the European Commission in the press release IP/04/382 dated 24 March, 2004.

applications, especially for work-group servers. Later investigations carried out by the European Commission revealed that Sun was not the only firm which had been denied this information; Microsoft's decision not to disclose information about Windows interfaces appeared to be part of a broader strategy aimed at driving competitors out of the market.

Rivals were prevented from developing products that were comparable to Microsoft's in terms of reliability, security and processing speed. Further investigations by the European Commission also revealed that the lack of information disclosure on Windows interfaces altered PC manufacturers' choice in favour of Microsoft's server products. On top of all these arguments, a series of internal documents that the European Commission found on Microsoft's premises confirmed the fact that Bill Gates' company was perfectly aware of the benefits deriving from this strategy, thus strengthening the allegations.

Accusations against Microsoft did not stop here, however; in 2000, the Commission extended its investigations in order to study the anticompetitive effects deriving from Microsoft's tying of Windows Media Player (WMP) with Windows 2000 PC operating system. The Commission concluded that the ubiquity which WMP had achieved as a result of being tied to the Windows OS, actually reduced the incentives of music, film and other media companies to develop content for alternative/rival media players.

Consequently, the Commission reported that Microsoft's tying of its media player had foreclosed the market to competitors and, ultimately, reduced consumers' choice; competing products which were not compatible with WMP were set at a disadvantage which was not related to their price or quality.

According to the European Commission, the two strategies of restricting interoperability to Windows OS and tying Windows OS with WMP were clear proof of Microsoft's attempt: *i*) to gain a leading position in the market for work-group server operating systems and *ii*) to eliminate competition on the market for media players altogether.

This latter aspect played a relevant role in the analysis conducted by the European Commission. According to the data available during the investigation, the market for media players was "tipping" in favour of Microsoft WMP and the Commission was convinced that this would have allowed Microsoft to acquire a dominant position also in related markets, such as those for encoding technologies, for software for on-line music distribution, for digital rights management technologies and so on. In the end, the fear of the Commission was that by building all these dominant positions Microsoft would have contributed to reducing competitors' incentives to invest in R&D activities in areas which were critical to the development and diffusion of information and communication technologies.

Box 8.1 – Cloud computing: the end of Microsoft dominance?[a]

Cloud computing (CC) refers to the use of computing resources (hardware and software) which are available in a remote location and accessible over the Internet; CC is considered the new killer app in the IT world, something which will dramatically change the entire industry.

In the case of CC, computing infrastructures are not in the user's hands, but are located far away, "in the cloud"; infrastructures are maintained by a supplier of CC services and consist of a series of servers which allow provision of computing resources to users (either individuals or firms) on a massive scale.

Following Fershtman and Gandal (2012), CC services can be classified as follows:

- infrastructure as a service: data storage and management services (computer servers);

- software as a service: Web-based applications (such as Gmail or Hotmail);

- platform as a service: essentially an operating system in the cloud such as Google AppEngine and Microsoft Azure.

Currently, the first two types of services are the most popular; in 2010, *The Economist* revealed that infrastructure and software services on the cloud generated more than 13 billion dollars in revenues. The market for platform services is less developed, but it is expected to grow fast in the next few years. Overall, CC services are estimated to reach 240 billion dollars in revenues by 2020 (Forrester Research).

The reason for this rapidly increasing popularity of CC services is simple: cost efficiency. Think of a business user: several estimates show that, on average, firms' IT maintenance accounts for around 80% of total IT expenditures; CC allows firms to cut this ratio down to 20%, and this gives IT departments the ability to invest more on the development of core business processes. Also individuals largely benefit from CC; for example, CC allows them to access personal files and data anytime and anywhere, or to share them with others without the need of having costly computing resources.

The most interesting type of cloud computing is platform as a service. So far this market has developed as a vertically integrated system, with the main actors (Google and Microsoft) directly providing complementary software (email services, office productivity suites and so on) for their platforms/operating systems (OS). Fershtman and Gandal predict that the market will evolve towards a separated vertical structure with platform owners supplying the infrastructure and several independent software developers providing services via the platform owner's proprietary cloud. According to this evolution, the market is bound to develop into a truly two-sided network where the two sides are individuals and application developers. Cross-side network effects are clear: users prefer the OS which offers the greatest variety of applications and programmers are willing to develop apps for the OS which is the most widely adopted.

CC is expected to change the shape of the market for operating systems; today, due to the predominance of network effects which has ignited the typical winner-takes-all dynamics, the market is dominated by Windows OS. Fershtman and Gandal claim that the transition to the cloud will allow for greater competition to emerge; this prediction is supported by the following two observations: *i*) data in CC are likely to be portable across platforms, thus increasing compatibility among different cloud OS, and *ii*) users' switching costs when changing platforms are negligible, thus making it much easier for consumers to shift from one cloud OS to another. These two characteristics are likely to increase market competitiveness and, possibly, to reduce the dominance of Microsoft in the OS market.

[a]Based on Fershtman and Gandal (2012).

At the end, the European Commission condemned Microsoft for abuse of dominant position. According to the Commission, Microsoft's anticompetitive conduct lasted for over five years and for this reason the final decision was very severe; not only did the company of Bill Gates have to pay a fine of 497.2 million euros but the Commission also imposed the following remedies:

- **interoperability**: Microsoft was obliged to disclose complete and accurate information to allow developers of non-Microsoft work-group servers to achieve full interoperability with Windows PCs and servers. In exchange for this information, Microsoft was entitled to receive a reasonable compensation in the case of information protected by intellectual property;[10]

- **tying**: Microsoft was required to offer PC manufacturers a version of its Windows operating system without WMP. In this way, the choice of which media player to install was left to consumers.[11]

The measures imposed by the European Commission have been highly criticised;[12] nonetheless the Microsoft case represents a milestone for antitrust intervention in network industries. In particular, the case highlights with great clarity how ICT markets need ongoing monitoring in order to prevent dominant firms from adopting anticompetitive practices. We will come back to these issues also in the following sections, when discussing access to intellectual property rights.

8.4   Antitrust policies and incentives for innovation

In ICT and, more in general, in industries characterised by extremely high rates of innovation, the application of competition laws may have strong effects on incentives to innovate. In the following section, we shall discuss this issue in greater detail while in Section 8.4.2 we focus on a more specific aspect, that is the relationship between antitrust legislation and intellectual property protection.

---

[10]In July 2006, the European Commission found that Microsoft did not fulfil this obligation and imposed an additional penalty payment of 280.5 million euros to the company from Redmond.

[11]Note that Microsoft maintained the possibility of offering also a version of its operating system with WMP. However, the two versions of Windows (with and without WMP) were required to be equally performing.

[12]Economides (2008) claims that in the end the remedies imposed on Microsoft did not have any relevant effect on consumer welfare; for example, the version of Windows without WMP was sold at the same price as the one with the media player and practically no computer manufacturer bought Windows without WMP.

> ## Box 8.2 – VisiCalc: the first Killer App for PCs[a]
>
> The story of VisiCalc goes back to the early 70s when the first personal computers were being developed. Early PCs were certainly more advanced than first-generation calculators thanks to substantial improvements of input and output systems and to the adoption of more user-friendly applications, such as the well-known BASIC software. Nevertheless, despite these impressive technological advances, in those years computers were still meant for expert users and not for the mass market.
>
> VisiCalc is the first killer application in the software industry. It represented a turning point that transformed computers from a hobby for enthusiasts into an important business tool for a wide range of people. The secret to success of this application consisted in exploiting the data processing ability of computers for a very specific problem, namely the development of a spreadsheet program, which soon became an essential tool for financial planning and for mathematical computations.
>
> VisiCalc made manipulations on large data sets an easy task. Complex series of operations could be performed and repeated in virtually no time at all. This application was much more powerful and flexible than the management software tools that were available at that time.
>
> VisiCalc was a breakthrough for the market with significant effects also on the sales of computers. The market share of Apple II, the first computer VisiCalc was installed on, started to soar just a couple of months after the spreadsheet was available. This fact convinced producers of microcomputers and of programmable calculators to install the software in their products.
>
> In only a few years, more than 1 million copies of VisiCalc were sold; more recent applications such as Supercalc, Lotus 1-2-3, Quattro, Multiplan and Excel have been strongly "inspired" by VisiCalc, another fact that confirms the great success of this application.
>
> ---
>
> [a]Taken from Di Domizio (2010).

8.4.1 Antitrust in dynamic industries

The aim of this section is to analyse the impact of antitrust enforcement on the dynamics of innovative industries; typically, competition in these industries differs greatly from the one that can be observed in more mature sectors. In industries characterised by high innovation rates, such as ICTs, firms often compete to acquire full control of the market; in the economics jargon, we say that firms compete not *within* the market but *for* the market. Innovation takes place as a series of winner-takes-all races where firms invest large amounts of money in research and development in order to invent a "killer application", a product which is so innovative compared to the existing technology that it immediately becomes the new industry standard. For example, cassette tapes replaced the 8-track, only to be replaced in turn by compact discs, which were undercut by MP3 players, which will in turn eventually be replaced by newer technologies. Schumpeter (1942) coined the expression *creative destruction* to describe this kind of industry dynamics.

On top of that, in high-tech industries, technology is usually characterised by low marginal costs and large fixed costs due to the fact that firms need to invest substantial amounts of money in R&D and in infrastructures.

The literature on the role of antitrust laws in highly innovative industries is extremely vast. As argued by many scholars, in such an economic environment, a rigid application of antitrust policies aimed at stimulating competition and preventing firms from exploiting their market power, may have a negative impact on the natural dynamics of innovation. According to Evans and Schmalensee (2002) there are at least two implications for antitrust analysis:

- **market power.** In high-tech industries the presence of market power is not a symptom of market failure but a necessary condition for innovation; successful firms need to earn high profits as a return for their substantial investments;

- **relevance of innovation.** The key determinant of industrial performance is innovation. Therefore, rather than static efficiency, competition policies must stimulate dynamic efficiency; in other words, antitrust legislation should provide firms with appropriate incentives to invest in R&D.

Therefore, the question economists ask themselves is whether or not antitrust enforcement in ICT industries should follow different standards for the definition of relevant markets or for the assessment of market power and of predatory strategies. According to Evans and Schmalensee (2002), dynamic industries should not be exempted from antitrust laws nor should they be subject to specifically tailored rules. However, the two authors believe that antitrust laws should take into greater account the specificities characterising these industrial sectors; according to Evans and Schmalensee, antitrust authorities tend to be too concerned with static efficiency: this approach often neglects the fact that the main source of value in dynamic industries is related to firms' ability to innovate.

Shapiro (2005) holds a rather different opinion. The author uses the U.S. experience to deny the fact that antitrust authorities focus essentially on static efficiency. On top of this, Shapiro argues that antitrust laws aimed at limiting dominant positions do not hamper innovation incentives; as the author says, indeed, "major innovations often come from lean and hungry firms introducing disruptive technologies, hoping to topple current market leaders, rather than from dominant incumbents who profit greatly from the status quo."

Fair competition and incentives for innovation

In order to understand better the relationship between antitrust policies and incentives to innovate, we devote this section to presenting a simplified version of the theoretical analysis by Segal and Whinston published in 2007 in the *American Economic Review*. In this work, the authors highlight the contrasting effects of a more stringent antitrust policy on firms' incentives to innovate in dynamic industries.

As we emphasised above, a crucial characteristic of high-tech industries is that innovation takes place as a series of winner-takes-all races; consistently, Segal and Whinston examine the effects of antitrust policies in an industry characterised by a sequence of inventions, where in each period an entrant firm which has developed an innovation replaces the incumbent and becomes the market leader. Antitrust policies play a double role: on the one side, they help the potential entrant by protecting it from the incumbent but, on the other, they lower the value of incumbency and, therefore, they reduce the entrant's incentives to invest to become the market leader. Segal and Whinston examine the net effect of these forces and emphasise the so-called *front-loading effect*.

The model by Segal and Whinston: the front-loading effect.
Consider a game with an infinite time horizon; in each period t, with $t = 1, 2 ... \infty$, only two firms, A and B, operate; let $\delta \in [0, 1]$ denote the discount rate.

In each period of time, one of the firms is the market leader while the other is the potential entrant; formally, consider a generic period of time t and, without loss of generality, assume that:

- firm B is already operating in the market and it is, therefore, the leader (the incumbent);

- firm A has not entered the market yet and, therefore, represents a potential entrant (the challenger).

At the beginning of period t, the challenger can undertake a research project; the project consists in an investment c which generates an innovation with probability $1/2$. We assume that the incumbent does not invest in any research activity.

If the research project is successful, then firm A enters the market and competes against firm B. A's innovation is a killer application that forces B to exit the market at the end of the period; therefore, in the following period, $t + 1$, the two firms reverse their roles: firm A becomes the incumbent and firm B plays the role of the challenger which, in turn, can invest c to develop a new killer application, an event occurring with probability $1/2$. If firm A does not innovate in t (either because it has not invested at all or because the research project was not successful), then it does not enter the market; in this case, firm B continues to operate as the incumbent-monopolist. Clearly, if in t firm A does not innovate, at $t+1$ the two firms do not reverse their roles: firm A still is the challenger and firm B the incumbent.

We can now define the profits obtained by the two firms in t. As mentioned previously, if firm A does not innovate, then B is the only firm operating in the market; in this case, firm B enjoys the monopoly profits, which, for simplicity, we normalise to 1. By contrast, if firm A develops the innovation, then it enters the market and competes against the incumbent. In this case, profits depend on: i) the intensity of competitive pressure, which reduces the profits of both firms and ii) the severity of the antitrust policy.

For simplicity, we do not explicitly model competition between the incumbent and the challenger but we use reduced forms to represent their equilibrium profits. Let $\gamma \in [0, 1]$ measure the inverse of competitive pressure (the lower γ the more intense competition) and $\alpha \in [0, 1]$ the severity of the antitrust law; we assume that, in period t, firms' profits are given by the following expressions:

- firm B's profits: $1 - \alpha (1 - \gamma/2)$,

- firm A's profits, gross of research costs: $\alpha\gamma/2$.

Profits are increasing in γ, the inverse of the intensity of competition between firm A and firm B; competition is fiercest when $\gamma = 0$, which represents the case, for instance, of two firms offering homogeneous products. As γ increases, competition becomes less intense (e.g. firms offer differentiated products) and, therefore, profits get larger. When $\gamma = 1$ firms are not competing against each other, as it will be clearer later on.

Let us now consider the parameter measuring the severity of the antitrust policy. A larger value of α indicates a more stringent antitrust enforcement that restricts the incumbent's behaviour and protects the challenger. As a consequence, the larger α, the higher the profits for the entrant and the lower those for the incumbent.

However, this is not the only effect of antitrust enforcement; a more severe antitrust policy (a high α), in fact, makes competition between the two firms more effective, thus reducing the overall industry profits. To see this, one can check that industry profits, i.e. the sum of the profits of the incumbent and of the entrant, are equal to $1 - \alpha + \alpha\gamma$ and decrease with α:

$$\frac{\partial(1 - \alpha + \alpha\gamma)}{\partial\alpha} = -1 + \gamma \leq 0. \tag{8.1}$$

Therefore, an increase in α not only shifts part of the incumbent's profits to the entrant, but also makes competition more effective, thus lowering industry profits. Note also that, as shown in expression (8.1), the more intense competition (i.e. the smaller γ) the greater the reduction of industry profits. More severe antitrust interventions do not have any effect on industry profits only when competition is absent ($\gamma = 1$); in this case, aggregate profits equal 1, regardless of how stringent the antitrust policy is and, therefore, a larger α simply reallocates profits between the two firms.

Table 8.3 summarises the above discussion and shows the profits for both firms in t and which role (incumbent or entrant) they play in $t + 1$.

	Firms' profits in t		Role of the firms in $t + 1$	
	Firm A	Firm B	Firm A	Firm B
A innovating	$\frac{\alpha\gamma}{2}$	$1 - \alpha\left(1 - \frac{\gamma}{2}\right)$	incumbent	entrant
A not innovating	0	1	entrant	incumbent

Table 8.3: profits in t and role of the firms in $t + 1$

The questions we are interested in are the following: when is it profitable for the entrant to invest in the research project? Does a more severe antitrust legislation induce the challenger to invest in R&D?

To answer these questions it is useful to make an observation which greatly simplifies our analysis. At each period t, the stage game is always the same: one firm plays as the incumbent and the other as the entrant and the profits are always as shown in Table 8.3. This means that the choice which is optimal at time t is optimal also at any subsequent period of time. Therefore, we need only to consider two possible strategies: i) the entrant always invests in the research project and ii) the entrant never invests.

The entrant decides whether to invest or not by comparing the pay-offs it gets in the two cases. The pay-off of the strategy "never invest" is clearly 0: the challenger does not incur any R&D costs nor does it obtain any revenues.

The alternative strategy "always invest" (namely, invest in t and in all the following periods in which the firm plays the role of the entrant) generates an expected pay-off that we denote by V_E. This pay-off can also be interpreted as the "value of being the entrant in t". Since, in case of success of its research project, the entrant firm replaces the incumbent, then in order to determine V_E, we also need to determine the value of incumbency, denoted by V_I.

Let us start by defining V_I; when the entrant chooses the strategy "always invest", the value of being the incumbent in t is:

$$V_I = \underbrace{\frac{1}{2}(1 + \delta V_I)}_{\text{entrant not innovating}} + \underbrace{\frac{1}{2}\left(1 - \alpha\left(1 - \frac{\gamma}{2}\right) + \delta V_E\right)}_{\text{entrant innovating}}. \qquad (8.2)$$

With probability $1/2$, the entrant fails to innovate and the monopolist continues to act as the incumbent also in the next period. In this case, it obtains $1 + \delta V_I$: the monopoly profit equal to 1 in t plus the present value of being the incumbent in $t+1$, δV_I. The second term in expression (8.2) represents the incumbent's profits when the entrant innovates and enters the market: in t the entrant and the incumbent compete against each other and in $t+1$ the incumbent becomes the challenger; formally, the incumbent's profits in case of entry (event which occurs with probability $1/2$) are: $1 - \alpha\,(1 - \gamma/2)$ plus the present value of being the entrant in $t+1$, δV_E.

Following a similar procedure, we can compute the value of being the entrant at period t; when the entrant chooses the strategy "always invest", V_E is:

$$V_E \;=\; \underbrace{\frac{1}{2}\delta\, V_E}_{\text{entrant not innovating}} \;+\; \underbrace{\frac{1}{2}\left(\frac{\alpha\gamma}{2} + \delta V_I\right)}_{\text{entrant innovating}} \;-\; c. \tag{8.3}$$

The entrant pays the R&D cost c and with probability $1/2$ the research project fails; in this case, the firm obtains no profits in t and in $t+1$ it will still be the entrant (thus obtaining a present value δV_E). With complementary probability, the project succeeds, the entrant innovates and enters the market. In t the firm obtains profits equal to $\alpha\gamma/2$ and in $t+1$ the firm will become the incumbent, thus obtaining δV_I in discounted terms.

We can now determine under which conditions it is profitable for the entrant to invest in the research project. Formally, the entrant invests when $V_E \geq 0$, that is when V_E is larger than the profits obtained from the strategy "never invest". By using expression (8.3), it follows that the entrant invests when:

$$\frac{1}{2}\delta V_E + \frac{1}{2}\left(\frac{\alpha\gamma}{2} + \delta V_I\right) - c \geq 0 \iff c \leq \frac{1}{2}\left(\frac{\alpha\gamma}{2} + \delta(V_I + \delta V_E)\right).$$

For the sake of simplicity, it is useful to define $P(\alpha) \equiv (\alpha\gamma/2 + \delta(V_I + V_E))\,/2$ as the "innovation premium": according to the above expression, for the challenger it is profitable to invest in R&D when the innovation premium is greater than or equal to the cost of the investment c. As expected, the innovation premium is a function of α, namely the severity of antitrust intervention; therefore, we can focus on $P(\alpha)$ in order to examine the effect of a more stringent antitrust policy, that is how a tighter regulation of the incumbent affects the incentives to invest in R&D activities.

Note that expression $P(\alpha)$ depends on the values of being the incumbent and of being the entrant at time t, V_I and on V_E; therefore, in order to proceed with the analysis, we need to determine these two values explicitly. By solving the system of equations (8.2) and (8.3), it follows that:

$$V_I = \frac{1}{4}\frac{4 - 2\alpha + \delta\alpha - 2\delta - 2\delta c + \alpha\gamma}{1 - \delta},$$
$$V_E = \frac{1}{4}\frac{\alpha\gamma - 4c + 2\delta c + 2\delta - \delta\alpha}{1 - \delta}.$$

Finally, by substituting these expressions into the function $P(\alpha)$, we obtain:

$$P(\alpha) = \frac{1}{4}\frac{2\delta(1 - c) + \alpha(\gamma - \delta)}{1 - \delta}.$$

Simple differentiation of $P(\alpha)$ with respect to α leads to the following result:

Result 1. *A more severe antitrust policy increases incentives to innovate if competition is not too fierce. Formally, $P'(\alpha) \geq 0$ if and only if $\gamma \geq \delta$.*

This result can be easily interpreted. Consider first the case of no competition between the incumbent and the entrant, formally $\gamma = 1$; in this case, since $\delta \leq 1$, a more stringent antitrust enforcement increases incentives to innovate.

As mentioned previously, when $\gamma = 1$, a more restrictive antitrust law only shifts profits from the incumbent to the entrant, without reducing industry profits. In this case, an increase in α has two contrasting effects on the entrant's incentives to innovate: *i)* it stimulates investments because in the case of entry the challenger receives a greater share of industry profits, *ii)* it reduces incentives to invest because the entrant anticipates the fact that it will enjoy lower profits once it becomes the incumbent. However, while the increase in profits associated with effect *i)* is immediate (it occurs on entry), the reduction in profits associated with effect *ii)* occurs one period later, when the entrant becomes the incumbent; time discounting makes the near-term effect *i)* the dominant one. This is why Segal and Whinston say that a more severe antitrust enforcement induces a *front-loading effect*; when $\gamma = 1$, a larger α increases the premium $P(\alpha)$, thus stimulating innovation.

When $\gamma < 1$, an additional effect must be considered: a more stringent antitrust policy lowers industry profits, as highlighted by expression (8.1). This fact reduces the entrant's incentives to invest: the entrant anticipates the fact that the overall profits collected in the entry and in the incumbency phases are lower due to the more severe antitrust intervention. This additional effect counterbalances the front-loading one and it is stronger, the more intense competition is (low values of γ).

Result 1 shows that the front-loading effect dominates when $\gamma \geq \delta$ (weak competition) while the intensity of the antitrust policy reduces incentives to innovate when competition between the incumbent and the entrant is fierce, $\gamma < \delta$.

8.4.2   Intellectual property and competition policy

In this section, we focus on another issue which is extremely important for highly innovative industries, namely the relationship between protection of intellectual property and competition policy.

As highlighted in Chapter 6, modern technologies such as wireless communications, computers and software involve the integration of a wide range of different technologies covered by many essential patents which are owned by several companies. In such circumstances, companies must form alliances, work together in standardisation committees, cooperate to gain access to other's technology and to make their own technology available to others. The focus of this section is on the analysis of two common forms of collaboration for IP management: patent pools and cross-licensing agreements. As discussed in the following pages, often these collaborations are fundamental to allow firms in high-tech industrial sectors to coordinate with each other; nonetheless, they are horizontal agreements and, as such, they also have potentially anticompetitive effects which may hinder market efficiency.

Access to third-party's intellectual property

In recent years, the overwhelming amount of patents granted worldwide along with the cumulativeness of innovation in high-tech sectors have increased the importance of accessing third-party's intellectual property. In order to develop their own products, firms often need access to IP rights protecting relevant technologies owned by third parties.

Also in these cases competition policy may have perverse effects on incentives to innovate. On the one hand, it is widespread opinion that a stringent enforcement of antitrust regulations imposing patent-holders to provide access to their technology may seriously hamper their incentives to innovate; inventors anticipate the obligation imposed by the antitrust authority and, therefore, expect lower benefits from research activities. On the other hand, intrusive antitrust policies are often considered essential in order to avoid the risk of *hold-up* of future innovations: later innovators who fail to access the existing technologies may not be able to develop their follow-on innovations.[13]

A series of recent antitrust cases concerns exactly these issues. The heart of the matter can be summarised as follows: when is it best to oblige a patent-holder to license her/his intellectual property? Should an IP holder be alleged of abuse of dominance when denying access to her/his technology?

Answering these questions is a complex matter. An insightful analysis has been

---

[13]See Chapter 6 for further details on the hold-up problem.

provided by John Vickers, former Director General of the Office of Fair Trading, the British antitrust authority; the author reviews some recent antitrust cases in Europe to examine the relationship between intellectual property and competition policy (see Vickers, 2009). Vickers highlights the fact that the decisions taken in different cases by antitrust authorities reveal some ambiguities and confirm the complexities of the subject.

In the 1995 *Magill* case, the European Commission required TV broadcasters to supply their copyrighted program schedules to a supplier of a weekly TV guide, a new product which was not offered by the copyright owners. The main motivation for the obligation to license was that access to the copyrighted information was deemed essential for the development of a new product (the TV guide).

In the subsequent 2005 *IMS Health* case, concerning the format for presenting German pharmaceutical sales data, the European Court of Justice established with more precision under which conditions an IP holder must grant access to her/his rights. The Court ruled that the obligation to license an IP right occurs only in exceptional circumstances and, in particular, when the refusal to license: *i*) impedes the development of a new product for which consumer demand exists, at least potentially, *ii*) is unjustified and *iii*) it excludes any form of competition on secondary markets. When these three conditions are satisfied, refusal to license an IP right is considered as abuse of dominance. On the contrary, when at least one of these conditions is not met, denying access is not illegal per se.

These arguments lead us back to the EU Microsoft case. In September 2007, the European Court of First Instance upheld the European Commission's decision; as discussed in Section 8.3, Microsoft was punished for refusing to disclose information related to the interoperability of its operating system. This decision does not seem to be completely in line with the three conditions established by the European Court of Justice in the IMS Health case. In particular, the need to identify a specific new product which cannot be developed (for example a complete TV guide in the Magill case) has been "downsized" to the need to prove the existence of technical limitations which may reduce rivals' innovation incentives. Quite critically, Vickers (2009) concludes that:

> The European Microsoft judgment has therefore left unclear when a dominant firm with IP rights must share them with rivals. Following the judgment, the answer in Europe appears to be: by no means as exceptionally as previously thought.

Patent pools, cross-licensing and antitrust

High-tech sectors are typically characterised by the presence of thick webs of overlapping intellectual property rights covering relevant technologies, the so-called *patent thickets*. As we argued in Chapter 6, patent thickets can seriously undermine R&D incentives and lead to the so-called *tragedy of the anticommons*. In some cases, innovators need to negotiate licensing agreements with an extremely large number of IP holders; access to the relevant technologies may be delayed, or even prevented, and this puts the innovation process at risk. Cross-licensing agreements and patent pools are two possible solutions to patent thickets.

Cross-licensing is an agreement between two or more operators according to which parties grant reciprocal access to their patents to avoid the risk of mutual patent infringement. The agreement may be free of charge or it can require the payment of a fee. Cross-licensing agreements often involve large patent portfolios; in this case, such agreements are particularly desirable since they greatly reduce the transaction costs related to licensing negotiations. A recent example of cross-licensing is the agreement signed by Motorola and Research In Motion (RIM, the producer of Blackberry) in June 2010. Following a patent lawsuit which lasted more than two years related to mutual accusations of patent infringement, the two firms officially "kissed and made up" by negotiating a cross-licensing agreement to grant access to each others' technologies.

Patent pools are very similar to cross-licensing, but typically involve a larger number of operators. Members of the pool agree to share their patents. In some cases, they may decide to pool not only existing patents but also any patent they will be granted in the future in the relevant technological field. Two well known examples of patent pools are the Radio Frequency Identification Domain (RFID) and the MPEG-2. The first patent pool is made up of around twenty companies; the second pool manages the patents related to the digital data compression technology introduced in 1994 by the Moving Pictures Experts Group and it is made up of more than twenty members.

As in the case of cross-licensing, patent pools aim at improving coordination among operators, reducing transaction costs and limiting the negative effects related to the presence of patent thickets.

If these agreements are so useful, why are we so concerned about them? The reason is straightforward: since patent pools and cross-licensing are horizontal agreements, they may favour anticompetitive conducts; in other words, they represent another source of potential conflict between IP protection and competition policy.

In the remainder of this section, we present a stylised model in order to shed light on these issues. As we shall see, whether or not the antitrust concerns are actually grounded depends on the nature of the patents involved in the agreement. If patents cover complementary technologies, patent pools and cross-licensing agreements are not anticompetitive; by contrast, when technologies are substitutes, these agreements may substantially reduce competition among market players.[14]

A model of cross-licensing with essential patents (complementary technologies).
Consider a duopolistic market where two firms, A and B, compete *à la Cournot*; they incur a marginal cost of production $c < 1$ and face a linear market demand $p = 1 - q_A - q_B$, where q_A (resp. q_B) denotes the quantity produce by firm A (resp. firm B).

Production is based on two patented technologies and each firm owns one of them. In this section, we look at the case of complementary technologies; in other words, we assume that both technologies are necessary to produce and, therefore, each firm needs access to the rival's technology. Access can be obtained via a simple licensing contract or through a cross-licensing agreement.

In what follows we present a two stage game. In the first stage, firms determine the terms for accessing each other technology; in the second stage, firms compete in quantities. As usual, we solve the game by backward induction starting from the second stage.

The market equilibrium without cross-licensing.
Suppose that the two firms have not signed a cross-licensing agreement. In this case, access to the complementary patented technology is obtained thanks to two simple licensing contracts. With the first contract firm A grants firm B the right to use its technology and, with the second contract, firm B does the same with firm A. Henceforth, we assume that licensing fees take the form of per-unit royalties and, therefore, increase firms' marginal costs. The profit functions of the two firms are:

$$\pi_A(q_A, r_A) = (p - c - r_B)q_A + r_A q_B, \quad \text{and} \quad \pi_B(q_B, r_B) = (p - c - r_A)q_B + r_B q_A,$$

where r_A (resp. r_B) is the per-unit royalty charged by firm A (resp. B) to the rival; therefore, $r_A q_B$ is the overall licensing fee which firm B pays to access A's technology (and $r_B q_A$ is the amount paid by firm A to firm B).

By differentiating the profit functions with respect to q_A and q_B respectively and then by solving the system of first order conditions, we determine the output produced by each firm as a function of r_A and r_B:

$$q_A(r_A) = \frac{1 - c - 2r_B + r_A}{3}, \quad q_B(r_B) = \frac{1 - c - 2r_A + r_B}{3}.$$

---

[14]The model we present is very stylised and can be also applied to the case of patent pools; for the sake of simplicity, in the text we refer to the case of cross-licensing. For further details on these issues see Shapiro (2001) and Lerner and Tirole (2004).

Going backwards to the first stage of the game, we can determine the per-unit royalty chosen by each firm to grant access to its own technology. By substituting $q_A(r_A)$ and $q_B(r_B)$ into $\pi_A(q_A, r_A)$ and $\pi_B(q_B, r_B)$, we calculate firms' profits as a function of r_A and of r_B only:

$$\pi_A(r_A) = \left(\frac{1 - c - 2r_B + r_A}{3}\right)^2 + r_A\frac{1 - c - 2r_A + r_B}{3};$$

$$\pi_B(r_B) = \left(\frac{1 - c - 2r_A + r_B}{3}\right)^2 + r_B\frac{1 - c - 2r_B + r_A}{3}.$$

These functions are concave in their arguments. Therefore, by differentiating them with respect to r_A and r_B respectively and then by solving the system of first order conditions, it is possible to derive the optimal royalty fees chosen by the two firms:

$$r_A^L = r_B^L = r^L = \frac{5(1 - c)}{11},$$

where superscript L denotes that we are in the case of licensing agreements.

Finally, by substituting r^L into the demand and the profit functions we derive the equilibrium price and profits:

$$p^L = \frac{7 + 4c}{11} \quad \text{and} \quad \pi_A^L = \pi_B^L = \pi^L = \frac{14(1 - c)^2}{121}.$$

Market equilibrium in the case of cross-licensing agreement.
Let us now consider the case where access to the two technologies is negotiated through a cross-licensing agreement. Unlike in the previous case where each firm sets the royalty fee on its own, here the terms of access to the two technologies are jointly decided by the two firms.

Under a cross-licensing agreement access to each other's technology is based on a reciprocal per-unit royalty, denoted by r. In this case the profit functions of the two firms are:

$$\pi_A(q_A, r) = (p - c - r)q_A + rq_B, \quad \text{and} \quad \pi_B(q_B, r) = (p - c - r)q_B + rq_A.$$

In the second stage the two firms, given r, decide the quantity to produce; by differentiating $\pi_A(q_A, r)$ with respect to q_A and $\pi_B(q_B, r)$ with respect to q_B and then by solving the system of the two first order conditions, the quantities produced by firms A and B, given the reciprocal royalty rate, are:

$$q_A(r) = q_B(r) = \frac{1 - c - r}{3}.$$

Going backwards to the first stage of the game, we can now determine the royalty jointly chosen by the two firms. We assume that they set r in order to maximise their joint profits $\pi_A(r) + \pi_B(r)$. By substituting expressions $q_A(r)$ and $q_B(r)$ into the profit functions of the two firms, it follows that joint profits are:

$$\pi_A(r) + \pi_B(r) = \frac{2(1 - c - r)(1 - c + 2r)}{9}.$$

This function is concave in r; by differentiating it with respect to r and then by solving the first order condition, it follows that the optimal royalty rate in the case of cross-licensing is:

$$r^{CL} = \frac{1 - c}{4},$$

where superscript CL denotes the fact that we are dealing with the case of cross-licensing. By substituting r^{CL} back into expressions $q_A(r)$ and $q_B(r)$, we derive the equilibrium price and profits:

$$p^{CL} = \frac{1 + c}{2} \quad \text{and} \quad \pi_A^{CL} = \pi_B^{CL} = \pi^{CL} = \frac{(1 - c)^2}{8}.$$

A simple comparison of the profits firms collect when signing a cross-licensing agreement, π^{CL}, with those obtained without cross-licensing, π^L, reveals the following:

Result 2. *When firms holding patent rights on complementary technologies sign a cross-licensing agreement, they obtain larger profits than when they sign two distinct licensing contracts.*

This result has a simple explanation: when the two firms sign two distinct licensing contracts, a standard double marginalisation problem arises. Without cross-licensing, in fact, the equilibrium price p^L is inflated by two margins and, at the end, it turns out to be excessively high (and the quantity sold to consumers is excessively low).

In order to understand this point better, take firm A, for instance; with a simple licensing contract, it sets a large r_A in order to increase its licensing revenues (first profit margin). The royalty r_A increases the marginal cost of firm B which, in turn, reacts by raising the price charged to consumers (second profit margin). A similar reasoning applies for r_B. As a result, the equilibrium price charged to consumers is too high because of the combination of the two margins; excessively high retail prices mean that firms sell too little and, therefore, obtain lower profits.

With cross-licensing, firms bypass the double marginalisation problem; they reduce the first margin in order to increase market sales. One can check that the royalty rate is smaller in the case of cross-licensing, $r^{CL} < r^L$; as a consequence, the equilibrium price is smaller ($p^{CL} < p^L$) and the quantity sold to consumers is larger. These facts allow firms to collect greater profits than in the absence of a cross-licensing agreement.

Clearly since $p^{CL} < p^L$ also consumers benefit from a cross-licensing agreement. The following result summarises these arguments:

Result 3. *Cross-licensing agreements involving complementary technologies increase both consumer and producer surpluses; therefore, they are socially desirable.*

This result is extremely important and reveals that cross-licensing agreements involving complementary technologies are likely to increase market efficiency. Therefore, coming back to our basic question on the potential conflict between cross-licensing agreements and market efficiency, we have shown that antitrust authorities should not be concerned with this form of horizontal agreements; on the contrary, cross-licensing involving complementary technologies should actually be promoted since it increases social welfare.[15]

Cross-licensing of non-essential patents (substitute technologies).
The effects of cross-licensing are very different in the case of patents protecting substitute technologies; in our model, this occurs when both firms are able to produce with their own technology, without needing access to the rival's patent.[16] We analyse this case by proceeding as in the previous section; we determine the market equilibria with and without cross-licensing agreement and then we compare them.

Suppose that firms sign a cross-licensing agreement. The equilibrium in this case coincides with the one derived with complementary technologies. When signing the agreement, it is optimal for firms to set the royalty fee at r^{CL} regardless of whether technologies are complementary or substitutes; therefore, p^{CL} and π^{CL} are the equilibrium price and profits also with non-essential patents.

Let's now consider what happens when the two firms do not sign a cross-licensing agreement. In this case, the fact that the two technologies are substitutes matters: each firm can produce without accessing the rival's technology and, therefore, without having to pay any royalty. In other words, with substitute technologies, when firms do not sign a cross-licensing agreement, their profit functions boil down to:

$$\pi_A(q_A) = (p - c)q_A, \quad \text{and} \quad \pi_B(q_B) = (p - c)q_B.$$

---

[15]It is straightforward to note that the equilibrium price in the case of cross-licensing is the same as in the case of a monopolist holding both patents. For this reason, Result 3 is particularly interesting; it represents a case of "efficient collusion": by eliminating the effects of double marginalisation, this collusion is beneficial also for consumers.

[16]Take, for instance, the case of two firms producing personal computers, each one holding a patent for a specific type of processor; if the two patented processors guarantee the same computing power then they can both be used to assemble equally performing PCs. Therefore, each firm can produce its own model by using its own technology without needing access to the technology held by the rival.

In this case, firms play a standard Cournot duopoly game, with linear demand and marginal cost c; straightforward computations reveal that the equilibrium price and profits are given by:

$$p^{nL} = \frac{1 + 2c}{3} \quad \text{and} \quad \pi_A^{nL} = \pi_B^{nL} = \pi^{nL} = \frac{(1-c)^2}{9},$$

where superscript nL denotes that we are referring to the case of non-essential patents and firms do not sign any licensing agreement (neither cross-licensing nor simple licensing).

We can now compare the two scenarios (with and without cross-licensing). Unlike in the previous case, when technologies are substitutes and firms do not sign a cross-licensing agreement, the double marginalisation problem does not arise; firms compete *à la Cournot* with marginal cost c. The equilibrium price is not inflated by the first margin (licensing margin) and firms end up selling large quantities at a relatively low price. In this case, with cross-licensing, firms impose each other a royalty rate which increases their marginal cost and induces them to charge a price above the (Cournot) competitive level.

In other words, with complementary technologies, a cross-licensing agreement works as a collusive device which softens competition. Clearly, a higher equilibrium price lowers both consumer surplus and social welfare.[17]

The following result summarises the previous discussion:

Result 4. *Cross-licensing agreements involving substitutes technologies increase firms' profits but reduce both consumer surplus and social welfare.*

Summing up, from the analysis of the two cases we have just presented, it follows that it is always profitable for firms to sign cross-licensing agreements, regardless of whether patents cover substitutes or complementary technologies; cross-licensing reduces the double marginalisation problem in the case of essential patents, while it softens competition when patents are non-essential. In turn, the welfare effects of cross-licensing crucially depend on the type of technologies involved. In the case of complementary technologies, the absence of a cross-licensing agreement leads to an extremely inefficient equilibrium due to the effect of double marginalisation; therefore, in this case, cross-licensing is welfare-enhancing. By contrast, with substitute technologies, cross-licensing works as a collusive device which, therefore, harms social welfare.

---

[17]It is straightforward to check that social welfare equals $W^{CL} = (3(1-c)^2)/8$ with cross-licensing and $W^{nL} = (4(1-c)^2)/9$ without cross-licensing; it follows that $W^{CL} < W^{nL}$.

8.5   Antitrust policy and two-sided markets

In recent years, antitrust authorities have been investigating more and more frequently cases involving two-sided markets. In Chapter 4, for instance, we mentioned the potential collusive role of the interchange fee in credit card markets. The interchange fee, used to regulate transactions among customers and merchants, is jointly set by the banks and other financial institutions belonging to the credit card association. The way the fee is determined has raised many antitrust concerns. Several authorities alleged that the collective determination of the interchange fee has allowed VISA, Mastercard and other major credit card issuers to keep prices at artificially high levels, thus constituting a form of price-fixing.

However, in Chapter 4 we showed that the interchange fee may also have a positive effect on market efficiency. In two-sided networks, prices on the two sides of the market must be appropriately balanced according to the strength of the cross-side network effects. In the case of a credit card association, the interchange fee may help banks and financial institutions to achieve this goal.

The example of credit cards provides a more general message: antitrust authorities should carefully take into account the peculiarities of two-sided markets and be aware of the fact that assessing firms' behaviour on the basis of a "traditional" antitrust perspective may lead to erroneous conclusions. Due to the presence of cross-side network externalities, consumer demand on the two sides of the market are closely intertwined; this fact implies that antitrust authorities should not consider each side of the market separately but, instead, assess firms' behaviour by looking at both sides jointly.

A couple of examples are useful to illustrate this argument better. Suppose a dominant firm is charging a very low price, below its production costs. By applying a standard antitrust approach, this behaviour would be considered a predatory practice aimed at eliminating competitors; the firm sacrifices profits in the short-run (when the predatory practice is in place) in order to benefit from larger profits in the future when, once predation has succeeded, the firm raises its price to enjoy monopoly profits.

This interpretation may be incorrect in the case of two-sided markets. In Chapter 4, we argued that, in order to maximise the benefit generated by the cross-side externalities, the firm needs to appropriately balance the prices charged on the two sides of the market; we showed that when the intensities of the cross-side externalities are highly asymmetric, it may be optimal for the firm to "subsidise" the side which generates greater value. Therefore, a price smaller than the cost of production on one side may be part of a broader strategy aimed at maximising the value of externalities, without any anticompetitive intents. In other words, the firm is not sacrificing its short-run profits (to force rivals out of the market), hence one of the basic requirements for the strategy to be considered as predatory is missing.[18]

Box 8.3 – Travelport–Worldspan, a merger between platforms[a]

In 2007, the European Commission (EC) unconditionally approved Travelport's acquisition of Worldspan Galileo in the global distribution system (GDS) market. A GDS is a computer reservation system through which airline companies can distribute their tickets to travel agencies; it allows travel agencies to search for information on prices and availability, to make reservations and to issue tickets for the flights of hundreds of airline companies.

A GDS is a two-sided platform which offers intermediation services to airlines (one side of the market) and travel agencies (the other side); a GDS makes it easier to manage the relationship with final users for instance in terms of booking, cancellation, ticket issuance, payment and so on.

In 2007, the GDS market was already highly concentrated with only 4 large companies operating globally (Sabre, Amadeus, Travelport and Worldspan). The merger between two big players, such as Travelport and Worldspan, further increased industry concentration giving rise to a giant operator with a market share above 45% (even up to 80% in countries such as Belgium, Great Britain, Holland and Italy).

Despite the substantial increase in market concentration, the European Commission considered antitrust concerns to be largely unfounded and, therefore, authorised the acquisition.

The EC assessment of the case was based on the observation that despite their large market shares, GDS platforms were not able to exercise a significant market power. A GDS platform should think twice before charging travel agents too large prices for its services; airline companies have different tools to "punish" the GDS for such an opportunistic behaviour. For instance, they can drastically limit the information provided to the GDS on their flights (timetables, prices, features), thus reducing the quality of the service the GDS is able to offer. Moreover, airline companies may decide to increase the mark-up charged to travel agencies which sell tickets through a GDS, reducing in this way the convenience of employing computer reservation systems.

Finally, the EC also observed that airline companies are making an increasing use of alternative distribution channels (such as selling tickets directly from their websites) that allow them to bypass GDS services.

Following these arguments, the Commission established that the market power of GDS platforms, even the very large ones, turned out to be extremely diluted; for this reason, the EC finally decided to approve the merger without imposing any remedy.

[a]Taken from RBB Economics (2008).

We can summarise this discussion as follows:

Observation 1. *In two-sided markets, a price equal to or smaller than the marginal cost is not necessarily a signal of predation.*

---

[18]See Evans (2003), Wright (2004) and Evans and Noel (2005) for further discussions on these issues.

The second example highlighting the potential failure of the traditional antitrust perspective applied to two-sided networks concerns the role of competition among platforms. As shown in Chapter 4, an increase in the number of platforms serving both sides of the market does not necessarily translate into higher market efficiency. With greater competitive pressure, platforms enjoy lower market power; this entails two conflicting effects on social welfare: on the one hand, greater competition among platforms (less market power) implies smaller prices for the consumers on the two sides and, therefore, greater social welfare. On the other hand, however, competition also reduces the ability of platforms to appropriately balance the prices they charge on the two sides of the network which goes to the detriment of market efficiency. As shown in Chapter 4, when the intensities of cross-side network externalities are highly asymmetric and such that a monopoly platform is induced to subsidise one side of the market, then the second effect may dominate, thus making competition socially undesirable. We can summarise this discussion as follows:[19]

Observation 2. *In two-sided markets, competition reduces the ability of platforms to balance prices, hence it may reduce social welfare.*

This last observation has extremely important consequences for merger analysis in two-sided markets. European regulations require mergers among large companies to receive the approval of antitrust authorities. The main concern with a merger is that the associated increase in industry concentration may significantly reduce the effectiveness of competition and, consequently, the level of social welfare. However, following the above observation, it is not necessarily true that greater concentration implies lower social welfare; therefore, the standard antitrust prescriptions on mergers may not be appropriate in the case of two-sided markets.

The general message we can derive from these simple examples is actually very clear: in two-sided markets, antitrust investigations aimed at assessing collusion, mergers and abuse of dominance need to be much more articulated than in the case of traditional markets. This is the reason why, in order to avoid wrong evaluations, antitrust authorities need to carefully consider the peculiar features of two-sided markets.

8.6   Net neutrality

The principle of net neutrality (or network neutrality), a cornerstone for the functioning of the Internet, is currently at the core of a heated debate both in the U.S. and in Europe.

---

[19]See OECD (2009).

According to the net neutrality principle, Internet Service Providers (ISP) should treat all data transmitted over the Internet in the same way; in other words, they should not discriminate users or charge them differently according to the content, the site, the platform they use, the application and the mode of communication.

In order to understand the meaning of net neutrality better, it is useful to illustrate very briefly how data are transmitted over the Internet. Take, for example, Internet telephony (VoIP), which we have already mentioned in Chapter 5 (see Box 5.2). VoIP enables the making of phone calls over the Internet without using the traditional telephone network; VoIP technology involves the digitisation of voice signals which are then encoded, packetised and transmitted as IP packets over the Internet. Each packet includes headers providing information on the delivery address and on the position of the packet in the transmitted sequence of information. Headers are, therefore, essential for the receiving side to correctly listen to the original voice stream.

VoIP is a typical example of synchronous communication, since it requires the simultaneous presence of both the caller and the receiver. Clearly, the connection speed between the two parties affects the quality of data transmission and, therefore, influences the possibility of reassembling packets instantly without risking delays or losses of parts of information. However, VoIP is not the only example of synchronous communication. Other more advanced services are on-line chats, video-conferences and on-line broadcasting, which allow us to watch live events.

Asynchronous communication, instead, does not require the simultaneous presence of all the different parties involved. Emails, uploading and down-loading of files, or video-streaming services are all examples of asynchronous communication. In some cases, the quality of the service may be greatly affected by connection speed also in asynchronous communication. Watching videos on YouTube, for instance, requires sufficient bandwidth in order not to damage the quality of the service.

All these examples are strictly associated with net neutrality. As mentioned above, net neutrality is certainly one of the most important principles of the Internet since its early days. According to net neutrality, all data packets transmitted over the Internet must be treated in the same way. ISP cannot discriminate by user, content or site and therefore video-conferences, TV programmes, on-line chats or emails etc. must be treated on even terms.

In recent years the net neutrality principle has been put under strong pressure; the increased popularity of broadband services available on-line has triggered a heated debate on the necessity of maintaining net neutrality. Large telecom operators which offer access to the Internet, such as AT&T, Verizon or Comcast, argue that they have invested enormous amounts of money in order to build and up-grade the physical infrastructure of the network. These operators report that most of the benefits deriving from their investments are captured by the providers of Internet services, such as Microsoft, Google, Yahoo! and others; these companies are able to offer very advanced services thanks to the better quality of network infrastructures. In short, ISP claim their right to enjoy part of the value generated thanks to their investments.

Without net neutrality telecom operators would actually be able to increase their profitability by discriminating packets sent over the Internet. For instance, they could offer access services of different quality at different prices to content providers. In turn, these latter companies, could select the quality of the service they need according to their willingness to pay and, then, compensate the larger access fees by charging higher prices to consumers (or by increasing advertising revenues). Clearly, content providers, such as Microsoft, eBay and Amazon, are strongly against the abolishment of net neutrality; also the Federal Communications Commission (FCC), the U.S. antitrust authority, is in favour of maintaining net neutrality, as confirmed on several occasions since 2006. Initially, Google, the other big player in the Internet arena, was also a strong advocate of net neutrality but, during the last few years, it seems to have changed its view on the issue (see Box 8.4).

Let's go into greater detail in order to understand the meaning of net neutrality more thoroughly; the issue can be examined from different perspectives and it is probably for this reason that the debate on the topic appears rather confusing and muddled. Moreover, the discussion is often influenced by ideological concerns according to which all information on the Internet should be available to everyone, without restrictions or discriminations of any kind. These concerns are certainly of paramount importance; however, in this section, we limit our discussion to a merely economic perspective, thus leaving aside considerations of any other kind.[20]

---

[20]With regard to this point, it is interesting to quote Barack Obama. In 2006, the at-that-time White House candidate reported:

> The topic today is net neutrality. The Internet today is an open platform where the demand for websites and services dictates success. You've got barriers to entry that are low and equal for all comers [...] I can say what I want without censorship. I don't have to pay a special charge. But the big telephone and cable companies want to change the Internet as we know it. They say they want to create high-speed lanes on the Internet and strike exclusive contractual arrangements with Internet content-providers for access to those high-speed lanes. Those of us who can't pony up the cash for these high-speed connections will be relegated to the slow lanes. So here's my view. We can't have a situation in which the corporate duopoly dictates the future of the Internet and that's why I'm supporting what is called net neutrality.

For a comprehensive discussion on net neutrality see Marsden (2010).

More specifically, Schuett (2010) reports that net neutrality imposes telecom operators the following two types of restrictions:

1) no second degree price discrimination; in particular, ISP cannot oblige a content provider to pay a per-packet-fee conditional on the overall quantity of packets sent over the Internet;

2) no packet discrimination; ISP cannot treat packets differently (in terms of price charged or quality of the connection) conditional on their type, source or destination.

Following restriction 1), a network is said to be neutral when content providers pay a fixed fee to access the network regardless of the number of data packets they send over the Internet. In other words, net neutrality implies the so-called *zero-price rule*: content providers pay a fixed fee and, therefore, any additional packet that they transmit over the Internet costs them zero.

According to restriction 2), the network is neutral when traffic management is not allowed (the so-called *non-discrimination rule* applies). ISP are, therefore, prevented from giving priority to some packets and/or delaying the transmission of others.

The economics literature on net neutrality focuses on the following questions. What are the effects on market efficiency of the zero-price and of the non-discrimination rules? In other words, how does net neutrality affect social welfare? Does net neutrality stimulate or reduce incentives to invest in network infrastructures or in advanced services? Contributions to the literature can be classified according to which rule they focus on: the zero-price rule or the non-discrimination rule.

One of the most interesting works on the topic is by Economides and Tåg (2012); the two authors study the consequences of the zero-price rule by looking at the Internet as a two-sided market; an ISP sells access services to content providers, on the one side, and to final users, on the other. According to this rule, ISP are obliged to charge a zero price for the marginal packet sent by content providers. The question, therefore, is the following: is this pricing strategy socially desirable?

As discussed in Chapter 4, balancing the prices charged to the two sides of the market in order to maximise the effects of cross-side network externalities is socially desirable. In some cases, this may require one side of the market to be subsidised through a very small price, possibly below the marginal cost of providing access services. In general, the zero-price rule limits the ISP ability to balance prices appropriately; for this reason such a regulation may not be desirable from the social welfare perspective. However, Economides and Tåg (2012) show that whether or not the zero-price rule is welfare-enhancing depends on several market features such as the intensity of cross-side network externalities, the degree of industry concentration and so on.

Box 8.4 – The Google–Verizon deal: a not very neutral net

At the beginning of August 2010, Google (the number one search engine and the owner of YouTube) and Verizon (one of the largest U.S. ISP) announced an agreement for an "open Internet framework" establishing common rules for Internet access.

This agreement gave rise to a lively debate. As it stands, it is no more than a deal between two large companies and it is not binding for anyone else. However, according to some commentators, given the relevance of the involved parties, the risk of the agreement serving as a model for amending/ruling out net neutrality is substantial.

The framework is composed of two separate parts. The first part highlights the general principles for Internet access, while the second contains a series of practical provisions. According to the first part of the document, Google and Verizon seem to be strongly in favour of net neutrality; they emphasise the importance of Internet access and they warn against discrimination among different types of content.

However, after this declaration of intent, in the second part of the document, the two companies reveal their real purposes; more specifically, it emerges that Google and Verizon are willing to guarantee net neutrality in all circumstances except for i) the provision of "additional services" and ii) mobile Internet access.

Following point i), a telecom company that offers Internet access without any form of discrimination should be allowed to sell additional and separate services (such as additional content over a dedicated super fast network) with different traffic prioritisation.

Point ii) establishes that wireless networks should be excluded from any provision except for the transparency requirement. According to Google and Verizon, in fact, the wireless sector is already highly competitive and it is evolving rapidly; ISP should be allowed to offer services with different traffic prioritisation, to slow down or even to stop certain data running over their infrastructure. Therefore, according to Google and Verizon's proposal, an ISP should be allowed to stop, for instance, peer-to-peer traffic from sites such as BitTorrent or even that originated from VoIP services.

Clearly, points i) and ii) seriously undermine the net neutrality principle and as such have been strongly opposed by those who believe that Internet access provision should not be discriminatory.

According to the study by Lee and Wu (2009), the zero-price rule is certainly beneficial for market efficiency. A positive price for the marginal packet would, indeed, increase barriers to entry for content providers with the risk of limiting the range of services available to the consumer. Moreover, Lee and Wu suggest that in several cases, such as in social networks, the service becomes effectively valuable only in the presence of a critical mass of consumers. In the absence of a mass of users, the social network service has little value, hence its bargaining position vis-à-vis the ISP is generally extremely weak. This fact suggests that the zero-price rule may be recommendable in order to protect content providers (as social networks) from the risk of opportunistic behaviour by telecom companies.

Consider now the non-discrimination rule preventing ISP from giving priority to certain data packets rather than others; in this case, telecom operators cannot offer access services of different quality. In other words, under the non-discrimination rule ISP are not allowed to adopt second degree price discrimination strategies, such as versioning. However, as discussed in Chapter 2, in some circumstances versioning may be socially desirable. Indeed, by offering several versions of the service (different qualities and prices for the service), a firm is able to enlarge its market share; more consumers purchase the service and social welfare increases. Lee and Wu, who have vigorously supported the zero-price rule, are, instead, in favour of abolishing the non-discrimination rule, provided that ISP continue to offer a baseline network access service of sufficient quality.[21]

Abandoning net neutrality also raises some relevant antitrust concerns; for instance, the vertical integration between telecom operators and content providers may favour the adoption of predatory practices. Telecom companies, which are often also leaders in the provision of Internet access, may abuse their position in order to favour their own content and applications to the detriment of competitors.

To conclude, several commentators believe that, in the near future, the net neutrality principle, as we know it, will be abandoned, at least to a certain degree. The questions that still remain open in the policy makers' agenda are related to how far this process will go and how the problems which are bound to emerge will be tackled. With regard to these points, the U.S. and Europe appeared to have adopted different approaches. European regulators seem to have embraced a "soft approach"; they are confident that competition will mitigate the risk of anticompetitive practices which may eventually emerge once network neutrality prescriptions are lifted. According to this perspective, the intervention of antitrust authorities is considered sufficient to guarantee a levelled playing field. By contrast, the U.S. appear to be more cautious towards the abolishment of network neutrality. Regulators believe that antitrust intervention does not represent an adequate safeguard against anticompetitive behaviours; antitrust sanctions may come too late since they are inflicted *ex post*, only once the abuse has been proved. In high-tech industries the promptness of intervention is often crucial to avoid the emergence and the persistency of dominant positions and to guarantee market efficiency.

---

[21]Lee and Wu (2009), however, warn against the risk of ISP drastically lowering the quality of the baseline service, thus making it useless for content providers.

References

Acquisti, A. and Varian, H. (2005). Conditioning Prices on Purchase History. *Marketing Science*, 24(3):1–15.

Anttila, E. (2006). Open Source Software and Impact on Competitiveness: Case Study. Unpublished manuscript, Department of Electrical Engineering and Communications Engineering, Helsinki University of Technology.

Armstrong, M. (2002). Competition in Two-Sided Markets. Unpublished manuscript, University of Oxford.

Armstrong, M. (2004). Network Interconnection with Asymmetric Networks and Heterogeneous Calling Patterns. *Information Economics and Policy*, 16:375–390.

Arora, A. and Fosfuri, A. (2000). The Market for Technology in the Chemical Industry: Causes and Consequences. *Revue D'Économie Industrielle*, 92:317–333.

Arrow, K. (1962). *Economic Welfare and the Allocation of Resources for Invention*. In: Nelson ed., The Rate and Direction of Inventive Activity: Economic and Social Factors, Princeton University Press, Princeton, NJ.

Arthur, B. (1989). Competing Technologies, Increasing Returns and Lock-in by Historical Events. *Economic Journal*, 99:106–131.

Atal, V. and Bar, T. (2013). Patent Quality and a Two-Tiered Patent System. Unpublished manuscript, Montclair State University, Montclair, NJ.

Athreye, S. and Cantwell, J. (2005). Creating Competition? Globalisation and the Emergence of New Technology Producers. Open University Discussion Paper in Economics, n.52.

Bailey, J.P. (1998a). Electronic Commerce: Prices and Consumer Issues for Three Products: Books, Compact Discs, and Software. Organisation for Economic Co-Operation and Development, OECD/GD(98)4.

Bailey, J.P. (1998b). Intermediation and Electronic Markets: Aggregation and Pricing in Internet Commerce. PhD. Massachusets Institute of Technology; Cambridge, MA.

Bakos, Y. and Brynjolfsson, E. (1999). Bundling Information Goods: Pricing, Profits, and Efficiency. *Management Science*, 45(12):1613–1630.

Baye, M.R. and Morgan, J. (2001). Information Gatekeepers on the Internet and the Competitiveness of Homogeneous Products Markets. *American Economic Review*, 91:454–474.

Baye, M.R., Morgan, J., and Scholten, P. (2006). *Persistent Price Dispersion in Online Markets.* In: Jansen ed., The New Economy and Beyond: Past, Present and Future, Edward Elgar Publishing, Cheltenham, UK and Northampton, MA, USA.

BCG (2011). Fattore Internet. Come Internet sta Trasformando l'Economia Italiana. Report prepared by the Boston Consulting Group.

Belleflamme, P. (2005). Versioning in the Information Economy: Theory and Applications. *CESifo Economic Studies*, 51:329–358.

Belleflamme, P. and Peitz, M. (2010). Digital Piracy: Theory. CORE Discussion Paper n. 2010/60.

Besen, S.M. and Farrell, J. (1994). Choosing How to Compete: Strategies and Tactics in Standardization. *Journal of Economic Perspectives*, 8(2):117–131.

Bessen, J. (2004). Holdup and Licensing of Cumulative Innovations with Private Information. *Economic Letters*, 82:321–326.

Bessen, J. and Hunt, R. (2007). An Empirical Look at Software Patents. *Journal of Economics & Management Strategy*, 16(1):157–189.

Bessen, J. and Maskin, E. (2009). Sequential Innovation, Patents, and Imitation. *RAND Journal of Economics*, 40(4):611–635.

Bessen, J. and Meurer, M. (2008). *Patent Failure.* Princeton University Press, Princeton, NJ.

Bhargava, H.K. and Choudhary, V. (2008). When is Versioning Optimal for Information Goods? *Management Science*, 54(5):1029–1035.

Birke, D. (2009). The Economics of Networks: A Survey of the Empirical Literature. *Journal of Economic Surveys*, 23(4):762–793.

Boldrin, M. and Levine, D. (2008). *Against Intellectual Monopoly.* Cambridge University Press, Cambridge, MA.

Bolt, W. (2008). The European Commission's Ruling in MasterCard: A Wise Decision? *GCP - The Online Magazine for Global Competition Policy*, APR-08(1).

Bonaccorsi, A., Piscitello, L., Merito, M., and Rossi-Lamastra, C. (2006). Profiting from "Open Innovation". Teece's Building Blocks Meet the Open Source Production Paradigm. In: Bonaccorsi and Rossi eds, Economic Perspectives on Open Source Software, Franco Angeli editore, Italy.

Bounie, D., Eang, B., Sirbu, M.A., and Waelbroeck, P. (2012). Online Price Dispersion: An International Comparison. Available at *SSRN*: http://ssrn.com/abstract=1625847.

Bourreau, M., Lupi, P., and Manenti, F.M. (2013). Old Technology Upgrades, Innovation, and Competition in Vertically Differentiated Markets. University of Padua, Marco Fanno Working Paper 0158.

Brown, J. and Goolsbee, A. (2002). Does the Internet Make Markets More Competitive? Evidence from the Life Insurance Industry. *Journal of Political Economy*, 110(3):481–507.

Brynjolfsson, E., Dick, A.A., and Smith, M.D. (2010). A Nearly Perfect Market? *Quantitative Marketing and Economics*, 8(1):1–33.

Brynjolfsson, E. and Smith, M. (2000). Frictionless Commerce? A Comparison of Internet and Conventional Retailers. *Management Science*, 46(4):563–585.

Cabral, L. and Kretschmer, T. (2007). Standards Battles and Public Policy. In: Greenstein and Stango eds, Standards and Public Policy, Cambridge University Press, Cambridge, MA.

Caillaud, B. and Duchene, A. (2011). Patent Office in Innovation Policy: Nobody's Perfect. *International Journal of Industrial Organization*, 29(2):242–252.

Carter, M. and Wright, J. (1994). Symbiotic Production: The case of Telecommunication Pricing. *Review of Industrial Organization*, 9:365–378.

Casaleggio Associati (2012). L'e-commerce in Italia – 2012. Available for download at www.casaleggio.it.

Cave, M. (2004). Remedies for Broadband Services. *Journal of Network Industries, Competition and Regulation*, 5:23–49.

Cave, M. (2006). Encouraging Infrastructure Competition via the Ladder of Investment. *Telecommunications Policy*, 30:223–237.

Cave, M. and Vogelsang, I. (2003). Access Pricing Investment and Entry in Telecommunications. *Telecommunications Policy*, 27:717–727.

Chesbrough, H.W. (2003). *Open Innovation: the New Imperative for Creating and Profiting from Technology*. Harvard Business School, Cambridge, MA.

Clay, K.B., Krishnan, R., and Wolff, E. (2001). Prices and Price Dispersion on the Web: Evidence from the Online Book Industry. *Journal of Industrial Economics*, XLIX:521–540.

Clay, K.B., Krishnan, R., Wolff, E., and Fernandes, D. (2002). Retail Strategies on the Web: Price and Non-Price Competition in the Online Book Industry. *Journal of Industrial Economics*, 50(30):351–367.

Clemons, E., Hann, I., and Hitt, L.M. (2002). Price Dispersion and Differentation in Online Travel: An Empirical Investigation. *Management Science*, IIL(4):534–549.

Cockburn, I. and MacGarview, M. (2009). Patents, Thickets and the Financing of Early-Stage Firms: Evidence from the Software Industry. *Journal of Economics & Management Strategy*, 18:729–773.

Cohen, W., Nelson, R., and Walsh, J. (2000). Protecting Their Intellectual Assets: Appropriability Conditions and Why U.S. Manufacturing Firms Patent (or Not). NBER Working Paper, n. 7552.

Comino, S. and Manenti, F.M. (2011). Dual Licensing in Open Source Markets. *Information Economics and Policy*, 23(3):234–242.

Comino, S., Manenti, F., and Nicolò, A. (2011). Ex-ante Licensing in Sequential Innovation. *Games and Economic Behavior*, 73:388–401.

Comino, S., Manenti, F.M., and Parisi, M.L. (2007). From Planning to Mature: On the Success of Open Source Projects. *Research Policy*, 36:1575–1586.

Conner, K.R. and Rumelt, R.P. (1991). Software Piracy: an Analysis of Protection Strategies. *Management Science*, 37(2):125–139.

Cusumano, M., Mylonadis, Y., and Rosenbloom, R. (1992). Strategic Maneuvering and Mass-market Dynamics: The Triumph of VHS over Beta. *Business History Review*, 66:51–94.

Daffara, C. (2009). FLOSSMETRICS: The SME Guide to Open Source Software. Document available at http://flossmetrics.org/.

Dasgupta, P. and David, P. (1994). Toward a New Economics of Science. *Research Policy*, 23(5):487–521.

David, P.A. (1985). Clio and the Economics of QWERTY. *American Economic Review*, 75(2):332–337.

Degeratu, A., Rangaswamy, A., and Wu, J. (2000). Consumer Choice Behavior in Online and Regular Stores: The Effects of Brand Name, Price, and Other Search Attributes. *International Journal of Research in Marketing*, 17(1):55–78.

Dessein, W. (2004). Network Competition with Heterogeneous Customers and Calling Patterns. *Information Economics and Policy*, 16:323–345.

Di Domizio, A. (2010). VisiCalc: Col Primo Spreadsheet il Computer Diventa Utile. AppuntiDigitali – il primo blog italiano sulla tecnologia.

Distaso, W., Lupi, P., and Manenti, F.M. (2006). Platform Competition and Broadband Uptake: Theory and Empirical Evidence from the European Union. *Information Economics & Policy*, 18:87–106.

Distaso, W., Lupi, P., and Manenti, F.M. (2009). Static and Dynamic Efficiency in the European Telecommunications Market. The Role of Regulation on the Incentives to Invest and the Ladder of Investment. In: Lee ed., Handbook of Research on Telecommunications Planning and Management, IGI Global, IL.

EC (2012). European Commission: Digital Agenda for Europe – Scoreboard 2012. Directorate-General for Communication Networks, Content and Technology.

Economides, N. (1996a). Network Externalities, Complementarities, and Invitations to Enter. *European Journal of Political Economy*, 12:211–233.

Economides, N. (1996b). The Economics of Networks. *International Journal of Industrial Economics*, 14:673–699.

Economides, N. (2008). Public Policy in Network Industries. In: Buccirossi ed., Handbook of Antitrust Economics, The MIT Press, Cambridge, MA.

Economides, N. and Himmelberg, C. (1995). Critical Mass and Network Size with Application to the US Fax Market. Discussion Paper EC-95-11, Stern School of Business, NYU.

Economides, N. and Tåg, J. (2012). Net Neutrality on the Internet: A Two-Sided Market Analysis. *Information Economics and Policy*, 24:91–104.

Elfenbein, D.W., Fisman, R., and McManus, B. (2013). Market Structure, Reputation, and the Value of Quality Certification. Columbia Business School Research Paper n.13.

Ellison, G. and Ellison, S.F. (2009). Search, Obfuscation, and Price Elasticities on the Internet. *Econometrica*, 77(2):427–452.

Evans, D. and Noel, M. (2005). Defining Antitrust Markets When Firms Operate Two-Sided Platforms. *Columbia Business Law Review*, 667:102–134.

Evans, D.S. (2003). The Antitrust Economics of Multi-Sided Platform Markets. *Yale Journal on Regulation*, 20:325–381.

Evans, D.S. and Schmalensee, R. (2002). Some Economic Aspects of Antitrust Analysis in Dynamically Competitive Industries. *Innovation Policy and the Economy*, 2:1–49.

Farrell, J. and Shapiro, C. (2008). How Strong are Weak Patents. *American Economic Review*, 98(4):1347–1369.

Fershtman, C. and Gandal, N. (2012). Migration to the Cloud Ecosystem: Ushering in a New Generation of Platform Competition. *Communications & Strategies*, 85(1):109–123.

Foray, D. (1994). The Dynamic Implications of Increasing Returns: Technological Change and Path Dependent Efficiency. *International Journal of Industrial Organization*, 15:733–752.

Foray, D. (2006). *The Economics of Knowledge*. The MIT Press, Cambridge, MA.

Fukugwa, N. (2011). How Serious is Piracy in the Videogame Industry? *The Empirical Economics Letter*, 10(3):225–233.

Gabrielsen, T.S. and Vagstad, S. (2008). Why is On-net Traffic Cheaper than Off-net Traffic? Access Markup as a Collusive Device. *European Economic Review*, 52:99–115.

Galasso, A. and Schankerman, M. (2010). Patent Thickets, Courts and the Market for Innovation. *RAND Journal of Economics*, 41:472–503.

Gallini, N.T. (2002). The Economics of Patents: Lessons From Recent U.S. Patent Reform. *Journal of Economic Perspectives*, 16(2):131–154.

Gambardella, A., Giuri, P., and Luzzi, A. (2007). The Market for Patents in Europe. *Research Policy*, 36:1163–1183.

Gandal, N. (1994). Hedonic Price Indexes for Spreadsheets and an Empirical Test for Network Externalities. *RAND Journal of Economics*, 25(1):160–170.

Gandal, N. (2002). Compatibility, Standardization, and Network Effects: Some Policy Implications. *Oxford Review of Economic Policy*, 18:80–91.

Giles, J. (2005). Internet Encyclopaedias Go Head to Head. *Nature*, 438:900–901.

Goodman, D.J. and Myers, R.A. (2005). 3G Cellular Standards and Patents. *IEEE WirelessCom 2005*, 13 June.

Goolsbee, A. (2000). In a World without Borders: The Impact of Taxes on Internet Commerce. *Quarterly Journal of Economics*, 115(2):561–576.

Goolsbee, A. and Klenow, P.J. (2002). Evidence on Learning and Network Externalities in the Diffusion of Home Computers. *Journal of Law and Economics*, 45:317–343.

Green, J.R. and Scotchmer, S. (1995). On the Division of Profit in Sequential Innovation. *RAND Journal of Economics*, 26(1):20–33.

Hagiu, A. and Halaburda, H. (2013). Expectations and Two-Sided Platform Profits. Harvard Business School, Working Paper 12-045.

Hall, B., Helmers, C., Rogers, M., and Sena, V. (2013). The Importance (or not) of Patents to UK Firms. NBER Working Paper n.19089.

Hall, B., Jaffe, A., and Trajtenberg, M. (2001). The NBER Patent Citations Data File: Lessons, Insights and Methodological Tools. NBER Working Paper n. 8498.

Hall, B. and Ziedonis, R. (2001). The Patent Paradox Revisited: An Empirical Study of Patenting in the U.S. Semiconductor Industry, 1979–1995. *RAND Journal of Economics*, 32(1):101–128.

Harhoff, D. and Wagner, S. (2009). The Duration of Patent Examination at the European Patent Office. *Management Science*, 55(12):1969–1984.

Heller, M. and Eisenberg, R. (1998). Can Patents Deter Innovation? The Anticommons in Biomedical Research. *Science*, 280:698–701.

Jaffe, A. (2000). The U.S. Patent System in Transition: Policy Innovation and the Innovation Process. *Research Policy*, 29:531–557.

Jaffe, A.B. and Lerner, J. (2004). *Innovation and its Discontents*. Princeton University Press: Princeton, NJ.

Katz, M.L. and Shapiro, C. (1985). Network Externalities, Competition, and Compatibility. *American Economic Review*, 75:424–440.

Katz, M.L. and Shapiro, C. (1986). Technology Adoption in the Presence of Network Externalities. *Journal of Political Economy*, 94:822–841.

Klemperer, P. (1995). Competition When Consumers Have Switching Costs: An Overview with Applications to Industrial Organization, Macroeconomics, and International Trade. *Review of Economic Studies*, 62(4):515–39.

Klemperer, P. (2008). Network Effects and Switching Costs. Two separate contributions to the new New Palgrave Dictionary of Economics. In: Durlauf and Blume eds, The New Palgrave Dictionary of Economics, Second Edition. Palgrave Macmillan, Basingstoke, UK.

Kouris, I. (2011). Unified Two-Sided Market Model. Unpublished manuscript, Department of technology and innovation RWTH Aachen.

Laffont, J.J., Rey, P., and Tirole, J. (1998a). Network Competition: I. Overview and Nondiscriminatory Pricing. *RAND Journal of Economics*, 29:1–37.

Laffont, J.J., Rey, P., and Tirole, J. (1998b). Network Competition: II. Price Discrimination. *RAND Journal of Economics*, 29:38–56.

Laffont, J.J. and Tirole, J. (2000). *Competition in Telecommunications*. MIT Press, Cambridge, MA.

Lakhani, K.R. and Wolf, B. (2005). Why Hackers do What they do: Understanding Motivation and Effort in Free/Open Source Software Projects. In: Feller et al. eds, Perspectives on Free and Open Source Software, The MIT Press, Cambridge, MA.

Latcovich, S. and Smith, H. (2001). Pricing, Sunk Costs, and Market Structure Online: Evidence From Book Retailing. *Oxford Review of Economic Policy*, XVII(2):217–234.

Lee, H.G. (1998). Do Electronic Marketplaces Lower the Price of Goods. *Communications of the ACM*, 41(12):73–80.

Lee, R.S. and Wu, T. (2009). Subsidizing Creativity Through Network Design: Zero Pricing and Net Neutrality. *Journal of Economic Perspectives*, 23(3):61–76.

Lemley, M.A., Lichtman, D., and Sampat, B. (2005). What to Do About Bad Patents? *Regulation*, Winter:10–13.

Lemley, M.A. and Shapiro, C. (2005). Probabilistic Patents. *Journal of Economic Perspectives*, 19(2):75–98.

Lerner, J. and Tirole, J. (2002). Some Simple Economics of Open Source. *Journal of Industrial Economics*, 50(2):197–234.

Lerner, J. and Tirole, J. (2004). Efficient Patent Pools. *American Economic Review*, 94(3):691–711.

Lichtman, D. (2006). Patent Holdouts in the Standard-Setting Process. *Academic Council Bulletin*, 1.3:1–13.

Liebowitz, S. (1985). Copying and Indirect Appropriability: Photocopying of Journals. *Journal of Political Economy*, 93:945–957.

Liebowitz, S.J. and Margolis, S.E. (1994). Network Externality: An Uncommon Tragedy. *Journal of Economic Perspectives*, 8:133–150.

Littlechild, S. (2006). Mobile Termination Charges: Calling Party Pays versus Receiving Party Pays. *Telecommunications Policy*, 30:242–277.

Machlup, F. and Penrose, E. (1950). The Patent Controversy in the Ninteenth Century. *The Journal of Economic History*, 10(1):1–29.

Maldoom, D., Marsden, R., Sidak, J.G., and Singer, H.J. (2003). Competition in Broadband Provision and Its Implications for Regulatory Policy. *SSRN eLibrary*.

Manenti, F.M. (2001). On the Impact of "Call-Back" Competition on International Telephony. *Journal of Regulatory Economics*, 20:21–41.

Manenti, F.M. and Somma, E. (2011). Plastic Clashes: Competition Among Closed and Open Payment Systems. *The Manchester School*, 76(9):1099–1125.

Marsden, C.T. (2010). *Net Neutrality. Towards a Co-regulatory Approach.* Bloomsbury Academic, London, UK.

Matutes, C. and Regibeau, P. (1996). A Selective Review of the Economics of Standardization. Entry Deterrence, Technological Progress and International Competition. *European Journal of Political Economy*, 12:183–209.

Meyer, P. (2007). Network of Tinkerers: a Model of Open-Source Technology Innovation. U.S. Bureau of Labor Statistics – BLS Working Paper 413, November 2007.

Morgan, J. and Sefton, M. (2001). Information Externalities in Model of Sales. *Economic Bulletin*, 4(7):1–5.

Narduzzo, A. and Rossi, A. (2005). *The Role of Modularity in Free/Open Source Software Development.* In: Koch ed., Free/Open Source Software Development, Idea group, Hershey, PA.

OECD (2007). *Giving Knowledge for Free. The Emergence of Open Educational Resources.* Centre for Educational Research and Innovation.

OECD (2009). Two-Sided Markets. Directorate for Financial and Enterprise Affairs Competition Committee. Available for download at http://www.oecd.org/daf/competition/44445730.pdf.

Parker, G.G. and Van Alstyne, M.W. (2005). Two-Sided Network Effects: a Theory of Information Product Design. *Management Science*, 51 (10):1494–1504.

Peitz, M. and Koenen, J. (2012). *The Economics of Pending Patents.* In: Harrington and Katsoulacos eds, Recent Advances in the Analysis of Competition and Regulation, Edward Elgar Publishing, Cheltenham, UK and Northampton, MA, USA.

Penrose, E.T. (1951). *The Economics of the International Patent System.* Johns Hopkins Press, Baltimore, MD.

Pluvia Zuniga, M. and Guellec, D. (2009). Who Licenses Out and Why? Lessons from a Business Survey. OECD Science, Technology and Industry Working Papers, 2009/5. OECD publishing.

Pozzi, A. (2009). Shopping Cost and Brand Exploration in Online Grocery. NET Institute Working Paper No. 09-10.

Raasch, C., Herstatt, C., and Balka, K. (2009). On the Open Design of Tangible Goods. *R&D Management*, 39(4):382–393.

RBB Economics (2008). Two-Sides to Every Story? Lessons from the Travelport/Worldspan Ec Case. RBB Economics Brief 25. Document available for download at www.rbbecon.com/wp-content/uploads/2012/06/rbb_brief25.pdf.

Rochet, J. and Tirole, J. (2001). Platform Competition in Two-Sided Markets. Unpublished manuscript, University of Toulouse.

Rochet, J. and Tirole, J. (2006). Two-Sided Markets: A Progress Report. *RAND Journal of Economics*, 35(3):645–67.

Rohlfs, J. (1974). A Theory of Interdependent Demand for a Communications Service. *Bell Journal of Economics and Management Science*, 5(1):16–37.

Rotenberg, J. and Saloner, G. (1986). A Supergame-Theoretic Model of Price Wars during Booms. *American Economic Review*, 76(3).

Rysman, M. (2004). Competition Between Networks: A Study of the Market for Yellow Pages. *Review of Economic Studies*, 71(2):483–512.

Rysman, M. (2009). The Economics of Two-Sided Markets. *Journal of Economic Perspectives*, 25(3):125–143.

Schmalensee, R. (2001). Gaussian Demand and Commodity Bundling. *The Journal of Business*, 57(1):S211–S230.

Schmalensee, R. (2002). Payment Systems and Interchange Fees. *Journal of Industrial Economics*, 50(2):103–122.

Schuett, F. (2010). Network Neutrality: A Survey of the Economic Literture. *Review of Network Economics*, 9(2).

Schumpeter, J. (1942). *Capitalism, Socialism and Democracy*. Harper & Brothers, New York, NJ.

Scotchmer, S. (2004). *Innovation and Incentives*. The MIT Press, Cambridge, MA.

Scott-Morton, F., Silva-Risso, J., and Zettelmeyer, F. (2004). Cowboys or Cowards: Why are Internet Car Prices Lower? Unpublished manuscript, University of Berkeley.

Segal, I. and Whinston, M. (2007). Antitrust in Innovative Industries. *American Economic Review*, 97(5):1703–1730.

Shapiro, C. (2001). *Navigating the Patent Thicket: Cross Licensing, Patent Pools and Standard Setting*. In: Jaffe et al. eds, Innovation Policy and the Economy. The MIT Press, Cambridge, MA.

Shapiro, C. (2005). Antitrust, Innovation, and Intellectual Property. Testimony to Antitrust Modernization Commission, available at govinfo.library.unt.edu/amc/index.html.

Shy, O. (1996). *Industrial Organization: Theory and Applications*. The MIT Press, Cambridge, MA.

Smith, M.D., Bailey, J., and Brynjolfsson, E. (2000). Understanding Digital Markets: Review and Assessment. In: Brynjolfsson and Kahin eds, Understanding the Digital Economy, The MIT Press, Cambridge, MA.

Tanaka, T. (2004). Does File Sharing Reduce Music CD Sales? A Case of Japan. Institute of Innovation Research, Working Paper n.05-08.

Varian, H. (1980). A Model of Sales. *American Economic Review*, 70:651–659.

Varian, H. and Shapiro, C. (1999). *Information Rules. A Strategic Guide to the Network Economy*. Harvard Business School, Cambdridge, MA.

Verdier, M. (2009). Interchange Fees in Payment Card Systems: A Survey of the Literature. *Journal of Economic Surveys*, 24(4):1467–6419.

Vickers, J. (1995). Competition and Regulation in Vertically Related Markets. *Review of Economic Studies*, 62:1–17.

Vickers, J. (2009). Competition Policy and Property Rights. University of Oxford, Department of Economics, Discussion paper 436.

Vogelsang, I. (2003). Price Regulation of Access to Telecommunications Networks. *Journal of Economic Literature*, 41:830–862.

von Krogh, G., Spaeth, S., and Lakhani, K.R. (2003). Community, Joining, and Specialization in Open Source Software Innovation: a Case Study. *Research Policy*, 32:1217–1241.

Whelan, E., Parise, S., de Valk, J., and Aalbers, R. (2011). Creating Employee Networks that Deliver Open Innovation. *MIT Sloan Management Review*, 53(1):36–44.

Wright, J. (1999). International Telecommunications, Settlement Rates and the FCC. *Journal of Regulatory Economics*, 15:267–291.

Wright, J. (2004). One-sided Logic in Two-sided Markets. *Review of Network Economics*, 3:44–64.

Index